"The most important popular psychology book of the year, from one of the most important psychologists in a generation, *Ordinary Magic* shows how to make your mind work for you, not against you, when tackling life's most meaningful questions."

—Kelly McGonigal, author of *The Upside of Stress*

"It might seem fantastical that a set of simple techniques can make people happier, improve romantic relationships, reduce child abuse, reduce the achievement gap in schools, reduce dropout rates in college, reduce recidivism among troubled teens, reduce school suspensions, improve interactions between the police and citizens, reduce global poverty, and much, much more. But in this brilliant book, the pioneering social psychologist Greg Walton explains how "ordinary magic" can accomplish all of this. Even better, he does so with an accessible, poignant, and engaging writing style that makes it the best of both worlds—a book that is fun to read and will change your life."

—Timothy D. Wilson author of *Redirect: Changing the Stories We Live By*

"*Ordinary Magic* is required reading for anyone interested in making positive change in the world—an essential how-to guide from one of the most important psychologists working on the challenge of behavior change today."

—Laurie Santos, professor of psychology at Yale University and host of The Happiness Lab podcast

"Do life's biggest problems feel insurmountable? Greg Walton has the answer in his remarkable book *Ordinary Magic*. Using cutting-edge behavioral science, he shows how to break big problems into bite-sized goals we can all accomplish."

—Arthur C. Brooks, Harvard professor and #1 *New York Times* bestselling author

"This is an inspiring book by one of psychology's greatest architects of how to change behavior for the good—in relationships, in one's personal life, in the schooling of minority and low-income students, in building institutional trust, even in how to reduce global poverty. The reader learns how, through the recursive processes they launch, small interventions can move hills and, in time, mountains. It's an exciting book whose time has come—a must-read by anyone interested in seeing our society improve."

—Claude M. Steele, author of *Whistling Vivaldi: How Stereotypes Affect Us and What We Can Do*

"*Ordinary Magic* breaks it down. Here are the secret ingredients to conjure the magic of more confidence, trust, and belonging for ourselves and others. Blending stories, engaging descriptions of research, and straightforward, evidence-backed advice, the result is a bold, accessible, and inspiring book."

—Hazel Rose Markus, co-author of *Clash!: How to Thrive a Multicultural World*

Ordinary Magic

Ordinary Magic

The SCIENCE *of How We Can*
ACHIEVE BIG CHANGE
with SMALL ACTS

Gregory M. Walton, PhD

HARMONY
NEW YORK

Published in the United States by Harmony Books, an imprint of
Random House, a division of Penguin Random House LLC, New York.

Harmony Books is a registered trademark, and the Circle colophon is a trademark
of Penguin Random House LLC.

Photograph of Elizabeth Eckford, page 69, reprinted with permission of the
Will Counts Collection, Indiana University Archives.

Library of Congress Cataloging-in-Publication Data
Names: Walton, Gregory M. (Gregory Mariotti), author.
Title: Ordinary magic / Gregory M. Walton.
Description: First edition. | New York, NY : Harmony, 2025 |
Includes bibliographical references and index.
Identifiers: LCCN 2024035626 (print) | LCCN 2024035627 (ebook) |
ISBN 9780593580899 (hardcover) | ISBN 9780593580905 (ebook)
Subjects: LCSH: Change (Psychology) | Adaptability (Psychology)
Classification: LCC BF637.C4 W268 2025 (print) | LCC BF637.C4 (ebook) |
DDC 158.1—dc23/eng/20241007
LC record available at https://lccn.loc.gov/2024035626
LC ebook record available at https://lccn.loc.gov/2024035627

Printed in the United States of America on acid-free paper

HarmonyBooks.com | RandomHouseBooks.com

2 4 6 8 9 7 5 3 1
First Edition

Chapter-opening illustrations by Mark Nerys
Adobe Stock illustrations: part-opening illustrations by Kal El BSF; minus sign and
check mark by Vector light Studio; spirals by Vitalii; smiley face emoji by martialred;
teacher and student by rashadaliyev; hand washing by aboutmomentsimages; paper
towel dispenser by Janis Abolins; people icons by Rudzhan; tears of joy emoji by Nijat;
postcard by o_a; notepaper and paperclip by MR; paper by weedezign

FOR LISA, LUCY, AND OLIVER.

And for kids everywhere, young and old,
learning and becoming together.

Contents

They say life is like a box of chocolates, and I'd agree. But it's also full of questions.

Can I do it?
Do I belong?
Am I enough?

Here are these questions. Here's why they come up. Here are the spirals they start. And here is how we can set them to rest.

Ordinary Magic

Prologue

One of my favorite books as a child was Crockett Johnson's *Harold and the Purple Crayon*. You might remember it. Harold is a little boy with a magic crayon. Whatever he needs, he just draws. When his absent-minded scribbling transforms into deep water, he quickly draws himself a boat and clambers aboard. When he's done sailing, he simply sketches a shoreline upon which to disembark.

If only we had magic crayons to create new realities for ourselves and erase the problems that cause our minds to spiral. But, of course, life isn't a storybook. There are no magic fixes for the problems we carry with us all day long. Never mind the world around us. There's no easy way to scribble out big feelings like shame and mistrust (*Am I a bad person? Are you a bad person?*). A poster that proclaims "You're #1" won't eliminate the fear of falling short (*Am I smart enough?*). You can't just "snap out of" impostor syndrome (*Do I belong here?*). There's no "nudge" for the kind of rumination that sparks vicious cycles of worry in a marriage (*Is our relationship in trouble?*). But, perhaps, if we understood these questions more deeply, why they come up and how they work, we could find answers that will set us free.

This book is about change, and how to achieve it. It's about how things go wrong in our minds and our lives, in our relationships and our communities—and how we can set them right.

Our focus will be on all the things that matter: our most important goals; our belonging in spaces we care about; our closest relationships; conflicts that threaten to rule our lives; our health. Often persistent problems can feel permanent, as if they were locked-in features that constrain us, hold us back. But in fact, we have vast opportunities for change. And the tools to achieve this change are at your fingertips.

I could tell you this whole story as a series of magic tricks. Here's one. Did you know that three questions can improve your marriage? No, really, just three. That's what happened in one study of Chicagoland couples. Seven minutes a pop every four months for a year made couples closer, more satisfied, and more intimate. "21 Minutes to Save a Marriage" was the headline. Here's another. Did you know a one-page letter could keep kids out of jail? That's what happened in Oakland, California, with kids coming back to school from juvenile detention. That letter cut recidivism by *forty percentage points*. A third: A San Francisco hospital sent former patients a string of postcards. That cut suicide rates by half over two years. So, yes, the "tricks" in this book can get you more love and sex, keep kids out of jail, and save lives. Ba-da-bing!

If you're feeling skeptical, experiencing that *waaaait a minute!*—this is "too good to be true"—feeling, I get it. I really do. So, we're going to slow down. That's why there's a whole book ahead.

Two and a half decades ago, when I entered grad school, there's no way I would have believed that this sort of change was possible. It completely violates our intuitions. What is this, some kind of weird action-at-a-distance? A crumpling of psychological mind space so something tiny and trivial here (*twenty-one minutes*) transforms something huge and far away (*the quality of your marriage a year later*)? Some of the stories I'll share will seem magical. More science fiction than science. The tools of change I'll describe seem so small, so quick, so easy it's hard to believe they really can produce enormous gains. But the data are real. In fact, these tools are the products of decades of basic work by ingenious teams. We have dynamic models that explain how and why these seemingly magical results happen. And the best part is, this is a power we can harness.

It's worth thinking, just for now, that we already know that big changes can come from humble beginnings. An hour-long surgery can change your life forever. Is there any reason a precise psychological exercise—something that helps you think through a question that has pressed and re-pressed on your mind—can't do the same? This book will present hard-won, peer-reviewed, well-replicated evidence to show why seemingly small moments can make a world of difference.

So, I could tell you this story as a series of magic tricks. But I won't. For that wouldn't do it justice. For you and me and all of us all around the world are not mere spectators in this drama, sitting in plush chairs in some fancy theater watching magicians perform onstage. No, all of us are actors in this show. The true value of the story I have to tell is to pull back the curtain and invite you in. I'll introduce you to the scientists and professionals who have designed these catalysts and conducted the basic research. In their stories, we'll see how transformative change is not just possible but, in fact, completely ordinary. It's ordinary magic. By the end of this book, I hope you'll find examples like these both commonplace and extraordinary all at once (as I do now). And I hope you'll find them useful (as I also do). For this science gives a new vision of what is possible for ourselves, for our relationships and our communities, for our institutions, and for our world at large. It helps us understand *how* extraordinary change can happen and what each of us can do to make it happen. So, this book is the big reveal.

There's another reason it would be wrong to tell this story as a series of magic tricks. We're not going to put a select few magicians onstage as models for the rest of us to marvel at. No one has a monopoly on the kind of wisdom needed to make change happen. We're all on a journey to understand ourselves and others more deeply, to see more clearly the circumstances that we and others are placed in. That's the wisdom that allows us to act. So, we'll learn from many different people in many different circumstances. And I'll share my own experiences—both my successes and where I've screwed up and learned. My goal is for all of us to learn together to become wiser in understanding the challenges that life presents and how we can navigate these challenges well. And critically, we'll learn from a science that clarifies the crucial processes and tests what actually makes a difference in the most rigorous ways possible.

For more than two decades now, I've been privileged to be part of a wonderful community based primarily in social psychology. It's a community focused on challenges in life and what helps people navigate them well. Much of this work has been conducted quietly, often beginning in laboratory settings far removed from the public eye. It's work with deep connections to all the major problem spaces in life: to school, and how we learn; to health, and how we thrive; to relationships, and how we connect; and to work, and how we achieve. At key points, psychologists and skilled professionals have come together to build, step-by-step, practices that short-circuit vicious cycles of doubt, rumination, and conflict. It's a way to bring science and practice together to create meaningful, measurable, and lasting improvement in people's lives.

So, I'll take you on a journey with me. I'll explain the science behind the seemingly magical results in detail, with vivid examples. I'll introduce you to the women and men whose collective insights have advanced this work one step at a time.

The mechanisms we'll uncover aren't like the butterfly whose flapping wings change the weather. It's not random. They're more like flicks that set off chain reactions. We can predict when troubling questions will come up for ourselves or others. We can learn how to answer these questions well. We know that this can make a difference in people's lives. And, increasingly, we can predict the settings in which these answers will be helpful and the settings in which they won't. This is wisdom you can take to the bank—to achieve your goals and to be a better partner, a better parent, or a better educator, health professional, or other professional for those you serve.

These precise psychological exercises? These tools of change? In my community, we have a name for these things. We call them wise interventions.

In one case, my colleagues and I found that just an hour helping new college students surface and work through the question of whether they could belong in college helped them stay engaged, build relationships with mentors, and achieve at a higher rate over the next three years. *Ten years out,* participants in our study were happier and more successful in their careers than peers in the control group. That's an hour to change a life.

Gains like these amaze us. But what we should really marvel at is the power of the underlying psychology: the potency of the questions that people are asking in specific contexts (*Can people like me belong in college?*); the viciousness of the spirals, both psychological and relational, one can go down when the answer seems negative (*Maybe not*); and the extraordinary opportunities we have to get to better answers.

Over the course of this book, we'll travel far and wide. We'll glean insights from research undertaken in my lab and labs around the world; from wise educators and other professionals; from a variety of individual people of deep wisdom; from my own kids and students; and from children's books, which I've always seen as inspiring interventions of their own. Some of the best picture books, books like Jacqueline Woodson's *The Day You Begin,* animate troubling questions about the most important issues we face—like identity and difference—and gracefully guide us to wise answers, an expanded sense of possibility, whatever our age.

Before we go further, it might help to say what we're *not* doing when we do wise interventions. We're not telling students, "You belong!" or giving out T-shirts that proclaim it. And we're not telling people what to believe and then blaming them if they don't.

At Stanford, I share a lab with my close friend and colleague Carol Dweck. Dweck is well known for her groundbreaking research on growth (versus fixed) mindsets of intelligence. I've conducted a good deal of research with her and others on growth mindset. It's one of the most important wise interventions I know.

Unfortunately, the word "mindset" has been subject to some misunderstandings. There's a current in the popular zeitgeist that casts "mindsets" as a matter of personal responsibility. I've had countless college students tell me they were told in high school that they "should have" a growth mindset, as if a student struggling in school who feels judged as dumb could just wield a growth mindset like Harold's magic crayon. But in many ways, we live in a fixed-mindset culture. A student might attend a "gifted and talented" program, take a test presumed to evaluate inherent ability, or be told, "You're so smart." That culture saddles students with a looming question, especially when they struggle, *Am I smart enough?*

When our culture places nasty questions on the table, we can't just will them away. The world is full of exhortations, "Believe that you belong," ". . . that intelligence can grow," ". . . in yourself." Just believe? I don't know about you, but when I feel a creeping doubt, I can't just ignore it.

It takes a process. Dweck calls it "a journey." It's because of this confusion I won't use the word "mindset" much in this book. And I won't use "believe" as a command. The questions we face are legitimate. *Do I belong? Can I do it? Am I loved? Can I trust you?* They come up at specific times, for excellent reasons. They come from our culture and our contexts. Then we must contend with them.

This is where wise interventions come in. They create the right space to think through real questions we face.

Often, others help us get to better answers. It's the good friend who helps you see that a challenge you face, a doubt you feel, is fundamentally normal, that there's nothing wrong with you, that there are ways to make progress. It's a way to release those catastrophic fears. You might have ten opportunities for a conversation like that today. And when we plan for this, when we anticipate the icky questions that come up and create opportunities for people to contend with them honestly, all of us can spiral up. That's what allows three questions to change a marriage, a letter to improve the trajectory of a child's life. The drama here is below the surface. The change is quiet. The magic is ordinary.

So, in school, tools like growth-mindset interventions offer students better answers to troubling questions they commonly face. A student fails a test. *Does this mean I'm dumb? No. Challenge is how you learn.* Students can *use* answers like these to good effect. With these tools we have more power than we commonly realize to make things better for ourselves, our partners in life, and our communities. All of us do. *Far* more power.

But that power has limits. For not every school is one in which all students can belong. Some schools are discriminatory. And not every classroom is one where every student feels safe acting on a growth mindset—taking on challenges, making mistakes, or raising their hand when they're confused. So, institutions have crucial responsibilities too, to create better climates for those they serve. Change happens on several tracks.

In part 1 ("Spirals"), I'll introduce the key concepts you need to understand wise interventions: What are core questions? When do they come up? How do they set off downward spirals? And, lacking magic crayons, how can we reverse this process to spiral up? Then, in parts 2 and 3 ("Me" and "You"), we'll dig into five of the biggest questions we face—and how we can answer them well to thrive. Questions about belonging (chapter 3); whether you can achieve your goals (chapter 4); your identity and how you're seen (chapter 5); your closest relationships (chapter 6); and trust and respect out in the world (chapter 7). Finally, in part 4 ("Us"), we'll step back to think about the world we live in together and what it will take to make it wiser and better for all of us.

My goal is that this book will serve as a wise intervention of its own: to help all of us see more clearly the questions our lives present, both the questions that you face and the questions that other people face. All too often these questions stay below the surface, under our radar, stealthy and working against us. There they fester. But by seeing these questions clearly, by surfacing them and understanding their logic, we can answer them.

So, this book is for everyone. And it's a story of science. As we explore, we'll see areas where our understanding is strong and well developed. I'll share how that knowledge developed. But we'll also find areas where our theories are so far less well developed, and we'll learn how scientists are seeking to fill the gaps, to revise our theories by learning from and with the people contending with "bad" things here and now.

Along the way, you'll meet many people. Some, I suspect, you'll be sympathetic to. Maybe they're in a situation you're familiar with, or one you've faced yourself. Others you might not like so much. Some do foolish or even terrible things. But this book isn't about casting judgment. It's about understanding the questions that come up for all of us, in our different roles and perspectives, as we navigate life in all its twists and turns. It's about following the logic of these questions, seeing where they lead, and learning how you can answer them well for yourself and help others do the same. For, in becoming a little wiser, we can do a little more good.

We've been taught that change is hard. That relationships take work. That there aren't shortcuts to self-improvement. There's truth in all of that. But when that truth is overstated, things can feel hopeless. It can make us resigned, as if we were stuck with problems. A life in science has taught me that we don't have to settle for incremental progress. A small initial insight, a small change in direction, can lead us to vast new lands.

PART 1

Spirals

Chapter 1

Spiraling Down

Single starting errors . . . multiplied through time
into a fan-shaped array.
—IAN MCEWAN, *LESSONS*

I was four years old when I first got caught in a spiral. At least it's the first one I remember. My family had moved from Michigan to California for a year and a half, and my new preschool had a "No running" rule, inside or out. I was a willful child with lots of energy, no friends, and little regard for dumb rules. So I spent every day chasing the other kids around the playground, breaking that rule. Most days ended with me in the bleachers in "time-out." I just wanted to play!

Things might have kept on muddling along that way but for a telling event on school picture day. At least it was telling to me. A teacher sat me right in the middle of the group and made a point to ask me, among all the kids there, to hold the school sign. *Why would she do that?* I wondered. *Was this supposed to make me like her, or this terrible school?* Slowly it began to dawn on me that maybe I'd become "the bad kid," the one who must be pacified, the trouble-maker.

But I wasn't a bad kid! They were the evil ones. My anger began to boil. A fine moral outrage rose up within me. No future child could suffer my fate. Impelled, I began to follow the director around as she showed the school to prospective parents—and told them exactly what I thought of the school.

For the director, that was it. She ushered my parents in for a meeting and told them I would not be welcome back. "We'll tell the other parents whatever you like," she said. My father, wonderfully antiauthoritarian, responded, "How 'bout the truth?"

Things don't go wrong just at once. Often, they start small, sometimes in tiny, almost imperceptible steps. A little feeling, a small thought, an action taken or withheld. But then they gather speed, and before you know it, they've spiraled out of control. You get locked in a conflict with a teacher and decide they're your enemy. Your partner is late for date night—again—and you decide they don't love you. You fail a test and conclude, "I'm not a math person."

How do we get there? And how can we get out of these cycles or, better yet, prevent them from starting in the first place?

I've thought a lot about spirals, both as a kid and now as a part-ner, a parent, and a general-purpose human being. And as a social psychologist, a teacher, and a professor, I've studied spirals, the bad thoughts and feelings that set them off, and what we can do about them. Through these experiences, I've come to appreciate three foundational ideas.

The first is that, almost all the time, the self-doubt and mistrust we experience don't just pop into our heads randomly. We're not crazy, with wanton worries, at least not most of the time. Our doubts are triggered. The situation gives you your worries. In preschool, I *was* getting in trouble every day. I had reason to wonder if I was seen as "the bad kid." That question was on the table. That's why the event at school picture day was telling to me. It wouldn't have been telling to my friend George. He wasn't getting in trouble every day. Or take a student in the first generation in her family to go to col-lege. She has reason to wonder whether she will belong in college;

her family hasn't previously. Then, if she's excluded from a party, say, or criticized by a professor, it will mean something a little different than it would to a student whose parents have advanced degrees. Our doubts are legitimate responses to the world as it is. That means we can't expect to excise them quite as a surgeon would a tumor. But we can learn to recognize them, to predict them, and then to contend with them.

The second big idea is that the doubts and worries that preoccupy us often take the form of questions—big, existential questions. Here are three of them:

> *Who Am I?* Questions about how we see ourselves and, often especially, how other people see us: *Am I seen as a bad kid?*
> *Do I Belong?* Your place in the spaces that matter most to you: *Do people like me belong here?*
> *Can I Do It?* Your goals and abilities: *Am I smart enough to do this?*

These aren't beliefs we hold with confidence. They're not firm knowledge of your faults and failings, at least not at first. They're things we're trying to figure out: fearsome prospects, threats in the air, specters of all sorts and kinds. They might start small, a little fear, a shadow of doubt, but then, when just the right thing (the wrong thing) happens, that fear looms before you. Then you must contend with it.

Do you know the white bear study? Years ago, researchers showed that if you tell people not to think about something ("Don't think of a white bear!"), they can't help but do it (Did you?). But when it's one of these mental bugaboos, that's even more true. *Am I seen as a bad kid?* First a question like this threatens to take over your mind. You might deny it or try to push it away, but it pops up again and again. It's all-consuming. That's because the question is important. It matters for your sense of who you are, for relationships you care about. So you want to figure it out.

After taking over our minds, questions like this threaten to take over our lives. They act like leading questions. They point us toward negative conclusions; then those conclusions can quickly become self-fulfilling. The sad irony is that when we act on the basis of these thin slices of evidence, we risk making our fears come true.

At my next and much better school, the teacher did a very California thing. She had all of us five-year-olds sit in a circle on the rug and asked each of us to share what we were feeling. When it got to my turn, I said, "I wish I was a bee and could sting all of you."

I did myself no favors berating my new classmates. Clearly, that question was still on my mind. But I got lucky. The teacher gave my parents a call, a kind call. My parents explained why I might be a bit mad, and the teacher reacted well. She pulled me closer. A downward spiral was averted. But I wonder, sometimes, how else that story might have gone. I was a little White boy and my parents were academics. Even by preschool we have stereotypes about misbehaving kids. Would a teacher have been so kind to a little Black or brown boy? Would she have pulled him closer? Or might she have thought, *Maybe he's a little troublemaker?*

One of my all-time favorite studies shows how spirals can start in relationships. The social psychologist Sandra Murray at the State University of New York at Buffalo brought couples into the lab where she'd designed a provocative situation. In one group, each person got a worksheet that asked them to list "important aspects of your partner's character that you dislike." So, both people wrote briefly and then moved on. Everyone was fine. No problem.

In Murray's second group, however, even though she said both people would do the same task, they actually got different instructions. One person was prompted to list their grievances, but the other was asked to list all the items in their home. That left the first person sitting there, watching their partner write away for nearly two minutes longer, on average. Imagine you're that person, watching your partner scribble on and on, filling page after page with your failings. *Ouch.*

Murray's study was designed to see how that experience might affect people with high versus low self-esteem. When you don't think highly of yourself—you think you're not so fun, not so attractive, not so kind—it's easy to doubt that someone else could think well of you. And in fact, when the people with low self-esteem saw their partners writing away, seemingly unable to stop, they rated their partners more negatively and felt distant from them.

Questions like *Am I really loved?* make us see the world differently, and if we see things differently, we react differently. If you read your partner's irritation as more evidence that they're tired of you—instead of, say, that they had a bad day—you might withdraw emotionally or lash out. That generates still more irritation from your partner—and more evidence for your pessimistic hypothesis: *Now I know I'm not loved.* Before you know it, you're spiraling down, out of control. Will that initial question come to define you, or at least your relationship?

But this cycle isn't inevitable, and that's my third point. This is a process, and that means it's not fixed. It's *answers* we are looking for when we face defining questions. When we find better ones, we can flip the script, free ourselves, and spark spirals that propel us upward. The things we worry about most are the issues that will define our lives: *Does my partner love me? Will I be a good parent? Can I accomplish what matters to me?* We can get better at anticipating these questions and recognizing them when they come up, both for ourselves and for other people. We can develop an ear for psychological questions. Then, by accepting these questions instead of suppressing them, we can find answers that are "wise" to our situations, answers that are legitimate and can help us thrive. In doing so, we can become more resilient: in Murray's study above, people who had high self-esteem were unfazed by watching their partners write on and on about their shortcomings. Maybe we can learn their secret.

The small but powerful tools that reverse these negative spirals? Wise interventions.

BREAKING IT DOWN

Could a postcard save a life? Could a red Volkswagen make you better at math? Could seventeen words increase the odds middle school students go to college? Could twenty-one minutes save your marriage?

Of course, all that seems ridiculous. It doesn't match the canonical wisdom about success. Big gains seem to require heavy lifting. Sometimes, internal gifts are presented as the deciding factor. The people who succeed are the smartest, the most brilliant, the geniuses among us. Or perhaps it's the people with the greatest self-control, those highly disciplined human beings who always resist the one tempting marshmallow in order to get two. Sometimes we're told it isn't about the person at all but being in the right place at the right time—growing up in the right neighborhood, going to the right school, having the right advantages.

The problem with all these accounts is that they aren't very useful. They don't help us see what we can do to make things better (Just be gritty? Become advantaged? Change neighborhoods?). But the fact is, sometimes small things move mountains. To understand how, we must dig deeper to understand exactly how spirals play out in our lives—how one thing leads to another, how we can gain confidence or lose it, build trust or erode it. Often these cycles start with a question.

Say you're a senior member of your team at work. You're twelve minutes late to the weekly staff Zoom. Once you've "joined audio," the first thing you hear is your old friend's voice. "There you are! So glad you could fit us in." You laugh and explain the disastrous traffic, difficult drop-off at your kids' school, or whatever it was that messed up your morning. The moment passes and the conversation moves on. You turn to the job at hand, focused and ready to go.

But what if you're a junior staffer, still feeling your way. Same thing happens: You're twelve minutes late to the weekly staff Zoom. Once you've "joined audio," the first thing you hear is the boss's voice. "There you are! So glad you could fit us in." A few colleagues chuckle. You consider making excuses—about traffic, drop-off, whatever it was—but the moment passes, and the conversation moves on.

Your mind doesn't, though. It's still ruminating. *Was that snark in my boss's voice? Were they talking about me before I logged on? Do I fit in here? Am I any good at this job?* You might not be fully aware of these questions. Your mind works quickly on multiple tracks at the same time. And those questions are nasty; they threaten your sense of belonging, your worth, and your value, at least at work. So you try to push them away, to suppress them. But they're still there. And once they've been triggered, it might feel like the evidence keeps pouring in.

Someone makes an inside joke in the chat. You don't get it. *I don't belong here.* Someone rolls their eyes while you're talking. *They don't respect me.* The boss ignores you for the rest of the meeting. *No one sees me.* Again, these thoughts may not be fully conscious. But there's no mistaking the fact that your motivation to get back to work has waned by the time you log off. What was it you were supposed to look into?

Next thing you know, you're idly messing around online when a text comes in from the person who rolled their eyes. "You ok? You seemed out of it at the meeting." You ignore it. But your mind doesn't. It's busy composing possible replies. The full spectrum from passive-aggressive to career imperiling. Eventually you pick up your phone. What will you text back?

This is how self-defeating spirals start and how they gather speed. Let's break down the moving parts:

1. A circumstance places a big question on the table—about identity, belonging, or adequacy: *You're new at work. You want to succeed and belong, but you wonder . . .* That question looms, latent and inactive, but present.
2. A "bad" thing happens: *Your boss is a little snarky.*
3. That question gets triggered: *You read the room for answers, drawing negative inferences from ambiguous evidence. You're distracted from the task at hand. Your pessimistic hypothesis becomes more entrenched.*
4. You act on that pessimistic hypothesis, making matters worse.

Maybe you send that colleague a snarky text back. And what do you know: When you see them a few days later, they're cold to you.

Now you aren't talking. Maybe you flub that assignment your boss gave you, and they lose confidence in you. Fast-forward a year and you're at a new job. Tensions are emerging with the new co-workers. Or are they? How will this story end? Do you have any control over it?

Yes, you do. We all do. Negative spirals or feedback loops like these aren't inevitable. In fact, there are very small things we can do both for ourselves and for others to nip them in the bud—and prevent catastrophic outcomes months and years into the future. Better yet, there are ways we can launch positive spirals—dramatically increasing our chances of future happiness, success, and flourishing. The very same processes can either propel us upward or pull us down.

To understand how all this is possible, let's get more precise about sequences like 1–4. There are three key concepts at play: "core questions" (No. 1), meaning making or "construal" (Nos. 2 and 3), and "calcification" (No. 4). Think of these as "the three Cs" of spirals—whether positive or negative.

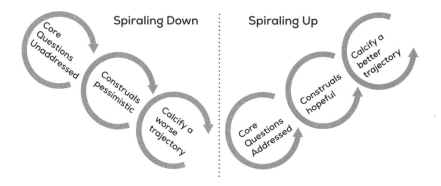

CORE QUESTIONS. There are the fundamental questions all of us face, at one time or another. For example: *Who am I? Do I belong? Am I enough?* I think of these questions as "defining" because they help define you and your life: your sense of self, what relationships you'll have, and whether you'll be able to do and be the things you aspire to. There might be long stretches when you don't think about a given question much because it's settled for you then. But at critical junctures specific questions flare up, unsettle, and preoccupy you. Then they begin to shape what you see and how you act.

CONSTRUAL. It's natural to think that we have an unfiltered view of the world. That light hits your eyes and you just see what's out there. But it's more that we *read* the world, interpret it, drawing inferences based on what's already in our heads. We pick up on themes that seem relevant or important to us, not noticing or screening out other details. "Construal" is the word psychologists use to describe this process, although I won't use that word much because frankly it's a mouthful of taffy.

This filtering can be so rapid, so automatic, so "natural" that it becomes invisible to us. One finding that helped me understand this looked at early language development. When babies are first born, they can distinguish every sound in every human language. So, a newborn baby in Japan, say, will perk up when a series of *l*s is interrupted with an *r*, a phonological distinction that isn't made in Japanese and one that poses notorious difficulties to adult Japanese speakers trying to learn English ("Hello" versus "Herro"). Or a baby learning English will notice the distinction between the English *th* (θ) and similar sounds in Hindi (त, थ), which are also nearly indistinguishable to adult English speakers. What happens? By the time babies turn one, they've learned which distinctions are made in their native language and which aren't. The first baby has learned to read the world as a Japanese speaker; the second as an English speaker. They've learned what they can safely ignore, so they can focus on the distinctions that matter for them. And now they can't "hear" what's not marked. (This is why a person learning a second language as an adult can have a leg up if they heard that language as a baby. They may not remember any grammar or vocabulary. But they might be able to hear the novel phonological distinctions that others struggle with.)

But it's not just in the course of development that we learn what's relevant to us and then read the world that way. It's every day, in every interaction, in all our little goals too. A friend once told me of an ingenious class demonstration that helped her begin to understand this process. A professor split the class in two and then spoke to the first half alone, telling them of his love for travel and a recent trip to Libya. Next, he spoke to the second half about shopping and how hard it was to find the right size shoe. Last, he brought the class together and said a single word. He asked the students to write it down. Students in the first group wrote, "Tripoli." Those in the second wrote, "Triple E."

Construal is like a kind of focus. As you look out at the social scene, what snaps to attention? By learning what people see clearly, how they read situations, we can learn what questions guide their view.

If you're anything like me, one of the most powerful guides is whatever could pose a risk to you, could threaten you. If you're walking through a forest where a tiger is said to prowl, you might hear that tiger in every rustle of leaves, see it in every sway of reeds. But in the social world, we don't all face the same threats. That's why my friend George wouldn't have minded if he'd been asked to hold the sign at our preschool's picture day. He wasn't at risk of being "the bad kid."

There's a lovely picture book by Brendan Wenzel called *They All Saw a Cat.* Wenzel depicts a cat on every page. Only it's never the same cat. A child sees a pet, warm and fluffy, worthy of a back scratch. A fox sees a fur ball to chase. But the mouse? It sees a demonic monster in blood red with looming yellow eyes, gnashing teeth, and sharp claws. They all see a cat. But only the mouse sees a threat.

When a core question is unsettled for a person, it functions like a lens through which you see the world. We seek answers that can help us resolve that question. *Is it true?* we ask. *Are my doubts and fears well founded?* Then, if a "bad" thing happens, it can seem like proof of your negative hypothesis. We aren't neutral observers on the lookout for evidence one way or the other. We're in the grip of confirmation bias, attuned to evidence that corroborates our preconceived theory.

Digging Deeper with Construal: Tifbits. Sometimes "bad" things are bad unto themselves: like an episode of depression, a racist comment, an infidelity, or failing a test. But it's only partly their inherent quality that makes these events bad. One thing is the depression. Another is troubling questions it might provoke, questions like *Is there something wrong with me?* or *Will I be able to accomplish what I want?* And sometimes those questions are what is most problematic. Suppose you fail a test. If it's a good test—that is, a valid test—that means you haven't learned the material yet. You might have to put in more work, or try a new approach to learn the material. That's too bad. But somewhere, in the back of your mind, do you think, *I'm dumb and I'll never get it?* Do you try to push that thought away, only to find it pop back up? Do you never want to look at the material again? *That* is what would make a failed test truly "bad."

I put "bad" in quotes to refer to this second kind of bad. That's when an event triggers or seems to confirm a negative hypothesis.

It can be easier to see how this triggering works when the event itself is neutral or even positive on its face. That was me at age four being asked to hold the school sign. There was nothing inherently bad about being asked to hold the sign. Or consider a quiet Friday night at home alone. Maybe you take a bath, read a book, or watch a movie. If you're a busy adult in the "rush hour" of life, that prospect might be pleasant, even blissful. But if you're in the first year of college, do you think, *I haven't been invited to anything. Am I being excluded? Will I ever make friends?* Those questions begin to pose threats, to define you and your prospects negatively.

So, a core question (*Am I seen as a bad kid?*) can be on the table for people in one case (me) but not another (George), and then the exact same situation feels completely different. This is a layer of complexity we'll return to again and again. For tricky as it can be to truly understand the questions that you face, it can be trickier yet to appreciate the questions that other people face.

Sometimes it's comical when one person sees a threat and another does not. Or a pet, which, of course, has its own concerns and ways of seeing the world. Once our dog, Tomato, lovable but dumb, became convinced that a stump caught in the surf was a fearsome sea monster out to get him. He spent a good five minutes chasing the stump, diving back whenever it attacked on an incoming wave.

Even after I'd hauled the log out of the water, he struck a defensive pose. I laughed, but for him that stump was the rustle in the leaves.

Of course, I'm not immune. When I was a kid growing up in Michigan, my family often took advantage of the long summer days to go canoeing, a week or more, on rivers as far afield as northern Ontario, great rivers that flow north toward Hudson Bay. So, from an early age, I was comfortable in a canoe, skilled in the intricacies of the "J" stroke, a strong paddler.

One weekend when I was about ten, we took a trip on the Sturgeon River, billed as the fastest in Michigan's lower peninsula. The outfitter gleefully reported that 80 percent of canoeists flipped at some point. "Plan on getting wet as many of our guests take an unplanned 'refreshing' dunk!" they said. The Sturgeon is a small, windy river with quick turns and, most dangerous of all, sweepers—spreads of branches that overlay the outside portion of a turn, right down to the surface of the water. That lets the current pass through unobstructed, but can trap a boat and turn it broadside. Then, with a little wobble, the current will rush in, and down you go.

All through the day we navigated the river with aplomb. We tracked the tight curves, back-paddled when necessary, and kept well to the inside whenever sweepers appeared, far from the swift current that could suck us into the danger zone. We swept past boat after boat of less experienced paddlers caught among the branches. I sure was proud when by mid-afternoon we hadn't flipped yet.

It was then that we approached a quick but unremarkable right-hand turn, no different from dozens of similar curves we'd already navigated. There was no sweeper, no hidden log just beneath the surface, no protruding rock to dodge. Just fast water, bearing right.

Paddling in the bow (the front), however, I felt some minor turbulence. The boat shifted left, stronger than I expected. That 80 percent figure flashed before my mind. Sure we were going under, I dove right in, the better to get out of the way. And *that*, of course, is what flipped the boat! My father paddling stern got dunked and came up sputtering—sputtering at me. All our gear floated off down the river. We lost a good hour, a pad, and a life jacket. And I lost any credibility.

Worried I'd flip the boat, I'd flipped the boat.

For me, it was just a momentary doubt, and all that got dumped was the boat. But for my brother, an inference ended a relationship. Living in New York City in his twenties, he met a woman through his work as a musician. Six months in, he thought the relationship was going well. Then, seemingly out of nowhere, she broke up with him. When he asked her to explain her reasoning, his now ex-girlfriend said, "Do you remember that time we went to Macy's?" My brother had a vague recollection of an entirely uneventful shopping trip.

"Yes," he said.

"I had to tell you to tuck your shirt in," she explained, pausing. "I can't be with you."

When my brother told me about this later, we christened it a "tifbit"—tiny fact, big theory.* It was silly, and we laughed. But I have always wondered: What did her reaction betray? What question was in her mind that made this event stand out among all the others? Why did an untucked shirt define for her who he was and how they could never be together? How did that reading then shift the trajectory of their relationship? We never did learn what questions were on the table for her.

With wisdom and kindness and a little distance, we can laugh at ourselves in situations like these. But we should pay attention. For beneath every tifbit is a real question, and it's almost always a reasonable one.

In my first year of college, I was biking back through campus one lovely fall day when I saw a large group of fellow students gathered enthusiastically around a truck from the California burger chain In-N-Out. Maybe they craved a taste of home. But in Michigan, where I was from, there are no In-N-Outs. I'd never heard of it. Feeling excluded from the burger party, I biked off in a huff to eat my lunch in the dining hall alone. I remember thinking, *I'm not standing in line for a burger!*

---

* We also coined an opposite term, "hufnot"—huge fact, no theory: "Sure we slept together. But it didn't mean anything!"

What was my problem?

As an eighteen-year-old, I certainly didn't want to think of myself as feeling that I did not belong in college. And I definitely didn't want to think that an In-N-Out truck could trigger that feeling. How ridiculous that would be. Who thinks they don't belong because of a burger truck?

It was ridiculous. Of course not knowing about In-N-Out didn't mean I didn't belong in college. But that's the point. For looking back now, I know the truth is I was homesick. I felt so far from home and all the people I knew and loved. So I wondered, *Will I make friends in California? Will I fit in?* Seeing all those classmates crowded together, eager to get lunch from a place I'd never even heard of, just triggered those anxieties.

Big responses to small experiences can help us see what lies beneath the surface. For a tifbit is never just a tiny fact. It's a clue to the bigger questions that define our lives.

CALCIFICATION. Calcification happens when our negative thoughts and feelings get entrenched—often as a consequence of our own actions. You have a bad date and think, *Am I unlovable? Will I be alone forever?* Pretty soon your next date isn't going well either. Rinse and repeat long enough, and you're stuck in a romantic rut. It could have happened to me at age four. Had I been judged a troublemaker, would I have come to love school, to love to read, to love to learn?

When you start to look, you can see spirals everywhere. You fail an important math test. You think you can't succeed, and stop going to class. You feel sick from a treatment designed to help you overcome an illness. You think it means your illness is especially strong and resistant and so avoid treatment. You have a fight with your kids. You think you're a "bad parent," and then yell at them even more the next time. This is self-sabotage, and one step at a time it costs us our achievements, our health, our relationships, and our well-being.

Yet if our struggles arise, in part, from the inferences we draw, we have an opportunity. With a little prompt, I could have known that almost everyone feels homesick at first in college, that we're all in some sense far from home, even the kids from California, that everyone was trying to find new communities. Maybe then I would have joined the line at the In-N-Out truck. I could have asked someone to tell me what In-N-Out was. Why do they love it? What is "animal style"? I'm sure they would have been thrilled to share. I probably would have had a better lunch. Maybe I would have made a friend, too.

Chapter 2

Spiraling Up

Why, Sal, that's nothing to worry about. That means that today
you've become a big girl.

—ROBERT MCCLOSKEY, *ONE MORNING IN MAINE*

One Morning in Maine, Robert McCloskey's classic picture book, opens in crisis. Sal has a loose tooth! " 'Ma-a-a-ma!' she cried. 'One of my teeth is loose! It will hurt and I'll have to stay in bed! I won't be able to eat my breakfast and go with Daddy to Buck's Harbor!' "

For Sal, the loose tooth provokes sharp questions: *Who am I now? Will I be able to do what I love?* That's when her mother intervenes. She doesn't dismiss Sal's concern or ignore it. She just helps Sal to a new way of understanding the predicament a loose tooth poses to a young child: "That means that today you've become a big girl."

Sal begins to try on her mother's answer for size. "Did your baby teeth get loose and come out when you grew to be a big girl?" she asks. Her mother reassures her, "Yes, and then these nice large ones grew in." Will baby sister Jane's teeth get loose too? "Yes, but not for a long time, not until she stops being a baby and grows up to be a big girl like you."

Out on the beach, Sal tells a fish hawk and then a loon, "I have a loose tooth!" When she meets her father, she shares, "Daddy! I have a loose tooth!" He affirms her mother's answer, "You're growing into a big girl when you get a loose tooth!" Offered a different answer to the deep questions a loose tooth posed her, Sal takes it up. "I'm a big girl," she says, "I can . . . dig a lot of clams, fast."

I thought of *One Morning in Maine* when our daughter, Lucy, had her first sprained ankle. "I can't go to school!" she wailed. My wife, Lisa, and I told Lucy all about our own long histories of sprained ankles, how they happen to everyone at one time or another, that the sprain would definitely get better, and that it was certainly not cause to stay home from school.

These are examples of wise interventions: graceful, often fleeting moments that help us answer core questions as they come up. For Sal, the question was, *Is a loose tooth a catastrophe?* For an adult in an intimate relationship, it might be, *Does my partner really love me?* For a parent struggling with a colicky baby, it could be, *Am I bad parent?*

In this chapter, we'll dig into the conceptual tools that undergird wise interventions. These are the tools you can use to launch upward spirals in your own life, for yourself, and for the people you love, teach, serve, and work with. To begin, I've found it useful to be explicit about what I mean by both "wise" and "interventions."

Some people associate "wisdom" with philosophy or religion. With ancient Greeks or Buddhist monks. And the word "wise" does have ancient roots. Aristotle distinguished "theoretical wisdom" (*sophia*) and "practical wisdom" (*phronesis*). But "wise" as my colleagues and I use it doesn't mean timeless advice about how to live a good life. It's not static and unchanging or rooted in the observations of Dead White Men. It has more in common with the "wise" in words like "streetwise." It's about being "wise to the situation," especially to the questions that come up here and now and for whom. It is responsive, dynamic, and specific. "Wise" in this sense is eminently practical. There's nothing old or far away about it. This is knowledge for doing: "know-how" to contend with the problems you face right now.

This use of the word "wise" comes to us from the gay community in San Francisco in the 1950s, where the sociologist Erving Goffman observed that people used the word "wise" to describe straight people who "got" gay people, who saw their humanity despite the prevailing homophobia of the time, and then interacted with them as normal human beings. Later, in the 1990s, my colleague and mentor Claude Steele described "wise schooling" as practices sensitive to the predicament of students laboring under negative stereotypes, practices that could help students succeed. Synthesizing these influences, I think of wise as being sensitive to the defining questions that people face about themselves, other people, and the social structures they seek to navigate. Wise interventions know when these questions come up. They help people answer these questions well.

Historians have a lovely term to describe social or cultural analyses that are detached from an understanding of their historical roots: "ahistorical." It's a bit of an epithet. In just this way, I'm going to use the term "a-psychological." It's the opposite of wise: it's being insensitive or tone-deaf to the psychological circumstance someone is in. It would be as if Sal's mother told Sal, "Just eat your breakfast. And don't forget to clear your plate!"

To use "wise" in this way means that intervening well is equal parts art and science. It requires thoughtful listening to limn the sometimes tacit yet defining questions that arise for people in a setting. It involves recognizing what answers are possible and developing graceful ways to help yourself or others toward these answers. Wise interventions require humility. There is no guarantee of success. They don't always work. Sometimes they backfire. (Wise doesn't mean "effective" or "better than other approaches.") But we can learn from these failures and try to do better. And for me, part of this wisdom is using the methods of science to see if the answers we offer really will make a difference in people's lives. Data matter.

"To intervene" just means, quite literally, to come between a cause and an effect to achieve a better outcome. Wise interventions aren't flashy spectacles worthy of reality TV. This is not confronting the family alcoholic with an "us or the bottle" conversation. Often, the influence of wise interventions is subtle, below the surface, more quiet rethinking than dramatic confrontation. Sometimes a well-designed intervention is so graceful, so seamless, that people don't even see it. In one study I ran in graduate school, an hour-long experience I created to quell a worry about belonging among new college students raised students' grades over the next three years. But at the end of college, almost no student remembered what they had done in that session three years earlier. Almost none thought that session had had "any" effect on their college experience.

So wise interventions are quiet, not loud. One reason is that the activities they involve are ordinary. Every day, we reflect on our experiences and think and talk through whatever is pressing on our minds. The difference is that science helps formalize the approach, and that lets us act with far more intentionality, clarity, power, and impact.

Another reason wise interventions don't loom large over us is that they are often preventative rather than reactive. They aim to prevent a problem from spiraling out of control, often by helping us set aside a persistent psychological question with grace and deftness. In that study of social belonging, we know the intervention improved students' grades and experience; it was a rigorous randomized controlled trial with a true control condition. But in a larger sense that one-hour session played a very small role. For what was the "real" cause of students' success? It was the upward spiral that the intervention unleashed. Once students felt more confident, they worked hard on coursework, developed strong friendships with classmates, and reached out to professors and developed mentors who guided and inspired them. The intervention was like slipping engine oil in the right place at the right time to clear an obstacle so the gears could come together, so a person and a system could succeed.

It's useful to distinguish wise interventions from other prominent techniques to shift behavior, especially "nudges." Nudges are small tweaks to a setting that make it more likely that people will act in ways someone wants. For example, it's marginally easier to acquiesce to a default than to opt out. If being an organ donor is the default, then you might get more donors than if people had to opt in. Similarly, if a cafeteria puts the apples at eye level and the cookies on the tallest shelf, it's easier to pick an apple. But nudges aren't "wise" in my sense. They don't even pretend to interface with the big open questions that seek to define us. Nudges treat people like water, whose flow must be directed by the "choice architect." This can be helpful in certain cases. I'm glad when a cafeteria is laid out so it's easier for me to choose healthy options. But tweaks like these don't make for lasting changes in people's lives. They don't give you something you can take with you to the next situation.

And if we tried to apply them to the defining questions of our lives, the results would be absurd. I wouldn't want my agency over the things that matter most to me to be "nudged." You wouldn't "nudge" a friend's marriage. That would be disrespectful and manipulative. Wise interventions, by contrast, take what we already want—the goals, relationships, and lives we are striving toward—and help us toward good answers to troubling questions that come up along the way. When we find these answers helpful, we can use them to flourish on our own terms. That's what Sal did when she picked up her mother's answer. She used it to dig a lot of clams fast and have a great day at Buck's Harbor with her father and sister Jane.

So *how* can you intervene effectively—in your own life, for yourself and for those you care about?

This chapter elaborates the basic template. At a high level of abstraction, the idea is (1) to figure out when a defining question predictably and reasonably comes up for you or for others, understand that question and how it shapes how you or others make sense of experiences, think, feel, and act; (2) if that question would lead one down a bad path, to develop a more positive answer, one that you or others could endorse as legitimate and put to good use; and (3) to learn how to offer that answer well, with grace and dignity, whether to yourself or to others.

STEP 1: LISTENING FOR QUESTIONS

Wise interventions always start with listening—listening not so much for answers as for the questions that arise in specific circumstances. We have to listen because, truth be told, we don't already know what we need to know. We don't know which questions matter, when, and for whom. We have to learn.

Most of the time, we're getting the kids to school. Preparing for the next meeting. Making dinner. Trying to find our keys. We're living our lives. Then, when core questions come up, we're blindsided. So, our first move is to anticipate *when* questions might come up. When should we make a special effort to listen for questions and understand them?

An acronym can help: "TICs," Transitions, Identities, and Challenges.

When to Listen

TRANSITIONS: RATS, SNUGGLES, AND EARLY BLOOMERS. First, it's often in transitions, when the world is in flux, that we're trying to make sense of things. It's no accident that it was in my first month of college that the line at the In-N-Out truck spooked me. I was just joining a new community. *How will people receive me? Will I make friends? Will I be able to work toward my goals?*

That's why some of the most powerful wise interventions focus on transitions. A classic study addressed teachers and the impressions they form of students very early in the school year—impressions that can quickly calcify to lock in productive or unproductive patterns of interaction.

This being psychology, the story, of course, begins with rats. In the 1960s, the Harvard psychologist Bob Rosenthal was teaching a class on learning. He'd taught his students about a research program at McGill University in the 1950s that had bred rats to be especially fast, or especially slow, at navigating a maze to earn a tasty treat. For their last assignment, Rosenthal told his students that they'd get to replicate the work from McGill. Each student would get five rats. Some students would get "maze-bright" rats: "[You] should find your animals on average showing some evidence of learning during the first day of running. Thereafter performance should rapidly increase." Others got "maze-dull" rats: "[You] should find on the average very little evidence of learning in your rats."

There was, in fact, a research program at McGill in the 1950s that had bred rats to be "bright" or "dull" at running mazes. But these weren't the rats that tricky Bob Rosenthal gave out. His students just got standard-issue lab rats. Rosenthal wanted to see what would happen if they just *believed* that their rats were "bright" or "dull."

When Rosenthal looked at the data, he found that those expectations made a big difference. When students were told that their rats were "maze-bright," the rats solved the maze in two minutes and twenty-one seconds, on average. They showed a sharp growth curve, "a monotonically increasing function." Every day, they did better than the day before. But when students thought their rats were "maze-dull," the rats took much longer, three minutes and twenty-eight seconds. After some initial improvement they plateaued. Same genetic line. Same task. Same practice. Different label.

What was happening? It looked like magic, and sometimes Rosenthal talked about it that way. But actually, it seems, it came down to snuggles. Students said they liked the "maze-bright" rats more. And they were more friendly and gentle with them. Was that helping the rats learn?

Now, who cares about lab rats and how long it takes them to navigate a maze? Not me! But I do care about kids and learning in school. And so did Rosenthal. Would what worked for rats work for schoolchildren?

After all, when a new school year begins, teachers might worry whether their students will grow academically. And they might have that worry especially for students who aren't at a high level yet, or who are stereotyped in our society as less able. So, Rosenthal went to South San Francisco, California, a working-class community just north of the airport, and gave out an official-sounding test (the "Harvard Test of Inflected Acquisition") that, he said, would identify those kids who were most likely to be "academic bloomers" that year. Then he gave teachers the results, identifying the likely "bloomers" in their class. Of course, unbeknownst to the teachers, this label was actually applied at random, just like the so-called maze-bright rats. Students themselves were told nothing. Yet eight months later, at year's end, kids labeled bloomers, especially those in the earliest grades, showed extraordinary gains in IQ scores, far outdoing the unlabeled kids. Teachers had elicited the growth they'd been led to expect.

Rosenthal's study unleashed a firestorm. Some took better expectations as the magic bullet education was waiting for, as if nothing else mattered. The belief a kid can succeed matters enormously, but it's more the engine oil than the engine. School requires many things, not just better expectations but well-designed lesson plans, skilled teachers, and committed administrators. There are no magic bullets.

In the research world, a generation came of age one part inspired by Rosenthal's work and one part dubious. So predictably, a wave of studies tried to replicate the results. Some "worked" (labeled kids did better); some didn't. We now know that there are key details of Rosenthal's study that mattered. First, he didn't tell teachers that students were "smart." That might backfire if a kid then failed an early assignment. He called kids "bloomers." The expectation was for *growth*.

Second was the timing, and this drives home the importance of transitions. Rosenthal gave the bloomer label within *the first week* of the new school year. It's during these early days when a teacher is trying to make sense of a new crop of kids (*Will this child learn and grow? Will that one? Or will he just goof off all year long?*). That's when a good label might stick and start a better spiral. But after teachers have set their views, a too-late label will wash away. In fact, in later studies when labels came after several weeks, they had little effect.

IDENTITIES: STEREOTYPES AND LIVER FOR DINNER. Part of the impetus for Rosenthal's work was the knowledge that, implicitly or explicitly, some children are labeled dull. The bloomer label was a way to undo that presupposition in the mind of a teacher. But more questions come to the table when *you* know that some aspect of your identity—such as your race, your gender, your age, or any other aspect of your self—could be the basis for people seeing you as less able than others.

It was research on identity that first showed me the incredible power of psychology. For me, it's a flashbulb memory. Sitting on the old white couch in my parents' living room at the age of fourteen, I read a story in *The Atlantic Monthly* about an amazing study by my now colleague Claude Steele. Steele and his collaborator Josh Aronson brought together Stanford undergraduates to take a challenging test. In a first case, they explained that the test was carefully designed "to provide a genuine assessment of your verbal abilities and limitations." Indeed, the problems came from the GRE, a test used in admissions to graduate school.

In this circumstance, Black students got only about five problems right in the time allotted, while White students got ten right. This despite the fact that all the students were well prepared, and analyses equated for any difference in preparation. It's a disparity found so often Steele would later call it "almost lawful."

For me at fourteen, it was depressing. In social studies class, I'd been learning about the persistence of inequality in America, despite many investments and programs. It was hard to reconcile the idealism of the American dream with the idea that other young people in my generation wouldn't have the same opportunities I had. It went without saying, it seemed, that there was nothing you could do in the short term to level the playing field.

But you could. For Steele and Aronson created another circumstance and then, on the exact same problems, within exactly the same time limit, Black students' performance soared. In fact, equating for students' preparation, Black students did just as well as White students, even a little better. What was the difference? It was just a little thing, it seemed. It was how the task was presented. In the second case, Steele and Aronson didn't call it a test. They said the problems weren't evaluative in any way. They were just a series of verbal puzzles, hard ones designed to help psychologists understand how people solve puzzles.

When I first learned about this research, it blew my mind. Something as basic as test performance, and an inequality as old as racial gaps in achievement, could be mitigated with a "simple" change in instruction. *What was this power?* I had to know.

Steele argued that the first circumstance created a "predicament" for Black students. Vast stereotypes in the United States pose people of African descent as less able than others. Less smart. That's upsetting. In our terms, a so-called evaluative test puts questions on the table. *If I do badly, will people take that as proof of the stereotype that Black people aren't smart? Will I let down my whole group?* Now, hundreds of experiments later, we know that the very desire to disprove a stereotype is distracting and makes it harder for people to perform well. Steele called it "stereotype threat."

In the second case, all Steele did was tell students that the task wasn't evaluative. But that's not a little thing at all. It's huge. Now questions that come from stereotypes need not come up. Now all students were free to perform well.

In just the same way, when you tell people that a math test has been specially designed to be "gender-fair," that women perform just as well as men, women's scores rise. If you ask people to read an article that refutes stereotypes about age differences in memory, older adults do better on memory tasks. One team even built a mini golf course in the lab. When they called it a measure of "natural athletic ability," playing on the stereotype of White people as unathletic, it took White students nearly twenty-eight strokes on average to navigate the course. But when they called it a measure of "sports intelligence," White students got through in just twenty-three strokes. Black students, who face the opposite stereotype, showed exactly the opposite pattern.

These are all examples of performance, intellectual or athletic. But stereotypes can also muck up everyday conversations. Say you're at a party with a diverse group and the conversation turns to a sensitive subject like affirmative action. If you're White, you could wonder, *Will I say something wrong? Could I be seen as racist?* If you're Black, you might wonder, *Will I be respected and valued? Will I experience racism?* Research finds these mutual questions can lead people to avoid tough topics, and make them awkward if they do engage in them. These questions undermine learning and mutual understanding. So when our identities are on the table, we should listen up. What risks does a person with a particular identity face? What questions are on the table for them?

In high school, for me, research on stereotype threat wasn't just fascinating. It was tantalizing. Could we harness this power? Could we make real-world situations more like the puzzles condition? Could that help kids succeed and make our world more fair and equitable? In many ways, that inspiration is the origin of this book, thirty years coming.

Identity isn't just about stereotypes, though, or how you might be seen by outsiders. People also want to fit in with their group. If you think a new behavior might put your standing at risk (*Is this what people like me do?*), you might hold back—even if that behavior is the right thing to do. Recognizing this question contributed, in its small way, to the American war effort in World War II.

During the war, the United States faced meat shortages, yet "cheap meats" like heart, kidney, and brain were going underused. The War Department wanted to get people to eat more of these organ meats, so it turned to Kurt Lewin for ideas. Lewin, a German Jew, had fled Nazi Germany for the United States in 1933 to become one of the founders of social psychology. He's one of my intellectual heroes.

So, in 1942, Lewin set to work interviewing people in a small midwestern community about their food choices. The first thing he saw was that almost all meals were eaten at home and housewives controlled what food came into the kitchen. Because housewives were the gatekeepers, he focused his efforts on them.

In one case, Lewin did the obvious thing, mostly to show it wouldn't work. He gave housewives compelling lectures about the virtues and importance of eating organ meats, including tasty recipes, detailed nutritional information, and the importance for the war effort. It was all led by the town nutritionist. Great stuff. No effect. Over the next week, exactly 3 percent of housewives served organ meats to their families.

Why didn't that work? What Lewin had seen when he'd talked with housewives was that these foods were stigmatized in this particular community. "Kidneys or certain viscera are considered . . . as food only for poor people," he wrote. Lewin saw that the prospect of serving these foods provoked questions for housewives. *Is this something people like me do? If I served these foods, how might I be judged?* No matter how compelling, the lecture didn't address these questions.

So, with a second group, Lewin engaged housewives in a group discussion. A facilitator talked about the war and the efforts of the government to change health habits. He asked the participating women, "as a representative group of housewives," what they might do to help, what obstacles stood in the way of serving organ meats, and how these obstacles might be overcome. At the end, the nutritionist shared the same recipes. Then, to close the conversation, the facilitator orchestrated a key detail. Women were asked for a show of hands. Who would serve organ meats to their families in the next week? As hands started to rise, a woman could see the norm of what "housewives like me" do shift. And if you raised your own hand, you'd be making a public commitment in front of your peers to the new norm. It was a way to answer those questions. *Yes. People like me can do this. No, I won't be judged poorly.* Over the next week, 32 percent of housewives served organ meats.

As Lewin later wrote, from one vantage point, these results were deeply counterintuitive. "Perhaps one might expect single individuals to be more pliable than groups of like-minded individuals," he wrote in an article published the year after his death. "However, it is usually easier to change individuals formed into a group than to change any one of them separately." To do that, you had to address the question of what it is that "we" do.

Identities can be tricky because they depend inherently on perspective. My question might not be your question, and your question might not be mine. And a question that comes up at one time might not come up at another. For certain members of my family there is no worry about eating heart and kidney. It's just, *More please.*

CHALLENGES. The third circumstance that often elicits core questions is when we face challenges, when things are hard, when we struggle or fail. Some challenges are obvious. It could be a bad test score. *Does this mean I'm dumb and will never learn?* But it could also be Sal's loose tooth. For me, there was the line at the In-N-Out truck; the tremble that made me flip the boat; and being asked to hold the school sign in preschool.

Tifbits.

There's nothing inherent in these events that makes them challenges. Sometimes, even if you live them, you have to figure out why they get under your skin. I didn't understand myself when I got pissy with the In-N-Out truck. I doubt the women in Lewin's study could have easily articulated the deeper barrier to serving brains to their families (*Is this something people like me do?*). They were just saying, "Yuck!"

It can be hard to see with clarity the challenges you face. Harder yet is understanding the challenges another person faces. So knowing when to listen isn't enough. We also have to learn to listen well, both to others and to ourselves. Suppose you're my brother, mystified at his ex's reaction to his untucked shirt. The proper response is not, "You're overreacting." The proper response is, "Please help me understand. What does this mean to you?" And then you have to listen.

How to Listen

PERSPECTIVE TAKING, PERSPECTIVE GETTING. When you or someone else has a big reaction to a small event, it's like an alarm bell. *Ding, Ding, Ding!* Something is up. You know there's a question to figure out. But how can you do that? In *One Morning in Maine,* Sal makes it easy. She says her worries out loud ("One of my teeth is loose! It will hurt and I'll have to stay in bed! I won't be able to eat my breakfast and go with Daddy to Buck's Harbor!"). But often things are more opaque.

The standard advice to understand other people better is to take their perspective. But often that's absurd. If my brother just tried to take his ex's perspective, it would have clarified exactly nothing. For an untucked shirt meant nothing to him. Sometimes perspective taking is presented as the cure-all to improve understanding and overcome conflict. But it's not.

A few years ago, a team of psychologists led by Tal Eyal at Ben-Gurion University of the Negev in Israel found that people consistently *believed* that if you tried to take someone else's perspective, you'd be better at understanding them—whether it was understanding a stranger's emotions or your spouse's preferences about what to do on a Saturday night. But people were spectacularly wrong. Across twenty-four separate experiments, Eyal found that making an effort to take another person's perspective didn't improve people's understanding of the other person. If anything, it made people worse.

How disconcerting is that? And if we have trouble understanding our spouses, it sure doesn't bode well for understanding people with vastly different lived experiences.

But in a twenty-fifth experiment, Eyal tried something different. She did what Sal did with her mother. She gave people a chance to talk.

The participants in the study were couples. In the key group, Eyal let them talk first for five minutes about what they liked and didn't. Would you rather spend a year in London or in Paris? Would you rather spend a quiet evening at home or go to a party? And with that conversation people became far more accurate at understanding their partners. Eyal concluded that we can't just take someone else's perspective. But we can get it. She called it "perspective getting."

Several years ago a close friend moved with her family to Dresden, Germany, to take a new job. Her husband was often away during the week working in Switzerland, leaving her to solo parent two young boys as she worked full-time. The kids could make their way home from school all right in the afternoon. The trouble was that sometimes they literally couldn't open the front door. It was sticky, and on hot days the wood would expand and the boys were just too small to shove the door open.

So my friend turned to a neighbor in the building, a retired woman who was usually home in the afternoons, and asked if she could help her kids out. The neighbor was hesitant, but one warm day that fall when the boys couldn't open the door, she let them in.

That night the neighbor knocked on my friend's door. To my friend's shock, the neighbor asked her to please never request that she open the door for the boys again.

Oh, the thoughts that coursed through my friend's mind! *That selfish woman! Why would she be so unkind?*

But she stopped. Was there something else? Was there something she didn't know?

That's when my wise friend made a small gift and brought it to her neighbor. She explained her circumstance. That she was a working mom. That she had meetings all afternoon and couldn't just leave work. That her husband was out of town during the week. She expressed her thanks for the woman's help that afternoon. And then she listened.

As they talked, my friend learned that her neighbor was deeply uncomfortable with the idea of opening someone else's door. It violated the very strong notion of privacy she held for a person's home, a value of particular importance in this area of Germany. As my friend listened, she saw the question on her neighbor's mind (*Will I be invading their privacy?*). And once that question was on the table, she found she could answer it (*Absolutely not!*). And then she found her own angry question (*Why would she be so unkind?*) evaporate.

With this new understanding, my friend and her neighbor became close friends. And the neighbor never failed to let the boys in when the door stuck.

If I'm a man, I can't just guess what it's like to be a woman. If I'm forty-five years old, I can't just guess what it's like to be fifteen and growing up today, or ninety and living in a retirement community. I can't even guess what it's like to be my spouse—and it's been lockdown and we've been living together 24/7.

But I can ask. And you can share. And I can listen. And if we do that well and sincerely, we can start to learn. So, maybe we do have a magic ingredient—language.

For the writer Ijeoma Oluo, finding the language to talk about race gave her community. Oluo begins her book *So You Want to Talk*

About Race by describing the centrality of race in her life, "one of the most defining forces," and the value she gains when she finds a community with whom she can share race-related experiences. "This is not just a gap in experience and viewpoint. The Grand Canyon is a gap. This is a chasm that you could drop entire solar systems into . . . [but] we can find our way to each other. We can find a way to our truths. I have seen it happen. My life is testament to it. And it all starts with a conversation."

Kurt Lewin left Germany in August 1933 with his wife and children. His mother and sister, who went to Holland instead of the United States, would be captured and killed by the Nazis. That May, Lewin wrote to a longtime colleague, Wolfgang Köhler, at the Berlin Psychological Institute, describing his decision. He began, "I think it is practically impossible for a non-Jew to gauge what being a Jew has meant for a person, even in the liberal era of the last 40 years." But then he goes on to describe this circumstance:

> There have probably been very few Jewish children of any generation who have not been singled out from the natural group of their peers between their 6th and 13th year. Quite suddenly and without any kind of predictable cause, they have been beaten up and treated with contempt. Whether instigated by teachers, by students, or simply by people on the street, these recurring experiences pull the ground out from under the feet of the young child.

So, Lewin begins to help his friend into his experience of the world.*

Sometimes when people are trying to share their experiences with people of different backgrounds, they use a linguistic device called "generic yous." It's a way to make your experience normal and general, so anyone can relate to it. Here's a story shared by an older man about his experience as one of the first Black students to

---

* It appears that this letter was never mailed, perhaps because it would have put both sender and recipient in danger. It was found among Lewin's papers by his daughter.

enroll at an all-White boarding school in Virginia in 1967. He's telling the story on *This American Life,* on National Public Radio—that is, to an audience with many White people. He speaks almost entirely in the second person:

> If you could imagine yourself being in bed, asleep, and somebody throwing your sheet over your head and you're suddenly being pummeled by a bunch of guys. That's pretty intense. At fourteen years old, feeling that you have no sanctuary at all, feeling that you're really not safe from getting beat up, and that you're doing it not just for yourself, but for a movement that's larger than yourself, taking that kind of beating, and it hurts when you get hit.
>
> Then you don't sleep the rest of the night because you don't know if they're coming back. You're crying. You're angry. You're hurt.
>
> The next day, when you go out to breakfast, you're looking around, trying to see if you can identify everybody that did it because of how maybe they're looking at you. You wonder if everybody else knows, and if they're laughing behind your back. It's humiliating, but it also made me angry. It made me hostile in some ways.

Only at the very end does the first person emerge. That second person is a way to invite others into your circumstance, to consider, "What might that be like?"

DETECTIVE WORK. Sometimes we don't have the luxury of talking directly about an experience. Sometimes it's more a process of figuring things out. Then you have to follow the clues. You begin with an idea of a question that might be on the table for a person at a given time. As evidence comes in, you update your beliefs. You put it together and, if the process goes well, an image is cast in sharp relief.

My grandmother Ginny died in the summer of 2015, following a long and joyful life. That December, my extended family gathered for a memorial in Rhode Island. Later we would scatter Ginny's

ashes in a favorite park along the shore where she and my grandfather David had liked to walk and watch the birds.

The night before the memorial, I was putting Lucy to bed. She
was three at the time, so I thought the whole thing might be a bit
confusing for her. I decided to talk with her some about what was
going on.

"Nini [Lucy's name for my mother] is going to be sad tomorrow,"
I said. "It's her mother's memorial." I paused. "Everybody dies."

"But I won't die?" Lucy said.

"Well, yes, you will, a long, long time from now."

"But *you* won't die?"

"Yes, I will, a long, long time from now."

Lucy was quiet for a long time. I wondered if she might be upset.
But then she said with perfect calmness, "Then there will be no
more people?"

"But there are the babies."

Lucy thought some more. And then she said, "It's like in and
out, in and out." And she made this beautiful circle motion with her
hands.

"Yes!" I said.

I had thought that death might be a fearsome prospect to Lucy.
That watching the memorial might provoke troublesome questions
for her. And I wanted to get ahead of that, in the safe space together,
just the two of us before bed. But I was wrong. For Lucy, it wasn't an
emotional topic at all. There was no big question or worry for her, at
least not then. She was just trying to understand the facts. I saw
then that talking through big, complex subjects is not something
we do just once but many times. There are many layers. It begins
with getting the facts on the table.

In that case, I projected a bit. I assumed that Lucy had worries
she didn't have. The conversation helped me learn my mistake and
understand her a bit better, as I think it helped her.

But more often, we're blind to the worries that someone else has,
because they're not our own. In the year after grad school, I took a
year off research to do a fellowship in the U.S. Congress. I ended up

working in the office of Senator Hillary Rodham Clinton. The experience was fabulous, and there were many adventures (and misadventures) along the way. Toward the end of the year, I staffed a meeting for Senator Clinton with the president of an Ivy League university, certainly a powerful person in his own right, along with the university's general counsel. It would be a friendly meeting, mostly a catching up. There were only a couple items on the agenda, and no major issues. So, for the most part, I was just looking forward to an interesting conversation.

The meeting was held in Senator Clinton's office in the Russell Senate Office Building. I sat on the long yellow sofa next to the senator across from our guests. As the conversation proceeded, I noticed that the president's leg kept jerking back and forth, up and down. It wasn't just a little swaying, but some real twitches. Big movements. *What's going on here?* I thought. *Is he okay? Is this some kind of medical event? Am I going to have to get the paramedics in here?* I was mesmerized by those legs, jerking this way, jerking that.

Only then did it dawn on me. "Ah shit! He's nervous! Of course he is! He's meeting Hillary Clinton!"

You might think it'd be easy to know what bothers you, what gets under your own skin. After all, who's more knowledgeable about your inner experience than you? *Ha!* If only we were so wise. The truth is that, often, we have no clue. You might also think that as a psychologist I'd have some special advantage in understanding myself. And you would be wrong. It's not just the In-N-Out truck. I regularly confound myself. Once, toward the end of grad school, a dentist asked me, "Have you been under a lot of stress lately?"

"No," I replied, completely truthfully.

"Are you sure?" he asked. "Because it looks like you've been grinding your teeth at night."

"Really?" I said. "I don't think so."

"I do," he said.

As I thought about this later, I realized there had been a lot going on. I was trying to apply for jobs and figure out what to do after grad school. A relationship had ended. I wasn't sleeping well at night. If I thought about stress scales, it added up to a lot. In fact, if I were my friend, I'd say I was definitely under a lot of stress. But I had no direct experience of it. It took the dentist to cue me in. So now I pay attention. If I'm grinding my teeth at night, I know I'm stressed out. And I ask myself why, what might I be stressed about? That's detective work. (And I got a night guard, so I'm not toothless when I'm sixty-four.)

It's easy to think that our privileged access to our internal experience grants us special insight. But sometimes it's just misdirection. We gaslight ourselves. Wrapped up in the day to day, we miss the big picture, fail to see the pattern in our responses. We're too close. To make it harder yet, core questions can feel like a growing stain on your life. Who wants to admit a question like *Will I ever get a job?* or *Will anyone love me?* Instead, we suppress these questions, pushing them down. But the worry doesn't go away. It stays hidden beneath layers of defensiveness and obfuscation, unrecognized and undealt with.

In many ways, basic research in social psychology is just a more structured way to listen to people, to hear them and learn the questions they face. Often, we start simple, just by asking people about their experiences, especially with transitions, times when identities might matter, or situations that might be challenging. It's what Lewin did with housewives in the Midwest. Or, if you're interested in the transition to college, you might ask college students to share a time they felt they really belonged, and a time when they weren't so sure. "Tell me a story," I'll ask. "What happened? What thoughts crossed your mind? How did you feel? How has your experience changed over time?"

Then, as our understanding builds, we might create structured situations to do just what I've suggested you can do in your life: to look systematically for when even "small" events might elicit a large response. In the first study I ran in grad school, I asked students to list eight friends who might fit in well in an academic field. It was a normal, everyday task, but it was carefully designed to be hard. The goal was to learn how Black students would read the difficulty of listing friends in an academic field: What would it mean to them? How would they *construe* it? I found it triggered them to doubt their belonging and potential in the field. They even discouraged another Black student from pursuing it. That response crystallized for me the question Black students faced at this predominantly White college: *Can people like me belong here?*

It's the same strategy Sandra Murray used in her study of couples. She put together a situation—you see your partner writing on and on, seemingly about your faults. Then she looked at how people with low self-esteem read that situation (*Maybe that means my partner doesn't love me*). And it's what Claude Steele did in his work on stereotype threat. He called a test "evaluative" and then looked to see how people who faced a negative stereotype read that situation (*Maybe I'll just be seen as a token of a negative stereotype*) and what that did to their performance.

STEP 2: SURFACING QUESTIONS, DEVELOPING ANSWERS

Once you've begun to recognize the questions people face in any given situation, what can you do? The first part is making these questions visible and understanding them together with others, which I'll call surfacing. The second is developing better answers.

Surfacing Questions

In March 2022, I had dinner at Café Einstein Stammhaus, a lovely old-world establishment in Berlin, Germany, with dark wood paneling and a fabulous Viennese cranberry schnitzel. I was there to help welcome a new cohort of undergraduates to their study abroad experience. I happened to sit with a young woman I'll call Julia. It was our first conversation together, and as we made our way through the schnitzel, I asked Julia about her life. She told me that she'd been a very competitive gymnast in high school, "but then I blew my knee out and COVID happened." There was something in the way she told her story, her complete frankness, that let me see clearly and then just ask the question that came to mind.

"Did that make you depressed?"

"Oh, definitely," Julia said, without missing a beat. "I mean, I was already seeing a therapist, but for sure."

I don't think a young person in my generation would have been so comfortable sharing a psychological problem. I know I wouldn't have been. I admired that in Julia. In that conversation, she put her circumstance on the table for me. She was completely open. Then we could both see it for what it was. You're seventeen, eighteen years old. You've organized your whole life around an activity; now you can't do it anymore. And you can't even see your friends. That's the situation. Might that make a person depressed? Of course it could.

In that conversation, Julia and I ratcheted each other up to achieve a common understanding of a difficult circumstance. That understanding firmly held, questions that might otherwise rear up, questions like *Is something wrong with me?* or *Will he judge me?* fall aside.

Surfacing means recognizing the psychological situation you're in, gaining clarity about the question or questions it provokes, understanding that these questions are a normal response, and talking and thinking through ways to make progress. That process might start with yourself but often this is work we do together, building toward a common understanding, as Julia and I did.

A great way to see the power of surfacing is to look at situations where it was lacking. One example is Claude Steele's work on stereotype threat. When I first learned about stereotype threat in the 1990s, it seemed as if the stereotype would just loom in a person's awareness. The threat was "in the air," in Steele's words. *If I do poorly, it might seem people like me are dumb!* But the early studies yielded curiously mixed evidence that students even reported more anxiety under stereotype threat. In grad school, I once attended a talk by Steele's collaborator Josh Aronson. Aronson shared how he'd talked with participants in the study afterward and told them about the theory of stereotype threat that he and Steele were developing. Even though Black students had performed so much worse when the problems were represented as "a test," Aronson relayed that

they had said, "to a T, 'Interesting theory. Didn't happen to me.'"
Black students were unaware of the question they faced or, at least,
unwilling to acknowledge this question to Aronson.

What we know now is that when people experience stereotype
threat, they *suppress* thoughts about the stereotype. They push them
away. In another study, my good friend Christine Logel at the University of Waterloo outside Toronto, Canada, asked women to take
an evaluative math test. First, however, she gave women a task in
which they had to identify whether strings of letters were words or
nonwords (it's called a lexical-decision task). Some of the words
were related to negative stereotypes about women (for example, "il-
logical," "irrational," "emotional," "weak," "failure"), and others were
not. Ironically, Logel found that when women were about to take a
math test under stereotype threat, just when you would think the
stereotype would be top of mind, they were actually *slower* to identify these gender stereotypical words. They were pushing those
thoughts away.[*]

When you think about it, this makes sense. After all, if you care
about a subject and really want to do well on a test, then that's what
you want to focus on, not some crappy stereotype. The problem is
that this effort at thought suppression itself takes up mental resources. In fact, Logel found that the *slower* women were to identify
words related to the stereotype the worse they did on the test.

So, suppression doesn't work. But could you contend with those
thoughts? In one of the sillier studies in the literature, Logel reasoned that if you surfaced the amorphous negative thoughts that
come up under stereotype threat and gave people a strategy to manage them, even an absurd strategy, this might free up mind space
and help people do better. To try this out, she suggested to women,
"Should you feel nervous, anxious, or worried you do not know
what to do while taking this test, please try and replace those

---

[*] Another reason we know women were pushing the stereotype away is that *after*
the test women who'd been under stereotype threat showed a rebound in accessi-
bility of the stereotype-related words. They sprang back in awareness, just as
thoughts of a white bear rebound after you try to suppress them.

thoughts with thoughts about a red Volkswagen." Women's performance *doubled*.

Later studies used a more direct approach. A lab study led by Michael Johns at the University of Arizona found that teaching people about stereotype threat caused women's score on a tough math test to jump from 36 percent correct to 53 percent. "Knowing is half the battle," he called it. Could that make a difference in the real world, where students are studying and learning over time? A team at San Francisco State University led by Avi Ben-Zeev taught 670 undergraduate students enrolled in challenging math, science, and engineering majors about stereotype threat. That way, if students experienced vague worries, they would know where these worries came from. *Why am I feeling anxious? It's not because I lack ability, am not prepared, or don't belong. It's stereotype threat.* That raised grades among Black and Latinx students over a full semester, eliminating the racial achievement gap. As the study taught students, "Knowledge is power." These gains are wonderful. But it's notable that students needed help to get there. Like me with the dentist, they needed Ben-Zeev's team to help them see their own experience clearly.

Surfacing helped me just the other day as a parent. My wife and I and our kids were leaving the Tech Interactive, a very cool museum in San Jose, California, when our son, Oliver, who was seven, got caught up in an exhibit near the exit. We were ahead of him and waited just a few seconds outside the doors before he came running after us, tears streaming down his face. I picked him up and hugged him. The thought crossed my mind to just say out loud the question I knew he'd ask. "You were scared you'd be left behind, right?" Oliver nodded, and I felt his small body relax. That's what the question was. It was reasonable. But the fear needn't hold.

We have no magic crayons. But when we bring the questions we face into the open and place them in the space between us, we can see these questions clearly. We can understand them, where they come from, how they're reasonable. And we can decide what they mean, what they don't, and what to do with them.

Developing Wise Answers

Surfacing is about understanding the questions with others. Sometimes that's enough, like with Oliver at the Tech Interactive. Just stating a question can normalize it and sap its power.

But other times, we need to dig deeper, to build up the answers that will expand our sense of what is possible and help us thrive. It's a process, and we might need good structures or help from others to go through it, especially when those answers are more complex.

First it helps to understand what wise answers are not. They're not BS. They're not sticking your head in the sand and denying reality. If you're a student struggling in math class, it won't do to deny this. Nor will it help a new parent overwhelmed by a colicky baby to pretend that everything is hunky-dory. Instead, wise answers acknowledge the circumstance a person is in and, fully recognizing this, reject whatever nasty implication that circumstance might put on the table for a person (*Maybe I'm dumb at math? Maybe I'm a bad parent?*). By staying grounded in the reality of the challenges we face, wise answers become authentic and legitimate. They become answers we can use to address these challenges.

We'll see many examples in the pages to come, and the details matter. But wise answers follow some broad channels. When Sal's mother says, "That means that today you've become a big girl," she shows Sal that losing a tooth is normal, that it happens to everyone, that it doesn't portend bad things, and that, in fact, it's a sign of growth. That's a lot of work, all at once.

When bad things happen in our relationships, in school, at work, or in our health, we need a growth mindset in the broadest sense of the term. That means avoiding negative labels, labels that imply a fixed, negative view of yourself, of other people, or of a situation you are in. We can use process terms instead, to describe an experience, not who you are or who someone else is, but what you're experiencing. This growth mindset also recognizes that other people too have faced your circumstance; that you're no snowflake, whatever the situation. It means recognizing causes of the bad thing that don't malign you or others as lazy, stupid, immoral, or otherwise bad; the obstacles you face are legitimate and others have faced them too. It means forecasting opportunities for improvement, identifying productive ways to face the challenge, not resigning yourself to a fixed negative future. It means, finally, recognizing opportunities that could arise in the context of the bad thing, to see what might be positive, meaningful, or useful, and thus not just something to be overcome but an opportunity.

We can break this down into five narrative principles:

- Principle 1: Avoid negative labels (*I'm not bad/You're not bad*)
- Principle 2: You're not the only one; you're never the only one (*It's normal*)
- Principle 3: Recognize causes that don't malign you or others (*I/you face real obstacles*)
- Principle 4: Forecast improvement (*It can get better*)
- Principle 5: Recognize opportunities (*Silver lining*)

These principles vary in whether they take leading or supporting roles. Sometimes one or more is absent. And they're always molded to the objective circumstance. Wise interventions don't obscure the truth. But in surfacing the truth, they also show us what's not true.

Just a few blocks from our home on the Stanford campus, nestled by Lake Lagunita along the jogging route I take with our dog, Tomato, is a small "contemplative garden." As Tomato and I approach the garden, I always take a pause. For this is the site where Chanel Miller, author of *Know My Name*, was assaulted following a campus party in January 2015.

An assault can seem to imply that you are a bad or tainted person, that you deserved it, that you'll never be loved again, that a victim is all you are. In the victim-impact statement Miller prepared for the court, she gave voice to this experience—and rejected it:

> You took away my worth, my privacy, my energy, my time, my safety, my intimacy, my confidence, my own voice, until today. . . .
> You made me a victim. . . . For a while, I believed that that was all

I was. I had to force myself to relearn my real name, my identity. To relearn that this is not all that I am. I am a human being who has been irreversibly hurt, who waited a year to figure out if I was worth something.

The clarity of Miller's writing is its power. *Here* is the experience. *Here* are the fearsome thoughts. They are not true. *Here* is what is true.

There's a reason we associate wisdom with age. With experience, we can learn better ways to think about the challenges life presents. Wise interventions help us age—in the best way. They give us a map. They help us see ahead and see clearly—to anticipate and recognize the questions we might feel or are in the midst of feeling in the face of a challenge. This wisdom assures us that what we're feeling is normal, and that we can make progress. In sharing and forecasting her experience, Miller provides an extraordinary service to others. But how did she get there?

STEP 3: OFFERING WISE ANSWERS WITH GRACE

None of us can simply shift our thinking at will. You can't just tell someone caught in a self-defeating cycle to quit it. We come by our modes of thought honestly. So, we need good reasons to adopt new views. That means wise interventions aren't just giving advice, or telling someone what they *should* do or believe. It's not a teacher telling a student, "You should have a growth mindset!" or a "friend" saying, "Why can't you just get over it?" Nor are wise interventions simply repeating some mantra ("I'm good enough, I'm smart enough, and doggone it, people like me!"). These are not blunt-force instruments that exist apart from a context; rather, they help people contend with the context.

Instead, wise interventions involve graceful ways to develop good answers, both in offering them to others and in committing to them yourself. Sometimes the approach is direct. But often, wise answers involve more *showing* than telling. It might mean a teacher or boss sharing their own worries about belonging and, in so doing, showing that it's normal to feel like an impostor at first, that this experience is not a chronic or permanent state of affairs, and how, with time, it will get better. Sometimes, it's seeing another person's process. In grad school, my adviser, Geoff Cohen, took pains to show me the work he went through in writing. Seeing the labor behind the simplicity and clarity of his words gave me a road map. My own early flailings were no reason to think I couldn't get there myself. For some of the most personal difficulties we face, wise answers come simply from the opportunity to reflect on well-structured questions.

The verb we use here is really important. I like "to offer." Wise interventions are not mind control. They're not manipulative. And this is not social engineering. You can't force someone to believe something or do something they don't want to (even if you wanted to, which you shouldn't). Wise interventions are not imposed from on high or shoved down people's throats. Rather, they anticipate the questions that reasonably come to mind in a situation and then *offer* people—in graceful ways appropriate to the relationship, the time, and the context—answers that could help them navigate that situation well. People can then take up that answer and develop it for themselves, or not, as they choose. You do wise interventions *with* people, not to people.

Even when we develop wise interventions just for ourselves, it is the same. You don't force an answer on yourself. You *offer* yourself an answer, a way of thinking. You spend some time playing with that answer, tossing it around in your head, trying it out in your life, until it feels just right for you and your circumstance, and then you use it to spiral up.

More Direct Approaches: Peanuts and Probation

If wise interventions are *offers*, it's important to understand the role that one person can play for another. What is their relationship? What is appropriate for one person to offer the other?

In *One Morning in Maine*, Sal's mother is a parent. She cares about Sal, she has Sal's best interest at heart, and she has more experience than Sal. That means she has standing to tell young Sal how to think about her calamity: "That means that today you've become a big girl." Our professional roles too offer opportunities to be direct. It's what Avi Ben-Zeev's team did at San Francisco State with undergrads experiencing stereotype threat. In fact, I think that if you're a professional, you have an obligation to get this right: to help the people you serve think about their experience and any "bad" news in a way that will be most productive for them.

Let's look at two real-life examples, one from medicine and one from education. They're both important unto themselves, but they also help us see what offering wise answers can look like in practice. If you're a professional, perhaps there are lessons you can take to your work. And if you've ever been in a situation like one of these, I hope these examples give you a little more clarity.

First example. Say you're a doctor and you're doing a new kind of exposure therapy for kids with peanut allergies. Basically, you start off patients with minute amounts of peanuts and slowly build up their tolerance. It's called oral immunotherapy, and it can desensitize children to peanut allergies. Sometimes patients experience mild side effects, annoying things but not life threatening, like an itchy mouth, nausea, hives, or stomach pain. So, you tell patients that these are unfortunate side effects of treatment. They're experiences to be minimized.

That's a-psychological. It's not sensitive to the predictable concerns a child has in this circumstance.

Say you're the child. For years, you've been told a single peanut could kill you. Then, like Sal and her loose tooth, even an itchy mouth might be a calamity. *Is this a sign the treatment isn't working? Does it mean that my allergy is very severe and resistant to treatment? Am I about to die?*

The Sean N. Parker Center for Allergy and Asthma Research at Stanford wanted to get this right, so it partnered with a team led by Lauren Howe, now at the University of Zurich, and my colleague Alia Crum. Together, they developed a different message: patients were told that mild side effects are a sign that their body is strengthening and the treatment is working, as some evidence suggests. In the study, fifty kids with peanut allergies were randomized to condition, mostly boys averaging just under eleven years old. Half got the symptoms-as-positive-signals message. Half got the symptoms-as-side-effects message (treatment as usual).

What happened? Kids in the symptoms-as-positive-signals group were less anxious about symptoms over *seven months;* they had fewer symptoms as dosage increased; and they produced more antibodies associated with desensitization. When a troubling question about side effects was addressed, treatment went better.

At one point, the research team asked participants for their advice for future patients. In the treatment-as-usual condition, one child simply said, "You know, hang in there." But a boy, about ten years old, in the symptoms-as-positive-signals condition had the following exchange with an interviewer:

> INTERVIEWER: So, what advice would you give for future kids who are going to go through this treatment who might be feeling kind of afraid they might have symptoms, how would you tell them to think about their symptoms?
>
> PATIENT: Um, when you have a symptom, it it it is actually meaning that your body is fighting off peanuts.

That's like Sal, picking up an answer that's useful. Now he's sharing that answer with another child who might benefit from his wisdom.

Every day, thousands of people get terrible medical diagnoses. They're told they have cancer, heart disease, a rare illness. Might people ask, *Is this a catastrophe? Is my life over?* Do these questions exacerbate illness and get in the way of treatment? Are there authentic and better ways to think about illnesses? How could medical professionals help people toward these ways of thinking?

Second example. Now you're a college administrator. One of your jobs at the end of each term is to review the transcripts of all the students at your college and identify those students whose work isn't meeting standards. Their grades are too low, or they aren't earning enough credits to maintain good academic standing. You send these students a letter informing them of this fact. You tell them they're being placed on academic probation. Here's the basic letter you've been sending:

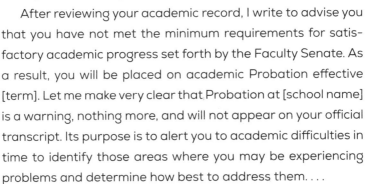

Dear [student name]

After reviewing your academic record, I write to advise you that you have not met the minimum requirements for satisfactory academic progress set forth by the Faculty Senate. As a result, you will be placed on academic Probation effective [term]. Let me make very clear that Probation at [school name] is a warning, nothing more, and will not appear on your official transcript. Its purpose is to alert you to academic difficulties in time to identify those areas where you may be experiencing problems and determine how best to address them. . . .

Placement on academic Probation is a part of the University's commitment to offer students support for—and guidance through—whatever difficulties they may have experienced. . . .

Best Regards,
[Administrator Name]
[Administrator Title]

Several years ago, a university reached out to our team. They'd built some great resources to support students on probation. They were confident they could succeed. But still they found that only one in four students got off probation at the first available opportunity, a year later. Why? What more could they do?

Say you're a student and you just got that letter. What might that be like?

To find out, our team, led by Shannon Brady now at Wake Forest University, began by interviewing students. She found that students said probation was, essentially, the worst experience of their academic lives. When Brady put students' stories of their experience with probation through automated language tools, she found they were more negative in tone than Nathaniel Hawthorne's *Scarlet Letter*, the paradigmatic tale of shame in American literature. They even rivaled *King Lear*, though they didn't quite reach the depths of the five saddest country songs of all time as identified by *Rolling Stone* magazine (a list that includes my personal favorite, "Whiskey Lullaby" by Alison Krauss and Brad Paisley).

Brady saw that probation provoked massive questions for students. *Am I one of the few losers who can't do it? Does anyone else struggle? Am I seen as weak and deficient? Does the university think I can recover?* Students were desperate for answers to these questions. But the standard letter didn't address them. In fact, it only made them worse. One student said,

> I overreached my preparation by taking [a difficult math class and a difficult physics class] in the same quarter. I failed both classes. . . . I was crushed and confused when I received the letter from [the] advising [office] that I had been placed on probation. . . . There was a lot of fear, anger and self loathing. . . . I felt like a failure and the vague impersonal language of the letter from some authority figure I had never met didn't help me at all.

The standard letter, too, was a-psychological.

So, working with the university, Brady set out to revise the letter. Many of the revisions involved just making explicit what was already in the hearts and minds of the administrators: that they viewed students with respect, that the university was ready to partner with them to address the challenges they faced, that they believed in them, and that success was possible. Some changes were easy. For instance, why the capital *P* for "probation"? Brady dropped that and revised the language further to emphasize process explicitly ("the academic probation process"). She made it explicit that students were not alone ("You should also know that you are not alone in experiencing these difficulties"). And she offered hope for return to good standing ("By working with their advisors, many [students] leave the [probation] process and continue a successful career at [school name]").

Other fixes were more subtle. One section seemed helpful at first: "Placement on academic Probation is a part of the University's commitment to offer students support for—and guidance through—whatever difficulties they may have experienced." But when Brady asked students about this, she found they experienced it as sarcastic (*whatever* difficulties). So she changed that section too to recognize the specific challenges she knew students faced ("There are many reasons students enter the academic probation process. These reasons can include personal, financial, health, family, or other issues"). Here's where the letter landed altogether.

Dear [student's first name],

After reviewing your academic record, I am writing to inform you that you have not met the minimum requirements for satisfactory academic progress set forth by the Faculty Senate. As a result, you will have an academic probation status beginning [term]. This process is simply designed to alert you to academic difficulties in time to help you identify those areas where you may be experiencing problems and determine how best to address them. It will not appear on your official transcript. . . . If you meet the requirements for satisfactory academic progress, this probationary status will end. . . .

There are many reasons students enter the academic probation process. These reasons can include personal, financial, health, family, or other issues. Our goal is to help you identify the factors that are relevant to you and to help you address them. You should also know that you are not alone in experiencing these difficulties. Many students enter and participate in the probation process each year, and by working with their advisors, many leave the process and continue a successful career at [school name]. . . .

We are confident that you can meet these standards. However, it is important that you take steps to address the causes of your academic difficulties. If these conditions are not met, you may be at risk for restricted registration status or suspension.

Best Regards,
   [Administrator Name]
   [Administrator Title]

Brady also included a second page with five stories from former students who'd gone through probation. It was a way to provide social proof that the experience of probation could be normal, that negative feelings were normal, and that growth was possible. Here's one:

When I failed an important math class, I was devastated. If anything, getting the probation notice made me feel worse. I thought I was the only one having a hard time. Eventually, I got up the courage to talk to my RA [resident assistant]. . . . He told me, "You'd be surprised how many times I've had this conversation." . . . I learned something important in the process, about how to face up to challenges, to reach out to others for help, and find a way forward.

—*"Michael," Junior*

Brady began to test out the new letter in small experiments. Students were asked to imagine getting placed on probation and receiving one letter or the other. In sample after sample, students said that they'd feel less ashamed and less stigmatized if they got the "psychologically attuned" letter rather than the standard letter. They even said they'd be less likely to consider dropping out. When asked to compare the two letters directly, 78 percent preferred the attuned letter. One student said, "[The attuned letter] seemed more human. [The original letter] seemed like it had been written by someone in the administration that the student would never ever meet, while [the attuned letter] more directly addressed the obvious concerns and anxieties that would arise if one were to receive this notice."

Obvious concerns? They weren't obvious to the administrators who reached out to us. These were committed professionals, good people, and fully motivated to improve students' experience. But they didn't grok the specific concerns students had, or see how they could address them, because, before our project, they'd never truly listened to their students.

Could this help students spiral up? To find out, Brady conducted a small field trial. Students being placed on probation got either one letter or the other. The first outcome was whether students met with an academic adviser promptly, as both letters asked them to do. With the standard letter just 43 percent of students showed up. The attuned letter bumped this up to 68 percent, connecting more students to resources. And a year later, Brady found that students who'd gotten the attuned letter were more likely to have returned to good academic standing, up to 43 percent from 26 percent. Rewriting the letter was no panacea. But it helped.

The attuned letter helped students for the same reason many people find the phrase "shit happens" reassuring: It punctures the perception that the shit one is currently experiencing is unique to you, rare, and damning. The fact that shit happens to other people too, probably more than you might think, and that it need not have enduring consequences, is reassuring. It means we're not alone and there's nothing wrong with us. There's just a problem to be solved.

Less Direct Approaches: Creating the Right Space

For Sal and her mother, for a patient and a doctor, or for a student and an educator, one person has standing to offer the other a better answer directly. But what if it's just two adults? Then a direct approach could come off as presumptuous: the "friend" who tells you who you are, or how you should think.

That's not appropriate. Nor is it fitting. People need to be able to develop answers for themselves. Then a less controlling approach can work better.

Sometimes the tiniest thing, at just the right time, can help a person answer a question. A few years ago, a friend told me over dinner how her tech company had closed the deal with a highly sought-after hire. Only several weeks after beginning work did the new employee reveal why she'd accepted the company's offer. It wasn't the salary or stock options, the free food, or the beer taps that opened at 4:00 P.M. Nor was it the work group or the project she would contribute to. It was a single slip of paper that no one else had noticed. On it was handwritten, "All Genders Welcome." Someone had taped that slip of paper to the single-use bathroom door down the hall from the room in which she'd interviewed. Apparently, an LGBTQ+ employee group had met in the same space a few weeks earlier. They'd put the paper up, and it had just stayed there. No one knew, but the candidate identified as transgender. That slip of paper served as a cue for her. It helped her begin to answer the basic question she faced: whether a trans person like her would be welcome at the company.

That was inadvertent. There the company got lucky. But when we can anticipate the questions that are likely to come up for a person in a situation, we can be intentional in offering better answers. Sometimes it might be a sign on the wall—a school or workplace being thoughtful about how to depict its community, what values to broadcast. But a sign goes only so far. With more complex questions, people need the right kind of space to think things through.

We've already seen one example of how to create this space. Lewin put a lot of thought into how to create discussion groups for women to consider how "housewives like me" might serve organ meats. He didn't just tell women that they should serve heart and kidney. Nor did he instruct women on how to think about this. Instead, he invited women to take on a leadership role, to think through how their community could make a change. And he created space in which women could talk through this change together. This was an opportunity for women to change their views, and to see those same changes reflected back to them in the words and actions of their peers.

When people face personal challenges, one of the best things you can do is offer models of how others have faced those same challenges: stories of how they too struggled, of worries they experienced, but how they persevered and made progress. That allows people to consider their own experience in this light, how it reflects that model or how it could, how their thinking is developing in the same way, how they're on the same growth curve. One of the best ways to do this is by inviting people to *give* advice in turn to those younger or less experienced than themselves. It's a way for a person to take on that leadership role.

Say you're a teacher. You've been teaching ten years. Sure, sometimes, kids get out of control and sometimes you get frustrated. Just the other day a student gleefully tossed whatever it was in the air again and again right in the middle of math class. You like this student, but all eyes on him, none on the math? You snapped. Almost automatically, you drew out that thick pad of referral slips you'd been handed at the beginning of the year and sent him off to the office, scheduled for detention with the assistant principal "of discipline." The next day he was sullen.

You know it wasn't your best moment. Was there another way? Will you have space to even consider this?

Say you're lucky. Some time later, your principal invites the faculty to participate in a program for experienced teachers like you. You get the chance to read stories from other teachers about their experiences working with kids when they misbehave. Teachers talk about discipline situations, how it's hard sometimes when kids act out, but how they've made progress by pulling kids closer, doing what they can to maintain positive relationships even when kids misbehave, not pushing them away. When you think about it, that's what you want to do too.

Some of the stories are from kids too. They talk about how they appreciate it when teachers listen to them, even if they don't always show it. One teacher tells a story about a time when he was a student and a teacher who'd given him detention didn't just sit there but listened to him and heard his point of view. He talks about how he tries to do that now with his students. Teachers talk about working through conflicts with students, trying to understand them, even when kids are irrational, even apologizing when necessary.

As you read the stories, you think more about your own practice. Now it's your turn. You're asked, "How have you learned to use an approach like this with your students, or are working toward it?" and "What do you do to maintain strong relationships with students, even when they misbehave?" Your responses will go to new teachers, just learning how to work with students when they misbehave. As you write down your thoughts, you think about practices you like, what has worked for you, and what hasn't. You think about how you want to show up for your students, even when they're disruptive. Before you know it, you've recommitted yourself to a better approach. And you feel proud to share your expertise with future teachers.

We call this technique "saying is believing." In it, people get stories that model an optimal way to think about a problem: not downplaying the challenge, but seeing it clearly, and seeing ways to make progress. Then they get space to explore that way of thinking for themselves, to consider how it might be true or fitting for them and build on what they might already be doing. That's offering. All the while people are treated as models for others rather than recipients of "an intervention," which could feel demeaning or controlling. Best of all, this approach leverages one of the most meaningful things to people: the opportunity to make a difference for others. When you've faced a challenge and are learning to work through it, it's an incredible opportunity to share your learnings with other people just beginning this process. That advocacy helps you recommit to your journey of growth even as it helps others begin theirs.

Creating this space can take time and planning, so these approaches can be less suited for spontaneous daily interactions. But having the right space at the right time can transform a person's life. It's particularly fitting when problems are systematic—like sky-high rates of discipline problems in school. In fact, this approach, tested in rigorous randomized controlled trials, has reduced suspension rates for thousands of students, especially students of color.

Sometimes, the touch is lighter yet. The right space might involve just the opportunity to respond to a well-put question. When people have had traumatic experiences, even the act of writing can help. It gives you a structure to work through how you want to understand something difficult: a way to construct a narrative with a beginning, a middle, and an end. You can look back on what you've written and edit it until it's just right for you, an apt description of something you have faced or are facing, what it really means, what it doesn't, and what you want to do with it. In fact, as research by Jamie Pennebaker shows, "expressive writing" can help us find closure with some of the most personal challenges.

So, it's not surprising that Chanel Miller achieved her growth and recovery in part by writing about her experience. And in writing, Miller created a model for others, a map for other people to make sense of their own experiences.

I saw Miller's impact for myself in the fall of 2021. I was teaching my Wise Interventions class at Stanford. At the end of a lecture on identity, I shared Miller's story. A few weeks later, I was holding office hours by Zoom, and a student I'll call Laura joined. We chatted for a while about her interests and research projects going on in the department that she might want to get involved in. It was a very normal conversation. Then Laura told me that she had appreciated the section on Chanel Miller, particularly because she herself had experienced a sexual assault during her sophomore year of college. And then she told me in broad strokes about her own process of recovery, a process that echoed Miller's experience. All of this she shared in a completely straightforward way. It was surfacing. It was normal. It was healthy. It was just like Julia's story in Berlin. Here's what happened. Here's what I experienced. Here's how I recovered. And that surfacing was made possible because Miller wrote about her experience with such clarity and because I shared her words in class.

Laura was just one person who benefited from Miller's story; I'm sure there are thousands of others. That's a silver lining. It's a reason why movements like MeToo matter. They're like society-wide wise interventions that help everyone in a circumstance understand that circumstance better, to know that even if you have experienced something awful, it doesn't mean you're awful, that it was your fault, or that your future will be terrible.

How Wise Interventions Fit

Wise interventions are a psychological approach to problems in our lives. So, at this point, you might ask, Is this just clinical psychology? Don't we have therapy to help people out of maladaptive ways of thinking? Indeed, we do, and it plays an important role. But a basic assumption of wise interventions is that we're fundamentally normal: We have a reasonable basis for entertaining troubling questions. They come from the circumstances we face. Clinical psychology, by contrast, is sometimes even called abnormal psychology. Going to therapy is commonly understood as what you do when something is wrong with you. Ironically, that presumption affirms the kinds of pejorative questions that give rise to problems in the first place. A Faustian bargain to get the support you need.

It's an issue even when therapists take a different view. A clinician I know sees this dynamic as so counterproductive that he wants to break up the whole model. "We can't hire enough therapists," he says, referring to the mental health crisis on university campuses. At minimum, he insists that therapists in his group begin sessions by asking, "What has happened to you?"—not "What's wrong?" Better yet, he believes, is to invest some of his resources in preventative work to address the big questions that young people face—*Who am I? Do I belong? Can I do it?* and *Will anyone love me?*—before they metastasize into clinical disorders. These are the questions, he finds, that young people want to address more than anything.

When Julia got depressed, she had very good reasons. She'd blown out her knee, couldn't do what she loved, and couldn't see her friends. When Chanel Miller questioned herself, she too had excellent reasons. She'd been assaulted, first by the perpetrator and then by a criminal justice system that interrogated her experience. Likewise, when students worry how their university might see them when they get placed on probation, they're not being irrational. Their thinking is not disordered. There is nothing wrong with them. These questions are reasonable. They're normal and predictable. That makes wise interventions broadly relevant, both to each of us as individuals and to social policy. When you learn, for instance, how people experience side effects from exposure therapy for a peanut allergy, you can anticipate what your own experience might be like in a similar situation, or what a loved one might experience if they were in that circumstance. That can help you respond. And it can help institutions too. When a doctor's office or a university groks the questions the people they serve face, it can learn how to offer better answers to people in the future. That's an opportunity for specific changes to institutional practices to help all of us thrive.

You might also ask, Do wise interventions just "psychologize" problems? If you're focused on how people interpret things, are you just "blaming the victim" while ignoring the "real roots" of problems? The worries behind these questions are one of the reasons I think it's so important to re-center the conversation on the dynamic of questions and answers. Often we use words like "interpret" and "mindset" (or "construe," the social psych jargon) to talk about these things. So, we might ask, How does a student interpret being placed on probation? But that would imply the process is all in the student's head. It'd be "her" interpretation, and if she were to get stuck in a bad way of thinking, it might seem to be her fault. It might even seem fixed, as though that interpretation were well rooted and hard to change. But basic psychological questions come from the circumstances we face; after all, the student has been told that her work is substandard, that she might even get kicked out. *How am I seen? Am I respected? Is there hope for improvement?* And these questions are dynamic. The student is trying to figure out the answers. They're not stuck—not yet. Then it's the university's responsibility to help students toward a better answer, one they can use to succeed.

Loaded questions are *a* root cause of problems. But they aren't the only cause of struggles. So, in helping people to better answers, wise interventions never act alone. They're part of a complex puzzle, the engine oil that helps an engine go.

In the pages to come we're going to see some truly remarkable findings. They show how these upward spirals can happen. Better achievement years later for students. Stronger marriages for couples. Less child abuse for kids. Lower rates of recidivism for convicted felons. But never do wise interventions act alone, and never are they "quick fixes." They typically reflect years of basic science and rigorous development and evaluation from teams of ingenious people. And even as we marvel at their power to cause positive change, a key question will also be to understand where these interventions won't work, why, and what we can do about that.

PART 2

Me

Chapter 3

Do I Belong?

I'd left my mama back in Brooklyn to go to a school
I'd never seen in a city I'd never been to.
—JACQUELINE WOODSON, *RED AT THE BONE*

A simple exercise on belonging helps
black college students years later.
—*SCIENCE NEWS*

I n the fall of 1981, a seventeen-year-old African American girl left her hometown of Chicago to enter Princeton University, following in the footsteps of her older brother, a star basketball player. The siblings grew up in a working-class family, in a one-bedroom apartment on the city's South Side, a mostly African American community. Their father worked at the city water plant, their mother was a homemaker, and in the summers sometimes they vacationed at a small cabin in Michigan. Neither parent had attended college. On both sides, family members had moved north to Chicago in the Great Migration of African Americans out of the South. At the time and still today, African American students constitute about 8 percent of Princeton undergraduates; it is an institution whose first *nine* presidents all owned slaves. What was that experience like for her?

This student was well prepared for college. She'd been on the honor roll all four years in high school and had graduated as salutatorian of her class. Four years later, having majored in sociology and minored in African American studies, she would be on her way to Harvard Law School. Yet her introduction to her senior thesis was blunt, "My experiences at Princeton have made me far more aware of my 'Blackness' than ever before. . . . No matter how liberal and open-minded some of my White professors and classmates try to be toward me, I sometimes feel like a visitor on campus; as if I really don't belong. . . . It often seems as if, to them, I will always be Black first and a student second."

Having spent four full years at Princeton, Michelle Robinson was still not sure whether she belonged.

Nine years earlier, in the fall of 1972, another student entered Princeton. Sonia Sotomayor was also the first in her family to go to college, a woman of Puerto Rican descent from the Bronx, New York. Forty-one years later, as associate justice of the Supreme Court, Sotomayor would recall, "[At Princeton, I felt like] a visitor landing in an alien land. . . . I have spent my years since Princeton, while at law school, and in my various professional jobs, not feeling completely a part of the worlds I inhabit."

And just in the spring of 2022, the soon-to-be justice Ketanji Brown Jackson told Senator Alex Padilla of California of her own experience going to Harvard in 1988: "It was rough. It was different from anything I'd known. There were lots of students there who were prep school kids like my husband who knew all about Harvard. And that was not me. I think the first semester I was really homesick. I was really questioning, 'Do I belong here?' 'Can I make it in this environment?'"

Michelle Robinson Obama, Sonia Sotomayor, and Ketanji Brown Jackson are among the most successful, respected, and widely ad-

mired members of their generations. If they experienced such profound doubts about belonging in college, it's safe to say the rest of
us aren't immune either. It's not just students at elite institutions.
Students attending all sorts of institutions, from big public universities to small colleges, have told me of their worries about belonging. One international student from Africa attending a small college
in rural western Pennsylvania gestured up at the sky in a focus
group to evoke the airplane that took her back and forth from home
to college, "Where am I?" she asked. "Just up in the air somewhere?"

When I have talked with staffers at the White House, they tell
me that questions about belonging are pervasive in their world,
too—precisely because of the awe and respect they hold for their
office. Members of the military and employees at brand-name Silicon Valley companies tell me the same thing. It's a bit like the opposite of the Yogi Berra–ism, "Nobody goes there anymore. It's too
crowded." When you value a space so much, when that institution
is so important for what you want to do and who you want to become, sometimes it's hard to believe you could truly belong there.

When I went to college, I had every advantage. It wasn't just that
I was White and middle class and from a college town. Even my
great-grandfather James Bissett Pratt was an academic, a professor
of philosophy at Williams College. One of his mentors was the eminent psychologist William James. It's a legacy I find obscene—
a form of wealth that few have. Yet still, I was struck by a bout of
homesickness early in college, as evidenced by my ridiculous tifbit
response to the In-N-Out truck I shared in chapter 1.

That was a trigger for me. What are yours?

For all of us face questions of belonging in one form or another,
at one time or another. For me in college, the context was just that I
was moving far across the country. But for millions of students,
questions about belonging have a particular painful resonance.
They come directly from the history and reality of exclusion in education along racial-ethnic and social-class lines. For it's not just *Do
I belong?* that students like Michelle Obama, Sonia Sotomayor, and
Ketanji Brown Jackson asked. The question was, *Do people like me
belong?* That question gets in the way of becoming.

"DO PEOPLE LIKE ME BELONG?"

Who belongs in the United States, who is an equal citizen, and who is welcome to participate in public life have always been fraught. At its founding, the United States included nearly 700,000 enslaved people of African descent. They were literally defined as three-fifths of a person. Thomas Jefferson, the lead author of the stirring Declaration of Independence ("All men are created equal"), would also write twelve years later, "Blacks, whether originally a different race, or made distinct by time and circumstances, are inferior to whites. Will not a lover of natural history, then, excuse an effort to keep them as distinct as nature has formed them."

The contradiction within Jefferson is reflected in the history of the United States: an epic, multigenerational battle between the forces for inclusion and those that would oppose them. We've see-sawed from the Civil War to end slavery to Jim Crow laws that resegregated public life. From the Chinese Exclusion Act of 1882, to the Immigration and Nationality Act of 1965, which removed discrimination in immigration policy, to the Muslim travel ban. From Black Lives Matter to backlash against talking about race in school.

Policies of exclusion are, of course, practiced by individuals and inflicted upon other individuals. In a 1962 essay, James Baldwin recalled an experience twenty-five years earlier, "I was thirteen and was crossing Fifth Avenue on my way to the Forty-second Street library, and the cop in the middle of the street muttered as I passed him, 'Why don't you n——s stay uptown where you belong?'" On January 6, 2021, a member of the White racist mob that stormed the U.S. Capitol accosted a passing Black bicyclist, "We're gonna take this country back—believe that shit. Fuck Black Lives Matter. What y'all need to do is take your sorry asses to the ghetto."

The civil rights movement was and is fought not just for integration but for belonging. Dr. Martin Luther King Jr. dreamed not of mere coexistence but "that one day on the red hills of Georgia, the sons of former slaves and the sons of former slave owners will be able to sit down together at the table of brotherhood."

Brotherhood.

In that dream, all people are accepted as full members of the community; all are included in its activities and supported in their growth; all are recognized and valued for their contributions and respected for their worth.

While fights for belonging have been waged in every aspect of public life, perhaps nowhere has this fight been more vicious than in school. Just a few months after Baldwin's essay, Governor George Wallace of Alabama would proclaim, "Segregation now, segregation tomorrow, segregation forever." Later that year, Wallace stood in the doorway at the University of Alabama to physically block the entrance of the first two African American students who sought to enroll there.

Just as Jefferson invoked "natural history" to justify racial segregation, racist exclusion in education hid beneath the cloak of scientism. From 1922 to 1945, my own psychology department at Stanford was led by Lewis M. Terman, a eugenicist whose main contribution to public life was to promulgate a belief as bizarre and breathtaking as it has been harmful: the idea that people have within them something deep inside, more or less fixed at birth; that this thing is highly variable across people and groups; that it more or less determines your capacities in school and life; and that it can be assessed using relatively brief instruments. Terman called this thing "intelligence." The instruments were standardized tests. Among the questions Terman developed to assess this intelligence was one that asked children to explain charming White middle-class proverbs like "One swallow does not make a summer."

If you got questions like that wrong, Terman placed you in various categories. Today, these category labels have become epithets. You might be called feebleminded, a moron, or even an imbecile. Yet it's not hard to imagine how people from diverse cultural groups might struggle with questions like this. As a citizen of the twenty-first century, I too had no idea what that swallow proverb meant until I looked it up. Does that make me feebleminded, or even an imbecile?*

Still, Terman plowed ahead with conclusions so sweeping they'd seem farcical if he weren't so self-serious. In a 1916 book, *The Measurement of Intelligence*, Terman writes,

> [Mental deficiency] represents the level of intelligence which is very, very common among Spanish-Indians and Mexican families of the Southwest and also among negroes. Their dullness appears to be racial.

For Terman the eugenicist, it was a quick hop and a jump to mass sterilization. In the next paragraph, he writes,

> Children of [low IQ] should be segregated in special classes and be given instruction which is concrete and practical. They cannot master, but they can often be made efficient workers, able to look out for themselves. There is no possibility at present of convincing society that they should not be allowed to reproduce, although from a eugenic point of view they constitute a grave problem because of their unusually prolific breeding.

So opines my former department chair and the future president of the American Psychological Association: If you can't pass the swallow test, you don't deserve good schools and, really, you shouldn't have kids. Good to know.

In his history of racism in psychology, *Even the Rat Was White*, the African American psychologist Robert Guthrie summarized how early Black academics took stock of the situation, "Eugenicists were correctly viewed as white supremacists using the concept of genetics as their weaponry against Black people."

Terman's conclusions are horrifying to read today. But they

---

* I learned it goes back to Aristotle, who wrote, "One swallow does not make a summer, neither does one fine day; similarly one day or brief time of happiness does not make a person entirely happy."

aren't so distant. The presumed importance of "intelligence," its putative power to define you and your potential, still echoes in the mind. A few years ago, I was speaking with a group of educators when, on a whim, I asked who could remember their SAT score, a test most would have taken decades earlier, judging from the quantity of gray hair in the audience. Nearly everyone in the large ballroom raised their hand. How absurd is that? Despite decades of professional experience, successes and setbacks teaching young people, these educators recalled their score on a test they had taken at sixteen or seventeen years old. For what it's worth, I can remember my SAT scores too (and my ACT scores), tests I took nearly thirty years ago. If you took these tests, do you remember your score? That's a tifbit if ever there was one.

What's one to think if public officials literally stand in the schoolhouse door to keep you out while the best-regarded scientists of the day caricature your entire community as less capable and less deserving of schooling than others? It's not subtle. Let us look anew at the first African Americans to integrate segregated schools. One can imagine the threat, the loneliness, the isolation they must have felt. What true heroes these young people were, carrying their books

Elizabeth Eckford, one of the first nine African American students to enroll in Little Rock Central High School, 1957. Will Counts Collection: Indiana University Archives.

to learn and become something new in schools that did not welcome them, pushing open doors for others to follow.

Today, a political movement essentially tries to justify the continued overrepresentation of Whites and the well-off in higher education by recapitulating Terman's old idolization of test scores as magic indicators of merit—as neutral, as unbiased, and as of determinative importance. This when we know that test scores are systematically biased against students of color; they literally underestimate their ability because of processes like stereotype threat. When we worship at the altar of standardized test scores, we effectively "launder" Whiteness. We convert it to ostensible merit.

This movement reinforces the history of racial exclusion in education. That history echoes. It echoed at my alma mater Yale University in the spring of 2018, when a campus police officer detained a Black grad student taking a nap in a common area, proclaiming, "You're in a Yale building and we need to make sure you belong here." This at an institution that displayed stained-glass images of slaves picking cotton through 2016, with no critical commentary; that resisted, until 2017, protests to rename a residential college named for John Calhoun, a nineteenth-century racist whose main claim to fame was defending slavery and who had no actual connection to Yale. Might a Black student be sensitive to the accusation she doesn't belong there? The student, Lolade Siyonbola, told officers, "I deserve to be here. I pay tuition like everybody else. I'm not going to justify my existence here." If that incident had occurred instead, say, at Howard University, a historically Black college, it wouldn't have been pleasant. But nor would it have carried the same ugly resonance.

It echoed one week earlier at Colorado State University, when a woman called police about two Native American teenage students on a campus tour, saying, "They don't belong." The students' mother, Lorraine Kahneratokwas Gray, said, "They were shocked. They were trying to figure out what they did wrong." That same year, Colorado State enrolled 28,691 students, of whom exactly 125 were Native American, or 0.44 percent. Gray said, "There's a part of us that feels like we don't ever want to go back there again. But maybe we feel an obligation to future generations to be pioneers in a sense, to make that presence and to effect that change."

This history of exclusion persists in clouds of doubt for students of color. That doubt hangs in the air and coexists with the profound hope and striving that students bring to college. For what Obama, Sotomayor, and Jackson experienced was not a confidence that they did not belong. They *had chosen* their universities. They *hoped* they could belong. And they *wanted* to belong. And, in some sense, as it turns out, they *could* belong; at least they could develop strong relationships on campus, find communities that welcomed them, and learn and grow. Obama, for instance, wrote her senior thesis under the tutelage of Walter Wallace, an eminent African American sociologist who had joined the Princeton faculty in 1971. Sotomayor was mentored by a history professor, Nancy Weiss Malkiel. She successfully advocated for the hiring of Latinx professors and for courses on Latin American studies and wrote a thesis on Puerto Rico's struggle for self-determination.

But when doubt hangs in the air then, like a shadow that could hide a monster in the dark, even mild experiences can reawaken the question, *Can people like me belong here?*

In 2014, Michelle Obama shared a story about her college experience with a group of college leaders:

> When I first arrived at school as a first-generation college student, I didn't know anyone on campus except my brother. I didn't know how to pick the right classes or find the right buildings. I didn't even bring the right size sheets for my dorm room bed. I didn't realize those beds were so long. So I was a little overwhelmed and a little isolated.

This is a remarkable story. Consider that, by 2014, Obama had been professionally successful for decades, first as an attorney and then in various public sector roles in Chicago. When she told this story, she was the First Lady of the United States and among the most admired people in America. The event she recalled happened decades earlier. And in this story, there are no villains. There is no racist George Wallace. There's not even another actor. It's just an inconvenience she faced, it would seem, an errand to be run. Why did it stick with her?

That was a trigger for Obama. It was her tifbit. *If I can't even get the sheets right, how can I expect to be fully included and valued, and pursue the opportunities that Princeton offers?*

My collaborators and I call this experience belonging uncertainty. It's a feeling of unsettledness, an up-in-the-airness, a persistent wondering, a "not feeling completely a part of the worlds I inhabit," as Sotomayor put it. It's a *question* about whether you can belong in a place that at once seems foreign and even hostile yet could transform your life. It's a feeling that goes to the heart of stigma. As the sociologist Erving Goffman wrote in 1963, "The central feature of the stigmatized individual's situation in life . . . is a question of . . . 'acceptance.'"

Questions of belonging refract history into the present. Ever the "wise Latina," Justice Sotomayor wrote in a case before the Supreme Court, "Race matters, because of the slights, the snickers, the silent judgments that reinforce that most crippling of thoughts: 'I do not belong here.'"

While history puts questions of belonging on the table for millions of people, it does not answer this question. It is answers that people are looking for.

BELONGING TIFBITS

I wasn't thinking about any of this, at least not directly, when I first entered grad school at Yale in 2000.

My first project was a curious one. I was going to ask Yalies about their interest in a particular field of study. Most students' interests at the time centered on the humanities and social sciences, so I thought I'd ask about computer science, a minor discipline on the sidelines for most undergrads. But first, I implemented a clever suggestion made by my new graduate adviser, Geoff Cohen. We'd ask students to list friends of theirs who might fit in well in the field. I think Cohen made the suggestion on the floor of his office, where many of our early meetings were held. A bout of back pain had made this the most comfortable space for him. It was a rather absurd place to begin a research project but perhaps appropriate. We'd build our way up.

Cohen and I were both interested in how students' social relationship to a field of study might affect their motivation. Later, we'd do research showing that if you had a personal connection as trivial as a shared birthday with a math major, that could increase your sense of belonging and motivation in math. But in this study, we were interested in how students might respond if it seemed as if they might *not* have friends in a field. Why then were we asking students to list friends they might have in computer science?

The trick was that we wanted to see how students would respond if they *had difficulty* listing friends. After some careful pretesting, we decided to ask students to list either two friends of theirs who might fit in well in computer science or eight friends. Two friends was easy. Our pilot participants had been able to list three or so on average. The question was, if you had difficulty listing eight friends, if you found yourself staring at empty slots, perhaps beginning to list people who you kind of knew wouldn't fit in so well in computer science, perhaps listing people who weren't really your friends, would you ascribe any particular meaning to this? How would students read that difficulty?

To find out, afterward we asked students a series of questions on what we would call their "sense of fit" in computer science: Did they feel they could belong in the field and do well there, would they enjoy it, and how much potential did they think they had to succeed there?

I ran students through the protocol one by one in our psychology lab, a lovely second-floor conference room. When Cohen and I looked at the results, we saw a clear divergence in students' response. White and Asian students were nonplussed by the friend-listing task. Sure, they had difficulty listing eight friends. But it didn't matter. They were reasonably positive about their fit either way. Black and Latinx students too were sanguine when they'd been

2 FRIENDS CONDITION	8 FRIENDS CONDITION
Subject Number: _____	Subject Number: _____
FRIEND FORM	**FRIEND FORM**
Please list **2** friends (first name, last initial) of yours who have personal characteristics, interests, experiences, or skills that might make them *likely to fit in well at Yale's Computer Science Department or in fact do make them fit in well.* You can think of friends here at Yale, from high school, or even among your parents, siblings, or other relatives, or among family friends, teachers, etc. Anyone who could be called a personal "friend" is a possibility.	Please list **8** friends (first name, last initial) of yours who have personal characteristics, interests, experiences, or skills that might make them *likely to fit in well at Yale's Computer Science Department or in fact do make them fit in well.* You can think of friends here at Yale, from high school, or even among your parents, siblings, or other relatives, or among family friends, teachers, etc. Anyone who could be called a personal "friend" is a possibility.
List 2 friends who might fit in well in computer science.	List 8 friends who might fit in well in computer science.
1) _____ 2) _____	1) _____ 2) _____ 3) _____ 4) _____ 5) _____ 6) _____ 7) _____ 8) _____

asked to list two friends. They didn't come into the study dubious they could do well in computer science. These were all smart young students. But they were reactive. When they'd been asked to list eight friends, they began to express misgivings about the field. Listing eight friends wasn't harder for them than it was for White and Asian students. The difference was that that difficulty struck a chord for them: it seemed to portend something larger.

I ran the study a second time, this time just with White and Black students. We got the same results. Again, White students were unaffected by the friend-listing task, but Black students showed a sharp shift. One bottom-line question asked students how much potential they thought they had to succeed in computer science relative to other Yale students, on a percentile scale. Black students who weren't asked to list any friends rated their potential at the fifty-second percentile, slightly above average. Those asked to list two friends were a bit more positive yet, rating their potential at the fifty-eighth percentile. But those asked to list eight friends rated their potential at just the thirty-first percentile.

And it wasn't just how students saw their own fit. It was also how they saw *other students'* fit. At the end, we asked students to advise peers considering computer science as a major. For the most part, everyone was encouraging. For example, when we asked students to advise a Black student, "Walter," fully 77 percent of Black students who'd been asked to list no friends or two friends encouraged him to go for it. But among Black students asked to list eight friends, just 30 percent were encouraging. Their concerns weren't explicit. One student just wrote, "I think Walter still needs to look at other fields." Maybe they weren't fully aware of the belonging issues themselves. But that difficulty listing friends seemed to mean to Black students not just that they might not fit well in computer science but that someone else in their group might not fit either.

It would take years for me to fully appreciate what the students in these studies were telling us. With time, I began to see the difficulty listing friends as just one challenge among many when students come to a new school. In another study, we asked first-year college students to complete a diary every night for a week. We asked students to describe "any events that happened to you today that made you feel positively or negatively about [school name] or about your experience here." Much of what students described was social in nature. Here are some of the negative experiences they shared. Call it a (bad) day in the life of a college student:

- *"My teacher canceled her meeting with me"*
- *"My usual friends weren't at dinner"*
- *"Not getting an e-mail back from a peer"*
- *"I felt bad that I haven't gone on any dates [in college]"*

- *"Not being recognized at awards dinner (when I deserved it)"*
- *"Dumped by girlfriend"*
- *"My boyfriend didn't call"*
- *"Stress over a paper"*
- *"I'm working on a paper that is due tomorrow and I have writer's block"*
- *"Found a dead mouse under a pile of my clothes"*

All bad events, no doubt, especially finding a dead mouse! But would these events hold a larger meaning to students? If you had a bad day, would that make you feel worse about college as a whole?

To find out, we asked students each night and the next afternoon some of the same questions gauging their sense of fit, but this time with regard to college in general: How much did students feel they belonged in college, could do well, and had the potential to succeed? Because we wanted to know how students' sense of fit fluctuated from one day to the next, we asked them how they felt "right now."

Then we put the data together. Did having a bad day tie to daily feelings of fit?

For White students, the answer was no. White students' sense of fit bounced up and down some over the week, of course, but it wasn't related to how good or bad their day was. Just 1 percent of the variance in their daily sense of fit was predicted by the quality of their days.

But for Black students, these two things went hand in hand. When Black students had a bad day, they reported a worse fit that night and the next afternoon. For them, fully *59 percent* of the day-to-day fluctuation in their sense of fit was tied to how good or bad their days were. After good days, Black students were confident they belonged and could succeed, just as confident as White students. But after bad days Black students reported a worse fit than White students.

These are tidbits, like Michelle Obama's ill-fitting sheets. If circumstances like a history of exclusion raise a core question, *Can people like me belong here?* then a bad day ("Stress over a paper," "My boyfriend didn't call") might seem like an omen. That sets the stage for a downward spiral. For if you're feeling you don't belong, it's going to be harder to reengage in that space, to reach out to friends, to talk with a professor.

We also developed a scale to tap into "belonging uncertainty" directly. As a point of comparison, we first asked students how much they felt they belonged in college in general:

1. *I belong at [college name].*

In our first sample, students of color (Black and Latinx students) and White students both generally endorsed this statement. Absent a threatening cue (difficulty listing friends, a bad day), everyone felt pretty good about their belonging in college.

Then we gave out two more statements. These asked students how much their experience of belonging varied with daily experiences:

2. *Sometimes I feel that I belong at [college name], and sometimes I feel that I don't belong at [college name].*
3. *When something bad happens, I feel that maybe I don't belong at [college name].*

Now, with the very same sample, we found a marked difference. Black and Latinx students said their belonging went up and down with daily experiences more so than did White students. Even as they felt they belonged in their college in general, they also said this belonging was vulnerable and subject to events. It was not firmly held.

These studies focused on belonging among Black and Latinx students. But there's nothing magical about being a student of color that puts you at risk for belonging uncertainty. It's really just how circumstances come together in a situation.

BELONGING UNCERTAINTY IN STEM

A few years ago, I was invited to give a talk at an engineering department at Stanford on gender and belonging. A previous speaker had been deemed "unscientific." So, I walked over from my building and joined a faculty meeting in progress. About forty people were in attendance. The chair of the department was a woman. But there was just one other woman in the room, sitting in the back, among thirty-eight men.

I decided to start with a study by my good friend and collaborator Mary Murphy, a social psychologist at Indiana University. To show how questions of belonging come up for women in math and science, Murphy had shown undergrads a video of a math, science, and engineering conference. She varied just the proportion of women depicted in the video. In one case, half the people were women. In the other, one in four were—a figure that, ironically, seemed wildly optimistic in the 5 percent women room I was in. Unsurprisingly, Murphy found that women anticipated they would belong less at the conference dominated by men. They were also less interested in attending it. My audience nodded along.

Next, Murphy showed that women also experienced a kind of "cognitive vigilance" in response to the male-dominated video; they remembered more trivial details about the conference, like its location and background features of the rooms. That's important. Imagine you're at a conference in your field but you're so on edge that you remember the irrelevancies—but not, perhaps, the content of whatever was presented. Again, my audience nodded along.

Last, I presented Murphy's third main finding: that the vigilance women experienced also had a physiological expression. Their hearts were beating faster and they were sweating more when they saw the male-dominated conference.

That's when the talk went off the rails.

I heard a voice at the back of the room. It was the second woman in attendance. "Of course they're more aroused," she said. "They just saw a bunch of men!"

Some awkward chuckles. People glanced around. But I was shocked. A sexist joke . . . by a woman . . . and what a bad one!

I wanted to stop the talk right there. I wanted to ask, "What compelled you to say that?" Really, I wanted to yell at the men, "What kind of environment have you created here? Look at that. This is your colleague. Are you not ashamed?"

But a thousand thoughts rushed through my mind. Was this how a woman proves she belongs in this space—by saying whatever dumb thing a man might say first? If I said something, would I put her on the spot? I really didn't want to do that, so I kept on with the presentation. I still don't know if that was the right move.

After grad school and a year in Washington, D.C., I moved to Waterloo, Ontario, a quiet town about an hour and a half west of Toronto. I went to Waterloo to do a postdoc with Steve Spencer, whose research on gender I had admired for years. Together with two of his grad students, Christine Logel and Jennifer Peach, we began to look at the experience of women in the engineering program at the University of Waterloo. It's one of the best programs in the world, sometimes called the MIT of Canada. The students who get in are incredibly capable. Yet we had reason to think not everything was right.

At Waterloo, students entered the engineering program enrolled in one of twelve majors, and these majors varied quite a bit. In some majors, like chemical engineering and environmental engineering, about one in three students were women, so a typical twenty-person class would have six or more women in it. But others, like mechanical engineering and software engineering, averaged just 10 percent women. So, in those majors, if you're a woman and you walk into a typical twenty-person class, there'd be just one other woman there, on average.

Mary Murphy's research suggests that underrepresentation might matter. And there could be a lot of reasons for that. People might just ask, *Why? Why are there so few people like me here? Is there something wrong with this place, or wrong for people like me?* Or, if you're the only one in a setting, it could seem like you represent your whole group. That's what Justice Sandra Day O'Connor felt when she served as the only woman on the Supreme Court for more than a decade. Justice O'Connor would later describe her experience when Justice Ruth Bader Ginsburg finally joined the Court in 1993: "It made an enormous difference [for me]. When I'd arrived there had been a large amount of media attention to the selection of a woman and then to see what that woman did, under all circumstances. . . . And the minute Justice Ginsburg came to the court, we were nine justices. It wasn't seven and then 'the women.' We became nine. And it was a great relief to me."

When it's on the table that you could be marginalized because of your gender, might everyday challenges loom large, just as they had to Black college students? At Waterloo, again we gave students a daily survey and asked what had happened to them each day, good and bad. The routine challenges students reported were predictable:

- *"I couldn't follow the Physics lecture"*
- *"Professor replying to me in a demeaning [way]"*
- *"Still feel [a] little bit lonely"*
- *"I cannot find any one of my friends that I have breakfast with during dinner"*
- *"Feeling homesick"*

In this case, to suss out how much weight students gave these experiences, we just asked them, "How important was this event?" on a scale from 1 (not at all) to 5 (very). Then we added up the importance scores students gave to all the negative events they experienced each day.

In the more gender-balanced majors, women and men both averaged about five bad-event-importance scores on a typical day, and there was no difference between them. When we looked at the majors dominated by men, men averaged slightly less, four and a half importance scores. But women averaged nearly eight.

Negative events loomed large to Black students at a predominantly White college, and they loomed large to women in engineering majors dominated by men.

And it wasn't just the importance women saw in negative events. Women in these same male-dominated majors also felt less confident they could handle daily stressors in school. Their level of self-esteem was both lower and more unstable, bouncing up and down. They weren't doing as well on a daily basis. They were buffeted about more by daily events.

IT'S JUST A TINY FACT . . . AND NOW WE SPIRAL UP:
"NOT KNOWING HAS CEASED TO BE A REFLECTION OF VULNERABILITY"

Back in grad school, as I thought about college, I realized that we don't do much to prepare students for the inevitable challenges going to college presents. It isn't because people don't care. When I came to Stanford as an undergrad in the fall of 1996, the RAs, the older students who staffed our dorm, greeted every new student with glee, shouting their welcome as we pulled up, luggage in hand, "Greg Walton: Welcome to Stanford! Welcome to Paloma!" It was thrilling but strange. There was a relentless, almost willful positivity. A woman came to our dorm early in the year. I don't remember who she was or why she was there, but she said something that stuck with me: "It's your freshman dorm! You're going to make your best friends for life here!" Maybe that was true for her, but it wouldn't be for me (I would make more of my college friends later). I remember thinking, "I thought my friends from high school were pretty good. But what do I know? I'm only a freshman."

There was nothing in my experience to say that college might be hard sometimes—that you might get homesick, that you might feel lonely, that you might get excluded or rejected, that you might get a bad grade, that a professor might be unkind. There was nothing to say that these kinds of things were liable to happen and that was okay. If you look at the movies, they always seem to cast college in the warm light of nostalgia, the funny pranks, the friendships forged, the freedom from parents, the parties, "the best years of your life." It makes it seem as if everyone is happy all the time, thrilled to be there, making lots of friends, doing great in class (or not caring if they're not), going somewhere exciting. That didn't set me up well when I felt homesick. The whole thing is a-psychological.

In grad school, I was also coming to appreciate my privilege in college on a deeper level. Sometimes I was homesick. But here are some of the questions I *didn't* ask. When people talked about "merit," I didn't wonder if they meant I didn't deserve to be there.

When I got a bad grade on a math midterm, I didn't worry people might think "people like me" couldn't do math. When I got critical feedback on a paper, I didn't ask whether my instructor had formed a biased judgment of me. I just got to work learning to write better.

Once a public policy professor came to dinner at our dorm and asked each of us what we were majoring in. Everyone else said political science or public policy, but when he got to me, I said philosophy (which would be my eventual major). He said, "Who's going to be the one without a job?" and started an ugly hiccupping laugh. I just thought he was a jerk; my father and my great-grandfather were both philosophers. They were employed. It didn't bother me.

So, I was homesick, but I didn't worry about whether I belonged in the academic spaces of college.

And that was really helpful. In high school, I was inspired by Claude Steele's research on stereotype threat. So, even before my first class, I emailed Steele and volunteered to work in his lab. I didn't wonder whether it was my place to email him or if my labors would be welcome. For several years, then, I worked with his doctoral student Joseph Brown, helping to recruit participants and run them through study protocols. Later, I did an honors thesis with Steele, exploring students' sense of belonging. Then, with his support, I applied to grad school. One step at a time I built relationships, developed skills, and joined a community of like-minded people: friends, mentors, and general partners in crime, some of whom I've known now for nearly thirty years, with whom I have learned, grown, and collaborated.

That's a very normal story. But it's revealing. In high school, I knew of the objective advantages I had, as a White person, attending good schools, living in a stable family and a middle-class community. I was outraged that other people in my generation didn't have those same advantages. But I didn't yet appreciate my psychological privilege—the troubling questions I did not ask that did not hold me back.

Those questions shouldn't hold anyone back. When circumstances raise the question, *Can people like me belong here?*, how can everyone get to good answers?

What if you pulled back the curtain? What if you showed students that challenges to belonging happen to everyone in the transition to college, at some point and in some form? That they're normal and get better with time and there are things they can do to build their belonging?

In grad school, I began to ask college students about their experiences of belonging in the transition to college—what they worried about, what was hard, and how their experiences had changed over time. As I anticipated, almost everyone had a story to tell, stories of challenge and of growth. Then Cohen and I spent hours writing and rewriting these stories to capture their essence. We made them into parables.

We began to share these stories in the spring of 2003. By this time, our lab had moved from the lovely second-floor conference room to a suite of small utilitarian rooms in the basement of the psychology department. Still, it was an upgrade. With more rooms, I could run more students at once.

In the study Cohen and I had designed, we'd bring Black and White students in the first year of college one by one to our basement rooms. We'd give them information and the stories drawn from our survey of older students. Our participating students would read these stories, spend time thinking and writing about them, and share their own story as advice for future students (the saying-is-believing component). Then they'd complete some surveys over the next week.

There were two conditions. In the first, the belonging exercise, the content focused on students' experience of belonging in coming to college: how it's normal to worry at first about whether you belong in college, but it gets better with time. And we would tell that story in multiple ways, from multiple voices.

We didn't tell students we were trying to fix their feeling of belonging. If you faced a persistent question about belonging, being told you need fixing is the last thing you want. Instead, we told students we wanted to learn from them as experts in the transition to college. We wanted their help for future students. We asked them to help us understand the stories we'd heard from older students, to tell us how worries about belonging had played out in their own lives, and to help us convey this to future students to help them in their transition. We'd treat our participating students as co-creators of an intervention for others, not as recipients of an intervention.

What was the content like? First, we gave the bottom line. We told students we had surveyed older students and found that many students worried at first about whether they belonged in college but that those concerns receded with time. For example, students read that previous students had worried during their first year "whether other students would accept them in the context of classes or course-work" and "that professors viewed their abilities negatively." But they also learned that "after their freshman year, most students come to feel confident that other people accept them," and that "their comfort in the academic environment has improved."

Next, we gave students the stories from older students describing their experience coming to college and how these experiences had changed over time. There were nine stories, just a page and a half in total, from diverse students, men and women, of all racial back-grounds. They described all sorts of everyday challenges and wor-ries. Feeling homesick or intimidated by professors. Having trouble making friends and feeling left out. Struggling in class and getting critical feedback. But each story described how students' experience got better with time. Here's one:

JUNIOR/SENIOR SURVEY:
A SUMMARY OF RESULTS

ILLUSTRATIVE SAMPLE OF FREE-RESPONSE REPORTS

"I love [school name] and I wouldn't trade my experiences here for anything. I've met some close friends, I've had some fan-tastic experiences, and I've certainly learned a lot. Still, I think the transition to college is difficult, and it was for me. My fresh-man year I really didn't know what I was doing—I made a lot of casual friends at parties and other social settings and I avoided interacting with professors in class and office hours,

I think because I was intimidated by them. It got a lot better once I chose a major I was excited about. I began to make close friends through classes and labs, and I started to get involved in research with one of my professors. Now I am happier than I have ever been at [school name]. It is really rewarding for me to feel like I belong in the intellectual community here."

—Participant #103, [dorm name], senior, White female

It's important that the stories came from diverse students. We wanted to show students that it wasn't just people from their group who'd faced challenges. We wanted Black students to see that White students too had worries about belonging—even students you might have thought had it all together ("Joe College"). Of course, we knew that students of color also face distinct kinds of challenges, including experiences of discrimination. That just wasn't the focus of this exercise.

We were trying to help students out of a fixed black-and-white mindset as they interpreted everyday experiences. If you got a bad grade or were excluded, we didn't want students to ask, *Does this mean I don't belong in college?* Instead, we wanted students to think about belonging as a process and then to ask, *How can I develop my belonging here? What relationships can I build that will be helpful for me? How can I find my community?*

Next, we asked students to share their own story. Why might students initially feel unsure about their belonging but overcome these fears with time? Could they illustrate their answer with examples from their own life, to help future students with their transition? Later, we told students we wanted to record them reading their essay as a speech to a video camera. These recordings, we said, could be shown to future students to help them in their transition to college. We gave students a chance to revise their essay before recording it. This way they had an opportunity to think more deeply about belonging, space to translate the lessons from other students to their own lives, and an opportunity to advocate for this way of thinking about belonging to other students.

Students took the task very seriously. They spent nearly *half an hour* writing their essays, on average. Their essays averaged about 550 words, more than four times longer than the average story they'd read. Eighty-four percent of students agreed to give the speech. Students described many experiences of non-belonging, from feeling ill-equipped for college classes to being intimidated by professors, to not having made close friends yet, to not knowing where they wanted to go academically. The essays are lovely. In reading them, you can see students working through challenges and building productive ways to understand them. Here's one from a Black woman with an interest in music.

YOUR TURN

In an effort to further understand how the transition to college takes place, we would like to ask you to describe why . . . students might feel initially unsure about their acceptance but ultimately overcome these fears. . . .

I remember loving the first night of college—excited by all the possibilities . . . but also being annoyed by the ever-present sense of superficiality. . . . No one seemed to want to show their vulnerabilities. . . . Countless days went by where I thought everyone else knew what they were doing; reading the junior senior responses made me realize that almost everyone thinks the same way. It's funny. . . . In music 210A, I felt like I was always the one without the answer. "Everyone else seemed to know it." But now in music 211B, I realize that there are indeed some people who always know the answer but I do—often—know the answer. Not knowing has ceased to be a reflection of vulnerability but has become a completely normal part of going to college. The same general idea applies to the social scene as well. In the first few months, there seemed to be this group of people in my entryway who bonded over drinking and partying. . . . I felt like they had everything going on, but that I was somehow a loser when I sat in my room Sat-

urday night watching a movie. But now, in second semester, that entryway group has broken up somewhat, as people are no longer desperate for some sense of family. I feel even respected for the fact that I was willing to do what I wanted to do. . . . You think a chemistry test is hard, only to find out that everyone else thought so too and subsequently having the professor reaffirm your opinion. . . . Last example: I am a violinist and I had a huge confidence crisis at the beginning of the year, as it seems that everyone else—including my roommate— had studied with amazing teachers. But even now, I realize that I'm not half-bad and that I'm improving. . . . It takes a while to understand that none of us have it completely figured out. That's what freshman year is about. Frankly, we won't have it figured out sophomore year either. But thankfully, we are all learning that we're in the same boat now and can thus be more understanding.

Some of the stories were downright hilarious. I laughed out loud when one student described how early in the year she'd learned of a classmate who'd written a book about Russian philosophy. Who does that? "At this point, intimidating was an understatement," she wrote. But later that year, late at night outside a campus party, she found the young scholar swaying, peeing against a wall, drunk. "Once you see the kid that wrote a book on Russian philosophy peeing on the wall—he doesn't seem quite so intimidating anymore."

That hour-long session in the basement suite was deeply meaningful for students. One wrote, "It was nice to know how common my experiences were." Another shared, "It's encouraging to know that so many students feel out of place freshman year but get over it." A third said, "It is comforting to see the commonality of experiences across all lines."

To understand the causal effect, we had randomly assigned half of students to do the belonging exercise and half to one of several control conditions. In these groups, students also read stories from older students and wrote about their experiences, but the focus wasn't on belonging. One addressed the physical environment of college—how students get used to the campus and weather with time. Another focused on learning study skills. It was designed to be a neutral experience. This first sample was small, just twenty-five Black students and thirty White students, but it was a place to start.

Over the summer of 2003 and into the fall, I felt my eyes slowly open as I read students' stories and analyzed the data they had given us. It was like peeling back the layers of an onion as we learned more about their lives and how the belonging exercise had begun to shift them.

The first thing I looked at were questions we asked immediately after the exercise. These assessed students' sense of fit in college— the same kind of thing we'd looked at in the friend-listing studies: how much students thought they belonged in college, how much they enjoyed academic work, how capable they felt, and how much potential they thought they had to succeed. For Black students, there was an enormous effect. In the control condition, Black students rated their potential to succeed at about the fiftieth percentile. But with the belonging exercise that shot up to the seventy-second percentile.

We also gave students a list of classes (for example, World Literatures, Physics of Flying), described half as being difficult but offering a strong opportunity to learn and half as "gut" classes—easy, but with less opportunity to learn. Which classes would you like to take? If the exercise helped students feel more confident in their belonging, would they be open to more difficult but edifying classes? Here too we saw a big gain for Black students. In the belonging condition, 57 percent of the courses Black students expressed an interest in taking were of the difficult/edifying nature, up from 36 percent in the control condition.

But most important was how students read their daily flow of experience, their construals. The daily diary survey I mentioned earlier was actually collected from these same students, but only those students in the control condition. There we found that fully 59 percent of the daily ups and downs in Black students' sense of fit was tied to the quality of their day. One woman in the control condition gave us a vivid example of this contingency. One evening she wrote, "Everyone is going out without me, and they didn't consider me when making their plans. At times like this, I feel like I don't belong here and that I'm alienated." It wasn't just that she'd been excluded from an outing. To her that exclusion meant she didn't belong in general.

When we looked closely at students' responses, we didn't see differences by race or condition in the adversities students faced. The belonging exercise didn't just make life easy. But what it did do was prevent daily challenges from functioning as tifbits. If challenges to belonging are normal when people come to college, if they happen to everyone and generally get better, then a bad day might just be a bad day; a tiny fact, no big theory required. In fact, with the belonging exercise, that contingency in Black students' sense of fit fell to 24 percent. When they had a bad day, they were better able to maintain the sense that they belonged in college in general, that they were capable, and that they had the potential to succeed.

As students' meaning making shifted, so did their behavior. Each nightly survey asked students about various behaviors that could help them get more involved in college life, build friendships and relationships with professors, and find a direction. Had they attended a review session or study group meeting? Had they asked a question in class or emailed a professor? How long had they studied? When we looked at the data, we found that Black students engaged far more in these behaviors with the belonging exercise. The effect size was nearly one and a half standard deviations (that's gigantic). One of the biggest increases was in emailing professors. With the belonging exercise, Black students reported emailing professors an average of 2.69 times over the week, as compared with 0.88 times in the control condition—a threefold increase. And they reported studying four hours and thirty-five minutes a day in the belonging condition, as compared with three hours and thirteen minutes in the control condition. In the first week after the one-hour session, Black students were studying more than an hour longer *each day*.

As a grad student, I found these findings remarkable, and they are. But there was something more I did not fully appreciate yet: spirals. For what might happen next? All of this is beginning to calcify a better spiral.

What will happen if students are studying more, talking with professors more, and feeling more confident and resilient on campus? What will the rest of their college experiences be like? What will their lives be like?

Cohen and I ran another cohort through the same protocol, and then, a month or so before students graduated from college, we surveyed them again. We also got their permission to look at their academic records from all of college, the full sweep through graduation. Now we had ninety-two students.*

If anything, the processes we'd set in motion back in the basement suite had accelerated. If you looked at students' term-by-term GPA over the three years after the exercise, from sophomore through senior year, the pattern in the control condition was discouraging. Black students' GPA took a little dip at the end of their sophomore year, on average, and then recovered, but mostly it was flat. There was no sustained growth with time.

But with the belonging exercise, Black students' GPA rose term by term, as though each term they acquired more resources, more capacities, more ability to succeed in a challenging college environment. Again, White students weren't affected, so the effect was to reduce the racial achievement gap. Altogether, that one-hour exercise in the first year of college cut the achievement gap from sophomore to senior year by half. And because this effect was really an upward shift in Black students' trajectory, the reduction was greatest senior year. That year, the treatment reduced the gap by 79 percent.

Because our sample was small, we obtained a second, much larger comparison group: all Black and White students in the same

---

* Because the college the students in this first study attended was highly selective, all of the students graduated. Later studies at other institutions would look at whether the belonging exercise could help students persist in and graduate from college when they might otherwise drop out.

class years as our students, but who hadn't participated in the study at all. Black students who'd gotten the belonging exercise outdid those peers too. By addressing a troubling question about belonging, a question rooted in the history of racism in education, we had unleashed learners, growers, and connectors.

And happier, healthier young people too. In that end-of-college survey, Black students who hadn't gotten the belonging exercise (those in the control condition) reported high levels of belonging uncertainty. A simple cognitive task revealed they were thinking more about words related to self-doubt ("dumb," "inferior," "loser," "weak") and negative racial stereotypes ("anger," "poor," "riot," "token," "welfare"). For them, a threat was in the air. And they reported being less happy than White students and less healthy too. It sure is crappy to feel like maybe you don't belong at the end of four long years of college.

But Black students who'd gotten the belonging exercise felt more confident they belonged. They were thinking less about self-doubt and racial stereotypes. They reported being happier and healthier. Later, when we got students' permission to access records from the university health center, we found that Black students averaged 5.33 visits to the health center in the control condition from their sophomore through senior year. That dropped by more than half with the belonging exercise, to 2.09 visits.

The end-of-college survey had one more surprise. You might think that, if the belonging exercise had so completely transformed students' experience, they'd be oh so thankful, it'd be their North Star, their guiding light.

Ha!

That's not how wise interventions work, nor the spirals they set in motion. In the last part of the survey, we asked students if they remembered the study they'd participated in back in their first year. Most said they did. But when we asked what they'd learned in the study, just 8 percent recalled the basic idea. And just 14 percent said that the session had "any" effect on their college experience. As one student said, "I soon forgot about it."

Students didn't credit their success in college to the intervention, and, actually, that would be ridiculous. For what was the "real" reason they succeeded? It wasn't the belonging exercise. It was the hard work students put in; the close friendships they formed; the opportunities their college opened to them, which they pursued; the mentors they found, who helped them chart their path. All the belonging exercise did was help students address a question they faced. Then students could begin the work of college: to study hard; to spend time with peers; to join student groups; to attend office hours and, yes, to email professors. Then students' efforts, skills, confidence, and relationships could grow in tandem. That's spiraling up.

So, the belonging exercise went under the radar. It did its work, and then it got out of the way. In fact, I made every effort in the years after the daily diaries to discreetly avoid our participants on campus, including one student who, memorably, tried to ask me out on a date.

A GOOD LIFE: *"THROUGH A LOT OF HARD WORK AND SOME LUCK I'VE ACHIEVED THE GOALS I SET FOR MYSELF YEARS EARLIER"*

These results were so astonishing that, even to me, they sometimes felt like magic. It was like looking at a visual illusion, something you can see in two completely different ways. I vacillated. When I thought about it from the perspective of social psychology theory— these are worries about belonging, here's what they do to a student, here's how you can address them—it made sense. One thing leads to another. . . . But whoa! If ever I slipped out of that perspective and reverted to "common sense," it seemed unbelievable, that strange action-at-a-distance. An hour in the first year of college had raised students' grades over *three years*? And made them happier and healthier?

Seeing this has helped me understand *how* change happens: through spirals. For life, and school especially, isn't just a box of chocolates. It's a series of escalators. If you can get on the right track, you can go places.

So, what happens next? After all, the point of college isn't to get good grades. It's to prepare you for a career and for life.

In the fall of 2011, years before she began her professorship at Wake Forest, Shannon Brady entered the doctoral program at the Graduate School of Education at Stanford. Before coming to grad school, Brady had worked for several years as a teacher on the Pine Ridge Indian Reservation in South Dakota, where she was recognized as "Teacher of the Year" in 2008. In 2017, when she would defend her dissertation at Stanford, her peers would honor her as a "rockstar," a "bundle of light and energy that brightens your day and guides you through life." In addition to taking on students' experience of academic probation, she directed some of her prodigious energy in grad school to following up on students in that first belonging study. How were they doing in their adult lives?

With dogged persistence, Brady combed our files, alumni records, and social media to find email addresses, old mailing addresses, anything to connect back with our participants, who had long since graduated. In the end, she was sending crisp $50 bills in the mail to folks who hadn't responded, just begging them to take a few minutes to please log in to our online survey to tell us about their lives. That got eighty of our original ninety-two students, or 87 percent, to participate. On average, they were twenty-seven years old. Anywhere between seven and eleven years had passed since they spent that one-hour session in our basement suite.

In the survey, Brady asked about broad dimensions of a good life: How satisfied and successful do you feel in your career (agreement or disagreement with statements like, "My job is meaningful")? How happy are you ("In most ways my life is close to my ideal")? How engaged in your community are you, such as in leading athletic, religious, cultural, or professional groups?

In addition to the scale questions, Brady asked people to just tell us about their lives, what was good, what was bad, and what was important to them. The responses from Black adults who had completed the belonging exercise years earlier were, almost to a person, inspiring. They reflected accomplishments, connectedness, and growing contributions to society. One student was completing a residency in preventative medicine. Another was preparing for a residency in neurosurgery. Several attended law school. One worked as a child advocate attorney. Others described volunteer work. One worked as an environmental policy adviser, realizing a long-held dream. Another taught in a low-income public school, saying, "I love it." One dreamed of saving lives through better data processing to identify diseases. On the following pages are some of their stories.

What about in the control condition? Here, Black adults were less likely to describe specific accomplishments and contributions, or even a clear direction. They were not unsuccessful. But there was more uncertainty and, frankly, more frustration and loneliness.

These stories are overwhelming for me to read. It was incredibly gratifying to see how the activity we had developed had freed young people to succeed in their lives. But it was heartbreaking to consider what might have been for those students who did not get the belonging exercise. Yet we needed that control condition to see if this exercise could really help.

Behind the stories were hard numbers. In one question, Brady asked people to rate their level of success in their careers compared with other graduates from their college. Black adults who'd received the belonging exercise rated their career success at the sixty-fifth percentile, while those in the control condition put themselves at the forty-seventh percentile. The same pattern emerged when we asked about the potential they anticipated in the future. And that greater confidence in belonging we saw at the end of college? It persisted into the working world. Black adults were more confident they belonged at work with the belonging exercise than without it. As one person in the control condition wrote, "The aspects of this job that I don't like include feeling like I am constantly being judged on what I do/don't know and feeling inadequate at times."

It wasn't just professional success. The stories Black adults told were also stories of joy. On a standard measure of life satisfaction, Black adults scored 5.41 (on a 7-point scale) with the belonging exercise, nearly a full point higher than those in the control condition (4.44). On a standard statistical measure, that's an increase of a full standard deviation. By comparison, winning $100,000 in a lottery gets you about 0.04 standard deviations in life satisfaction over a decade. By that math, each person in the control condition would have to win $2.5 million to achieve the gain in life satisfaction that those randomized to the belonging exercise experienced.

For many people, a good life is an active life, a life of community, of service, of giving back, of working with others toward a common good. These were also themes Black adults in the belonging condition described ("I am also very busy with my volunteer Bible education work"), and they came out in the numbers as well. On average, Black adults reported being "very involved" in about three times as many community groups with the belonging exercise than without. They also reported holding leadership roles in more groups.

How did this spiral happen?

Given the premium placed on grades in college, you might think it was better grades that led to these improvements. But no. College grades only modestly predicted these outcomes. One control-condition student even said, "Speaking to a recruiter, I was reassured that my résumé, pedigree, and grades were certainly not the problem. It was just the way the cookie crumbled for me."

What made Brady a great teacher on the Pine Ridge Indian Reservation was her constant attention to her relationships with her students; she showed them that she cared for them, that she believed in them, that she would help them get where they wanted to go. And when she looked closely at our data, she saw that's what really mattered. Mentorship.

When Brady asked people if they'd had an academic mentor in college, just 43 percent of Black adults in the control condition said they had. When she asked if that mentorship had continued after college, just 4 percent said yes.

But among Black adults who'd gotten the belonging exercise, 84 percent said they'd had a mentor in college. Thirty-seven percent

Spiraling Up (Belonging Condition)

Spend a couple of minutes writing about your current life, including what you are doing, how you are doing (both the positives and the negatives), and what is important to you.

"I go to a great law school and have some really good friends. I never imagined that I would get a job at a law firm and have the opportunities I have in front of me."

"I am also very busy with my volunteer Bible education work."

"It is my third year in the organization [a low-income public school] and I love it. The kids work harder than I have ever seen kids work before."

"The more I get into database management and modeling, [the more] I consider moving into medicine and bioinformatics. My mom died of cancer in 2011. The detection of that could have been much earlier had the hospital had a predictive model in place that reads blood work results. Building models to predict a car accident is okay—building a model to prevent cancer would rock."

"I dreamed of working with notable environmental law professors to study environmental justice issues and creating policy at EPA to address climate change. Fast forward to now, and I work at EPA crafting environmental justice and climate change policy and have a year left before graduating from law school, having studied environmental law with renowned professors that are now my mentors. Through a lot of hard work and some luck I've achieved the goals I set for myself years earlier."

Not So Much (Control Condition)

Spend a couple of minutes writing about your current life, including what you are doing, how you are doing (both the positives and the negatives), and what is important to you.

"Life is just ok—it ebbs and flows . . . right now it is not great. . . . I will have an uphill battle securing a good [medical] residency. . . . I also feel like I have few friends or people I can turn to when I am stressed and that when I do look to them for advice, I tax them so much that they don't really want to be around me."

"I'm the collateral damage of a bad economy. Some people lucked out, some people didn't. Anyway, I try not to ask myself 'why me?' too often."

"I'm still burned out from 1L [the first year of law school] so it's hard for me to keep the enthusiasm going."

"It has been a struggle for me, but medical school is supposed to be difficult. I try to keep things positive, but I find that when I take a break, I become even more behind . . . that has led to a lot of stress and disappointment."

"I wish I were further along a career trajectory and could see a clearer path of growth and development."

"I am currently working to improve my outlook on life. . . . I do feel left out of events that my friends may be participating in. . . . I've been utilizing Facebook more in order to see what's happening with my friends and to feel more included in what they're up to. I have been pacing myself with Facebook since I feel it can be quite overwhelming as I feel others may have it better than me."

said this mentorship had continued after college. And they said this mentorship was more important too (4.11 versus 2.87 on a 5-point scale). Remember that bump in emails to professors? Perhaps some of those emails had helped build these connections.

The stories Black adults told conveyed this difference. With the belonging exercise, Black adults credited mentors with supporting them through hard times and into their careers. Their stories were detailed and powerful. Here are two:

The first semester of my freshman year was very difficult for me. I was struggling academically, didn't feel like I fit in, and was unhappy with my major. I really did not feel like I belonged. At the halfway point in that semester I was totally miserable. Around that time, I began to spend more time speaking with my freshman counselor. We really bonded, and she helped me to realize that I did belong. Thanks to her, I was able to connect better with my peers and perform better academically. We've kept in touch ever since.

One of the most meaningful mentorships came from my Math professor. I started in basic mathematics, but was interested in [engineering]. However, on the first math mid-term, I almost failed the test. I went to speak to the professor and, when he learned I wanted to be an engineer, he said "well, basic calculus is the foundation of all engineering, so you'd better shape up," or something like that. It actually really discouraged me at first. But, then I spoke with my mom and realized that I just needed to get back to basics. I started going to math tutor sessions . . . and also bought a basic geometry/trig book to help me remember the basics. In fact, the next two mid-terms, I scored the 3rd or 4th highest in the class and ended up acing calculus. Along the way, the professor saw my improvement and started mentoring me. He and I would talk after class, not just about the class, but more about life, in general, and my interest in engineering, specifically. He helped me tremendously and we stayed in touch, even as I left his class in the Spring. He nominated me for a scholarship and in general kept in touch with me throughout the next year, until he retired.

By contrast, Black adults who hadn't had the belonging exercise just described a lack of mentoring:

> I wouldn't say I received any mentorship—not for lack of interested professors, but I didn't really seek it.

> I don't think I necessarily had a mentor-mentee relationship with anyone. I definitely looked up to and sought out advice from older brothers in my fraternity, but it wasn't until having graduated that I realized the importance of meaningful mentorship relationships.

Like Michelle Robinson, who entered Princeton in 1981, Sonia Sotomayor, who entered Princeton in 1972, and Ketanji Brown Jackson, who entered Harvard in 1988, the Black students who took part in this study were extraordinary young people with every opportunity before them. When troubling questions about belonging were addressed, many of these students were able to find mentors who helped them chart a path into adult life. But when they weren't, that made it harder to build the kinds of relationships students would need to succeed later in life.

SPIRALING UP IN STEM: *"I AM NOT ALONE. THE HIGH STANDARD AT UW IS REALLY A WAY FOR THEM TO PUSH US."*

When I moved to Waterloo in August 2006, I was desperate to learn if we could replicate these basic results. For if "one swallow does not make a summer," nor does one study prove a point. Was the belonging exercise a one-hit wonder? Or could it work again, with a totally different population?

Moving to a small Canadian town was hard at first. It felt very slow, and I knew essentially no one. But fortunately, I also knew that everyone worries at first about whether they belong in a new place and it gets better with time.

Even more fortunately, my new postdoc adviser, Steve Spencer, paired me with one of his senior grad students, Christine Logel, as office mates. Christine's social spirit was irrepressible, even though she'd just had a baby. Having no social life whatsoever, I would literally go anywhere with Christine: grocery shopping, clothes shopping, walking through the mini zoo with her and her baby daughter. I remember feeling so grateful to Christine for taking pity on and spending time with me. Only years later did I find out that *she* felt grateful to me! On the job, we were officially work husband and wife and each other's greatest admirers.

Logel is a brilliant social psychologist, and one thing she understood was the culture that women faced in engineering. So, starting in the spring of 2007, together with Spencer and another grad student Jennifer Peach, we began to explore women's experience of belonging in engineering with a series of listening sessions. We certainly heard stories of homesickness, academic challenges, and feelings of intimidation. But another theme that came up time and again was whether you could still be female in such a male space. One woman told us, "[A female professor discouraged us from publishing] a 'classy' calendar of women in engineering: '[Don't] present yourselves as women first if you want to be taken seriously as engineers.'" If you wanted to belong in engineering, did a woman need to renounce her femininity?

Women struggled with this question and felt its tensions. But they also described learning. One said, "You can still be one of the guys and be feminine. Realizing that is a big jump you have to make. I really like being one of the guys, I don't want to give that up. There was this fear that if I get too girly, they'll exclude me from that club. It was a matter of finding I could be both."

Logel knew from her dissertation research how quickly male-female interactions could go sideways in engineering. She'd found that just in regular conversations about engineering, male engineers tended to flirt with women, especially men who were a little more sexist. They'd sit a bit closer to a woman, look at her body a bit more, and act a bit more confidently. That raised gender stereotypes for women and made them do worse on an engineering test. The devil was that women liked the flirting men more.

As we reflected on what we'd heard, we decided to complement the basic themes that Cohen and I had developed with stories that surfaced the particular challenges of fitting in as a woman in engineering.

Here are two of the stories we told. In the first, "Mike," a senior student in mechatronics, describes his experience facing some of the basic challenges to belonging:

> My first year, I think, I was intimidated. I dreaded group work. I worried other engineers wouldn't take me seriously or listen to my ideas. But then one of my professors assigned a project that I was excited about. . . . So I spoke up more in my group and shared more ideas. For the most part, people were eager to listen. . . . Now I love group work—dividing up a complex project, helping each other out. . . . I've contributed to solving problems in engineering, and I'm proud of that.

If you are a woman reading this story, it might help you see that even senior men, whom you might think have it all together, can feel judged and intimidated at first and need a process to work through this.

The second story straight up surfaces the reality that, yes, a woman might not fit in with men when they're performing their gender identity. But that's okay, as Fatima, a civil engineering student, learns:

> Initially my transition to university wasn't bad. I enjoyed most of my classes. But it took a while to get to know my classmates. I remember once in my first term having lunch with some other civil engineers. They spent 90% of the time talking about hockey, about which I know next to nothing. I felt like I didn't belong. It was discouraging. But over time I got to know my classmates bet-

ter, individually and as a group. Once I remember talking about the TV show *Monster Machines,* which I have to admit I love. We had a great time sharing stories about the different episodes. Even though I don't share their love of hockey, I realized that we do have a lot in common—an interest in how things work—and that's why we're all engineers. My major has turned out to be a lot of fun. I have made good friends with a number of my classmates, and I feel like I really belong here at UW.

As Fatima shows, you needn't be a hockey nut to belong in engineering. It can just be a tiny fact.

We began to deliver the belonging exercise (or control materials, which focused on study skills) in the fall of 2007, with students beginning their first year in engineering. We showed the stories in a brief slideshow, including audio recordings of senior engineering students reading them to increase their impact. Then we asked students to describe their own experiences so far, their worries and progress. At the end, we asked students to write a personal letter to help a future student in their transition. Just as the Black (and White) students had done in the first study, what the engineering students wrote was wonderful, moving, and impactful. They described specific challenges that come up in the transition to engineering, thought through how to understand them, and identified productive next steps. Here's one letter, written by a woman in computer engineering:

Dear future UW Frosh: First of all, congrats on getting accepted into UW. I can assure you that UW is definitely the best university to be in. In my letter, I'll share some of my experience as a 1st-year engineering student. Hopefully you'll find it helpful.

Going into UW, I was very excited and nervous at the same time. . . . First of all, I didn't know if I was "good enough." . . . I know that I will be surrounded by hundreds of top students from all over the world. To be honest, the workload at UW is extremely heavy. I felt very stressed and disappointed when I "failed" one of my quizzes, for the first time in my life. However, I soon found out that everyone's on the same boat as me. That is, I am not alone. The high standard at UW is really a way for them to push us to become a better engineer. In fact, I am really glad that I am being challenged here at UW.

Secondly, most people are worried that they wouldn't fit in with the community, I was too. But then I realized that everyone is new to UW, everyone is looking for friendships. . . . My tip to you is, take initiatives, introduce yourself to the person beside you, you'll be surprised that they are very eager to talk to you as well. . . .

One more thing, don't worry about being the only girl in your engineering program. You won't be, but you will be the minority for sure. There are only 10 girls in my 128 people program. So don't be intimated by all those guys, don't feel that you aren't as good. Instead, feel special, male engineer students and profs actually respect female students a lot. Again, just be yourself and enjoy the process, it's once in a lifetime. Good luck! ☺

The whole session was over in forty-five to sixty minutes.

Altogether, we ran students from three cohorts through the procedure, in the fall semesters of 2007, 2008, and 2009, to obtain a sample of 228 students. As I began to analyze the data as a whole in the summer of 2010, I found a pattern that would not have surprised Mary Murphy. The problems women faced were all in the male-dominated majors, those averaging 10 percent women. In the more diverse majors, women were doing well. Their grades were strong, just as high as men's, they felt they belonged, and they were confident they could succeed. There the belonging exercise had no effect. It wasn't needed. These weren't the circumstances that placed persistent questions about belonging on the mind.

But women in the majors grossly dominated by men were struggling. The most important bottom-line outcome was students' grades over the first year. In these majors, women in the control condition averaged a 65 on Waterloo's scale, barely clearing the minimum needed to stay in engineering, 60. By contrast, men averaged 75 with or without the belonging exercise. Women also reported they belonged less, felt less able to succeed, and said they enjoyed their classes less than men, both immediately after the randomized materials and about four months later, in a spring semester survey. And these were the same students who found daily slings and arrows especially "important."

But with the belonging exercise, women's GPA rose all the way to 77, an average mark so high it nearly reached the standard for the Dean's Honors List, 80. Immediately, they felt they belonged and more confident in their abilities. Over the next several weeks, no longer did negative daily events loom large. Women felt more confident they could handle daily stressors, and their self-esteem was higher and more stable. By the second semester, they were more confident they could succeed in engineering and said it was easier for them to imagine becoming a professional engineer.

At the same time, women's friend groups shifted. In the control condition, women in the male-dominated majors reported in the spring term that just 43 percent of their close friends on campus were male engineers. That's far below the 90 percent representation of men in their classes. These women also told us they'd been hearing more sexist jokes about female engineers on campus than they had earlier in the year. (Remember that bad quip from the faculty meeting at Stanford?) But women in these same majors who'd done the belonging exercise said that 75 percent of their friends were male engineers. And they reported no increase in hearing sexist jokes. They were more integrated with their classmates. That's a social circumstance a student can use to spiral up.

STORIES OF BELONGING—THEIR POWER, THEIR LIMITS: *"THE STORIES THAT WE TELL . . . HELP US CREATE, AND LIVE, IN THE WORLD THAT WE WANT TO LIVE IN"*

After the results from Waterloo, the belonging exercise still felt a bit like magic, but it also began to feel more ordinary. Today, belonging interventions have been tested more than a dozen times in rigorous trials, with tens of thousands of students. Some adaptations have focused on students' experience entering broad-access colleges—institutions that serve as critical vehicles for upward mobility for millions of Americans—and increased the rate at which students maintain enrollment and make progress toward a degree. Others have been adapted for introductory biology and physics courses in college, key gateways to careers in science, and eliminated group disparities in the STEM pipeline. Yet others have been implemented earlier, in the transitions to middle and high school, improving students' trajectories through school. We have also learned how to deliver belonging exercises online, a way to reach many people efficiently. One series of trials found that online belonging and related exercises before college reduced inequalities in persistence and grades through the first year by 30 to 40 percent with full institutional cohorts. We'll dig into these innovations in chapter 8.

Belonging stories have also become part of our culture. A scholarship competition, We Belong in College, invites students to share "a time you struggled to or through college, how you persisted, and any advice you have for students with similar challenges." In one picture book, Elisa Kleven's *The Apple Doll,* little Lizzy whispers a secret to her favorite apple plucked from her tree, "I'm scared to start school. . . . What if I don't make any friends?" but comes to find her way in kindergarten. In *New Kid* by Jerry Craft (winner of both the Newbery Medal and the Coretta Scott King Award), a student of color navigates the chichi Riverdale Academy.

It hit me how ubiquitous belonging stories have become in the fall of 2021. It was the return to full-time in-person schooling following the COVID-19 shutdown. Early in the school year both of my kids, Lucy and Oliver, heard the picture book *First Day Jitters,* by Julie Danneberg, read aloud by their teachers. In the story, Sarah doesn't want to go to the first day of school. "I'm not going," she says. "I don't want to start over again. I hate my new school. . . . I don't know anybody, and it will be hard." After much cajoling from her father, Sarah arrives at school, meets the principal, and is ushered into the classroom. Only then do we learn that Sarah is not a student at all. She's the teacher! Most beautifully, after reading the story, one teacher disclosed to her class that she too felt nervous about starting a new year and meeting new students, especially after COVID. It's a detail that made me smile. Even the teacher is nervous at first.

I've long admired the late neurologist and writer Oliver Sacks. Sacks once wrote, "Our only truth is narrative truth, the stories we tell each other and ourselves—the stories we continually recategorize and refine."

Sacks is talking here about the past, about memory. But when we tell belonging stories, we are forward-looking. We are forecasting what our experience in a setting might be like: recategorizing and refining what opportunities it might hold. What it might require of us. As the Native American activist Kim TallBear, a professor at the University of Alberta, says, "The stories that we tell not only come out of the world that we live in. [They also] help us create, and live in, the world that we want to live in."

Yet that vision also has to be legitimate. For some stories are mere fables. They're just fairy tales.

If you're offered a positive, growthy story about your prospects in a setting you really want to belong to, you're probably going to consider that vision. You might try it out in your interactions with other people. You'll kick the tires on the idea, so to speak. Is this way of thinking true here, and true for people like me? Can I use it to help me build relationships and work toward my goals?

But suppose that vision is just a fantasy. What if you try to make friends but no one includes you, not ever? What if you reach out to professors, but no one responds? What if your supervisor at work always credits your ideas to someone else, even after you've raised the concern.

Not all belonging trials have succeeded. It's *not* magic. Sometimes, stories aren't enough. Exercises like the belonging intervention depend on whether people actually can come to belong. Is there a Walter Wallace available to mentor Michelle Robinson, if only she reaches out? Is there a Nancy Weiss Malkiel available to support Sonia Sotomayor? It's crucial that schools and employers make sure that every person in their community really does have the support they need.

When we're trying to plow new ground, to break a glass ceiling one blow at a time, it's easy to wonder, *Can people like me belong here?* Then we're vulnerable. Every hassle, every slight, every struggle, can seem to confirm your fear. Can we create a culture in which we share, not hide, our struggles, where we can see everyday challenges on the path to belonging as the tiny facts that they are? And can we create the institutions, norms, and relationships where this path really is available to everyone?

KNOW IT. OWN IT. USE IT.

Know your questions. Use your answers.

Here is the question this chapter has covered.

Do I/people like me belong here?

This exercise has two parts. You can do either part or both, as you like.

Part 1: Think about yourself, your life and circumstance.

Pick a community in which this question is relevant for you, a place you're part of and want to belong to but one that sometimes also elicits some uncertainty, where your belonging feels up in the air. It could be a school, a workplace, or even a community group. *Then write down your answers to these questions:*

1. What's a tifbit (tiny fact, big theory) you've experienced relevant to this question—something small that happened that you had a disproportionate response to? How does that tifbit reveal how this question comes up for you, what exactly the question is for you?
2. Why is that question normal and reasonable for you, given your circumstance—but not necessarily true (or not the only way to think about it)?
3. How can you answer that question in a way that will be healthy and productive and authentic for you? What's a better answer, and how can you *offer* yourself that answer and try it out?*

Part 2: Think about someone else, someone you care about: a friend, a family member, someone you work with or for.

Consider their life and circumstance. Pick a context in which this question is relevant for them. *Then write down your answers to these questions.*

1. ˮWhat's a tifbit they've shown relevant to this question? How does that tifbit suggest how this question comes up for them, what exactly the question is for them?
2. Why is that question normal and reasonable for them, given their circumstance—but not necessarily true (or not the only way to think about it)?
3. Given your role and relationship, how can you help this person answer that question in a way that will be healthy and productive and authentic for them? What's a better answer, and how can you gracefully *offer* that answer to them so they can build it out for themselves and use it to spiral up?* *For instance, describe your own worries about belonging in a related situation, and how you worked through these.*

---

* Remember the principles for thinking through "bad" events:

Principle 1: Avoid negative labels (*I'm not bad*)

Principle 2: You're not the only one; you're never the only one (*It's normal*)

Principle 3: Recognize causes that don't malign you or others (*I/you face real obstacles*)

Principle 4: Forecast improvement (*It can get better*)

Principle 5: Recognize opportunities (*Silver lining*)

DIGGING DEEPER
BUILD YOUR BELONGING

If you have a little more time, and a buddy to talk with.

This second exercise is a more structured way to help you think about belonging, how it works in a community you're part of, and how you can build it. It's adapted from a class I teach for first-year students at Stanford.

As in the first exercise, begin by identifying a community you want to belong to but one that sometimes also elicits some uncertainty, where your belonging feels up in the air. It could be a school, a workplace, or a community group.

Step 1: Understand Another Person's Experience of Belonging

Find *one* person in this community with whom you'd like to have a conversation about belonging. Ideally this person has a little more experience than you in the community.

Tell this person that you'd like to talk with them about their experience in the community. If they are willing, ask them questions like these:

1. *What was a time or experience in* which you felt you really belonged in this community? *What happened? What did it mean to you? Why did it mean this?* Emphasize that the experience need not be objectively "large" but should be meaningful to them.

2. *What was a time or experience in which* you felt that maybe you did not belong in this community? *What happened? What did it mean to you? Why did it mean this?* Again, emphasize that the experience need not be objectively "large" but should be meaningful to them.

3. *How has your experience of belonging in this community changed over time, from when you began through the present?*

Ask any follow-up questions you like. Say, "Tell me a story about that."

Consider taking notes or recording (with their permission). Then write down what your interviewee told you. Describe their experiences, how they understood them, what you learned from talking with them, and what more you'd like to learn. This writing is a way for you to consolidate your thoughts.

Step 2: Reflect on Your Own Experience of Belonging

Almost everyone worries at first about whether they belong when they come to a new community. However, the specific kinds of worries people have, and the specific triggers for these worries (tifbits), can vary.

Reflect on your experience coming to this community. Consider your background, the community you came from, your family, your prior experience, and your various identities.

- *What are ways you have experienced belonging so far in this community?*
- *What are ways you have experienced worries about belonging so far in this community?*
- *What triggers for these worries have you experienced? Why were you sensitive to these triggers? What did they mean to you? What does that tell you about your belonging worries?*
- *Why might these worries about belonging be normal and reasonable and experienced by other people too, maybe more than it might seem? How might they relate to your background and identity?*
- *How might these worries change over time? What can you do to help them change for good?*

Take a few minutes to write down your answers to these questions.

Step 3: Do Something to Support Your Belonging

This step has three parts.

1. Reread what you wrote for Step 2. Identify one specific thing you could do to grow your belonging in this community. It could be any of the following:

    - Start a conversation with someone you'd like to get to know better, such as a potential friend or mentor or someone you look up to.
    - Do something to connect your interests, values, identity, and/or background to this community.
    - Participate in or help organize a social event involving this community, ideally an event that draws on or is related to something that matters to you.
    - Get involved in something in the community you enjoy or care about or that connects to your identity.
    - Tell your own story (How? To whom?).
    - Something else.

Jot down what you plan to do, why you plan to do this, and how you hope it goes.

2. Go do it.
3. Reflect on what you did and how it went.

    - How did it go? Did it go the way you expected, or were there surprises?
    - What did it feel like?
    - What did you learn?
    - What might you do next?

(When my students do this exercise, they almost always find it goes better than they expected.)

DIGGING DEEPER
CRUMPLE PAPER BELONGING

Have a small group?

This last exercise is inspired by a spontaneous moment in a class I taught years ago when I first came to Stanford as a professor. It's a way to have a productive conversation about belonging in a group.

In class, I asked first-year students to write privately about their experiences of belonging at Stanford, including worries they felt and how their experience was changing over time. I told students not to include their name or any other identifying information so they could be completely forthcoming.

Then I collected what they wrote, shuffled up the papers, and handed a few back to be read aloud. What was amazing was that you didn't have to hear more than one or two. All the stories were the same. They differed in the details, of course, but they all expressed the same worries and hopes. It was deeply moving. No one was alone.

Later, our team developed a version for a first-year dorm at Stanford, working with resident assistants. Then a team led by Kevin Binning at the University of Pittsburgh learned to embed exercises like this in large introductory science courses and found, using rigorous field experiments, that this improved students' attendance, grades, and even persistence in college. My friend Patricia Chen, an educational psychologist at the University of Texas at Austin, does a version she calls "Crumple Paper Belonging." After doing their writing, everyone crumples up their sheet of paper and throws it in the middle of the table to be read aloud.

Here's a version for students coming to college. But you could do it with any group where people might want to belong but be nervous at first. Feel free to adapt it for any community in which you think it might be fitting.

In this version, I'm assuming there is a facilitator, with a script (in *italics*) and instructions for them. In the dorm at Stanford, the facilitator was a resident assistant, a "near peer." So that person began by sharing their own experience of belonging as a kind of model. But you can also just start with Step 2, where students do their own private reflections.

Step 1: Open and Share

We all know that [college name] is a special place. Still, the transition to college can be tough. For many of us:

- *This is the first time living on our own, away from our families and high school friends.*
- *We are constantly meeting new people and wondering if they will become our new friends.*
- *Life isn't as structured as it was in high school: How do we manage our free time?*
- *There are tons of opportunities and groups; we have to figure out where we fit in.*
- *We have to figure out how to navigate college classes, how to get to know professors, and sometimes how to handle disappointing grades.*

It can be easy to feel overwhelmed or to sometimes wonder to yourself, "Do I really belong here?"

When I first came to college . . .

[A brief story about worries about belonging that the facilitator felt, and how their experience changed over time.]

These kinds of experiences are normal in the transition to college. Everyone goes through them, and they get better with time as you adjust to college.

Step 2: Write

Today, we'd like each of you to reflect on some of the experiences you've had so far in coming to college. So, please take a few minutes to write about the experiences and challenges you've faced. You can think about experiences meeting other students, taking classes, adjusting to dorm life, or interacting with professors. Coming to college is a big transition! Please write about some of the difficulties you have experienced and how some of these difficulties have begun to change with time.

Really try to express your story—what it's been like for you. Be as specific as you can about the particular events or experiences you've had. But please don't include your name or any other identifying information. When you're done, we'll collect what you've written, and the responses will be all mixed up and we'll read some aloud.

WHAT HAS COMING TO [COLLEGE NAME] BEEN LIKE FOR YOU?

Many students experience difficulties and worries coming to college, from living in a new place, to trying to make new friends, to finding their way in a new academic environment.

Take a few minutes to write about the challenges you have experienced in the transition to college, and how these experiences have begun to change over time.

Please, don't include your name or other identifying information.

Step 3: Share and Discuss

Collect the responses, and then hand out a few to students to read aloud.

Begin an open discussion about what you're hearing in the responses. You could ask:

- *What experiences, feelings, or themes are common across some of the responses we read?*
- *It seems like a lot of people are writing about how they _____. I know that for me, I felt that way but thought that everyone else*

had everything under control. Why do you think that sometimes we don't realize that other people also have our same worries or are struggling in ways that we are too?

- *Think back all the way to the beginning of the year. How have your experiences or the experiences we heard about been changing?*
- *Looking forward to the future, how do you expect these experiences will continue to change? What can we do to help them change for good?*

Try to include everyone: Go around the circle if necessary. Don't tell anyone what they should feel. Instead, validate students' responses. Recognize both commonalities and differences in students' experiences, in both the nature of students' experiences and their timing (for example, "It often happens at different times and in different ways for different people").

Chapter 4

Can I Do It?

When you learn new things, neurons connect in the brain.
—OLIVER, AGED SEVEN

Know how I did it? When I wanted to stop, I just kept going.
—LUCY, AGED FOUR

November 3, 2022, Philadelphia. The crucial Game 5 of the World Series between the Phillies and the Houston Astros. The series was tied at two games apiece. On the mound for the Astros was Justin Verlander, one of my favorite players and among the best pitchers of his generation. Verlander had come up with my hometown team, the Detroit Tigers, and brought them back from years of mediocrity to win the American League pennant in 2006 and then again in 2012. An old-fashioned workhorse, Verlander had the wondrous quality of strengthening as the game went on, often throwing his hardest, most dominant pitches in the later innings.

Unfortunately, Verlander's success in the regular season hadn't been matched in the postseason. Just six days earlier in Game 1 he'd given up five runs in a 6–5 Astros loss. In fact, in eight World Series starts going back sixteen years, Verlander had never won. As he faced the Phillies' left fielder Kyle Schwarber leading off Game 5, he stood tied with the Oakland Athletics' disco-era Catfish Hunter for the most home runs given up in World Series history—nine, all painful.

So, of course, on the second pitch, the catcher signaled for an inside pitch, but Verlander's fastball slipped into the middle of the plate and Schwarber didn't miss. Line drive deep into the right-field seats. Home run. The 45,693 Phillies fans in attendance went wild, and the unfortunate record was all Verlander's. If you watch the highlight, you can tell he knew right away. Alone on the mound, a short hop at the end of his delivery, a grimace, and then he tosses his right hand in the air as if to say, "Ahh, sh——!"

You've spent your whole life playing baseball. You've dreamed of playing in the World Series since you were a young child. There is no higher stage. Yet you've struggled here time and again. It's become your bugaboo.

You might think Schwarber's home run would be just the start of another Phillies barrage. But no. Verlander would gather himself and go five strong innings, allowing just three more hits against six strikeouts and not another run in a 3–2 Astros victory. It was his first World Series win, at age thirty-nine. Two days later back in Houston, the Astros would win Game 6, and Verlander and the Astros were World Champs.

Why didn't that home run derail Verlander? If ever there was a time for a tifbit, that would have been it. Interviewed after the game, Verlander described his experience after Schwarber's moon shot:

> Initially, you're like, that sucks. But as a starting pitcher, been there, done that. It just sucks because of the moment and obviously all the questions and weight. You have to rely on the hundreds of starts and thousands of pitches I've thrown before and just kind of say, "OK, I've given up leadoff home runs before. It's not going to be indicative of what's going to happen the rest of this game, by any means. Let's see what happens."

Wow! On that stage, in the few seconds before the next hitter steps up, Verlander is able to surface and then reject the ostensible implication of Schwarber's home run: "It's not going to be indicative . . ." Verlander is six feet, five inches and able to throw a baseball a hundred miles an hour. But skill isn't everything. I'd bet a good deal that his psychological presence is a big reason he's on his way to the Hall of Fame.

When we're working toward goals big or small, it's inevitable that we'll encounter roadblocks along the way. Struggles, dead ends, exhaustion, stress. To keep going, we can't treat those roadblocks as proof we don't have what it takes.

WHAT TO DO AND WHEN TO DO IT

People are doers: "Dream-singers, / Story-tellers, / Dancers," in Langston Hughes's lovely 1923 ode to the African American community, "My People." We're not content to just sit and be. We want to learn, to accomplish, to make a mark, on our own or with others, to build a better life for ourselves, and to contribute positively to the lives of others. But we don't always act effectively toward our goals.

Why not?

Sometimes we just don't think through *how* to accomplish a goal. Then creating a structure to plan out exactly what you'll do and when you'll do it can help get a job done. In a classic study, giving college students frightful images of tetanus made no difference in their likelihood to show up at the campus health center to get a tetanus shot. With or without the scare tactics only 3 percent of students showed up. What helped was when students got a map with the health center circled and a simple question asking them when they might be free. Now 28 percent came. Those students didn't need more reasons. They just needed to plan out the concrete steps to get it done. This approach, called implementation intentions, can help corporate workers get annual flu shots too. And college students do better when prompts help them decide exactly when and how they'll prepare for exams.

At other times, it's not even obvious what behaviors will make a difference. We tell preschoolers to eat their veggies all the time, but have you ever explained why? One study found that using kid-friendly language to share a bit about how nutrition works (for example, food is made up of lots of different things, and your body needs all these different things to work and grow) increased preschoolers' selection of vegetables at snack time. As a global community, all of us had to learn what makes a difference in preventing COVID-19 (mask wearing, social distancing, vaccines) and what doesn't (quarantining your mail, drinking bleach).

But even if you know what behaviors will make a difference, and even if you plan out exactly when and how to do them, there's no guarantee you'll succeed. All the time we don't. You're up on the mound. You know what you've got to do (hit the damn corners!) but serve up another meatball. In this chapter, we're going to zoom in on three big questions that can pop up and get in the way as we try to accomplish goals: *Can I do it? Do I need a break?* and *Is this really my goal?* Can we recognize these questions? Can we learn to answer them well?

PART 1: "CAN I DO IT?"

When I was a kid, playing baseball was maybe my favorite activity. Mostly I played shortstop, but I also pitched on occasion. Briefly (very briefly), in the spring of eighth grade, I mysteriously developed a sharp break in my fastball, a jump that devastated hitters. It's to my everlasting regret that I lost that break just that summer and never recovered it. But that spring, I was in the zone. I well remember one game. We'd opened up a big lead, but the other team had the audacity to attempt a comeback. By the last inning, our lead was down to one with two runners on and one out. Coach brought me in to pitch. I wasn't thinking, *Can I do it?* I was thinking, *I'm going to dominate these suckers!* And I did. Two strikeouts and the game was over.

It's not when things are going swimmingly that we ask the icky questions. But fast-forward a few months and I was getting hit all over the yard. That's when I needed Verlander's presence. For it's during struggles, when things aren't going right, that we ask troubling questions.

I've long thought that my mother is one of the best intuitive psychologists I know. When I was going to college, I remembered the stories she told of the loneliness and frustration she felt in her two years at a small New England college, which led her to transfer to the University of Michigan. Those stories helped me put my own challenges in college in context.

But I also know my mother's deft wisdom extends far beyond what I can easily see. Sometimes I get a peek at her skills when I watch her interact with our kids. Not long ago, as we were preparing dinner together, seven-year-old Oliver was struggling to peel an orange. My mother said with kindness, "Oh, that's hard to do with little fingers, isn't it?" In that short phrase, she anticipated the question Oliver might not even know he could be asking (*Am I just bad at this?*) and helped him to a better answer (*It's just that my fingers aren't big yet*).

I am my mother's son. So, when our kids were little and learning to walk but tripping over every third sidewalk imperfection, I always liked to say, "Good fall" or "Good catch." Falls are inevitable; what we should value is the recovery.

The trouble of being a klutzy new walker, however, pales in comparison to the problem of struggling to learn a new skill, whether you're a student in school, an adult at work, or just trying to pick up a new language for a trip. It might take some toddlers longer to learn to walk than others, but in general we think that every child will get there. But in society, loud voices proclaim that some people are just smarter than others and therefore more deserving of learning opportunities. In chapter 3, I introduced the early Stanford psychologist Lewis Terman, who pushed an extremist view of IQ on the United States and thence the rest of the world: the idea that some people (and groups) are just smarter than others, that these differences determine life outcomes, and that they can be assessed in short tests.

The causal structure of skill development is itself opaque. One person is so good at math, while another struggles. Why? Then along comes a prominent "scientist" with "objective" tests who proclaims it's simple! It's just a quality inside you—"intelligence"—and you either have it or you don't. That's a catchy notion. Then, when you see someone good at math, it's easy to think they were just born that way, that math must come easy to them, that there's something different in how their brain works that automatically differentiates complex equations or does whatever else it was that impressed you. Less visible might be the work the person put in, the opportunities they had, the teachers who helped them to key insights. Stanford students call it "duck syndrome": it looks like everyone else is gliding smoothly across the lake when really we're all paddling frantically under the surface.

It's hard to overstate Terman's influence in education. It's present in the habitual ways we praise kids as they try to learn ("You're so smart!"), how we sympathize with them ("It's okay. Not everyone can be good at math"), and how we catastrophize setbacks ("Oh no!"). It's present in how we structure schooling: in gifted and talented programs and standardized tests said to evaluate "aptitude," which we then use to dole out educational opportunities. These practices make a spectacle of dividing the ostensibly smart and deserving from the dumb and undeserving. They are spectacularly a-psychological.

These practices have a long legacy. The first major application of IQ tests was in World War I, when Terman worked with others including Robert M. Yerkes, then president of the American Psychological Association, and Henry Goddard, director of research at the Vineland Training School for Feeble-Minded Girls and Boys in New Jersey,* to devise and administer intelligence tests to more than 1.7 million soldiers. Featuring such questions as "Velvet Joe appears in advertisements of . . . (tooth powder)(dry goods)(tobacco)(soap)," the team labeled about half of army recruits "morons" or worse, recommended 8,000 for immediate discharge, and reserved training opportunities for the privileged few. (Do you, like me, have no

* A school for the "feebleminded"? WTF!?

idea what the answer is? Would you, like me, be a moron?) After the war, the Princeton psychologist Carl Brigham adapted the Army Testing Project to create the SAT for the College Board, which has now been in the business of sorting students for college for nearly a hundred years. It's absurd, but Terman had such faith in tests like these he maintained "there is nothing about an individual as important as his IQ, except possibly his morals."

What do ideas and practices like these do to a student going about the daily business of school? You're taking on new material, trying to learn something you don't understand yet. You misstep. *Am I smart enough?* James Baldwin wrote, "The great force of history comes from the fact that we carry it within us, are unconsciously controlled by it." It's like a little ghost of Terman hovers inside you, whispering at every turn, *Maybe you're a moron.* Will you keep going and find another way? Or will you heed that whisper?

Terman, Yerkes, Goddard, and Brigham were selling what's now called a "fixed mindset" of intelligence, a term coined and an idea developed by my close friend and colleague at Stanford Carol Dweck. You might think that a fixed mindset would hurt mainly the people labeled as dumb, but actually it hurts all of us. Dweck tells the story of her own experience in elementary school in New York City, where a teacher literally sat her class in IQ order. As a child, Dweck didn't fully appreciate the harm this caused her. But several years later as an adolescent she had occasion to return to the school, to walk back through the old halls, to see her classrooms. She describes the experience as feeling like "a ghost," as if every other quality of hers, her zany personality, her interests and goals, her commitment to others, were stripped away, irrelevant in the face of whatever her all-important IQ score was. It took a long "growth-mindset journey" for Dweck to undo that damage.

A few years ago, the Stanford Graduate School of Education professor Jo Boaler, an expert in math education, made a short film, *Rethinking Giftedness.* Boaler interviewed college students who'd been assigned to gifted and talented programs early in their schooling. These programs define some kids as "gifted" and then give them special classes and curricula.

One student described the experience this way: "We took a weird test that was nothing like I'd ever done before, and then after that some of the kids that took the test were pulled out of class to go to a special class." She then added, "Being gifted to me meant that it was something that was in me already. It was not something I could work at, but it was something that came from within me, and had been identified from this test when I was seven." For many of the students Boaler interviewed, that label transformed routine challenges in school into a terror. "Well, the first time I really struggled at something was at memorizing my times tables," the student said. "That made me feel terrible, and my mom went to talk to my teacher, and everyone was freaking out that I couldn't do something. And struggling meant that maybe it was running out. Maybe I was getting towards the end of that thing that was within me and I couldn't go any further. So, it was really scary."

It's no surprise that "being gifted" meant it was already within you. That's what Terman *taught*. It's the premise of gifted and talented programs. The crazy notion that struggling with your times tables might mean your magic talent is running out follows from this logic. It makes a setback a tifbit. It works in just the way a history of exclusion transforms other routine challenges in school, like not bringing "the right size sheets" for a dorm room bed, into omens of non-belonging.

This is tragic. School should be joyful and growing and wonderful—even, and especially, when something is hard at first, a challenge to dig into, an area in which to grow. But was it for you? Is it for your child? Always? As much as it could be? For so many of us, Terman and his cronies turned school into one tifbit after another. Another student Boaler interviewed said, "As soon as I slipped up, as soon as I made a small mistake, the kind of feeling that came around was that I wasn't gifted, that I'm not a gifted individual when it came to mathematics." A third shared, "I wasn't supposed to ask questions, because I was already supposed to know how to do everything." That directly harms learning.

In 1998, Dweck published a classic study with Claudia Mueller showing how labels can backfire. First, Mueller and Dweck gave

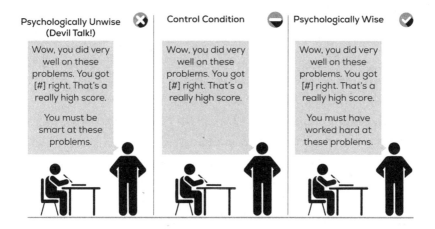

fifth graders some hard but solvable puzzles. When the students were done, the experimenter praised them. In the key condition, she said, "You must be smart at these problems."

That might feel good in the moment, but it's devil talk.

Next, kids got a second set of puzzles. These were so hard everyone had the experience of failing. What Mueller and Dweck wanted to know was what inference would kids draw from this setback? Would it serve as a tifbit?

It did, but only if students had first been told they were oh so "smart at these problems." Then children inferred that they just didn't have the ability to solve problems like these. Maybe they weren't so smart after all. And they didn't stop there. They began to endorse the view that intelligence is fixed (either you have it or you don't). They shifted their goals away from learning and toward just choosing things they could do easily. When given a third set of problems, the same difficulty as the first, they struggled, performing worse than they had on the very same kinds of problems just a few minutes earlier. And if they had the chance to misrepresent their score, they were more likely to lie about it. A shit show, frankly. That's spiraling down in thirty minutes or less.

But it needn't be so. When Mueller and Dweck said instead, "You must have worked hard at these problems," kids didn't presume that struggling on the second set of problems meant they couldn't do it. They thought it meant they had to work harder, to find another way.

They held fast to their growth mindset (the idea that you can grow your intelligence, no matter where you start, by working hard, getting help, and finding good strategies). They said their goal was to learn. On that third set of problems, they did better, not worse (they were learning!). And they weren't tempted to lie about their score.

Labels like "smart" can make you un-resilient, precisely because they transform everyday events like struggling with new material into tidbits, possible proof you might not have that magic ingredient needed to succeed.

Terman's legacy pops up in the most ironic places. I once spoke to a group of journalists at a university in Texas about growth mindset and belonging. Literally the room next door housed the university's gifted and talented program. I entered the lobby and turned right. But if you went left, you'd be in the business of sorting the geniuses from the rest of us.

Another time I spoke to a group of faculty at a welcome-to-the-new-school-year event at a small university in Indiana. The local inn at which my hosts kindly put me up gleefully proclaimed, "Where SMART people stay." I even took a picture and put it in my talk the next day.

Our kids' elementary school tries very hard to promote a growth mindset. These efforts are substantive, sincere, and often excellent. I loved it when Oliver, aged seven, came home from school and shared that "when you learn new things, neurons connect in the brain." And at back-to-school night when Lucy started kindergarten, the principal spoke beautifully about belonging, and even showed a short video of Jo Boaler talking about growth mindset in math. But then I walked out of the room. The school sign always displays a silly joke. That day it said,

Why are the fish so smart?
Because they swim in schools.

A fixed-mindset joke?

Then I got to Lucy's classroom and met her teacher, who would turn out to be wonderful. Yet one of the very first sheets of paper we parents were handed asked in bold letters, "What kind of smart is your child?" and proceeded to list all the different ways a kid could be "smart." Oh, I threw up my hands!

We're fighting the ghost of Terman everywhere. It's that shiver that passes through you when you get a disappointing score on a standardized test, when someone expresses surprise you didn't do better.

The year Lucy started kindergarten, our local school district voted to rename our middle school, which had long been named for Terman himself (Terman Middle School). Imagine trying to learn algebra in a school named for a guy who thought the main goal of education was to separate the smart kids from the dumb kids. Then you struggle to get your head around, say, absolute value. Should you too be "segregated in special classes and be given instruction which is concrete and practical"? Will you be placed in some little corner of the school, deemed a "moron"?

It's because the presumption that intelligence is fixed is so often the default that we must be very intentional about dismantling it. Later in kindergarten when Lucy got over the first hump of learning to read, she and her classmates started to say "easy-peasy" to describe books they already knew how to read. But that conflates how hard it can be *to acquire* a skill with how easy it is *to execute* a skill once you've mastered it. Consider speaking a second language: hard to learn but easy to do once you know how. But if you conflate the two, it turns the learning process into a tifbit (*If it's so easy for everyone else [to do], why isn't it easy for me [to learn]?*).

So, Lucy and I talked about that, about recognizing, expecting, and valuing—truly honoring—the difficulty of learning a skill like reading. What an extraordinary thing it is that young kids do! That means that even when it's easy for someone else *to do* something, it might be hard for you *to learn* that thing. The learning process might be filled with bruises or embarrassment. But that doesn't mean you won't get there.

All of us can be vulnerable to this mistake. Sometimes people say a great leader just has "it." Do we see the efforts and mistakes that went into developing those leadership skills?

It helps to make the value of learning explicit. Carol Dweck and I have a joint lab group (Dweck-Walton Lab) that serves mostly as a space for grad students, postdocs, and visiting scholars to share their work and ideas, to get feedback, and to learn from and with one another. We call it "half-baked lab" and make a point at the beginning of each year to emphasize that we welcome research ideas at every stage of baking, from earliest inception, just a curious thought, to nearly complete, and use feedback and discussion to "bake" them.

It's ironic given our research that we felt the need to be so explicit. But we had seen the lab morph before our eyes into a series of polished presentations where at times speakers seemed more concerned with showing off than with listening and growth. And as the implicit bar rose higher, fewer people even wanted to present. "Half-baked" became a hedge to prevent that slippage.

I've seen this slippage in corporate cultures too. Once, a grad student and I interviewed two employees at a big Silicon Valley tech company. They kept using the term "supersmart," so I asked about that:

ME: What's valued more here: supersmart or working very hard?
EMPLOYEE 1: Working very hard.
EMPLOYEE 2: . . . Um, no . . . Supersmart.
EMPLOYEE 1: . . . Yeah, supersmart.

You could tell they wanted it to be working hard. They knew that was the "right" answer. That was the culture they wanted. But at the end of the day, they knew that "supersmart" was what was valued. That's a culture gone awry.

It needn't be so. At the computer chip maker Nvidia, the CEO, Jensen Huang, implements the "radical belief that failure must be shared." As The New Yorker reports,

In the early two-thousands, Nvidia shipped a faulty graphics card with a loud, overactive fan. Instead of firing the card's product managers, Huang arranged a meeting in which the managers presented, to a few hundred people, every decision they had made that led to the fiasco. (Nvidia also distributed to the press a satirical video, starring the product managers, in which the card was repurposed as a leaf blower.) Presenting one's failures to an audience has become a beloved ritual at Nvidia.

That's a culture where people can learn.

As an academic, I probably spend more of my time writing and helping grad students and younger scholars with their writing than anything else. And writing poses special challenges. Like parenting, it begins with a bang. There's nothing more daunting than a first draft, a blank page looming before you, nothing on it, nothing to build on.

That blank page can be terrifying.

You go to the place you like to write. Your home, with your fuzzy slippers. Your office, door shut. A coffee shop. You open your blank page. You stare at it. You write a few sentences. They're awful, just awful, awkward, not right, so you slash them. Your mind wanders. You check your email, peruse a website. You try again. You're there for three, four, five, even six hours. Now you're leaving that place, thinking you've wasted your entire day. You've spent however many hours and all you have is one measly paragraph, and it's not very good. *It's crap here, crap there,* you think. *I'll never be able to write this thing.* But before you know it, you've written Draft No. 2 in your head.

I think of the experience of writing a first draft as like swimming through some especially thick liquid. Maybe molasses. You have to fight for every inch. You might feel like you're making hardly any progress. But later, when you have a clean draft and are polishing it, editing and sharpening, it might feel fast flowing, more like slipping downstream through a smooth brook. Knowing and accepting that it will be slow at first, sometimes excruciatingly, is the first step to making progress. And as you do that time and again, you get better. You learn.

I've long loved an essay by the nonfiction writer and writing instructor John McPhee. Originally published in *The New Yorker,*

McPhee's "Draft No. 4" tells the story of the time his daughter Jenny, then a senior in high school, told him of the distress she felt at how long it was taking her to even start a school writing assignment. McPhee decides to write her a letter:

> Dear Jenny: The way to do a piece of writing is three or four times over, never once. For me, the hardest part comes first, getting something—anything—out in front of me. Sometimes in a nervous frenzy I just fling words as if I were flinging mud at a wall. Blurt out, heave out, babble out something—anything—as a first draft. With that, you have achieved a sort of nucleus. Then, as you work it over and alter it, you begin to shape sentences that score higher with the ear and eye. Edit it again—top to bottom. The chances are that about now you'll be seeing something that you are sort of eager for others to see. And all that takes time. What I have left out is the interstitial time. You finish that first awful blurting, and then you put the thing aside. You get in your car and drive home. On the way, your mind is still knitting at the words. You think of a better way to say something, a good phrase to correct a certain problem. Without the drafted version—if it did not exist—you obviously would not be thinking of things that would improve it. In short, you may be actually writing only two or three hours a day, but your mind, in one way or another, is working on it twenty-four hours a day—yes, while you sleep—but only if some sort of draft or earlier version already exists. Until it exists, writing has not really begun.

One of my first grad students, Priyanka Carr, described the first stage of writing as the "vomit draft." You "throw up" everything you know, bits of ideas and text, relevant quotations, references, placeholders, random associations, and put it all in the same document. You make no effort to write that well; just get everything out on the page. If you get feedback at that stage, it'd be silly if that feedback was on the quality of the writing. Is it badly written? Of course, it is! Is it badly organized? Certainly!

But what that document does is expand your working memory

capacity. You can start to see all the parts together and their relation-ships. And then you can begin to organize your thoughts, and write them out. Now I share that metaphor with every student. Produce the vomit draft first! And that's how I began this book.

In 1970, two psychologists at Yale University, Michael Storms and Richard Nisbett, published a curious study in the leading journal in the field. They gave people a sugar pill and said it would make their minds race. The goal was to help people fall asleep faster. *Huh?*

Suppose you have a big presentation tomorrow. You're lying there, stiff as a board, heart pounding. Boom-boom. Boom-boom. *What if I can't fall asleep? What if I'm exhausted tomorrow and embarrass myself? I have to get to sleep—now! What is wrong with me!*

Surely these thoughts aren't relaxing. Storms and Nisbett wanted to find out if they truly make it harder to fall asleep. And if they did, could you interrupt them to help people fall asleep more quickly? To learn, they recruited people in New Haven, Connecticut, who identified as insomniacs. These people, mostly students at Yale, reported taking nearly forty-five minutes to fall asleep, on average. Storms and Nisbett gave them each a pill to take before going to sleep. They said the pill would help the researchers in their study of dreams. But actually, it was just a sugar pill. What was important was the side effects they said the pill would cause. In the key condition, Storms and Nisbett told people the pill would "increase your heart rate and . . . your body temperature. You may feel a little like your mind is racing." You might think this expectation would make it even harder for people to fall asleep. But Storms and Nisbett thought it would help. For this way, if you're lying there and your heart thumps and your mind starts to race, you can attribute the experience to the pill, not to something wrong with you. Just as they predicted, in this condition people fell asleep nearly twelve minutes faster than they had previously.

Another group was told exactly the opposite: that the pill would "lower your heart rate . . . [and] decrease your body temperature . . . it will calm down your mind." Now the logic reverses. *My heart is pounding despite the calming pill. There must be something really wrong with me!* Now it took people an extra fifteen minutes to fall asleep.

Storms and Nisbett talked about "exacerbation" cycles. If you ask, *Is there something wrong with me?* that exacerbates insomnia. We'd call it spiraling down.

Twelve years later, the psychologists Tim Wilson (whose dissertation adviser was Nisbett, and who would later become a mentor for me) and Patricia Linville began to suspect that something similar might happen when students come to college, only on a longer timescale. You get some bad grades early. Do you wonder, *Maybe I'm not college material?* Do those thoughts hurt students' success? And could you interrupt them to help students succeed?

To find out, Wilson and Linville didn't give students a sugar pill. They found another way to offer students a better answer to the questions posed by early struggles. Working with first-year students first at Duke University and then at the University of Virginia worried about their academic performance, they shared information and stories from older students who described how they'd received worse grades in the first year than they had anticipated but how their grades had improved with time. The implication was that early struggles were normal, that they didn't reflect anything wrong with you, that things could improve. This information was presented as the results of a general survey. That way students weren't treated as in need of help, and the experience wasn't shaming. In a first study, this raised students' GPA through the next school year and reduced the rate at which students dropped out from 25 percent to 5 percent. In later studies, Wilson and Linville incorporated what we now call saying-is-believing tasks, such as inviting students to write essays to high school students describing why academic difficulties are normal early in college, how these difficulties reflect transient factors like "not knowing how to take college tests" or "unpleasant living conditions," and how they can get better. It was a way to address a core question (*Am I college material?*), to offer more hopeful construals of everyday challenges (*They're normal and improve with time*), an idea students could use to calcify a better trajectory (by staying engaged in learning). These exercises consistently raise grades for struggling students.[*]

Modern-day growth-mindset interventions don't just offer students better answers to troubling questions posed by a rocky term or two. They offer an entirely different view of intelligence itself: not as a fixed quality that lies within you as Terman taught, but as a capacity that can grow ("like a muscle") with hard work, good strategies, and help from others. Ironically, it's a return to the original European notion of intelligence. In the late nineteenth century, as poor children flocked to Paris with varying levels of education, the French psychologist Alfred Binet sought to develop a tool to measure where kids were so they could be matched with the right educational opportunities. Reflecting this fundamental growth orientation, Binet saw a lack of opportunities as an illness: "after the illness, the remedy." Drawing on this legacy, growth-mindset interventions seek to help us move from between-people comparisons (*Am I as smart as . . . ?*) to within-person comparisons (*How can I get better?*). Then struggles and setbacks become how we learn, not a sign of inability.

The development of growth-mindset interventions has been one of the major successes in psychology and education over the past twenty years. And just like Storms and Nisbett's work on insomnia, and Wilson and Linville's on academic worries in the transition to college, this science teaches us two things at once. First, when we see a growth-mindset intervention improve students' success, we learn that questions like *Can I do it?* directly harm students' prospects of success. Second, we learn as a practical matter how to develop better answers and if this will really make a difference for students.

Josh Aronson, Carrie Fried, and Catherine Good developed the first growth-mindset intervention at Stanford in 2002. Using a procedure a bit like Wilson and Linville's, they invited undergrads to

---

[*] If you're noticing a similarity with the belonging intervention described in chapter 3, you're right. Wilson and Linville helped inspire the belonging intervention.

serve as pen pals for a struggling middle school student. In the key condition, the participants were encouraged to help the student see intelligence as a capacity that can grow "like a muscle," watched a brief video that discussed how intelligence can grow throughout life, and were asked to incorporate examples from their own life to illustrate this idea in their letter for the middle schooler. Actually, there was no middle school student, and the letters exchanged were orchestrated by the researchers. Yet as compared with two control conditions, the experience raised grades for the college students the next term.

In another early trial, Lisa Blackwell, Kali Trzesniewski, and Carol Dweck created a six-session workshop for seventh graders in New York City. Students read and discussed how the brain can grow "like a muscle." The effect was to reverse an ongoing decline in math grades. Teachers also noticed this uptick in students' motivation. When asked to identify students who'd shown greater motivation, they called out threefold more students who'd done the growth-mindset workshop, as compared with students assigned to a control workshop focused only on study skills. Here's how two teachers described these changes in motivation:

> Your workshop has already had an effect. L., who never puts in any extra effort and often doesn't turn in homework on time, actually stayed up late working for hours to finish an assignment early so I could review it and give him a chance to revise it. He earned a B+ on the assignment (he had been getting C's and lower).

> M. was [performing] far below grade level. During the past several weeks, she has voluntarily asked for extra help from me during her lunch period in order to improve her test-taking performance. Her grades drastically improved from failing to an 84 [on] her recent exam.

That's important, and not just because it confirms the effectiveness of the intervention. If your teacher sees you trying harder in school, they're more likely to go to bat for you—accelerating that upward spiral.

Sometimes people talk about "giving" students a growth mindset. But that's not what these exercises do. It's not like someone trying to persuade you of something. Rather, they share compelling scientific information, stories from other learners, and that vivid muscle metaphor. Then they create space for students to think through for themselves what a growth mindset might mean to them, how they could use it going forward, either in discussions with peers or in written reflections. It's why I use the verb "to offer." It's an opportunity to think for yourself about your experience in a new light. That's freeing, not controlling.

Today, rigorous growth-mindset interventions have been implemented with students around the world. But these early trials were small; together, the Aronson and Blackwell studies reached just 170 students. At Stanford, one of my first grad students, Dave Paunesku, was impatient. Tens of millions of students go to school every year wrought through with questions like *Do I belong?* and *Am I smart enough?* Paunesku felt viscerally what we should all feel—that it is an outrage; it is flatly obscene that questions like these should hold students back from becoming who they want to be. Equally, it is unacceptable that these questions should gum up our education system and prevent educators from realizing the full impact of their work in creating learning opportunities for young people.

Paunesku saw the promise of the ideas behind the Aronson and Blackwell studies, but he also saw that, practically speaking, these were boutique solutions to a massive societal problem. To truly make a difference, we don't need skilled surgeons working on a case-by-case basis. We need something more like a public health of schooling.

To help us get there, Paunesku would reinvent this work not once but twice. First, in grad school, he pioneered new methods that used technology to reach far more students in randomized controlled trials, even students far from research centers. These methods would ultimately power trials of both social-belonging and growth-mindset interventions with tens of thousands of students in the critical transitions to high school and to college. As important, this work would let us see boundary conditions: to learn where these interventions work and where they do not. For there are no magic bullets. Dismantling the legacy of Terman doesn't just mean offering students better ways to understand the challenges of school. It also means dismantling this legacy in the minds of adults, and in the culture and practice of education as a whole. So, with time, working through an organization he co-founded while still in grad school, PERTS (the Project for Education Research That Scales), Paunesku would also develop tools to help teachers create classroom environments that support belonging and growth for millions of students. We'll explore these tools in the Floodlight: Making School Wise.

PART 2: "DO I NEED A BREAK? NOW? NOW? NOW?"

When our kids were little, we took them to a campus preschool by bike. When they were babies, we stuffed them into a trailer where they rode along in style. But when they got older, they got their own bikes. Chugging home at the end of a long day on tiny twelve-inch wheels, they'd get tired sometimes and want to stop. I still have traumatic memories of kids sitting on the curb two blocks from home and twenty minutes past dinnertime refusing to go another inch. "I'm tired," they wailed. They treated tiredness as a reason to stop. (Tifbit alert!) So, I tried to change the meaning of tiredness for them. I took to saying, "It's when you're tired and you keep going that your muscles get stronger." Then, if the kids complained, I'd say, "Now is when you can get stronger!"

It didn't always work but I think it helped.

At one point, our route home involved a steep hill. Lucy, aged four, was challenging herself to climb the hill as high as she could. She would get going as fast as possible and then do her best to navigate the hill's steep, tight turns. Sometimes Oliver and I would bring chalk and mark on the sidewalk how far she'd gotten. One time, Lucy not only beat her previous record but crushed it. As Oliver and I whooped and cheered, she said triumphantly, "Know how I did it? When I wanted to stop, I just kept going."

Many challenges require persistence. You've got to keep going. But what if a voice in your head pops up every two seconds to say, *Do I need a break?*

Loud voices in our culture proclaim that our gas tanks are small—that your willpower, or your ability to persist in working toward goals, is limited and rapidly runs out. It's like we all have range anxiety. You're working hard to study a new concept in school, to complete a project at work you're excited about, or to finish a race strong. *Do I need a break? . . . Do I need a break? . . . Now? . . . Now? . . . Now?* Asked enough, will you give in?

Some of these voices are literally commercials. For generations, corporations have sold junk food as a tasty break. "Have a break, have a Kit Kat" or "You deserve a break today" (McDonald's). The very notion of a "coffee break" comes from a 1950s campaign by the Pan-American Coffee Bureau.

Lately, these voices have become more insistent. In 2010, Snickers launched a much-lauded global campaign, "You're not you when you're hungry." Ad after ad showed people incompetent, rude, ridiculous, and hilarious, only returning to their normal, well-behaved selves when they got a candy bar. With variations for different groups ("You act like a diva when you're hungry," "You're a cranky old man when you're hungry"), now we're told we *need* a candy bar or we'll be out-of-control social morons. The campaign has been credited with raising global Snickers sales. But it also worms an idea into our collective heads: that we're weak things in constant need of breaks and refreshments.

Just as Terman lent credibility to the question *Can I do it?* so science has lent credibility to the question *Do I need a break?* In a famous 1998 study, cited more than seven thousand times, the psychologist Roy Baumeister found that when people had to resist tempting chocolates and eat radishes instead, they quit a subsequent puzzle more quickly. Baumeister concluded that "the self's *capacity* for active volition is limited" (my emphasis) and that "a range of seemingly different, unrelated acts" all draw down the same, limited resource. Baumeister calls this "ego depletion." It's the idea that you've got this thing called willpower. But it's easily used up, and then you need to eat or rest or you'll lose control. This idea has been promulgated widely, including in Baumeister's 2011 book with the deeply ironic title *Willpower: Rediscovering the Greatest Human Strength*.

I call BS. The idea that we're weaklings in constant need of a break is a myth. It's just not true. And frankly, I find it offensive. Depleted by a few minutes' concentration? I think not. Consider the extraordinary things we do. I well remember as a child my mother reading me the gripping second book in the Bounty Trilogy, *Men Against the Sea*, the tale of Captain William Bligh's incredible, real-life open-boat voyage across thirty-six hundred miles of the South Pacific following a mutiny in 1789. But it's the ordinary too. The sustained focus required to produce a great dissertation—something I see every day with grad students. Consider what you do in your life when you care about something. A few minutes of focus is not going to "deplete" you. It's not going to render you "incapable." We can do more.

In social psychology, Baumeister's work provided a great service. It reignited interest in "self-regulation"; that's the question of how people regulate their own behavior to accomplish goals, a.k.a. willpower. In 2016, I would debate "ego depletion" with Baumeister at a social psychology conference in San Diego. But it took Veronika Job, a Swiss social psychologist now at the University of Vienna, to show what's really going on.

In the fall of 2008, Job came to Stanford to start a postdoc with Carol Dweck. We quickly became fast friends and collaborators. Job's interest in self-regulation was, of course, informed by Baumeister's work. But as Job, Dweck, and I thought about it, we began to suspect that it might be the *idea* that willpower is limited that is the real constraint. If you think that willpower is narrowly limited, might that turn every effort (like resisting a cookie) into a tifbit? *Do I need a break? Do I need a break?* Job began by developing statements to measure how people think about willpower. Here are two of them:

A LIMITED WILLPOWER THEORY	A NON-LIMITED WILLPOWER THEORY
Strenuous mental activity exhausts your resources, which you need to refuel afterward (e.g., through breaks, doing nothing, watching television, eating snacks).	When you have been working on a strenuous mental task, you feel energized and you are able to immediately start with another demanding activity.

If you agree with the first statement, you've bought what Snickers and Baumeister are selling. We called it a "limited theory of willpower," the idea that willpower is narrowly limited and rapidly runs out. You might start fast, but you've got range anxiety. If, on the other hand, you endorse the second statement, you have what we called a "non-limited theory of willpower." It's not thinking that willpower is *un*limited. It's just that you don't think it's so narrowly limited and might even be energizing. You can keep going.

Job ran a series of studies a bit like Baumeister's radish study. In one, she gave people a first task that was either easy, rote, or one that required a few minutes' concentration. Then she gave people a cognitive task that was challenging for everyone, and looked at how they did. For people who endorsed the limited willpower theory, Job found just the pattern Baumeister would expect. When the first task required focus, people made more mistakes on the second cognitive task. You might say they were depleted.

But for people who endorsed the non-limited theory, it didn't matter what they did first. They performed well either way on the cognitive task. They kept up their efforts. They weren't "depleted" by a few minutes' focus.

Maybe people who think one way or the other are just different from each other? Maybe their bodies work differently? Was *the idea* that willpower is limited really what was causing people to let up?

To find out, in another study Job experimentally evoked the idea that willpower is limited with some people, and non-limited with others. She gave people easy-to-agree-with statements that prompted one way of thinking or the other, and asked people if they endorsed them.

PROMPTING A LIMITED WILLPOWER THEORY	PROMPTING A NON-LIMITED WILLPOWER THEORY
Working on a strenuous mental task can make you feel tired such that you need a break before accomplishing a new task.	*Sometimes, working on a strenuous mental task can make you feel energized for further challenging activities.*

The reasoning here is that agreeing with one statement, or the other, makes that notion active in your mind. This activation produced the same results as Job's earlier study. Only when people were prompted to think of willpower as limited did their performance collapse on the second cognitive task. People prompted with the non-limited theory kept up their performance.

If people aren't literally depleted, if they have the capacity to keep going, what's going on? How does having the limited willpower theory hurt performance?

In a third study, Job asked people how tiring they found the first task. When it required concentration, everyone found it a little tiring—no matter the willpower theory. But did that matter? Only when people had been prompted with the limited theory. Then a bit of tiredness predicted worse performance later. Feeling tired had become a reason to let up; it'd become a tifbit. But when people had been prompted to think of willpower as not so limited, feeling a little tired was irrelevant to performance.

That was in the lab, but you can see the same pattern in people's daily lives: thinking about willpower as limited makes it harder to complete goals you really care about. In one study, Job tracked college students in California over an academic term. She found that students who endorsed the limited and non-limited theory didn't differ when they had a light term. But when students faced more demands on their time, those who endorsed the limited theory procrastinated more; they ate more junk food; they were more likely to show up late for appointments; they had more trouble controlling their temper; and they bought more crap they knew was too expensive for them. And, when they took a heavy course load, they got worse grades.

Now we know that a limited willpower theory makes it harder for people to sustain their efforts on challenging learning tasks, and then they learn less. It makes people less likely to achieve their goals, and that undermines well-being. If you have to work hard at something, it makes you want to rest, prompting glowing thoughts about a hammock or a comfy sofa and making you lounge longer if you get the chance. But it also makes people "too exhausted to go to bed": when people endorsed the limited theory, they were more likely to procrastinate after a stressful day and delay going to bed. And it's not just sleep that gets dysregulated. In another study, Job found that people with type 2 diabetes who endorsed the limited theory were less apt to adhere to their treatment plan.

And those Snickers ads? The irony is that they make themselves true. If you think that willpower is limited, then a lack of sugar becomes another tifbit. In one study, when Job prompted people to think of willpower as limited, drinking sugary lemonade helped them keep going, performing well on the next task. Lemonade sweetened with a sugar substitute didn't have the same effect. That was the case even though people couldn't tell which drink had real sugar in it and which didn't.

But it isn't actually the sugar you need. For when Job prompted people with the non-limited theory, sugar made no difference. They kept performing well no matter what. Not having sugar wasn't a physiological problem. It wasn't a real capacity deficit that the sugar filled. It was more like the sugar turned off an excessively early warning light that you're running out. We don't fully understand how, but the limited theory tuned people to sugar on the tongue.

American culture teaches a limited theory of willpower from an early age. It's not just commercial culture or scientists promulgating ego depletion. It's reflected in our very organization of schooling. In *School's In: The History of Summer Education in American Public Schools*, Kenneth M. Gold, dean of education at the College of Staten Island, argues that a limited theory contributed to the creation of summer as a season of leisure:

> For [nineteenth-century school superintendents], a grave danger came from exerting too much energy towards learning for too long a period of time. . . . Most educators condemned excessive educational practices, and they identified a variety of negative results that would ensue from too much schooling . . . [especially] mental fatigue. . . . [School reformers in the nineteenth century] strove to reduce time spent studying, because long periods of respite could save the mind from injury. Hence the elimination of Saturday classes, the shortening of the school day, and the lengthening of vacation. . . . Teachers were cautioned that "when [students] are required to study, their bodies should not be exhausted by long confinement, nor their minds bewildered by prolonged application."

But that view is not dominant everywhere. In another study, Krishna Savani at Hong Kong Polytechnic University and Job looked at South Asian Indians, a culture that prizes self-control in daily life, where students study far more, on average, than American students. Savani and Job found that Indians believe, on the whole, that exerting self-control is energizing, not depleting. And it need not be the case anywhere. We don't yet have the kinds of interventions for willpower theories that we have for growth mindset; the studies I've described are all either short-term lab studies (where researchers temporarily prompt one view or the other) or longitudinal studies (which track how natural variation in people's views predict their outcomes over time). But we're learning how we can offer people healthier ways to think about their efforts, and from an early age. In one study, the psychologist Kyla Haimovitz wrote a simple picture book describing a child who came to find waiting energizing:

> Lucy waited and waited and it was hard. But the longer she waited, the stronger she felt! "I can keep on going," Lucy thought. "If I can wait a few minutes, then I can keep waiting."

(In a clever twist, the book was personalized so the main character's name matched the participating child's name.) After reading the book, four- and five-year-old kids in a California preschool waited 40 percent longer for a tasty treat. Once willpower became something that could be energizing, children searched for and found strategies to accomplish their goal.

In the summer of 2015, as Serena Williams won at Wimbledon, her sister Venus was asked if she'd ever thought Serena would reach twenty Grand Slam titles. Venus said, "I don't think we thought about any limits. When you're a kid, you don't think about limits. You dream. That's how it's happening now. Dreams are coming true." The Williams sisters were lucky. But far too many children grow up being told about their limits, implicitly or explicitly. The limits of their intelligence, the limits of their willpower. This narrative holds us back far more than any actual limitations, because it provokes discouraging questions at critical junctures: *Does this mean I'm dumb? Is it time for a break?* As a society we used to think that people were limited in what they could learn, that it was the rare child who could do calculus or learn to read. Those ideas held people back. They underestimated our capacities, how resourceful and persevering we can be. More than a hundred years ago, William James wrote, "We live subject to inhibition by degrees of fatigue which we have come only from habit to obey." But we can free ourselves. As James wrote a few pages later, "Ideas set free beliefs, and the beliefs set free our wills." Or as James Bond puts it, "I don't stop when I'm tired. I stop when I'm done."

PART 3: "IS THIS REALLY MY GOAL?"

The other day my wife, Lisa, and I were at a parent-teacher conference with a beloved fifth-grade teacher. At the end of the conversation, we spent a few minutes talking about school in general in the wake of COVID. In her experience, we asked, which had suffered more: kids' academic development or their social-emotional growth? Both, she said. Then she described how more students than ever were just opting out of learning. She'd introduce a new lesson, and a student would just check out: "I'm not going to do that. I don't like math."

What was she to do? What would you do?

You'd be forgiven for saying, "I'd tell them how important math is" or even "I'd make them do it." These are often our go-tos. But sometimes the trouble is just that other people push goals on us—without actually helping you take on those goals for yourself. It might be parents ragging on a kid to "eat your broccoli." Or a boss telling you to do something that seems pointless. *Is that really my goal? Or is it just something other people want me to do?* If you're a rebellious teenager—anything like I was (um, am)—the more other people order you around, the more you resist.

So, what's one to do? Practice so-called reverse psychology? Should a dad make a scene of gorging himself on junk food and outlaw broccoli? Should a teacher say that, yes, math is totally lame, and kids should just skip it?

Earlier in this chapter I described some studies that help people think through *how* to get things done, like a tetanus shot. That helps. But sometimes we need better reasons too. We need to think through *why*. In that tetanus shot study, scare tactics weren't right. But there are other kinds of reasons. For people, some of the most powerful reasons to put forth effort are social.

Helping: Learning to Swim, Hand Washing, and Science Class

A few years ago, volunteering in our kids' preschool, I happened upon a bright and cheerful picture book, *Noah's Swim-a-Thon*, by Ann Koffsky. Noah loves his summer camp—everything in it, kickball, painting, singing Shabbat songs. Everything, that is, but the pool. Noah is not induced to swim by a counselor's promise of a sticker ("I already have plenty of stickers"), by the prospect that the fish will hear him blowing bubbles ("Silly. There were no fish in the pool"), or by the chance to learn to swim ("Now why would I want to do that? If I swim, my whole body will be wet. I'll feel goose-bumpy, stingy, and stuffy all at the same time").

The story turns when the camp director announces a swim-a-thon. Each lap campers swim will earn prizes—and "prizes you will be GIVING!" "There are many children who can't afford to come to a wonderful camp like this," the director explains. "They don't get to play kickball, make arts and crafts, and sing Shabbat songs in music like you do." "No kickball? That sounded terrible to Noah." Noah learns campers will recruit family and friends to donate a small sum to the "Help Kids Get to Camp" *tzedakah* fund for each lap they swim. Let's let Koffsky take it from here:

> That night, when Noah was hanging his dry bathing suit and towel up, the swim-a-thon flier fell from his camp bag onto the floor.
>
> His mom picked it up. "Hey Noah, what's this?"
>
> Noah told her all about the swim-a-thon, the prizes, and the *tzedakah* for the kids who couldn't go to camp.
>
> "Are you going to do it?" she asked.
>
> "I'm not sure. Swimming makes me feel goose-bumpy, and the prizes aren't such a good reason to feel goose-bumpy."
>
> "That's true. The prizes aren't a good enough reason," his mom agreed.
>
> "But maybe, y'know, the kids and the *tzedakah* might be a good enough reason," Noah said softly.

His mom smiled and handed Noah a book and the telephone.

"Here. This book has the phone numbers of Bubbe, Zayde, Cousin Max, Aunt Adina—all our relatives."

Noah makes call after call. He puts in the effort at camp to learn. In the end, on the big day, with cheers from all the campers, he swims a single lap and earns $25 for the *tzedakah* fund.

You might think that what motivates people most is themselves. Generation Selfie, always looking out for No. 1. Of course we care what happens to us. But often we underappreciate the opportunity to help other people out, or to work toward common goals with others. To be together. To do together. The trick for people like our beloved fifth-grade teacher is how to connect everyday tasks like working hard in school to social motives, and that involves offering reasons instead of dictating them or ordering people around.

A clue as to how fundamental social motivations are for people comes from research on some of the earliest forms of social behavior. One study orchestrated opportunities for one- and two-year-olds to help an adult, such as to retrieve an object the adult had dropped that was out of the adult's reach. When prompted by just a reciprocal exchange (for example, passing a ball back and forth), children helped the adult on three out of four tasks, on average. Helping seems to bring its own rewards. Other research finds that toddlers show more happiness when they share a toy than when they play with a toy alone, and when they give a treat than when they receive one. What terrible twos?

It's adults too. Following smaller-scale experiments showing that spending on other people increases happiness more than spending on yourself, a massive cross-cultural study found that prosocial spending predicts greater happiness in 120 of 136 countries around the world. Researchers began to entertain the hypothesis that the effect of giving on happiness might be universal. Even Broadway's caught the tune. As *Avenue Q*'s "Money Song" goes, "The more you give / The more you get / That's being alive!"

If helping is fundamental, would well-placed reminders of the opportunity to help others make it more likely that people do key behaviors? In one study, Adam Grant at the University of Pennsylvania placed signs on hospital soap dispensers encouraging doctors and nurses to wash their hands. There were three conditions: a standard sign developed by hospital staff; a reminder that hand hygiene can protect you; and a reminder that hand hygiene can protect patients. All three signs reminded staff to wash their hands. But only the third sign answered the implicit question, *Why should I wash my hands?* with *To help other people.* After weighing the amount of soap left in dispensers before and after the signs were installed, Grant found that only the third sign increased soap use.

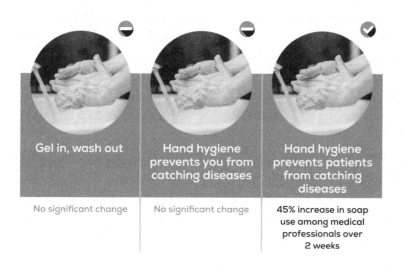

Gel in, wash out	Hand hygiene prevents you from catching diseases	Hand hygiene prevents patients from catching diseases
No significant change	No significant change	45% increase in soap use among medical professionals over 2 weeks

It's not just healthcare workers. In other studies, when university fundraisers read stories about how scholarships made a difference in students' lives, or when they had a chance to have a five-minute conversation with a scholarship recipient, they raised more money over the next month.

This same social motivation can help learners connect the dots. Chris Hulleman is now a professor of psychology and education at the University of Virginia. He's also a dad, a former teacher, football coach, and social worker, and a grandson of tenant farmers in the Midwest. Hulleman went to grad school at the University of Wisconsin, where he worked with the eminent psychologist Judy Harackiewicz. Together, they developed an ingenious approach to the problem faced by our fifth-grade teacher. You don't tell students anything. You ask instead. You give kids space to articulate for themselves why foundational schoolwork might be useful for them and people in their lives.

Hulleman and Harackiewicz got started in 2009, working with science classes in two local high schools. They created a short writing assignment for students to do beginning in the second week of the semester, a few days before each test in the course. Some students were just asked to summarize the topics covered in the course so far. But others were asked this question:

> How might the information be useful to you, or a friend/relative, in daily life? How does learning about this topic apply to your future plans?

They called this the "utility-value" intervention, because it focuses on the usefulness of course content: what you can do with what you learn.

Unsurprisingly, many students took the opportunity to describe how science could help them help others. One student in a biology course focused on "the eight characteristics of life":

> The reason I chose characteristics of life [is] because when I grow up I want to be a doctor. Doctors need to know about the characteristics of life in order to help their patients. This information can help me when I have to take advanced biology in college. My brothers are always getting sick and knowing about homeostasis and virus[es] can help me find out why they're always getting sick. And I want to be a laboratory technician. They need to know about DNA and stuff.

In chemistry, a student focused on graphing:

> Graphing is [an] important part of life because when you're trying to compare different data the graph is the best way to go. For an

example, my grandmother and aunt work at a retirement home and they need to decide dosages per day, meals, and etc. Graphing out all the data they have will [help them] come out with a resolution. This applies to college where I want to go someday.

Hulleman and Harackiewicz found that drawing this social connection made class better for students, especially students who were less confident in their abilities. They found more interest in their science classes and got higher grades.

Next, Harackiewicz and her collaborators learned to integrate this approach in large introductory science classes in college—the kinds of classes where a student's dream to become a doctor, a scientist, or an engineer might flower or die. Again the utility-value exercise improved grades and persistence, in some cases with the greatest benefits for students of color and first-generation college students. It's a way to reduce inequalities on the pipeline from student to scientist.

She's also found that sharing tips with parents about talking with teens about the usefulness of math and science coursework— for example, maybe don't; just leave this glossy brochure out where your kid can see it—led students to take an extra semester of elective math and science in the last two years of high school and boosted their scores on the math and science section of a college prep exam (the ACT).

There's a crucial detail in all this work. It's not telling a learner that something matters. If you're a teacher and you're proud of the content you're about to impart, bragging about how important it is might be tempting. But that can backfire. In one study, Elizabeth Canning found that telling students how valuable a math task was actually undermined interest and performance for less confident students. It's as though the student hears, "This is super important! You have to learn this!" If you're not so confident, you might freak out. Instead, it's an offer. You can scaffold the student. Seed some ideas about why the content is important. Maybe share why it's important to you or, better yet, a few stories from prior students about the value they found in the material. But then let your students articulate the value they find in the topic for themselves. That's more helpful and more authentic. "Teach it, don't preach it," Canning called it.

Many of us deeply desire to make a difference for others. To get there, we might have to work through a long and winding path to gain the critical foundational skills. When that path gets steep, how can you remind yourself why that learning matters to you, the difference it can help you achieve? When it's a learner you're supporting, how can you ask them so they can find their own reasons?

Togetherness: Norms, Paper Towels, Healthy Eating, and Pajama Making

It's not just helping that motivates us. It's also doing together. In another supercute baby study, researchers played a cooperative game with babies, such as holding a toy trampoline together on which to bounce a wooden block. Then they paused their participation. Infants as young as fourteen months old spontaneously tried to reengage the adult in the game. You might think the babies just enjoyed the game and needed the adult to do their part. But it goes deeper than that. Together, Luke Butler, a professor at the University of Maryland, and I ran a study with slightly older kids. We led four-year-olds to simply believe they were working on a tough jigsaw puzzle with another child, or that they were taking turns on the puzzle. Just the *idea* that they were working together led preschoolers to persist 36 percent longer on the puzzle and to like it more.

Perhaps, then, our fifth-grade teacher could just say to the math-resistant child, "Everyone is doing it. We're doing it together."

This approach is not without promise. After all, volumes of research have shown that social norms can be one of the most powerful sources of motivation. If other people are doing something, you might want to do it too. But there's a peril here. To navigate this peril, we have to understand *how* norms motivate us—and how they might not.

Here's the worst version of "Everyone is doing it." It comes off as an order: "So you should too." And of course, that is exactly the problem. For many of us, the feeling that someone is trying to order you around is what elicits resistance.

It's a feeling I know well. Of all my many fails in middle school, my biggest regret is when a not-so-beloved teacher told me to take my hat off.

"Why?" I asked.

"Take off your hat."

"Why?"

"Take off your hat."

"Why?"

"Take off your hat or go to the principal's office."

I paused.

For years I've fantasized of just walking down the hall and going to the principal's office. I'd await my loathsome teacher there. The principal would call my parents. And then, with perfect composure, I'd say, "Don't I at least deserve a reason to follow your dictates?" That's my dream. There are variations on it. Sometimes I sit in the office for hours, refusing to return to class until I get an apology. But in reality, I took the damn hat off.

So, in *Noah's Swim-a-Thon*, Noah's mother takes a light touch. She never tells Noah what to do or how to think. It's the same when we talk about what "most people" are doing. For if we don't, it's easy for things to go sideways. In one study, Lauren Howe, Priyanka Carr, and I posted signs in bathrooms around campus. The signs conveyed that "65 percent of people at Stanford" were reducing their paper towel use and asked bathroom-goers to do the same. That invocation of a norm did no good at all: no reduction in paper towel use. When we dug deeper, we found that people said signs like that made them feel "annoyed," that they felt "pressured," and that someone was "trying to manipulate" them. Telling our Stanford community that "most people are doing it" and merely asking them to do the same provoked an unhelpful question, *Are people trying to order me around?*

But norms needn't come off as orders. Instead, they can be more like an invitation to join a community working toward a collective goal—a bit like the four-year-olds working together on a jigsaw puzzle. So, in other bathrooms (selected at random), we posted a different sign. It showed the same norm, but this sign was explicit in inviting people to work with others. "Let's do it together," it said. "Join in!" It showed people together, not apart. That cut paper towel use by 14 percent.

It was the same in other studies when we showed people posters with norms about donating to charitable causes or reducing personal climate emissions. Only "working together" posters, which invited people to "join in" and "work together," got people on board. When we asked people about these signs, they didn't feel pressured. They just felt welcomed to join a community working toward worthy goals. And that provided a satisfying and motivating answer to the question, *Is this really my goal?*

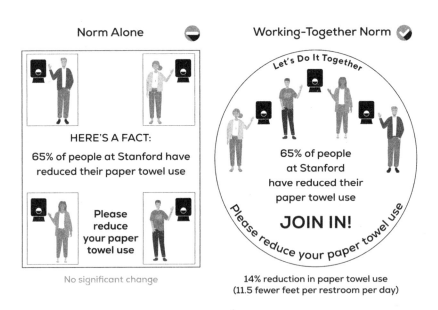

Norm Alone

HERE'S A FACT:

65% of people at Stanford have reduced their paper towel use

Please reduce your paper towel use

No significant change

Working-Together Norm

Let's Do It Together

65% of people at Stanford have reduced their paper towel use

JOIN IN!

Please reduce your paper towel use

14% reduction in paper towel use
(11.5 fewer feet per restroom per day)

The paper towel study was inspired, in part, by a famous earlier study. You might have heard of it. In that study, a team put up signs in hotel bathrooms conveying that most guests reused their towels at least once. That increased the rate at which new guests did too. Usually, this study is interpreted just as evidence that people follow norms. But rarely noticed is that the signs didn't just convey a norm. They also invited people to work together for a common cause. They said in big capital letters, "JOIN YOUR FELLOW GUESTS IN HELPING TO SAVE THE ENVIRONMENT. Almost 75% of guests . . . [use] their towels more than once." Our studies suggest this detail was critical.

Okay, let's get back to the really hard problem. Your fourteen-year-old won't eat anything but Flamin' Hot Nacho Cheese Doritos. What should you do? Leave a glossy brochure from the local farmers market on the kitchen table calling out the health benefits of fruits and vegetables? Perhaps that's not quite right.

You might feel like a nag telling your kid to eat better. Even leaving out a brochure might feel passive-aggressive. Adolescence is practically defined as a period in life when people are seeking out their own identity, independent of their parents. So teenagers are notorious for doing exactly the opposite of whatever their parents tell them to do—like rebelling by eating junk food.

But let's stop and think about that. Is there anything more conformist than junk food? This is an industry that spends *billions* annually pitching poor health to children, targeting especially vulnerable people like the less well-off.

There's a social motive a teen could get behind. What if you told teens the truth? Could their resistance to authority motivate healthy-eating?

Working in a large public middle school in exurban Texas, Chris Bryan, David Yeager, and Cintia Hinojosa flipped the script with their hilarious "exposé intervention." First, they gave eighth graders investigative journalism exposing the deceitful and manipulative marketing practices food companies use and how Big Food engineers its products to be as addictive as possible (maximum "crave-ability"). Here's some of what kids got.

THE EXPOSÉ INTERVENTION (EXCERPTS)

The companies that make the unhealthy food spend billions of dollars trying to get people to overeat. The reason is simple: the more people eat, the more money they make. If people only ate when they were actually hungry—or if corporations just let you choose what you and your body wanted to eat—they would make a lot less money. So, instead, they spend lots of money to come up with new ways to trick our brains into eating more than our bodies want, and more than our bodies can handle.

Why do the companies go after kids? Previous company executives have admitted that it's because they are easy targets. Children that young usually believe what adults tell them. Corporations put ads on Saturday morning cartoons for the most sugar-packed, addictive junk foods. They teach kids as young as 3 and 4—who don't know any better—that eating lots of junk foods is cool, fun, and normal.

Our brains are naturally designed to tell us to stop eating when we've had enough. But they have laboratories and hire scientists to figure out the brain's blind spots. Then they create foods that cause the brain to crave more and more sugar and fat, even when we're not hungry.

[Pictures of four food industry executives, all middle-aged White men in business attire]

[Name] is a former tobacco executive who oversaw Kraft. He calls himself "a bit of a fitness freak." So he avoids the sweet drinks and fatty snacks that his company sells.

Here we see how controlling food marketers are and the harm they cause. It's implied that thinking that junk food is cool is childish and that the pleasure of junk food results directly from the nefarious activities of these companies. And the people who run the companies are hypocritical douchebags. I don't know about you, but I'm not so far away from my adolescent self that this doesn't get me mad. It's a way to raise a critical consciousness.

The brilliance of this approach is that it simultaneously leverages adolescents' hatred of being told what to do (manipulative junk food companies!) and their prosocial goals (working together to help others). *So why am I eating healthy foods? To stick it to the man, to make my own choices, and to help others.*

Students learned that other kids were "shocked and angry" about manipulative food marketers. Then they were invited to describe how "students like them" can "fight back" (that is, saying is believing). In one version, kids had a chance to doctor junk food ads by using digital tools to "make it true," which they did, typically by inverting the ad's meaning. One student took a McDonald's ad, which proclaimed, "THE THING YOU WANT WHEN YOU ORDER SALAD" over a hamburger, and added, "SHOULD BE SALAD." A second scrawled "diabetes" over a Doritos ad, yielding "Doritos diabetes shots." A third wrote over an ad of a celebrity pitching soda with "I don't actually drink it" and "doing it for money," and replaced "obey your thirst" with "obey your body." The goal was to give young people practice immunizing themselves against ads. That way every time you saw an ad, you'd think of its manipulation and hypocrisy, not coolness and pleasure.

Compared with kids in a control group, who got standard information about food, weight, and health, the kids randomized to read the exposé materials chose healthier foods in the school cafeteria over the next three months, especially boys, who showed a 35 percent overall improvement in the health profile of their daily snack and drink purchases. A healthier diet over three months from a twenty- to forty-minute reading-and-writing activity!

So maybe leave some investigative journalism out for your teen to see: on evil food companies, the harm they cause, and how teens can resist, stick it to the man, and stand up for what's right by eating their veggies!

If you want to create change, it's almost always better to create an experience where people are working together for a common cause—not ordered around. It's a lesson the Harwood Manufacturing Corporation discovered back in 1939.

Harwood had a problem. The company had been in business for decades making pajamas and other garments. But a new plant in Marion, Virginia, was not thriving. Employees worked on a piece-rate system: the more they made, the greater their pay. The trouble was, whenever the product changed, it took forever for workers' productivity to recover. Turnover was high too.

Harwood was a family business run by Alfred J. Marrow, whose father and grandfather had founded the company back at the turn of the century. Marrow, as it happened, was good friends with Kurt Lewin. They'd met five years earlier when Marrow was completing his dissertation and considering a career in science. In fact, it was Lewin who convinced Marrow he could merge his academic interests with business. As Marrow would recall,

> I decided to follow Lewin's advice. I realized that with the power of chief executive, I could set up research programs that would provide insights into the management of people in organizations and thereby discover new ways to get people to attain their potential and work at their best.

That was Lewin's mission too. So two of Lewin's students, Lester Coch and John French, began to work with Marrow at the Marion plant. One of the first things they observed was that, ironically, it was the experienced employees who were the slowest to adapt to changes, slower even than new and presumably less skilled employees. In one case, when Coch and French tracked experienced employees, they found that their productivity didn't recover as long as thirty-two days after a product change had been introduced. Moreover, they observed "marked expressions of aggression against management" and "expressions of hostility against the supervisor, deliberate restriction of production, and lack of cooperation." People weren't just quiet quitting. Seventeen percent of workers actually quit within forty days.

Coch and French called it "resistance to change." And they had an idea why. At Harwood, as at many companies, when a change was in order, standard practice was to just call employees together and tell them what to do. Employees were being shut out of the process. Change was foisted upon them.

Instead, they suggested, why not bring employees together and have a conversation: talk through the change, discuss why it was needed, how the marketplace was changing, and how best to achieve the change. It needn't be so top-down. It could be a participatory form of management.

Marrow agreed to test it out. The results were striking. Coch and French found that when change was talked through in a discussion, employees' productivity recovered quickly. By day fourteen after the change, the average production rate exceeded the company quota. "The attitude was cooperative and permissive," they write. And no one quit in the first forty days. It led to headlines such as " 'Human Relations' Raises Sales 300%," on February 16, 1948, in *The New York Times,* with Marrow lauding "democracy in industry."

These were small studies, and 1948 is a long time ago. But I don't think people like to be ordered around any more today. In a 2022 study, Sherry Wu, a psychologist at the University of California, Los Angeles, found that twenty-minute weekly participatory work groups in a Chinese factory, in which supervisors listened as workers discussed their work and shared ideas and goals, increased productivity among 1,752 workers over a six-week period by 11 percent, and cut quitting twelve weeks later, from 33 percent to 15 percent. Workers also felt more satisfied and more in control on the job.

In modern-day tech companies too, when co-workers treat people in ways that invite their contributions, listening to their ideas, helping them build on them, this powerfully increases a sense of fit and commitment to the company, especially for women who risk being marginalized. Gregg Muragishi, who has led this research, calls this kind of treatment "microinclusions." If you want people to work as a team, it helps to treat them as part of the team.

There can be a profound disrespect in telling other people what to do, especially as children become adolescents and then adults and seek to make their own choices and pursue their own goals. In *Hairspray*, teenagers sing "Mama, I'm a Big Girl Now": "Stop, stop telling me what to do-o / Don't, don't treat me like a child of two-o." That doesn't mean we make choices alone, that there's no role for the people around you. We all need parents, teachers, mentors, peers, teammates, and managers. But just telling Johnny "Math is important" or "Everyone is doing it" or "Just do it" won't cut it. People need real reasons, not "because I said so." And at the end of the day, what they really need is to work through why something is important *to them*. Often that means how it can help them do well by others or work with others.

So far I've been assuming that when your parents urge you to eat your veggies, the veggies are actually good for you. Or when you sign up for an introductory science course, that course really will be useful for you, that, at least in theory, it could help you make a difference in other people's lives. But that critical consciousness about junk food marketing—sometimes we need that in school too. For it's not always the case that the people pushing you to learn are well intended, that what they're teaching is right for you, that you just need space to uncover the value that material has for you. That's not always true, not for everyone, not all the time.

Recently, teaching a group of new Stanford students, I asked about classes they'd taken in high school relevant to communities of color. In high school, I'd taken classes like Japanese Literature and Chinese Literature; even in American Literature, many of the authors we read were African American. So I was shocked when one student of color said she'd never read a non-White author in high school. Then a student from Sudan declared, "I can tell you all there is to know about the 1917 Russian Revolution. But I never learned anything about my own community." A Latina student volunteered that she'd read one book in high school "outside the canon." Which book was that? I asked. *Invisible Man,* she said. Surely, I thought, Ralph Ellison was in the canon. He's in my canon, at least.

Who is learning for? It's for the learner, I thought. When learning is, in fact, relevant to learners—to who they are, to who they're trying to be, and to what they want to do—people respond. In one study, when struggling racially and ethnically diverse students in San Francisco took an ethnic studies course in ninth grade, this increased the rate at which they stayed enrolled, attended class, and earned credits through high school. That single class boosted high school graduation rates by sixteen to nineteen percentage points.

In March 2019, I had the opportunity to tour Polaris Charter Academy, an amazing school in Chicago run by EL Education. It's in a tough neighborhood; even the day we visited, there was a lockdown when a man with a gun was seen outside the building. But the school was beyond impressive. One exhibit showcased a project eighth graders had done on redlining, the historic practice by which the U.S. government supported development in some (predominantly White) neighborhoods while denying this support to other neighborhoods. Students went to the very same address on the very same street, only one on the North Side of Chicago (predominantly White and wealthy, where development was supported) and the other on the South Side (predominantly Black and working class, not supported). They took a photo at each address and discussed what the contrast revealed: what redlining had done to communities of color.

Of course school will be more engaging for students when it helps them understand themselves and their families and communities better. When it's clear how school is for them, at least sometimes. This is called culturally relevant pedagogy.

There are times when the irrelevance of the curriculum is passive: just a default repetition of topics and assignments, even as a student body changes, say. But at other times it's intentional—a policy of erasure. Then the harms go well beyond boredom or disengagement. An infamous example are Indian boarding schools:

institutions, common around the turn of the twentieth century in the United States and Canada, designed expressly to erase Indian cultures, Indian identities, Indian heritage. It was not subtle. These schools went under the motto "Kill the Indian, Save the Man." In some cases, Indian families resisted assimilationist policies by withholding children, full stop, from schooling. In other cases, acts of resistance were symbolic, like wearing one's hair long.

There's no doubt we want to get stuff done—to achieve, to strike out Kyle Schwarber and win a World Series. But there's more than that. Learning isn't just about what you can do. It's also about discovering who you are, understanding the communities you belong to, your identity, your values, your people, your history. But it's not just bad schooling that threatens people's sense of self. It's whispers all around, insinuating, implying, suggesting who you might be and who you might not be, whispers that seek to define you, whispers that wreak confusion. Yet we'll see the power of speaking back, of telling your own story.

KNOW IT. OWN IT. USE IT.

Know your questions. Use your answers.

Here are some of the questions this chapter has covered.

Am I smart enough—or is my intelligence running out?
Is my willpower limited?
Is this really my goal?

Pick one of these questions. Then do either part 1 or part 2 or both with regard to this question.

Part 1: Think about yourself, your life and circumstance. *Then write down your answers to these questions.*

1. What's a tifbit (tiny fact, big theory) you've experienced relevant to this question—something small that happened that you had a disproportionate response to? How does that tifbit reveal how this question comes up for you, what exactly the question is for you?
2. Why is that question normal and reasonable for you, given your circumstance—but not necessarily true (or not the only way to think about it)?
3. How can you answer that question in a way that will be healthy and productive and authentic for you? What's a better answer, and how can you *offer* yourself that answer and try it out?*

Part 2: Think about someone else, someone you care about: a friend, a family member, someone you work with or for. Consider their life and circumstance. *Then write down your answers to these questions.*

1. What's a tifbit they've shown relevant to this question? How does that tifbit suggest how this question comes up for them, what exactly the question is for them?

2. Why is that question normal and reasonable for them, given their circumstance—but not necessarily true (or not the only way to think about it)?

3. Given your role and relationship, how can you help this person answer that question in a way that will be healthy and productive and authentic for them? What's a better answer, and how can you gracefully *offer* that answer to them so they can build it out for themselves?* *For instance, describe your own experience with a question like this, and how you are or have worked through this.*

---

* Remember the principles for thinking through "bad" events:

Principle 1: Avoid negative labels (*I'm not bad*)

Principle 2: You're not the only one; you're never the only one (*It's normal*)

Principle 3: Recognize causes that don't malign you or others (*I/you face real obstacles*)

Principle 4: Forecast improvement (*It can get better*)

Principle 5: Recognize opportunities (*Silver lining*)

DIGGING DEEPER
TAKE YOUR GROWTH-MINDSET JOURNEY

If you want to build your growth mindset.

Everyone is exposed in one way or another to a fixed mindset, the idea that you just have a certain amount of intelligence and there's not much you can do about that. That idea can hold us back.

But you can take a growth-mindset journey. At the end of that journey, you can fully recognize that intelligence grows with hard work, good strategies, and help from others. You'll know deep down inside that mistakes and struggle and feedback are how we learn. Then you can take charge. You can make progress on building the skills that help you become who you want to be and to do and achieve what you'd like.

I.   **WHAT ARE YOUR FIXED-MINDSET TRIGGERS?** These are the events that make you think, even a little, "I'm just not good at this," to feel discouraged or judged when you make a mistake, or to want to avoid material like that in the future. These are tifbits!

Describe a few of your fixed-mindset triggers. What are they? Why do they come up this way for you? What do they make you think or feel? What do they make you do?

2.   **WHAT CAN YOU DO TO HELP YOURSELF WHEN YOU HAVE FIXED-MINDSET THOUGHTS AND FEELINGS?** Here are some ideas. Which might be right for you?

Honoring the Challenge of Learning

- Reflect on how the brain changes when you learn: how it lights up when you make a mistake, how neurons rearrange and revise their connections when you work hard on challenges you can't do yet, how that change in the brain (a.k.a. learning) makes it easier next time you take on that material or skill. Imagine that change in your brain!

- Reflect on how other people too struggle at first when learning difficult new material or skills, even people who are accomplished now, even when their struggles aren't visible. Everyone has to learn to tie their shoes—and, say, to do complex math, to write well, to program, or to gain a second language. Remember that *learning* something new is always harder than *doing* what you already know.
- Talk to another person who can share their experience of growth and learning in the area that's hard for you. Ask them about the challenges they faced, their struggles and worries, and how they overcame these.
- Reflect on how much you have already learned, obstacles you have already overcome. Name the strengths you have developed, and describe how you can apply them to the next step.
- Give advice to a person younger than you. Tell them about the challenges you've faced, your struggles and worries, and how you have overcome these or are working to do so.
- Remember that those fixed-mindset thoughts and feelings are just thoughts and feelings. They aren't necessarily true. Imagine seeing them and then watching them float by. Then get back to what matters to you.
- Whenever you think, "I can't do it," add the word "yet."

What are good ways you can honor the challenge of learning? How and when can you do this well? Write down some ideas for yourself.

How to Learn

- Identify what strategies you could use to learn or get better, and think through which of these might be most useful for you.

- Talk with someone who knows and can help you think through different strategies.
- Talk to another person who can help you get unstuck.

When you're in a difficult learning situation, what are good ways you can explore different strategies to learn? Whom can you talk with to unlock strategies and get you unstuck? Write down some ideas for yourself.

Why You Learn

- Reflect on why you care about what you want to learn, why it's useful or meaningful to you, and what it can help you do.
- Reflect on the model you want to set for people younger than you, people you care about, who can look to you when they undertake their own growth-mindset journey. What image do you want them to have of you?

Learning can be hard, but it's also sacred. It's how we become. In the best cases, learning is joyful, thriving, a process of becoming who you really want to be. How can you keep the pleasure of learning close in your mind? How can you keep the model you would like to set for others present for yourself?

If you help lead a setting and want to help others in their growth-mindset journey.

1. **SHARE YOUR PROCESSES, WARTS AND ALL.** If you're more experienced than others, it's easy for other people to think that you always know what you're doing and always have. Then it's good to share your processes. Show people the hard work you put in to make a project succeed. Show them the different strategies you use, the blind alleys you walk down, and how you learn from these and come back out the other side. Show them your hard work and commitment. Don't just show them the finished product on the other end.

2. **SHARE YOUR PATH TO LEARN, TWISTS AND ALL.** It's easy for people to think that your path to success was a straight line. That learning was easy for you. Then it's important to share your struggles, mistakes, and setbacks— and how you have or are working through these. Write and share a "failure" résumé listing all the jobs you did not get, all the projects that failed, all the rejections you received. Encourage others to share their own. The first year I applied for academic jobs, my grad school classmates and I pinned all the rejection letters we received on a bulletin board in the lab. It was a big board. But by spring it was full!

3. **INSTITUTE PRACTICES TO KEEP THE CULTURE FOCUSED ON LEARNING.** Nvidia promotes the idea that "failure must be shared"; the whole point is to learn. *Never let a failure go wasted!* Have team meetings to talk through what happened when a project has failed. Carol Dweck and I

call our lab half-baked so the purpose of the lab is clear—to take ideas and projects at any stage and "bake" them into what they can become. How can you make the value of learning explicit for the people you work with and the settings you're in?

Chapter 5

Who Am I?

. . . here?
. . . now?
. . . in your eyes?
. . . really?

I walk away to remember who I am.

–VIENNA TENG, "GOODNIGHT NEW YORK"

There will be times when you walk into a room and no one there
is quite like you until the day you begin to share your stories.

–JACQUELINE WOODSON, *THE DAY YOU BEGIN*

One of my favorite picture books of all time is Lindsay Mattick's 2016 Caldecott winner *Finding Winnie*. It's the true
story of Mattick's great-grandfather Harry Colebourn, the soldier
who brought the bear who would become Winnie-the-Pooh to England during World War I. It's bedtime. Lindsay is snuggled with
her son Cole, his arms wrapped around a teddy bear. Cole asks for

a story. "What kind of story?" Lindsay asks. "You know. A true story. One about a bear."

So, Lindsay tells the story of Harry Colebourn. How he was a veterinarian in Winnipeg, how he took care of horses, and how he entered the service to help in a war "far, far away." How he bought Bear from a trapper on a train platform in White River, Ontario. How he took care of Bear, how he named her Winnie, how Winnie became "the Mascot of the Second Canadian Infantry Brigade," and how he brought Winnie to England. How, when he went to the front in France, he left Winnie in the London Zoo, where she would be safe. ("I'll always love you. You'll always be my Bear.") And Lindsay tells Cole the story of Christopher Robin, who came to the zoo with his father, Alan Alexander Milne. How Robin met Bear, how they became "true friends" and inspired the stories his father wrote, how Winnie became Winnie-the-Pooh, the most beloved bear in the world.

"But what about Harry?" Cole asked.

So, Lindsay tells Cole that after the war Harry visited Winnie and saw "she was truly loved. And that was all he had ever wanted." So he returns home to Winnipeg "and his life as an animal doctor. Before long, he was married and had a son named Fred."

Mattick then traces her lineage, with generations beautifully depicted by Sophie Blackall as branches on a tree, from Colebourn through herself to Cole.

"And then I had a son. When I saw you, I thought, 'There is something special about this Boy.' So I named you after your great-great-grandfather: Captain Harry Colebourn. I named you Cole."

"That's me?" said Cole in a whisper.

"That's you."

"And that's Winnie?"

"Yes," I said. "That's Winnie."

"And it's all true?"

"Sometimes the best stories are," I said.

Cole's eyes grew big, and he said nothing for a long time. Then he hugged his own bear close and let out a yawn that reached far away, and they both turned over and fell asleep.

I loved reading *Finding Winnie* to our children when they were little. For it's not just the meaning of a loose tooth that a parent helps a child with. It's who he or she is. Who their family is.

There are times when the stars align. When you return to an old familiar activity; to a place that means so much to you; to the people you are closest to: when you return to who you are. You're home.

It helps to hold that close. For as a child comes of age, a storm might blow in. A storm of stories and images, sometimes said aloud but often implied; whispers that seek to define you, to say who you are and broadcast that image to the world. You might get lost in that storm. So it's good to have a firm hold on yourself; to know yourself. So you can tell your own stories. So you can free yourself.

I used to think that identity was a hard-edged thing, fixed, rigid. I remember trying to write a personal statement in college applications. *Who am I?* I wondered. But that never got me anywhere. For identity is more like Play-Doh. It's squishy, shape-shifting, curves all over the place, more swirling "me" than rigid "I." It's better to ask, *Who am I here? Who am I now?* or *How do you see me?* Our selves are multiple and contested. Many voices clamber to speak for you, of you. You don't always have control.

In college I was boarding a Virgin Atlantic flight in San Francisco bound for London when the lead flight attendant came over the PA system and said in a lovely accent. "My Scottish grandmother told me to introduce myself whenever I spent the night with someone," he began, "and since we'll be spending the night together, let me tell you a bit about me."

In that spirit, let me tell you a bit about me.

In our family is a book, a memoir by my grandmother Vendla, my father's mother. She tells the story of her life: How her family moved cross-country from Minnesota to Arizona in 1922 in a Model T Ford, when she was thirteen, to homestead in the high desert in the eastern part of the state. How she taught in one-room schoolhouses in Sedona and elsewhere in Arizona in the early 1930s, met my grandfather, settled in Kansas, and fought together through the dust storms of the Great Depression. "Powdery dirt settled on everything including me," she wrote. "It stiffened and grayed my hair, gritted between my teeth, settled in my ears and nose." It's the story of how they hand built a cabin of adobe on land deeded her from the old family ranch in Arizona and how as teachers in Fresno, California, they returned to Arizona every summer with their four kids, my father among them, to restore the cabin after years of neglect, and to search for ancient Indian pottery, arrowheads, rattlesnakes, and other collectibles. It's a place I grew up going to, one Lisa and I have brought our kids to time and again, a place of family and connection. I suspect that you too have mementos and places in your family, treasures you might share with your children. In telling us where we come from, these things tell us who we are. They show us our strengths to face up to challenges, our kindness, and our values. They help to root us should a storm blow in.

PART 1: WHO TELLS YOUR STORY?

In *Finding Winnie*, Lindsay Mattick begins to tell Cole his story. Here I got to tell you a story of mine. But who gets to tell your story?

The other day, I was playing a silly game of make-believe with my friend's son Eli. Eli was about three, so I said, "Eli, you're silly."

"No, I'm not," he said. "I'm Eli!"

That's right. For who among us hasn't felt defined by others at one time or another, perverted, or put in a box? That's irksome to say the least.

So this is what we're attuned to: How are you seen? You hear your name across a crowded room. Nothing but your name. *What are they saying?* You have to know. In 1902, the sociologist Charles Cooley wrote, "The mere presence of people . . . an awareness of their observation, often causes a vague discomfort, doubt, and tension. One feels that there is a social image of himself lurking about, and not knowing what it is he is obscurely alarmed." A generation earlier Charles Darwin wrote, "It is not the simple act of reflecting on our own appearance, but the thinking what others think of us, which excites a blush."

In this chapter we're going to see many ways people get defined. Circumstances that provoke ugly questions, like *Am I seen as . . . a bad kid? . . . fat and ugly? . . . dumb? . . . a weak victim?* We'll see how these images can confuse us (*Am I really . . . ?*), how they can distract us, and how they can hurt us. But we'll also see how we can fight back and, with the right platforms that let us speak at just the right time, how we can win this fight and spiral up.

I've never felt more like an American than the time I've spent living outside America. In college, I studied abroad for a few months at Oxford University. I spent much of the time feeling gauche, a fish out of water, the Ugly American amid the sophisticated Brits. At my college, there was the chichi welcome event, with a platter of enormous prawns and an incredible white wine; and the peculiar tradition of High Table, where students stood in respect at long tables in the ancient dining hall as our tutors (the professors) processed up to a table several steps above ours and a Latin prayer was read before dinner. There was the posh woman I sat next to on the flight over returning from a ski trip to Colorado who gave me a list of all the fabulous places I just had to eat at in London, exactly one of which I could afford once, maybe.

The experience reached its zenith when I met the queen. It was entirely by happenstance. I was walking home from tutorial one Sunday morning. These are the kinds of weekly one-on-one classes that Oxford and Cambridge are famous for. As I passed through the central part of campus, by the Bodleian Library, established in 1602, toward the even older Church of St. Mary the Virgin, the streets were quiet. Approaching the church, however, I saw a row of barricades and a small crowd. I joined a group and asked what was going on.

"Her Majesty is receiving the service in the church there," an older woman said with obvious delight. "And she'll be coming this way."

Well, I thought! I could spare ten minutes for the queen. So, I joined the group, which turned out to comprise an older Canadian couple and a middle-aged American woman. The Canadian couple was giddy. "You know she's our queen too!" they said.

Soon enough Her Majesty appeared, walking along the way, greeting her subjects. Wearing a perfect bright yellow hat with a matching yellow jacket and handbag, she was gracious and immaculate. When she got to our little group, she asked the Canadian couple, "And where might you be from?"

"We're from Canada, Your Majesty. We are so pleased to meet you."

"Splendid," said the queen.

And then the American woman piped in. "And I'm from America," she said, in a high nasal tone.

"Oh!" said the queen. And she put her nose in the air and walked away.

Ahhh. It was mortifying . . . I felt like the Ugly American.

As we walk about the world, sometimes it feels as if we face mirrors at every turn. Only they're not regular mirrors. They don't show us as we really are, as we want to be, as we hope to become. They're fun-house mirrors. This one makes you look fat and squat. That one long and gangly, an awkward monster, all limbs and joints flopping about. None is the real you. No one would believe them. Or would they?

As the nineteenth century turned to the twentieth, the sociologist W.E.B. Du Bois captured the pervasiveness and particular quality of this experience among African Americans, writing in *The Atlantic,* "It is a peculiar sensation, this double-consciousness, this sense of always looking at one's self through the eyes of others, of measuring one's soul by the tape of a world that looks on in amused contempt and pity."

These images hurt. And they get in the way. One study, inspired by Claude Steele's research on stereotype threat, sought to mitigate that sense of viewing yourself from the outside, from a malignant point of view, in a particularly important context, high school students taking an Advanced Placement test for calculus. In typical conditions, students were asked to report their race, ethnicity, and gender right before the test. In this case, just 32 percent of Black girls passed the test, receiving a score of 3 or higher. But for a second group, the test designers put those questions *after* the test. The intention was to take the spotlight off identity as students began the test: to remove one reason a Black girl could worry, *Might people think a person like me doing calculus is a joke?* The rate at which Black girls passed the test bumped up to 38 percent. That's an organization beginning to take responsibility for the implicit questions it provokes. And it's more students earning college credit.

One of the troubles with questions like *Am I seen as a joke?* is no one says them out loud. If they did, it'd be better in some ways. At least it'd give you something to reject. It's the insidiousness, the ambiguity, that lets questions creep into the mind and hang in the air. Then they might even seem like your idea. They might seem true. *Maybe I am a joke?*

That's why surfacing helps. It's gaining that critical consciousness: getting clear on how you might be seen—on the narrative "out there"—so you can reject it with others.

What Story Is Told? (and Is It True?)

All of us have countless identities: age, gender, national origin, religious affiliation, race, ethnicity, sexual orientation; affiliations with schools or companies, with regions or neighborhoods; and our personal backgrounds. There are stories in our cultures about all these identities. Some might put you at risk, make you look bad, or deny you the help or support you need. Here are two cases where the story out there is almost palpable.

Am I (Seen as) a Bad Kid?

In the spring of 2023, a grad student working with me, Rhana Hashemi, was interviewing young people in Oakland about their experiences getting caught with drugs in school. Hashemi had worked through her own issues in high school to become a leading drug educator, committed to reducing harms and helping kids in their relationship with school. On this particular morning, she was interviewing a student, Grayson (a pseudonym). She asked Grayson to write down his experience coming back to school after having been caught selling marijuana:

> After I got caught it felt like that was it. I remember that the only thought in my head was that I would always and forever be a drug dealing, drug addicted high school dropout. And honestly, the hardest part was that I always had this strong sense that this path, of dealing and smoking all the time, would never lead me to where I wanted to be (even though I had no idea where I was sup-posed to be ☺) and even more so, it was actively hurting myself, my future, and the people that I loved and cared about. But even though I wanted to do right; I still felt like a bad kid. And feeling like I didn't belong in the one place [school] that could help me just pushed me further and further away from the help that I really needed.

A bad kid? Another student, Jordan (also a pseudonym), an eighteen-year-old high school senior, described how that narrative seeps into the mind and the downward spiral it starts.

> There's what I call a false narrative that they put on people where it's like you're given this whole idea that all these drugs are bad to these kids that are young, and they believe what you have to say because you're an adult. What an adult says is what we have to believe, right? So we hearing it from an adult that "oh this is bad for us and this and that we're bad kids when we're doing it" can really impact how that kid's gonna think, they're gonna believe ok well if they're telling me all this stuff about me because I got caught then crap, I'm gonna be beating up on myself. Then I'm a bad kid, this and that, can really self-harm a kid, give him depres-sion, lead him down different holes, lead them to other drugs. And then they'll feel like they're just disappointments. I've heard certain stories of people getting caught and it ruined their whole image on themselves.

A bad kid? What if Grayson or Jordan was a child you love? What if they were you? Whatever their costs, drugs shouldn't make a kid "a bad kid."

Charles Cooley, one of the sociologists I mentioned earlier, coined a famous metaphor: the "looking-glass self." It's the idea that you're looking in a mirror and see in the reflection whom society sees. But there's not just one mirror. It's more like you're in a bathroom with mirrors all around. They reflect you and each other in an endless stream, an infinity of images. Many agents are creating these images, both you and your friends and the people who love you but also other people, some careless, some ill-intended, some even vicious. It's easy to get confused, lost inside that kaleidoscope. It's hardest yet when you're a young person just developing your sense of self.

Sometimes, we have to walk away to remember. And it helps if you have compadres you can walk with, people who care about you and who believe in you, who can help as you build and rebuild your sense of self, as "me" becomes "I," as you seek to become the person you want to be. "It really wasn't until I met my counselor, that I felt a shift," Grayson says. "She was so genuine in her care for me that I couldn't help but give in, and eventually, with her support, I started going to school again and cutting back on my drug use. Having someone that I knew believed in me and wanted me to do well, made all the difference."

Like Chanel Miller, Grayson and Jordan are cutting through the haze, with the help of skilled counselors, partners who can help them see the operating narrative, the question on the table. And then they can say, "That's false. Here is what is true." Theirs is hard-earned wisdom. It's surfacing. And it's the first step.

Am I (Seen as) Fat and Ugly?

Streams of images heralding thin women flow through old-fashioned media and Instagram alike into the minds of girls and women. It's easy to see how that might prompt questions like *Am I fat and ugly?* or *Do I have to lose weight for people to like me?* A prominent theory in psychology, self-objectification theory, says that images like these create shame, even when a person has a normal human body. They suck up mental resources and reduce attention to internal experiences, because you're seeing yourself from the outside, a spectator on yourself. In a classic study, the psychologist Barbara Fredrickson found that just asking women to wear a swimsuit rather than a sweater increased feelings of shame, triggered a motivation to restrict eating, and hurt women's performance on a math test.

When we're exposed to alter images that prompt crappy questions (*Am I fat and ugly?*), it helps to gain that critical consciousness. What are these images? Where do they come from? What's really true? In one example, Erin Strahan at Wilfrid Laurier University in Ontario, Canada, developed a program to critique thin body ideals for adolescents. In two eighty-minute sessions with twelve- and thirteen-year-olds, she called out the source of these ideals in popular media (Who's getting rich off this?), showed how absurd they are (Here's how ridiculous Barbie would look if she were a full-size woman. . . . She'd topple over!), and gave kids a way to challenge them, by creating posters rejecting thin body ideals. A week later tween girls based their self-worth less on their appearance, felt more satisfied with their bodies, and worried less how others saw them. In the control condition, girls' relationship to their bodies was less healthy than boys'. But with Strahan's program, on most measures it was just as healthy.

Fighting Back

It helps enormously to get clear on the questions you face for yourself. But sometimes that's not enough. For these images aren't broadcast just to you. They're to the whole world. What, then, do people do when they find that they, or their whole group, is marked, conspicuous, spotlighted as weak or lacking?

We fight back. We fight for the image of ourselves and our group. Chanel Miller proclaims, "Know my name." After the fatwa was issued against him, Salman Rushdie describes "a 'me' floating around that had been invented to show what a bad person I was. 'Evil.' 'Arrogant.' 'Terrible writer.' . . . I've had to fight back against that false self." People who identify as transgender demand to use the bathrooms of their choosing and to be referred to using the pronouns of their choice. Those on the autism spectrum advocate for "neurodiversity." Women build community for "girls who code." In the eighteenth century, early abolitionists distributed posters depicting a man in chains ribboned with the phrase "Am I not a man and a brother?" Later civil rights leaders would declare, "Black is beautiful." Today we say, "Black Lives Matter."

These movements are birthed in pain: Drug addict. Slut. Fat. Dumb. Social movements give us compadres with whom to fight back. As the Black Lives Matter founder Patrisse Cullors says, "Black Lives Matter reminds people that black people are human, but more importantly, it reminds black people that we are human."

When these movements succeed, it can feel like a psychological earthquake. I well remember the homophobia of America in the 1980s and 1990s, my childhood: the dirtiness of the image of gay bathhouses, the "closet," the willful ignorance of the AIDS pandemic, and most of all the overriding shame imputed to non-straight people. One 1997 study found that gay men who were out of the closet yet sensitive to social rejection showed a faster progression of HIV to AIDS. That's spiraling down. Homophobia certainly hasn't disappeared. But marriage equality and raucous gay pride parades in middle-American cities—this was unimaginable to me at least then. That matters. Say you're fourteen years old and just coming to terms with the fact that you're gay. Your city hosts a gay pride parade. *Who am I?* This could be me! *Who are we?* This could be us! Your sexuality might become a source of pride and community, not shame and isolation.

In psychology, researchers set up specific situations to probe the tender spots of our identities. Then we can see how people battle back. It's a way to listen for the questions that people face. In one study, the social psychologist Emily Pronin at Princeton University gave female college students in math an article claiming that men were better at math than women. Women responded by disavowing those qualities of being female that seemed incompatible with math. No, I do not gossip. No, I do not flirt. No, I do not wear makeup. No, I do not want children. *I'm not that kind of girl.*

In another study, the psychologist Sapna Cheryan approached Asian Americans, so-called perpetual foreigners in American society, on a college campus. She asked a single question, "Do you speak English?" Then she asked what American television shows they remembered from the 1980s. People spent more than twice as long listing shows than when they hadn't been asked about English (*The Cosby Show, The Brady Bunch, The Wonder Years, The Golden Girls, Saved by the Bell . . .*). *I'm an American.*

In April 2008, *Vogue* created a controversy with an infamous cover likening LeBron James to King Kong. How might African Americans respond to an image like that? To find out, my colleagues Lauren Howe and Karina Schumann and I created an ad that juxtaposed an image of an African American security guard with a gorilla. African Americans responded by asserting that they experienced more distinctly human emotions (for example, nostalgia, romance, regret) and less emotions associated with other animals (fear, anger) and that they had more complex selves. *I'm a full human being,* they said.

These are tidbits. The responses reveal the questions beneath the surface: *Am I seen as . . . serious at math? . . . an American? . . . fully human?*

This fight is healthy, it's eminently reasonable, and it can help. But no one should have to compromise a desire to have a family to be taken seriously in math. And this fight itself can be costly. For often the images we see as we walk about the world are cloudy, ambiguous, contradictory, in flux. People don't generally walk around with billboards on their heads broadcasting their truest, ugliest thoughts ("You're just a girl. You're dumb at math"). What we see are shadows, impressions, and, sometimes, mirages. And if we're fighting with shadows, it's hard to know what actually matters and what doesn't. It's the ambiguity that sucks up mind space. As Cooley wrote, it's the "not knowing" that disturbs.

How can we take back control?

PART 2: THE DAY YOU BEGIN

I can admit it freely. I have a mad crush on Jacqueline Woodson. I get it. It'd never work out. But I especially adore Woodson's picture book *The Day You Begin*. It's one of my favorite books of all time. It's so damn wise; it has taught me so much. I've read it to my kids, of course (they are so annoyed with me), to my daughter's third-grade class (over Zoom during the COVID lockdown, when it literally brought her teacher to tears as she recalled her own experience as an immigrant), and to my own students. Actually, whenever I can, I don't read it myself. Instead, I show a video of Woodson reading it. No one could do it better.

The Day You Begin brings us into the world of elementary school. It's a world where every child feels different, deficient:

> There will be times when you walk into a room and no one there is quite like you. Maybe it will be your skin, your clothes, or the curl of your hair. . . . There will be times when the words don't come. Your own voice, once huge, now smaller when the teacher asks *What did you do last summer? Tell the class your story. We went to France*, Chayla says. *These shells come from a beach in Maine . . .* [But] you can only remember how the heat waved as it lifted off the curb, and your days spent at home caring for your little sister.

Yet Woodson shows us the strength we have within and how to bring that strength forth:

> There will be times when the climbing bars are too high, the run is too fast and far, the game isn't one that you can ever really play. *I don't want him on our team. You can watch. Maybe you can have a turn later.* There will be times when the whole world feels like a place that you're standing all the way outside of. And all that stands beside you is your own brave self—steady as steel and ready even though you don't yet know what you're ready for. There

will be times when you walk into a room and no one there is quite like you until the day you begin to share your stories.

My name is Angelina and I spent my whole summer with my little sister, you tell the class, your voice stronger than it was a minute ago, *reading books and telling stories and even though we were right on our block it was like we got to go everywhere. Your name is like my sister's,* Rigoberto says. *Her name is Angelina, too.* And all at once, in the room where no one else is quite like you, the world opens itself up a little wider to make some space for you. This is the day you begin.

Angelina speaks, and as she does, she gains a platform. Others listen, and they affirm her.

Often, when we lack power, we can't speak. And the people who have power, the people who matter for our outcomes, they can't hear. Then we get defined. So, one of the most important things we can do when people are in challenging circumstances is to create space: space that anticipates the goodness, values, and strengths of a person or a group of people; space that invites those people to tell their stories of this goodness and strength and how they apply them to the challenges they face; space that allows all of us to hear and affirm the stories they share, who they are, and who they seek to be. This voice lets us invert identities. It's an alchemy to turn the weak to strong, the bad to good.

Let's see some examples. As you think about these cases, I hope you will think about how you can create this space when others need it, when their identity is in the cross fire. And when it is you who is at risk, how can you take this space to tell your stories, to spiral up?

One of the researchers we'll meet next is Christina Bauer, a social psychologist at the University of Vienna, and a good friend. But when Bauer was a kid growing up in the 1990s in a tiny village in

Bavaria, there wasn't even a bus stop to the local *Gymnasium,* the academically oriented high school. No one in her village had ever gone there before. Bauer's father was a mechanic at a local car parts factory, her mother a homemaker and part-time cleaner of commercial buildings. When she was seven, Bauer remembers the entire village, all working-class people, coming together to help her parents build a new house, a beautiful home, so they could move out of her grandmother's place.

When she was a child, Bauer's father never let her think that she was any less than people with more money or privilege. He told her of his bosses at work, "You have to remember—these people are no different from us. They don't shit different dirt than we do" ("*Die scheißen auch keinen anderen Dreck als wir,*" a local saying). And she remembers the pride he took in his work and expertise. Once a wealthy insurance person came to their house because a neighbor's horse had escaped into their garden causing damage. The insurance person blew her father off and said he should just throw some soil in the holes caused by the horse and everything would be fine. Bauer's father, who is usually very kind and calm, threw him out of the house, shouting, "Obviously, you'd think that, because you've never had a shovel in your hand."

When Bauer turned ten, she had to decide what course to pursue in the rigidly tracked German educational system. She could attend the local *Hauptschule,* as her father had, a vocational track, or the mid-level *Realschule* like her mother. These were the tracks her friends would pursue, including her best friend Sabrina (a pseudonym). But only the *Gymnasium* would open doors to a university education. Her grades were high enough. Her mother left the choice to her. For months Bauer wanted to stay with her friends. But a week before the deadline, she came home from school and announced, "Mom, I thought about it, and I think I want to go to *Gymnasium.*" Perhaps it was the first-grade teacher who always said she should go to *Gymnasium.* Perhaps it was her grandfather, whose biggest wish was that a family member would attend *Gymnasium.* Or perhaps it was the strength her father imparted to her. Her mother said, "Yes, I think it's better." And so, her parents wrangled the bureaucracy to get a new bus stop.

"I remember Sabrina," Bauer told me, looking back. "We did everything together. But we had such different lives from then on. She has had a lot of really difficult life circumstances, including an addiction to drugs."

But for Bauer, the bus set in motion a new spiral. After a successful experience in the local *Gymnasium,* Bauer entered university still holding her thick Bavarian accent. In the first week, a classmate sitting at her table said, "I don't know why people speak with a Bavarian dialect. It just sounds so stupid." But Bauer remembered her father's strength, and knew her own.

Refugees Tell Their Story: "I'm not a weak victim. I'm strong and agentic."

In 2022, the English-Swedish photographer Anastasia Taylor-Lind took a portrait of a Ukrainian mother and daughter for *National Geographic.* The pair had hidden from Russian attacks in a Kyiv bomb shelter for six days, so terrified they couldn't sleep. When Taylor-Lind took the photo, she says, "The mother looked at me and joked, 'Do you want me to look like a refugee now?'"

What might that look like? And how might that feel?

Viet Thanh Nguyen knows. Author of the fabulous novels *The Sympathizer* and *The Committed,* Nguyen came to the United States from Vietnam as a refugee at the age of four. In *The Committed,* he writes, "Boat people were victims, objects of pity fixed forever in newspaper photographs. . . . If the price of being human was to be recognized through being pitiful, then to hell with humanity!"

Weak victims. This is so often the story we tell of refugees and of people in poverty. A newspaper article reads, "Many refugees are so traumatized . . . that they lack capacity to apply . . . [for] asylum." A charity solicits, "Millions of families around the world are struggling to overcome hunger, poverty, and injustice." *Those poor people.* But no one wants to be pitied.

Bauer and I began working together in 2015 just as an earlier movement of refugees to western Europe from countries like Syria, Kosovo, and Afghanistan was peaking. The next year, Bauer saw the weak victim narrative in action while working as an intern at the Roland Berger Foundation in Munich. It was expressed not in coldness or in hostility but in warmth—warmth of a debilitating sort. Bauer remembers a boy named Arafat, about seventeen years old. Like many boys, Arafat liked to play video games late into the night. Predictably, in the morning he preferred sleeping in to going to school. One morning Arafat came into the communal kitchen, late as usual. Yet the social worker whose job it was to make sure he got to school on time just gave him a hug and said, more to Bauer than to Arafat, "He's so poor. He really needs the extra sleep because of all he's been through." Bauer told me,

> That stuck in my head. It contrasted with the way I perceived the boys. That was never the narrative Arafat told, that he couldn't get up in the morning because he was a refugee. It was because he played video games too late. I have no doubt that [the social worker] really wanted the best for the boys and for Arafat in particular. But I felt like she wasn't doing him a favor with that. He really needed to learn the language, to catch up. He wasn't doing super well in school. I can only imagine what the teachers thought in this more conservative area, about this boy coming late to school every day.

Need it be so? For there is a counternarrative.

My favorite movie is *Casablanca,* and while there are many things I love about it, I adore the agency and the strength of the characters. There's Rick (Humphrey Bogart), who runs the café and sticks his neck out "for nobody" until he does. There's Ilsa (Ingrid Bergman), who tells Rick, "I don't know what's right any longer. You'll have to think for both of us, for all of us." But is that her way of helping Rick do the right thing? Then there's Victor Laszlo (Paul Henreid), the resistance fighter who escapes the Nazis (again). All of the characters are tough. They're refugees, displaced and impoverished, but fighting the Nazis and triumphing. Perhaps one reason

Casablanca works so well is that many of the actors and extras were, in fact, European exiles and refugees. The actor Dan Seymour reported that between takes of the scene in which the refugees drown out the Nazis by singing "La Marseillaise," many of the actors were crying. "I suddenly realized that they were all real refugees," Seymour said. This was their story, and they told it to the world.

In this story, refugees are strong and tough.* Actually, they might be the strongest, toughest people in the world. (Have you hidden from Russian attacks in a Kyiv bomb shelter for six days?) What if you invited modern-day refugees to tell their stories?

As Bauer was working toward her dissertation at the Freie Universität of Berlin, she began a partnership with Kiron Open Higher Education, a non-profit organization based in Berlin devoted to offering refugees educational opportunities. In preparation, she began to interview students with refugee backgrounds about their experiences. While refugees certainly described challenges, when Bauer asked, they also described strengths they had developed as refugees. Yet these strengths often went unrecognized. For some refugees, this erasure was so upsetting that even when it occurred outside school, it demotivated their pursuits of education ("to hell with humanity!").

Working with refugees, Bauer and I began to retell these stories of strength and how refugees applied them in school. There's nothing remarkable about the stories we told. Here's one:

> [My experience as a refugee] was difficult, but I have learned to stand on my own feet. . . . This ability to do things on my own has also helped me a lot at University. For example, when I don't understand something, I don't just wait for somebody to help me. Instead, I go online and try to figure it out myself or I contact the discussion forum.

Bauer invited a new group of refugee students to read these stories and then to tell their own stories in turn for future students. What

---

* And ingenious, like Kurt Lewin!

advice would they give? How could future students use what they had "learned as a refugee to succeed" in school? That's a way to offer students space to build for themselves a better answer to the question they faced: *Who am I? I am strong and capable. . . .* Students seized the opportunity. One refugee from Syria said,

> On the way to Europe a lot of things happened unexpectedly. So, I had to learn to adapt to the situation, embrace changes, and always roll with the punches. . . . This was an eye-opener and a beginning for a personal . . . revolution that [led] to liberation and personal growth.

Another was almost poetic:

> When I arrived in Europe, I was like a Middle Eastern seed placed in a European environment. A weak seed with only hope in life, it has many challenges ahead. I started to learn the language by myself . . . and I began to look for work.

Could this storytelling help as students began schooling in Europe? To find out, Bauer began by recruiting refugees through social media and asking them to imagine beginning a program of study. Then she shared either the stories of strength or neutral materials focused on study skills. Refugees who got the stories of strength and told their own story in turn expressed more confidence that they could succeed in the program. And they were more willing to take on challenges that could help them learn.

So far so good. Could this trigger an upward spiral? Could it help refugees do the hard work necessary to gain the skills to succeed in, and contribute to, a new society? Bauer embedded the exercise as a ten-minute addition to Kiron's standard onboarding process with refugees starting coursework. That way students could feel it in their bones: *Kiron sees me as strong and capable. I am strong and capable.*

Months later, when Bauer looked at Kiron's records, she found that students who'd gotten the strength stories, rather than the randomized control materials, had engaged 23 percent more in Kiron's learning environment over the next year, as assessed by total log-ins. And over seven months they had successfully completed 39 per-cent more courses.* A question about identity had been on the table: *Am I (seen as) a weak victim?* Left hanging, that question dragged refugee students down. Ten minutes addressing it helped them make progress. That's magic. And it's ordinary.

It's easy to mistake disadvantage for disadvantaged; adversity for weakness. We see a refugee, imagine all the challenges they have faced, and assume they are weak and need our help. There might be truth to that. But if that's all we see, we miss the strengths that people also develop. As Bauer says, "In general, I feel like once you get to know the individual behind the label, you see their strength and agency."

People with Disabilities Tell Their Story: "I'm not dis-abled. I'm skilled."

Here's another example. Aren't disabled people just *dis*-abled? It's sure easy to think so. In a 2015 study, the social psychologist Arielle Silverman gave sighted people experience in a blindness simulator. Volunteers had to navigate a room with a blindfold on, pour a glass of water, and write their identification number on a chalkboard, among other tasks. You might think a few minutes playing blind would increase empathy for blind people. Perhaps it did. But it also led people to judge blind people as less capable of independent work and living. Silverman, who is herself blind and confidently strides across college campuses with her trusty cane, concluded that the simulation gave sighted people "the initial . . . failure experi-ences of *becoming* disabled, rather than the competencies and adap-tations of *being* disabled." Who's really blind?

In this study, Silverman is starting a conversation. She's helping sighted people get perspective, inviting them into her world, to begin to see the skills a person develops when they live with blind-ness.

---

* Because of a data glitch, the course completion results were available only for seven months, not the full year.

When I was a kid, I was a big fan of the University of Michigan pitcher Jim Abbott. Born without a right hand, Abbott nonetheless dominated the college game, won an Olympic gold medal, reached the majors, and even threw a no-hitter with the Yankees in 1993. At Michigan, I once saw him pick a guy dancing off third base with a bluff, a false bobble of the ball. In his memoir, *Imperfect: An Improbable Life,* Abbott describes some of the work he did as a child to learn to navigate the world without a right hand, beginning by ridding himself of an onerous hook:

> The best it [the hook] did for me was to grant the motivation to be rid of it, which meant working the right arm I had until it became more reliable. My true arm was thin and slightly short and lacked the mobility of my left arm, but it had some life in it. Not having fingers was problematic, but my wrist worked okay. With my right arm, I could push things around, wedge things between my forearm and body, trap things, hold things steady, carry things with some nimbleness, and that all seemed to be a reasonable place to start. I was forever staining the right side of my shirts, where I cradled oranges in order to peel them and bike parts to fix them and baseballs in order to pitch them. I dropped a lot of stuff. I was frustrated when the easiest tasks required two hands, and so were nearly impossible for me. But it was better than the alternative, better than being Captain Hook. I'd left that behind; where, I didn't know and didn't care.

This is the work, the strength building, we don't usually see. It's a skill that served Abbott well in high school when an opposing coach had the first eight batters bunt against him. After the first batter reached base, Abbott threw out the next seven in a row.

If you ask people with various kinds of disabilities, they'll tell you all about how their disability has helped them, what it has taught them, the strengths it gives them. Deaf people might brag how sign language can be invaluable in loud environments like outer space—and, therefore, why deaf people would make for better astronauts. Stutterers might share how stuttering has helped them listen better and given them more empathy for others. Yet so rarely do we ask and elicit these stories of strength and instead persist in stale old narratives of disadvantage. How much is that the real disadvantage?

What would it mean if, instead, people contending with disabilities had platforms to share their strengths, so all of us could hear? What could contributing your voice and sharing your learnings do for a young person learning to live with a disability? And what could hearing these stories do for those of us without disabilities?

People with Mental Illness Tell Their Story: "Depression is compatible with making progress on things that matter to me."

Just as we miss opportunities to celebrate the strength building that happens with physical disabilities, so too we often trade in limiting narratives about mental "weakness." Depression affects nearly one in three Americans at some point in their lives, not just Julia, my dinner buddy at Café Einstein Stammhaus. It's not only about sadness. It's also a lack of energy. Sometimes depression can be so debilitating that people struggle to get out of bed. So, perhaps, it's not surprising that in one control condition Bauer found that 71 percent of people who had experienced depression thought the strengths necessary to pursue their goals did not describe people with depression well. Is that simplistic narrative another trap?

So, Bauer and I asked a psychotherapist and people who had experienced depression about strengths people develop through depression. We then reworked their stories to share back with other people. Here's one:

> [My depression] has been extremely difficult. . . . At the same time, [it] has also taught me some important things. . . . I've learned to better deal with negative thoughts and feelings. When my wife died, I thought this was the end of the world—I just didn't want to live without her. . . . But I realized that life does go on and I should make the most of it. . . . Dealing with depression is a long journey, and surely not an easy one; but . . . it's been making me stronger and better able to deal with other challenges.

We then told several hundred people who had experienced depression that we knew that "going through a depression is often very hard." But we shared these stories and asked them what they had learned through their experience of depression, and how these skills could help them pursue goals in their life. It was a way to see strengths without denying challenges.

Again, people seized the opportunity. One person wrote, "I know that when things seem impossible they can get better. The lowest point I've reached can be moved on from. So I know that no matter what I can get out of it."

Then people spiraled up. When we asked people about goals they were working toward, they mentioned things like "succeed in my job interview," "cut down on alcohol," "exercise 3 times a week," and "use less social media." Bauer found that the opportunity to engage with the strength stories made people more confident they could achieve their goals, as compared with people who just got standard information about depression. And two weeks later, when we asked how much progress they'd made toward their goals, people in the strength condition said they'd gotten further (64 percent complete versus 43 percent).

Why did that work? With the strength stories, people saw the qualities required to achieve their goals as better describing people with depression. *Is depression incompatible with making progress on things that matter to me? Absolutely not.*

First-Generation and Low-Income College Students Tell Their Story: "My social class background is a source of strength, not just weakness."

Poverty is many things. It's a lack of money, sure. It might also be having less time and attention, or less social capital, less access to networks that could help a person advance. It might be not having a bus to the local *Gymnasium*. But part of poverty is also that alter image of weakness. It's the classic "disadvantage," an image well buttressed in our society, including by slicked-up outfits like *The New York Times*'s campaign for "the neediest cases," rebranded only in November 2023. To say that's a-psychological doesn't do it justice. For years it's made me gag.

If you talk with people, they'll tell you all about the strengths they built from working-class experiences or experiences in poverty. That was Christina Bauer's story. Would eliciting these strengths help students succeed in college? Building on earlier laboratory studies, Bauer developed stories of the strengths working-class students can bring to college:

> I'm where I am because of my hard work, not because of my parents' money or anything like that. My family and I had it more difficult than many others, but I've still been doing reasonably well at school and university, which even exceeds my grandpa's dream that someone in our family would finally go to college.

In one study, when Bauer asked students how their social-class background affected their experience in college, first-generation college students talked almost exclusively about challenges. Only 19 percent mentioned even a single strength. But when students got the chance to read and reflect on these stories of strengths, 42 percent described strengths like developing a motivation to work hard or being able to deal with challenges. Then students put those strengths to work. When Bauer shared these stories in an introductory biology course, that ten-minute experience raised grades among first-generation and low-income students over the semester, compared with a randomized controlled group.

It's a result that echoes an earlier finding from Nicole Stephens at Northwestern University. Stephens developed a one-hour panel discussion to surface the differences in students' experience in college along class lines. One panelist, a first-generation college student, said, "I've been through a lot in my life. . . . It gave me perspective that made [school name] a lot easier to tackle. Midterms and papers seem hard, and they are, but at the same time they just seem like another drop in the bucket, and I love that perspective." Difference need not be weakness. Compared with attendees at a panel that offered standard advice, first-generation students who (at random) attended the panel that surfaced social-class differences and made them okay earned higher grades over the first year of college. That cut the social-class gap in GPA by 63 percent. Ordinary magic.

PART 3: MORE TRAPS IN SEEING

When circumstances pose a person as weak, it can make a world of difference to see their strengths. But there are other traps we must avoid too.

Not Seeing At All: "Am I even seen?"

A friend of mine once told me of a time he volunteered at a soup kitchen in the Tenderloin, a poor neighborhood in San Francisco. One week he served a client with a distinctive hat. So the next week he noticed when the same man returned with the same hat.

"Hey, how you doing?" he said. "I remember you from last week."

The client, a grown man, broke into tears. "You're the first person to see me in a week."

There's a reason the silent treatment is so painful. From birth, we're utterly dependent on others, the canonical social animal. But it's not just nutrition a baby (or an adult) needs. Developmental psychologists find that just a few minutes after birth infants orient toward people, preferring to look at dots arrayed in a face-like pattern (two dots above, one below), compared with an alternative (one dot above, two below). Neuroscientists map a special region of our brains devoted just to processing faces. And if babies aren't snuggled, they show gross deficits in brain development and physical and social functioning, even if they receive adequate milk and warmth.

Even as adults we find the most basic experiences more absorbing when we do them with others. In one clever study, volunteers found chocolate tastier when they sampled it with another person than when they ate alone.* Remember the study I mentioned in chapter 4, where preschoolers found a jigsaw puzzle more fun when they thought they were doing it together, as compared with

---

* They also found bitter chocolate worse when they tasted it with others. Other people don't make things taste good. They make things taste *more*.

when they thought they were taking turns? Another study found the same pattern for adults.

So other people are inextricably wound up in us: how we experience the world, how we develop, and what motivates us. And when you think about it, that makes sense. Nearly every important goal we have—from raising a child, to starting a business, to creating a work of art—requires people to come together. Our sociality is so central to who we are that some scholars maintain that the ability and the motivation to share intentions with others *is* the secret sauce that distinguishes humans from other primates. It's what allows us to develop culture and pass it on, and to learn to live and thrive in the most wildly different environments on Earth, from the Arctic to the Kalahari.

That makes the feeling of being invisible—so excluded you are unseen, and not just by an annoying sibling but by the entire human community—extraordinarily distressing.

Terrell Jones, an outreach worker fighting drug addiction in New York City, recalled his own experience in the lowest moments, of being spat on by neighbors, "Imagine having that be the only interaction you have with another human all day. I was like an alien, like I had two heads coming out of my neck. And I wanted, more than anything, to fix it."

Loneliness, the subjective feeling of being alone, of being disconnected from others, of being invisible, is one of the strongest predictors of bad health, stronger even than major health risk behaviors like smoking.

So, when people ask *Does anyone even see me?* even the smallest acts of recognition can go a very long way. A remarkable study worked with people who'd been admitted to one of nine psychiatric facilities in San Francisco with a depressive or suicidal state between 1969 and 1974. After addressing the acute crisis, clinical staff wanted to protect patients from a(nother) suicide attempt. What they tried was super low-tech. They sent periodic postcards to patients, beginning about thirty days after they'd left the hospital. The notes were very simple. Here's one:

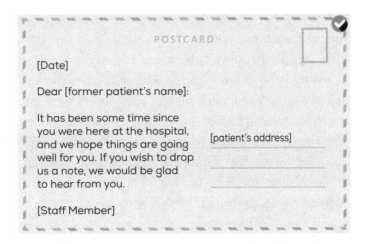

POSTCARD

[Date]

Dear [former patient's name]:

It has been some time since
you were here at the hospital,   [patient's address]
and we hope things are going
well for you. If you wish to drop
us a note, we would be glad
to hear from you.

[Staff Member]

The notes just acknowledged the patient and expressed support. They didn't ask anything at all of them or even request a response. Patients received one note a month for the first four months after they'd left the hospital, and then more along a schedule that gradually tapered off over five years. There was a total of up to twenty-four notes, as long as the patient's address didn't change. Each note was worded differently, individually typed, and responded to any response received from the prior notes. In the control condition, patients got the usual hospital treatment, but no postcards.

Years later, an evaluation team gathered data about mortality from the California State Department of Health, coroners' records, death certificates, clinical sources, and family members. Reporting the results in 2001, they found that patients in the postcard group were *half* as likely to have committed suicide over the two years following discharge, as compared with patients who got business-as-usual treatment. It was a drop in the suicide rate from 3.5 percent to 1.8 percent. The benefits then tapered off.

When I first read this study, I found it shocking. But then I read another. A similar approach with patients who'd been admitted for self-poisoning in Tehran, Iran, cut suicide attempts over the next year from 5.1 percent to 3.0 percent. Then a third study appeared. A team in New South Wales, Australia, had found a series of caring notes cut psychiatric readmission by a third over five years.

There is a power here. You can begin to see this power in how former patients in the first study responded to the notes. One person wrote, "Your note gave me a warm, pleasant feeling. Just knowing someone cares means a lot." A second shared, "After I threw the last letter out I wished I hadn't, so I was glad to get this one." A third wrote, most poignantly, "You will never know what your little notes mean to me. I always think someone cares about what happens to me, even if my family did kick me out. I am really grateful."

To be seen. How can we learn from this work to better see and support people who have faced a mental health crisis, not just as hospital staff members, but as a community of friends, family members, and neighbors?

Seeing Blindly: "Am I seen right?"

If you love a young person, you want to help them see themselves well, to answer that question, *Who am I?* in the best possible way. We saw how Lindsay Mattick introduced her son Cole to his family, and how Christina Bauer's father modeled a strength and dignity that served her well.

But sometimes we go overboard. Sometimes our praise is wanton, inauthentic, illegitimate. Still today many elementary school classrooms are peppered with hollow proclamations like "You're No. 1!" That's a leftover from the so-called self-esteem movement— the idea that gained prominence in the 1970s that, in its most extreme form, pinned essentially all personal and social problems on a lack of self-esteem. But undeserved praise doesn't help. In fact, it hurts, as my friend and colleague Eddie Brummelman at the University of Amsterdam shows in streams of research with snappy titles like these:

- "My Child Is God's Gift to Humanity: Development and Validation of the Parental Overvaluation Scale (POS)"
- " 'That's Not Just Beautiful—That's Incredibly Beautiful!': The Adverse Impact of Inflated Praise on Children with Low Self-Esteem"

Brummelman is good with a turn of phrase. But the point is serious. Why is excess praise problematic for kids? A particularly self-congratulatory child might begin to endorse such an exalted view of themselves. Then any setback or criticism becomes a threat to resist. Indeed, Brummelman finds that excessive praise promotes narcissism for kids who begin with higher self-esteem. Meanwhile, a more balanced child may wonder, *Do I have to live up to this image? If I don't, am I a failure?* Brummelman finds that people tend to give inflated praise most to kids with low self-esteem. But that can make kids avoid challenges, for then any challenge might reveal that you don't meet that standard. In fact, inflated praise predicts *lower* self-esteem over time for these kids. It seems to accomplish exactly the opposite of what it's aiming for.

Wanton praise isn't seeing another person truthfully or helping them become. It's not legitimate. The best a kid can do with that is ignore it.

Instead, Brummelman argues that building healthy self-esteem takes three things: (1) realistic feedback, (2) a focus on growth, and (3) unconditional regard. When young people face challenges, they need feedback to help them meet those challenges: where they are and how they can take the next step. They need to know that you believe in their potential. And they need to know that you love them no matter what.

One of my first projects with Brummelman looked at this third element. We asked adolescents in the Netherlands to share a time when "peers still accepted and valued you even though you made a mistake or did something stupid." One fourteen-year-old shared that she "made a lot of mistakes" on a task with a friend "but we are still good friends and she still values me." Several weeks later, when the first report cards of the year came out, we looked at kids who got low grades. Those who did the unconditional regard reflection a few weeks earlier, as compared with either of two control tasks, felt stronger, less ashamed, and more secure.

Unconditional regard is also essential in families. But you don't get there with overblown talk. I well remember one friend's mom proclaiming in all seriousness that her son, my friend, was the absolute smartest and most beautiful child in the world. Or it's the parent who explains that his kid really is gifted, and that's why they're in a special school. That's not just a shaky foundation for schooling. It's a shaky foundation for worth and for love.

With our kids school-aged in 2021, it was pretty much guaranteed that our household would become fans of Disney's *Encanto*. It's a lesson in unconditional regard. For in Mirabel's family, everyone has a shiny "gift." A brother can see the future, an aunt can change the weather, a sister has superhuman strength. Everyone has a gift but Mirabel.

So Mirabel feels inadequate, unappreciated, and unable to contribute. As the tension grows, the family home crumbles around her. But in the end, it is Mirabel who rebuilds the family on a stronger foundation. "I think it's time you learn," she sings. "You're more than just your gift." Her *abuela* joins in: "The miracle is not some magic that you've got. The miracle is you, not some gift, just you." With that, and with the help of the village, the family rebuilds its home. As the movie closes, Mirabel and her grandmother stand arm in arm, and the family presents Mirabel with a gift: a shiny doorknob engraved with the letter *M*. They invite her to look into its reflection: "We see how bright you burn / We see how brave you've been / Now, see yourself in turn / You're the real gift, kid, let us in / Open your eyes / *Abre los ojos* / What do you see?" Mirabel replies, "I see me / All of me." And so Mirabel's family reflects back for Mirabel the gift that she has given them.

PART 4: GUIDES AND GUARDRAILS:
NOUNS AND VERBS

So far this chapter has looked at times when a nasty shadow looms over you: a perversion of who you are; a weakness; an invisibility; or even a hollow inflation. That's disruptive.

But identities can also keep us honest. They give us guides and guardrails. Sometimes remembering who you are can help you make sure you're behaving the way you want to be and how you want to be seen.

In grad school, I got interested in some of the subtle ways we use language to infer what is, and is not, central to a person. An adviser, Mahzarin Banaji, now at Harvard University, introduced me to a series of studies led by Susan Gelman, a developmental psychologist at the University of Michigan. Gelman gave five- and seven-year-olds descriptions of another child's preference. She varied just the grammatical structure through which the preference was described. Here's an example:

1. *Rose is 8 years old. Rose eats a lot of carrots. She eats carrots whenever she can.*
2. *Rose is 8 years old. Rose eats a lot of carrots. She is a carrot-eater.*

The first statement uses verbs to describe Rose's love for carrots. But the second characterizes Rose as "a carrot-eater." It uses a noun phrase. Gelman found that kids inferred that Rose No. 2's preference for carrots was stronger than Rose No. 1's. For example, if her parents tried to stop her from eating carrots, they thought Rose No. 2 would be more likely to keep right on eating carrots. If Rose is "a carrot-eater," carrot eating is an essential part of Rose. As Gelman and her collaborator Gail Heyman wrote, "Language may help turn an arbitrary characteristic into a trait."

In grad school, I wondered whether people would do the same thing for themselves. Would you infer that one of your own preferences is more core to who you are, if you happened to have described it using a noun phrase? To find out, Banaji and I concocted a study that, we told participants, was about handwriting. First, we asked people about their preferences. What kind of dessert do you like to eat? What kind of pet do you like? What sport? Then we gave people a series of sentences, one for each preference, with a blank in each sentence in which to write in their preference. Here are some examples, with the blanks underlined and my personal preferences filled in.

1. I eat *chocolate* a lot.
2. I am a *chocolate*-eater.
3. I enjoy *dogs* a lot.
4. I am a *dog* person.
5. I enjoy *baseball* a lot.
6. I am a *baseball* fan.

Then we asked people to rewrite each sentence three times using their "natural handwriting style." The trick was that, at random, some of the sentences used verbs (1, 3, and 5), and others used nouns (2, 4, and 6).

Finally, we asked people about each preference. Tell us: How strong is your preference for chocolate? How likely would it be to change if your friends liked something else? We found that when people were led to describe preferences using nouns, they rated these preferences as stronger, as more stable, and as more resilient. The effect was smaller than the inferences people drew when they considered someone else's preferences. It was about one-third the size. But it was there.

"Could I Be 'a Voter'?"

It took Chris Bryan to take this work to another level. Bryan is now a professor at the University of Texas at Austin, but I still remember our first meeting together early in 2006, on the sidelines of a social psych conference in the bright sunshine of Palm Springs, California. Bryan had emailed me interested in the language effects I was observing. He thought they might have an application to civic behavior. But it wouldn't be until the spring of 2008 that we began working together in earnest.

That November would see the election to the presidency of an obscure senator from Illinois, Barack Hussein Obama. As Bryan and I began our collaboration, we knew that, for a campaign, winning so often comes down to the challenge of turnout. But for a person, voting can just seem like a hassle. There are forms to fill out and candidates to sort through. Then it's managing schedules on Election Day: get teeth cleaned, get oil changed, pick up kids . . . vote? It might seem like just one more errand to run.

But what if voting would make you "a voter"? In a democracy, that's a wonderful kind of person to be. I don't know about you, but whenever I pull the lever, push the button, or seal the envelope to confirm my participation in our regular national decision-making process, I get a warm and fuzzy feeling. A voter! A voice, a tiny one but coming together with millions of others in our national process. I think of all the other people participating from coast to coast, in small towns and big cities. And I remember all those who fought and fight to give us self-governance. All day and into the next I wear the "I voted" sticker proudly. One is on my laptop now.

Could the prospect of becoming "a voter" make it more likely people would vote? To put this idea on the table, Bryan and I created a ten-item survey. In one version of the survey, each question described voting using nouns, a kind of person you could become (like No. 2). In the other, the questions described voting using verbs, an act you could do (No. 1).

  1. *How important is it to you to vote in tomorrow's election?*
  2. *How important is it to you to be a voter in tomorrow's election?*

Using language in this way is very different from the other interventions in this book. It's a way of *introducing* a question to people in a setting. *Do I want to be a voter?*

That November, the day before the presidential election, Bryan handed out one version of the survey or the other to a small sample of eligible California voters. Examining state records months later, he found that 82 percent of those who got the survey with the verb questions voted—but 96 percent of those who got the noun form did—an increase of fourteen percentage points. The next year, he ran a similar but larger study the day before the 2009 New Jersey gubernatorial election (which elected Chris Christie). Turnout rose again, here from 79 percent to 90 percent.

These are some of the largest gains in voter turnout ever observed in rigorous research. If deployed only by the losing side, gains like these would easily reverse close elections. A 10 percent increase in turnout among supporters of Senator Hillary Rodham Clinton in the 2016 presidential election would have won her six additional states (Arizona, Florida, Pennsylvania, Michigan, North Carolina, and Wisconsin), turning a 304–227 Electoral College loss into a 328–203 defeat of Donald Trump. Similarly, Joe Biden's victory in the 2020 presidential election would have reversed had turnout among Trump's supporters risen 10 percent. Perhaps that's why "be a voter" messaging has spread across the globe (just google it).

These effects have held up in subsequent trials, especially elections that actually matter, where being "a voter" would have resonance. However, timing does seem important. If the experience is too distant from the opportunity people have to vote, it might not have the same effect. There's also no guarantee that the passive exposures produced by "be a voter" campaigns have the same effect as when people actively consider and respond to survey questions.

Still, Bryan's work shows how nouns can help us stay true to our ideals. It's as if the noun statement holds up a well-designed mirror to a person: *Is this who you'd like to be, how you want to be seen?* For most of us, being "a voter" feels great. So when we see that mirror (*Would you like to be "a voter"?*), we're more likely to vote.

Course Corrections Don't Come from on High: "Would I Be 'a Cheater'?" / "Have I Cheated?"

Just as nouns can provide us with guides for the people we want to be, they can also give us guardrails to prevent us from becoming the people we wouldn't want to be.

In a series of lab studies, Bryan gave people a clever task on which they could cheat to earn a few extra bucks. When he said, "Please don't cheat," some people still cheated. In fact, cheating was no lower than when he said nothing at all about not cheating. But when he said instead, "Please don't be a cheater," there was no evidence at all of cheating. So nouns can also keep us honest. They're like warnings. *Is this who you really want to be, how you'd like to be seen: a cheater?* For most people, that's a cue to pull back.

Much of this chapter has focused on ways we're maligned, how our images can be abused in the social sphere, and how we can reclaim who we are. But you don't need the cheater study to see that people are capable of terrible behavior, of being dishonest, hypocritical, jerks, or worse.

To stay true to our values, we also need to see where we could go wrong. And to course correct, we need to see where we have gone wrong. This kind of seeing often requires a gentle touch, a grace from others, a showing, not telling. For if someone berates you—if they use your worst moment to define you—you're liable to feel maligned. You might feel you have to defend yourself, and then reject the truth of what they have to say. Shaming doesn't give a person the space they need to feel the kind of shame that could help them course correct. It closes people off. So, when a person *might* cheat, a label could prevent that. But when a person *has* cheated, it helps to give a person grace as you raise the problem.

It's important to note here that, in general, psychologists think that all emotions have function, at least in the right context, even negative emotions like shame (or anger, or jealousy, or sadness . . .). They were literally selected for to help us navigate a complex social life. But even if shame can help a person mend a harm, *shaming* might be counterproductive.

I saw this for myself in a new project led by a grad student, Kimia Saadatian. Saadatian was focused on how universities communicate to students about honor code violations, like allegations of cheating. When she looked at the standard letter one university sent students to notify them that it was opening an investigation, she found it legalistic: "A concern has been filed about you in regards to a possible violation of the honor code"; "You have the right to be considered innocent until found responsible beyond a reasonable doubt." That's a-psychological, just as the standard letter to notify students of their placement on academic probation was in chapter 2. It doesn't address the worries a student might have when they get a letter like this. It just seems to define you as a presumptive cheater.

Working with students who'd gone through an honor code investigation, Saadatian revised the letter. The substance of the policy and investigation didn't change. But the letter became more personal; it emphasized the university's goal for the process to be a learning one and its faith in students' ability to work through the process to address the concern. In part it read,

> The goal at our office is to articulate and realize the standards that we have developed, revised, and endorsed together as a community. As such, when concerns arise, we work through each circumstance to identify what happened and help all of us do better as we strive to meet and affirm the standards we hold for one another.

Saadatian calls it "belonging and growth-secure." In an initial study, she found that students responding to this letter took the investigation just as seriously and were just as engaged with it as students who got the standard letter. But with the secure letter, students felt less judged. Their motivations were different too. They were less motivated to defend themselves, more motivated to learn from the process, and more motivated to avoid future infractions. They were also more motivated in their courses going forward and more hopeful they could achieve their goals in college.

And they felt more ashamed. When a potential misbehavior was treated with kindness, when the news was delivered without labels, people could see a potential misbehavior for what it was and begin to self-correct.

Violating an honor code pales, of course, in comparison to some of the ways people can hurt each other. But even in the most extreme circumstances, it's best not to joust with someone. That just makes them dig in. Far better is to hold up a mirror that lets them see for themselves how extreme, or how harmful, their views or behavior really are.

One kind of stigma is when people assume that you're weak and deficient, or when they don't see you at all, when you're invisible.

When it's you who is seen as weak and deficient, or who is unseen, how can you tell your own story, a story that acknowledges challenges you face but also highlights your strengths and goodness? When it's someone else who is seen as weak and deficient, or who is unseen, how can you invite them to tell their story and affirm it?

Another kind of stigma is when one person has hurt another. When this was you, how can you recognize this? And when it was someone else, how can you help them to see this and give them space to acknowledge it? How can we have grace both for ourselves and for others to become better?

KNOW IT. OWN IT. USE IT.

Know your questions. Use your answers.

Here are some of the questions this chapter has covered.

Am I (seen as) weak or bad?
Am I seen?
Am I loved just for who I am?

Think about a time when one of these questions was relevant to you (Part 1) or someone else (Part 2). Identify an aspect of your or the other person's identity that was or is at play. Then do either part 1 or part 2 or both with regard to this question.

Part 1: Think about yourself, your life and circumstance. *Then write down your answers to these questions.*

1. What's a tifbit you've experienced relevant to this question—something small that happened that you had a disproportionate response to? How does that tifbit reveal how this question comes up for you, what exactly the question is for you?
2. Why is that question normal and reasonable for you, given your circumstance—but not necessarily true (or not the only way to think about it)?
3. How can you answer that question in a way that will be healthy and productive and authentic for you? What's a better answer, and how can you *offer* yourself that answer and try it out?*

Part 2: Think about someone else, someone you care about: a
friend, a family member, someone you work with or for.
Consider their life and circumstance. *Then write down your
answers to these questions.*

1. What's a tifbit they've shown relevant to this question? How
   does that tifbit suggest how this question comes up for
   them, what exactly the question is for them?
2. Why is that question normal and reasonable for them, given
   their circumstance—but not necessarily true (or not the
   only way to think about it)?
3. Given your role and relationship, how can you help this
   person answer that question in a way that will be healthy
   and productive and authentic for them? What's a better
   answer, and how can you gracefully *offer* that answer to
   them so they can build it out for themselves?* *For instance,
   describe your own experience with a related question, and how
   you are or have worked through this.*

---

* Remember the principles for thinking through "bad" events:

Principle 1: Avoid negative labels (*I'm not bad*)

Principle 2: You're not the only one; you're never the only one (*It's normal*)

Principle 3: Recognize causes that don't malign you or others (*I/you face real obstacles*)

Principle 4: Forecast improvement (*It can get better*)

Principle 5: Recognize opportunities (*Silver lining*)

INVERTING IDENTITIES

Want to take back control of identities or experiences that cast you as bad or as weak?

This exercise is designed to be done in a small group, but you can also do Step 1 yourself, just for yourself. Or you could do it on your own and then share with others, perhaps inviting them to share too. If you do it in a group, there could be a special meaning to doing it both in a group of people with similar identities or experiences and in a group of people with different identities and experiences.

Step 1: Write

Everyone writes a response to this prompt:

> *Think about an identity or experience you have or have had that is often represented in negative ways (for example, as weak or as shameful). It could be a particular social group identity (for instance, age, gender/gender identity, national identity, place of origin, sexual orientation, social class, race, or ethnicity), a mental or physical illness or disability, or something that has happened to you. Name that identity or experience (but without identifying yourself, unless you want to share it with the group).*
>
> *Even if this identity/experience can be difficult or pose challenges sometimes, it's probably also a source of strength and pride and personal growth. What strengths have you developed from or working with this identity/experience? How have you applied these good qualities to work toward goals you care about?*
>
> *When everyone is done, we'll collect what everyone has written and some of the responses will be read aloud.*

STEP 2: ANONYMOUS VERSION (CRUMPLE PAPER!)	STEP 2: NON-ANONYMOUS VERSION
Make sure everyone completes Step 1 without identifying themselves. When everyone has finished writing, crumple up the papers, and throw them in the middle of the table. Then start to read some of what people wrote out loud.	If you feel comfortable, you can also invite people to read their own responses out loud, if they like.

Discuss. What did it feel like to write? To share? To hear? What themes are you noticing? What lessons would you like to take away? Consider how stories get told about our identities. What is really true? How can you stay in touch with what your identities and experiences mean to you? How can we listen better to others, and understand their full stories? Make sure to applaud everyone for sharing.

Sharing Beyond the Group. If you help lead this setting or group, you can tell people in Step 1 that you'd like to share their stories, if they are willing, more broadly (ask them to make a special mark in a corner—for example, "Okay to share"). Then find an appropriate forum in which to share these answers so others can see, like a physical or digital bulletin board. (Make sure any identifying information is removed, unless the author wants it there.) Invite other people to add their stories there too.

Reducing Global Poverty

In part 2, we have explored the many forms the foundational questions *Do I belong? Can I do it?* and *Who am I?* can take. Here we'll address these questions at another scale.

We live in a world of vast inequalities: inequalities in basic health, infrastructure, and economic opportunities; inequalities in social status, standing, and dignity. In this world, what is the appropriate stance a person with more can take for a person with less?

For inequality provokes a thicket of questions. If one person has less, does that make them less? If they receive aid, does that make them helpless? We'll see how a complex, multifaceted intervention can navigate through these questions to make progress on one of the hardest and most important problems in the world.

AM I (SEEN AS) LESS THAN?

Growing up in Jackson, Mississippi, Catherine Thomas saw experiences of poverty and inequality all around. From the age of fifteen, Thomas, who is now a psychologist at the University of Michigan, volunteered at a free clinic run by local medical students serving people without insurance. For a time, she planned to go to medical school too. But the longer Thomas spent at the clinic, the more disturbed she became at the underlying factors that drove people there in the first place. In Jackson, the neighborhoods with more were literally across the railroad tracks from the neighborhoods with less.

In college, Thomas began to gain a broader perspective. She read a famous thought experiment from the philosopher Peter Singer, the parable of the drowning child. Suppose your daily commute takes you past a shallow pond. One day, you see a child thrashing about, at risk of drowning. It's wet and muddy, but you could easily pull the child out. Do you have an obligation to help? Singer used this case to ask whether it's any different if it's a child living across the globe. "That really hit me," Thomas told me. "I thought of the obligations we have to redistribute wealth. No one should be in extreme poverty." At the same time, Thomas was learning how far a dollar can go in low-income communities around the world.

But Thomas was also asking critical questions about *how* we help. For in college too she saw programs that disturbed her: "voluntourism" programs that seemed more for the benefit of Western college students than the communities they ostensibly served. Those programs seemed to Thomas to reinforce power dynamics, to lock in inequality.

Inspired by a feminism acquired from her mother, by courses in gender studies and anthropology, and by research suggesting that engaging people's hopes and agency could unlock poverty traps, Thomas realized that seeing problems and caring are not enough. Intentions are not impact. She wanted to learn how you could advance women's empowerment in ways that would be organic, that began with dignity. So, in the summer after her first year at the University of North Carolina, Thomas volunteered for an organization in Togo run entirely by local women. In helping to organize community events focused on microfinance and women's economic empowerment, Thomas could begin to learn what would resonate with communities from the bottom up. It was a commitment she would bring with time to our graduate program at Stanford.

. . .

Like Thomas, I had the opportunity to see poverty close at hand as a teenager.

In August 1992, when I was fourteen years old, I traveled with my family to Rampi, a remote village in Indonesia. My mother was spending the year in Yogyakarta, a city in central Java, doing field research on the role of the *pasindhèn,* or solo female singer, in Javanese gamelan music. It was my parents' desire to get off the beaten path, and my mother's fluency in Indonesian culture and in both the Indonesian and the Javanese languages, that let us travel widely. So that August, a string of flights brought us to Tentena, a village on Lake Poso in central Sulawesi. My parents then made arrangements with "missionary airlines" to fly to Rampi. That is, they called up the local Canadian missionary and got him to give us a lift in his tiny propellor plane. Without his help, it would have been a two-day hike. I remember the tiny plane banking over the jungle and small fields, splitting mountainous hills. In Rampi, we'd have the chance to hike these hills, and maybe find ironwood and sandalwood trees.

When the plane bounced down once, twice on the dirt airstrip, the entire village, it seemed, showed up to watch. Kids and adults alike hung over a loose wooden fence. The villagers were eager to show us their community, including a new building they were constructing. And after my mother shared her interest in Indonesian music, at dawn the next morning three older women showed up in full regalia to provide us with a traditional performance.

There was no guesthouse in Rampi and nowhere to eat, so we were staying in a small hut at the airstrip. We'd contracted with a local woman to bring us meals. I'll call her Salma. My mother still remembers their first conversation.

"How many children do you have?" she asked. In Java, this question is a bit like "How was your journey?" It's mainly a time filler, a way to feel each other out.

"We have four children," Salma said.

My mother then asked the next question: "How old are they?"

"Five, four, and one," said Salma.

My mother felt the pang of the absence. Only then did Salma explain that one child had died. To say that she had four children felt to us a way to honor the fourth child, to keep this child alive.

A few days later, a headman from another village arrived, having heard that an American family was visiting. After some small talk, my mother asked, "What's the most difficult problem you face as village headman?" His answer: "Fevers like cholera and typhoid that cause so many children to die. Adults get those fevers too. And even though they don't always die of them, they are too sick to provide the kind of help we need in our village: to build a new school or a clinic."

We knew then what had happened.

At fourteen, all this made quite an impression on me. I felt the smallness of problems in my life, and the obligation to help. But it also made me think about how we help.

For most of us, I suspect, "alleviating poverty" calls to mind something vague, whatever "the neediest cases" funds, maybe buying someone a goat. But what does the other end of that exchange *feel* like? What questions might getting a handout provoke? What would the headman in Rampi have felt if we had just expressed our pity and cut him a check? The money might help. But the disrespect makes me sick. One refugee, resettled in Britain following the war in the former Yugoslavia, shared, "When I have to go to the Social Benefits Agency, I feel—'oh, look at yourself how low you are now, you used to be a normal person.' . . . I never had any kind of complexes in my life, but this has become a social complex."

It's a catch-22, a bit like that faced by a student in a mental health crisis. You're in a difficult circumstance and you need help. But as one hand gives, the other pats you on the head and says, "You poor, poor person." *Am I (seen as) less than?* What pain is in this question. Yet how common is this in how we treat others. In one study, Thomas looked at the mission statements of the thirty largest cash transfer programs in Africa. She found that 97 percent emphasized the weakness and vulnerability of those in poverty. This is profoundly disrespectful.

One purpose of aid is to meet an immediate need. A child is starving. You give her food. A man is sick. You give him medicine. But with chronic, systemic poverty, the problem is broader and far more complex. So, your goal has to be bigger: It is to help people become, to meet the challenges they face and make progress in their lives, as they define it. Then aid must build people up. It cannot diminish them.

When questions like *Am I (seen as) less than?* are on the table, the best aid is explicit in recognizing that the goals and projects and cultures and ways of doing things of the recipient are just as valuable as anyone else's. We give aid because your goals matter. And because we know that with the right resources you are powerful to achieve these goals. Having less does not mean being less. (Nor is having more being more.) Then the helper recedes. It's not about you. In the best help, the helper becomes invisible.

In Yogyakarta, the cultural center in Java where my mother lived, my parents had purchased a number of *wayang kulit* from a local craftsman. These are the exquisite shadow puppets used in all-night *wayangs,* or puppet theater, in Java. After a dinner, the craftsman brought puppet after puppet out for us to view. The decisions and negotiations stretched long into the night, concluding well after my brother and I had gone to bed. Even accounting for cultural differences in bedtimes and the love of negotiating in Java, staying up all night seemed excessive to me. But then my mother and I did some math. With a few basic assumptions, we estimated that this single sale might have accounted for *one-third* of the annual income of the craftsman. It wasn't just the work that was to be treated with respect. It was the transaction too.

It was easy for my parents to honor the culture and agency of the *wayang kulit* craftsman: to value his work and negotiate seriously over it. But when people are in poverty, when it's outright aid they need, can we structure this exchange too in a way that honors the recipient's culture, agency, and values? Who they are and who they can become, their goals, their power to achieve them, and their way of doing so.

It helps, to start, to give aid in a form that is fungible, something people can use flexibly, as they see fit—like cash, with no strings attached. But it also matters how you talk about the aid you give. In a 2020 study, Thomas, my colleague Hazel Markus, two economists, and I gave people in Kibera and Kawangware, low-income settlements in Nairobi, Kenya, small cash transfers. All we varied was how we described these transfers. One message mimicked the big aid organizations: "The Poverty Alleviation Organization," we said, had the goal of "reducing poverty and helping the poor meet their basic needs." The second message emphasized recipients' agency: "The Community Empowerment Organization" had the goal of "enabling people to support those they care about and help communities grow together." Same aid. But when we honored recipients' agency, people felt they were seen more positively by others; they were more confident they could control their finances; they even anticipated achieving more upward mobility over the next two years. And when we gave people the choice to watch videos teaching business skills valuable in the local economy, like how to finance a business expansion, or fun clips like soccer highlights, they chose to learn more skills.

The typical ways we give aid are self-defeating. Disrespect holds people back. Thomas's study in Nairobi begins to show how we can get out of this catch-22: by showing, in deed and in word, that the aid we give is to help people become, on their terms.

That study did not look at outcomes over time. In the next step, building on the work in Nairobi, and adapting the techniques Kurt Lewin developed more than eighty years ago to help midwestern housewives change what they served for dinner, Thomas and her collaborators would create what may be the most cost-effective multifaceted approach to poverty reduction ever documented in the history of the social sciences.

WHO COULD WE BECOME? WHAT COULD WE DO?

Just south of the Sahara is a borderland known as the Sahel. It's an arid region dotted with trees. Camels and goats wander half wild.

Stiff wooden walls surround family compounds, keeping wild animals out at night and people safe. In the heat of the day, women pound millet by hand, raising and lowering beams, up and down, up and down.

Villages in the Sahel are some of the most remote and isolated in the world. The average woman has seven children, no formal education, and no personal cell phone. She is not literate, and she has no means of transportation (car, bike, motorcycle). It's a seventy-three-minute walk to the market, on average, and twelve minutes to a water source. In this world, everything you know you learn by word of mouth. When Catherine Thomas and her team surveyed women in the Sahel in 2019, she found that just 2 percent of them had slept outside their village for work in the prior year. Some had never left the village.

In 2017, Thomas had joined a partnership led by the government of Niger in an economic development program in the Sahel. As climate change makes subsistence farming more precarious, the government wanted to encourage more women to develop small businesses. In an effort to learn more, Thomas traveled to Niger and, in an intense period of listening with local collaborators, including Abdoulaye Sambo Soumaila, a Nigerian economist, she asked women what mattered to them, what could support them in starting or expanding a small business, and what might hold them back. At one point Thomas asked women to choose which of four qualities mattered most for success. Two are the kinds of qualities those of us in Western countries usually prize: "hard work" and "self-initiative." But only one in three women in the Sahel chose one of these. Instead, they pointed overwhelmingly to the other two qualities: "peace," or social and inner harmony, and "good relationships."

As Thomas dug deeper, she saw that the success of women's small businesses hinged on their reputation and relationships. If a woman got on poorly with others, she might be ostracized. Older women might even be accused of witchcraft and pushed out of the village entirely. Thomas began to see specific questions that might hold women back from developing a business: *Will I be alone? Will*

I offend my community or violate my cultural values? Will I be (seen as) an immoral woman? Will I have conflicts with others? When people received aid, these questions were nested within that larger question, *Are we (seen as) less than?*

To begin to address these questions, Thomas worked with local artists and collaborators to develop a twenty-minute video telling the story of Amina, a woman who starts a business processing and selling hibiscus (or *bissap*) juice after a drought. In the video, Amina consults with her mother-in-law, a cousin, and her husband to develop the business. Its success allows her to send her children to school, and she shares what she has learned with other women in her village.* Throughout Amina's story, business is represented as done in partnership with others, as consistent with community values of respect and social harmony, and as helping people contribute to their communities and their growth.

Thomas wanted to use this video to start a community conversation. Drawing on the discussion groups Kurt Lewin developed in World War II to encourage middle-class housewives to serve "cheap" meats to their families, Thomas structured this conversation by treating communities as leaders in making a change and inviting people to talk through how they were making this change.

Say your name is Fatima, or Fati for short. You live in Wakawa, Niger, many hours from the capital, Niamey. You're thirty-eight years old and have seven kids. You've never been to school. You have no cell phone or means of transportation, and you are not literate. It's five kilometers to the local market. You have a small business, sometimes selling millet biscuits or grilled goat.

Like everyone else in Wakawa, you see a stranger, someone you don't know personally, rarely, maybe once or twice a month. (How often do you see a stranger, say at the grocery store?) So it's an honor, one day, when an emissary from the village chief calls at your home and shares that some people from the government and a nonprofit

---

* You can watch the full video in the original Zarma or Hausa with French subtitles (vimeo.com/241966553/477b0933bd, vimeo.com/216225407/41843032c1) or a four-minute clip with English subtitles (vimeo.com/251731247/a94aa34d87).

organization have come to visit your village. They're showing a film tonight! You're invited to come and bring your husband and another person, a cousin, sister, co-wife, friend, or child. You and your husband decide to bring your daughter, Haoua.

That evening, as the sun goes down, you come to the community meeting space. This is a round area in the middle of the village with sticks dug into the ground to keep the animals out. There's a blow-up screen, a generator, lights, and speakers. Everyone is there, maybe 250 people in all, including the chief, the imam, and all the village elders and business leaders. Nothing like this has ever happened in Wakawa before. A facilitator begins:

> Your community had been selected to participate in the Adaptive Social Protection Program in the Sahel. You have been identified because we believe that you have the necessary potential to use this program well and you are able to develop as a united community. We know that your community, like others, faces many challenges, such as droughts and floods. These challenges make food security and health difficult. But we know that you come together to find the strength to meet these challenges. It is said that "unity is strength."
>
> We hope that tonight you can share some of the practices that have made you successful in your adaptation. The social safety net program intends to support the hard work of your community. We believe that due to the solidarity of this community, community members will share new ideas and skills and support each other. When this happens, this community can become a model for other communities in this area.

Your village could be a model. What a thought! (You're certainly not poor people getting "aid" from rich outsiders.)

After showing the film, the facilitator opens a conversation: "We want to listen to different members of the community because we believe that everyone has an important specific experience to share." Community members are asked about parts of the film they liked and how they relate to their lives. At one point, you raise your hand

and say how you liked how Amina worked with her husband and family to build her business.

The facilitator then asks about "traditions of adaptation" in your community, "stories of your parents, grandparents, great-grandparents, or ancestors who changed their practices and way of life in response to changing conditions." One elder describes how community members took up new livelihood strategies after a drought, women starting to grow and sell vegetables from their gardens. Another describes efforts to increase women's access to markets, and to help more children go to school. Next, the facilitator asks about challenges that could come up and what your community can do to meet these challenges. One woman shares how women can create savings groups. A man talks about how family members can plan and work together and teach each other, like how Amina learned to make *bissap* juice from her cousin and then shared her experience with her community. Everyone who wants to speak has their turn. Then the facilitator brings the meeting to a close:

> Thank you for sharing how this community intends to grow and ensure a better and safer future for its children and grandchildren. We will be back to visit you over the next few months. When we return, we will ask you how you are doing, how you responded to the challenges you faced, and how you learned from each other. You are one of the few villages selected for this program. If this community makes good use of the program, we hope we can expand it to other villages so that more communities can learn from your success. We believe this community can become a leader by achieving these goals and growing stronger together. We are together. (Or, in French, *On est ensemble!*)

Thomas and her collaborators designed the discussion this way to build consensus and community support for women's entrepreneurship. That way, if Fati wanted to expand her business selling millet biscuits, she would know she'd be seen as normal, not abnormal, and as advancing traditional values, not violating them; and she could do this in partnership with others. The meetings lasted an hour and a half, on average, but in some villages the conversation went as long as three hours. Afterward, women got access to a weeklong life skills training program developed by an organization from Benin called CESAM (Le Centre de Suivi et d'Assistance en Management). The program included building skills like goal setting, effective decision making, and problem solving, while also reflecting on community values and how these can be expressed through work.

This was a massive project. Together with the government of Niger, the World Bank, and her economist collaborators, Thomas was able to reach thousands of households across Niger. A subset of these, 22,507 people in 4,712 households in 322 villages, participated in a randomized controlled trial. Because of the poverty these communities experienced, one of the goals was to test whether just giving people money and other economic supports (for example, business trainings) would help. All of the households were already getting regular cash payments from the government designed to shield economic shocks. That amounted to 10,000 West African CFA francs (XOF) each month ($15.95 in U.S. dollars, or $38.95 adjusting for purchase costs). That income, over a year, added up to about 11 percent of the average annual household spending in these poor, rural communities. This was the first group. Thomas and the team compared it to three other groups, to see what would help most.

The second group got the regular payments plus the program Thomas and her collaborators designed. The third got the regular payments plus a single huge lump-sum cash grant and economic supports. That grant was 80,000 XOF, or $127 ($311 adjusting for purchase costs). That's *88 percent* of the average annual household spending. (What's 88 percent of what your household spends in a year? What could you do with that?) The fourth group got everything: the regular payments, Thomas and colleagues' social psychological program, and the huge grant and economic supports.

What made the biggest difference for women's entrepreneurship and economic security? No doubt the cash helped. Six and eighteen months later, families that got the huge lump-sum payment and economic supports had more money and greater food security than families that just received the regular cash transfers. Women also felt more empowered. They reported to local survey teams better mental health, more confidence they could solve problems and achieve goals in their lives, and more control over household decision making, including how to use money they earned. Extreme poverty can suck you down; money certainly helps.

But what was remarkable was that the program Thomas and her collaborators designed achieved the same benefits, even without that large payment. Families showed the same and sometimes even larger gains in finances, confidence, and well-being. And, instead of seeing the benefits stagnate, with the social psychological program households improved over time, from the six-month follow-up to the survey at eighteen months. In the cash grant villages, families seemed to invest the cash primarily in extra livestock. They achieved financial gains quickly, but their finances didn't improve much more after that.

In villages that got the social psychological program, on outcomes like daily finances, food security, and mental health the benefits were sometimes smaller at six months. But they doubled at eighteen months. The evening event and the weeklong life skills training addressed questions that held women back, *Will I be (seen as) a "bad woman" if I start a small business? Would it pull me away from my community? Are we (seen as) less than?* Helping women and their communities set these questions aside unleashed women's entrepreneurial energy; then families developed a new economic base and spiraled up over the next year and a half. What's more, individuals and families were spiraling up together. Women in these villages were more interested in caring for the village; they felt closer with their partners (they held their hands closer together in describing their relationship) and more comfortable disagreeing with them; and they were less likely to say they had enemies in the village. Family members were also more likely to join women in growing businesses.

Of course, a lack of capital can hold people back too. The fourth

group that got both the lump-sum payment and the social psychological program tended to show the greatest benefits, especially on
economic outcomes, at the eighteen-month follow-up. But it was
more expensive, and budgets are limited. So Thomas and her collaborators' program has become a model for governments in low-
income countries that want to scale up evidence-based safety net
programs. Already it's been extended elsewhere in West Africa, to
Burkina Faso, Senegal, and Mauritania. Any community, I suspect,
can benefit from coming together to think through how to adapt as
our world changes. I wonder what difference it could make for
women like Salma in Rampi.

PART 3

You

Chapter 6

Do You Love Me?

Charlotte had written the word RADIANT, and Wilbur really
looked radiant as he stood in the golden sunlight. Ever since the
spider had befriended him, he had done his best to live up to his
reputation. When Charlotte's web said SOME PIG, Wilbur had
tried hard to look like some pig. When Charlotte's web said
TERRIFIC, Wilbur had tried to look terrific. And now that the
web said RADIANT, he did everything possible to make
himself glow. It is not easy to look radiant, but Wilbur
threw himself into it with a will.

–E. B. WHITE, *CHARLOTTE'S WEB*

The 1996 film *Jerry Maguire* opens with Jerry, a slick sports
agent played by Tom Cruise, in crisis. His client, a hockey
player, is recuperating in the hospital. "This is his fourth concus-
sion," says the client's son. "Shouldn't somebody get him to stop?"
Jerry tries to blow the son off. "It'd take a tank to stop your dad," he
says, checking his phone. The kid stares at Jerry. "Fuck you," he
says, and walks away.

That sits with Jerry. Several days later, he stays up late writing a corporate mission statement on ethics in representation. "The answer," he writes, "was fewer clients. Caring for them, caring for ourselves." As he writes, he begins to uncover a new dimension to his self. "I have lost the ability to bullshit," he says. "It was the me I'd always wanted to be."

Distributing that mission statement gets Jerry fired from the firm he helped build. Walking out, he invites anyone to join his new practice, "something real and fun and inspiring and true in this godforsaken business." The whole staff watches, a mix of sympathy and glee. Just one person joins him: Dorothy Boyd, a single mom played by Renée Zellweger.

Jerry Maguire is a love story, but it's not Jerry whom Dorothy falls in love with. Not quite. She falls in love with the person Jerry might become. As she confesses to her sister Laurel, "I love him for the guy he wants to be, and I love him for the guy he almost is. I love him."

In the very best relationships, each person sees the other person more positively than anyone else sees them—funnier, kinder, more intelligent, more generous, and more attractive than even they might think they are. Maybe it's how you hope them to be. Wonderfully, your partner sees you in the same way: as you hope you could become. That helps you each overcome the doubt that can pervade an early relationship. It tempers conflict as relationships develop. And it helps both of you become better versions of yourselves. It's as if your partner holds up a beautiful mirror just for you. You look great in that mirror, better than you ever thought possible. It's so lovely—and just right for you. You want to live up to that image, to become that person your partner envisions.

Some say "love is blind." But Sandra Murray, the psychologist at the University at Buffalo, who has led much of this research, says it's more that love is "prescient." Actually, love makes itself true. In one study, Murray tracked dating couples over a year. The more couples idealized each other (the more they saw their partner in line with their ideal), the more satisfied they were and the more likely they were to stay together. And one of the reasons their relationships strengthened was that people grew; they began to become the person their partner saw. You're Wilbur and you're becoming radiant, just as Charlotte sees you. You're Jerry, and you're becoming a genuinely good man, just as Dorothy sees you. At *Jerry Maguire's* iconic climax, Jerry tells Dorothy, "I love you. You complete me." That's spiraling up.

Murray's research teaches us that relationships are about more than the truth in some static and confined sense. Murray finds that married couples are no happier when they understand each other more accurately. Instead, to grow a relationship, we must break free from the here and now and imagine who we can become. We must inspire and be inspired. Murray writes, "As time passed, intimates appeared to create the partners they desired by idealizing them, turning self-perceived frogs into the princes or princesses they perceived."

So, relationships take faith. It's not a blindness to your partner's faults, or seeing them as perfect. As we'll see, blind faith is a recipe for disaster in relationships; it doesn't help couples keep each other in check or work out problems. Instead, launching that upward spiral takes a faith in your partner's essential goodness, in who they really are deep down on the inside, a faith in who they can become and who you can become together. With that faith firmly held, Murray shows, you're less likely to jump to the worst conclusions in a fight. "You were late" need not become "You're a selfish person." A mistake need not breed contempt. An untucked shirt like my brother's at Macy's need not mean "I can't be with you." It gives couples grace to work through conflicts and mistakes, to be imperfect, to become better. The result is that the more you and your partner see each other through that rosy lens, the more satisfying and secure your relationship becomes. Murray's work shows us that the usefulness of a way of thinking might matter more than its accuracy in some abstract sense. Thinking is for becoming.

At their heart, all relationships are is spirals. How I think about and behave toward you shapes how you think about and behave back toward me.

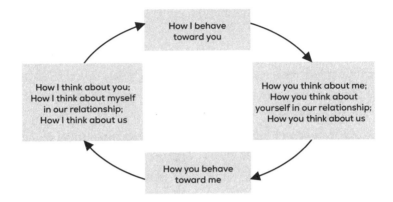

But spirals can take us up—or down. In Shakespeare's *Othello*, Desdemona's father, Brabantio, plants a seed of doubt in Othello's mind early in Act I, warning, "Look to her, Moor, if thou hast eyes to see. She has deceived her father, and may thee."

It is this seed that Iago cultivates and then reaps. He is a master manipulator, but he never acts outright. He hints, he drops clues, he fertilizes Othello's anxiety. In Act 3, Othello says, "I heard thee say even now, thou lik'st not that, when Cassio left my wife. What didst not like? And when I told thee he was of my counsel in my whole course of wooing, thou cried'st 'Indeed?' And didst contract and purse thy brow together as if thou then hadst shut up in thy brain some horrible conceit."

Othello begs, "I prithee speak to me as to thy thinkings," but still Iago holds back. "Though I am bound to every act of duty, I am not bound to . . . Utter my thoughts? Why, say they are vile and false."

What Brabantio sows and Iago cultivates in Othello is a question, *Will Desdemona betray me? Has Desdemona betrayed me?*

For years in introductory psychology courses at Stanford we have put on readings of David Auburn's play *Proof.* I've come to love the play, and the readings too. The lights are up; there is no stage, costumes, or blocking. It's just terrific local professional actors, script in hand, having rehearsed with a director for maybe a few hours. You can sit in the first row and become fully immersed in the dialogue and relationships. In some ways, I prefer it to fancy professional productions where you're at a remove from the words themselves. For our students, it's a different way to discuss big topics in psychology like mental illness and gender stereotypes.

What I've come to appreciate most watching *Proof* time and again is its treatment of trust or, really, mistrust. The play begins with Catherine grieving the death of her father, a brilliant mathematician, whom she cared for over the course of a long illness. Following his death, in the wake of a spark of romance with Hal, one of her father's last graduate students, Catherine gives Hal a key to a locked drawer containing an extraordinary mathematical proof that, Catherine says, she wrote. But Hal doubts her. He wonders if it's her father's work instead, despite his illness and despite the fact that he hadn't done any serious math in years. So Hal looks for proof. In the end, he comes to believe Catherine. But then it's too late.

HAL: Come on, Catherine. I'm trying to correct things.

CATHERINE: You *can't*. Do you hear me? You think you've figured something out? You run over here so pleased with yourself because you changed your mind. Now you're certain. You're so . . . *sloppy*. You don't know anything. The book, the math, the dates, the writing, all that stuff you decided with your buddies, it's just evidence. It doesn't finish the job. It doesn't prove anything.

HAL: Okay, what would?

CATHERINE: *Nothing*. You should have trusted me.

Spark out; relationship stillborn. Sometimes you have to assume a better relationship so it can become. Or to paraphrase George Michael, you gotta have faith, faith, faith.

Hal should have begun by trusting Catherine. But it's not faith alone that a relationship needs. You also have to learn how to be together.

When our dog, Tomato, was a puppy, Lisa enrolled him (and us) in various puppy training classes. One of the tips we learned was to stick our hands in his little mouth with all those supersharp puppy teeth and let him chomp down—"the jaw of death," as the trainer described it, with a little too much glee for me. At every graze of a tooth, she went on, we were to shriek in pain. For Tomato had to learn that people are wimps, that he had to have an especially soft mouth for us softies. So, we didn't just have faith that Tomato wouldn't bite us or our friends. We taught him how to play his part in living with people. We asserted our needs in a language—shrieks of pain—that he could understand.

Have you ever tried to take a nap with someone, whether a small child or a grown adult, and this fool repeatedly rolls over taking the blankets with them? You've got to tell them to stop, or you'll be sleeping out in the cold!*

To spiral up, relationships take good faith and idealization. But they *also* require standing up for yourself and coordinating so everyone's needs are met.

In relationships, fights can provoke troubling questions. *Are we in trouble? Do you love me? Is my partner a jerk?* We'll see how helpful it can be to set aside those questions. But the solution isn't to just ignore problems and not fight. Then problems will fester. *Good* fights can help you work out what you each need and how to live together.

There are some truisms in relationships, like "don't sweat the small stuff" and "forgive and forget." But James McNulty, a psychologist at Florida State University, has made a career of showing the boundaries of these usually healthy tendencies. In one study, he tracked couples in northern Ohio over the first two years of marriage. The more that one partner tended to forgive the other, the more satisfied they were in the marriage over time—but only if the partner rarely behaved negatively. If, on the other hand, your partner is being a jerk, a high level of forgiveness just lets that continue. Another study begins to show how couples can forgive while addressing problems: by directly demanding change in a partner's be-

---

* There's a reason the most famous op-ed of all time, Amy Sutherland's 2006 piece "What Shamu Taught Me About a Happy Marriage," is about using the techniques of animal training on your spouse. It's not so different. See Amy Sutherland, "What Shamu Taught Me About a Happy Marriage," *New York Times,* June 25, 2006, www.nytimes.com/2006/06/25/fashion/what-shamu-taught-me-about-a-happy-marriage.html.

havior. A team led by Michelle Russell at the University of North Carolina, Greensboro, videotaped problem-solving conversations among newlywed couples to see how much each person explicitly demanded changes to benefit themselves or the relationship (for example, "Do not do that anymore"). Tracking couples over the next four years, Russell found that what was most harmful was if a partner expressed forgiveness but did not ask the partner to change their problematic behavior. But if couples forgave while demanding change, their partners were more likely to compromise and to become more considerate over time.

The directness is important. McNulty warns that "*indirect* negative behaviors (e.g., sarcasm)" predict lower satisfaction and greater problems over time. "Confronting problems negatively but indirectly," he writes, "provides ambiguous information regarding the necessary course of action and thus tends to be ineffective at resolving problems." It might also feel hostile.

In *Othello,* the drama hinges on the fact that Othello never has an honest conversation with Desdemona about his doubts. As the audience, we know, of course, that Desdemona is faithful. Yet how does Othello address this question? It's not until Act 4 that he talks with Desdemona directly, but by then he's already convicted her in his mind. He calls her "a subtle whore," "a strumpet," and "false as hell." That ship has sailed.

PART 1: RELATIONSHIP INTERVENTIONS

Hopefully, you don't have Iago whispering in your ear (or your partner's ear!). Hopefully, you and your partner begin with trust, not mistrust. But if you're like me, relationships can be confusing, and you don't always understand what you feel or why you're feeling it. Why has a relationship that was once warm and close become awkward and distant? Why is someone you care about ignoring or rejecting you? What do you feel? What do they feel? And why?

Sometimes you might feel like a unicorn, as if no one else has ever felt what you feel. Every relationship is unique. But whatever you feel, I guarantee you other people have been there before. Probably far more than you think. In fact, there are predictable triggers, a lawfulness, even, to the questions we ask in dating relationships; in marriages; even, sometimes, heartbreakingly, in the relationship of a parent with a baby. The tools of science can help us track these questions, name them, and understand why they come up and how they affect a relationship. Then we can anticipate these questions and decide what to do with them.

One of the most powerful ways to learn about relationships is through intervention. When we develop exercises that help people work through relationship questions, we can track how the answers we offer (or don't) affect the course of relationships. These exercises have some distinct qualities, qualities that reflect the nature of relationships. First, both people in a relationship generally want that relationship to work. There's little we care about more than the success of a marriage or being a good father or mother to a child.* That means that when spirals go awry, things can hit the fan fast—consider the carnage that is the end of *Othello* (four dead characters onstage). But it also means that helping people set aside a pressing question can have particularly lasting benefits. The upward spirals here too are potent.

The second distinct quality draws from the fact that these exercises focus on spirals—the dynamic between two people. Each person is just a portal into this dynamic, so exercises can address either one person in a relationship and the questions they face or both people.

And third, because relationships are so personal, exercises to help people think through relationship questions take an especially light touch. They never ever tell people what to think or how to act. Instead, they typically feature leading questions that simply invite one or both people to reflect on their relationship in a new way.

---

* Volumes of research in the social sciences justify an interest in relationships in terms of how they undergird other things like mental and physical health. Those things matter. But relationships are their own reward, so that's our focus here.

Working Through Doubts: More Than Words

Let's start with dating.

You've gotten through the first stage. The initial noticing. A quiver of attraction. A text sent, awaiting a response. Perhaps you pluck petals: "She loves me, she loves me not." Maybe you sing along to Whitney Houston in your car ("How will I know if he really loves me?") or the classic "Shoop Shoop Song" ("It's in His Kiss"). You're now "official." Congratulations! You have entered the honeymoon phase.

Now, suppose, your partner is idealizing you. In their eyes, it seems you can do no wrong. You are brilliant, beautiful, kind, and loving. The cat's meow, never an ungracious moment, never an unkind thought. Never boring. Never unfun. Immune to warts. No pimples. Who you've always wanted to be.

Sounds great, right? And wouldn't Sandra Murray's research suggest you're ready to become that person, to idealize your partner in return, to become that couple you've always imagined? Spiral up and away—*3, 2, 1, blastoff!*

There's a catch, of course. In chapter 1, I described one of my all-time favorite studies—a classic in which Murray brought dating couples to the lab and one person, it seemed, wrote on and on about the other person's faults. Murray found that people with low self-esteem reacted badly to that. They denigrated their partner and felt distant from them. Their partner writing on and on was a tifbit to them. It seemed to reveal a dirty truth. How they were really seen.

Self-esteem plays a really important role in relationships, and not just in how people respond when they get poked. For if you think you're not so hot, it's hard to believe that anyone else will either. *Am I lovable? Could anyone truly love me?* Then it's not just that everyday challenges loom large, evidence of a partner's lack of love. It's also harder to see a partner's true love in everyday pleasures.

When I was a postdoc at the University of Waterloo, I became good friends with Denise Marigold, a leading researcher in the study of relationships. No one has taught me more about relationship spirals and how low self-esteem can muck them up—or what you can do about this.

What Marigold did was to think very clearly about what dating relationships look like to a person with low self-esteem, especially in that dreamy honeymoon stage. Let's begin supposing you're high in self-esteem. You agree, "I have a number of good qualities" (an item on the classic Rosenberg Self-Esteem Scale). The notion that your partner idealizes you is welcome, an affirmation, consistent with how you view yourself, perhaps a challenge to live up to. Your partner is helping you see your good qualities and realize them. You're spiraling up.

But what if, instead, you think, "I am no good at all." Perhaps you think, "I do not have much to be proud of," or that you might be "a failure" (all self-esteem items).

Again your partner prattles on, extolling just how wonderful you are. In this state of mind, you wonder, *Do they really love me? Or is it just words, just something they have to say?* Perhaps you see that rosy lens and just know it's not true. *That's not me!* You feel like an impostor in your own relationship. *I'm not sure whom you're dating, but that's not me.* The more your partner praises you, the more false it seems. *Do they even know me? Are they deluded? What will they think when they see the real me?* Your partner's praise has become a tidbit, driving you down.

Working with John Holmes and Mike Ross, two of the wisest and most jovial psychologists around, Marigold set out to learn how to help people with low self-esteem truly take a compliment from a dating partner—to experience it as a genuine reflection of their partner's love, as "more than words," as the team would write in a seminal 2007 paper. Could that help couples on an upward spiral?

Marigold knew that browbeating people wouldn't work. "No, really, she loves you. She really does. She thinks you're the best. I promise . . ." *Blah, blah, blah.* People with low self-esteem are well practiced in resisting that. In fact, earlier research had shown that favorites of the self-esteem movement, like telling people how wonderful they are, can backfire for people with low self-esteem. That just exacerbates the questions they face: *What will they think when they see the real me?* Also ineffective: getting people to repeat silly mantras like "I am a lovable person." It's easy to think, *But what if I'm not?*

So you can't force it. And that way of treating people is, I think, shallow. It doesn't take people's concerns seriously. Nor does it give people a structure to work through the evidence pertaining to the question at hand. In the end, Marigold took an approach strikingly similar to what Chris Hulleman, Judy Harackiewicz, and Elizabeth Canning did to help students find interest in math and science coursework. She asked a single well-framed question.

Working with young people mostly in "exclusive" dating relationships, she asked everyone to recount a recent compliment from their partner. A first group was just asked to "describe the event." Here one person lower in self-esteem wrote, "I had donated money to the Pakistani earthquake relief fund. I donated in mine and my partner's name, although the money was mine. He felt extremely happy and said I was generous." This person recounts the compliment, but she doesn't go further. She doesn't link the compliment to her partner's enduring love and admiration. She's stuck in what was said, in what happened in the past. In fact, in this condition, Marigold found that people with low self-esteem tended to use the past tense somewhat more than people with high self-esteem ("he *said* I was generous").

By contrast, people with high self-esteem were more than willing to connect a compliment to a partner's enduring love. As one person said, "I painted a picture for him, and he said that I was talented and that I was very creative. He admired my creativity and my ability to project my thoughts and feelings through painting/art." Not stuck in the past here. This woman reads her enduring good qualities in her partner's praise. If you already think you're great, you need no help taking a compliment.

Unsurprisingly, when Marigold asked people how secure they felt and how they saw their relationship as a whole, those with low self-esteem looked worse. They were less likely to agree, "I am confident that my partner will always want to look beyond my faults and see the best in me" or "I am extremely happy with my current romantic relationship."

In a second group, Marigold asked people to describe the concrete circumstances in which the compliment was given. Maybe people with low self-esteem weren't really thinking about the compliment. But that didn't help. The same gaps emerged in this group.

The critical change involved a single, elegant question. Marigold asked participants to: "Explain why your partner admired you. Describe what it meant to you and its significance for your relationship." This prompt, which Marigold calls "abstract reframing," doesn't tell people that a compliment has a global meaning. That wouldn't be an outsider's role. But it *presumes* this and then invites people to respond to this perspective. Now people began to take it up. One person with lower self-esteem wrote, "She admired me because she knew I was really busy with schoolwork, but when she called and asked for help, I stopped what I was doing to help her. I think this showed that she could rely on me if she ever needed help, and it showed how much I love her [and] am willing to do for her."

Stuck no more. And now we get liftoff. Immediately, people with low self-esteem felt more secure and rated their relationship as higher quality. That improvement persisted through a follow-up survey several weeks later. And it wasn't just a change in people's heads. When Marigold asked the partners of people with low self-esteem, they said that their partners (the participants) had behaved more positively toward them since that initial reflection. Likewise, people with low self-esteem reported that their partners too had behaved more positively back toward them. A single well-put question had improved the relationship spiral. Now the relationships of people with lower self-esteem looked just as healthy as those of people with higher self-esteem.

The details of Marigold's work teach us a lot. Thinking about a compliment alone didn't do the work. *Everyone* was reminded of a compliment. Nor did it help even to invite people to think about *whether* a compliment could reflect a partner's love. Marigold showed this with a fourth group, whom she asked to "Explain whether you think what your partner said indicated that he/she admired you. Consider whether it was meaningful to you and significant for your relationship." That was like a true-or-false question, and it produced no benefits. People with low self-esteem could consider whether a compliment had a broader meaning but then just think, *Not really*. It also isn't the case that people with low self-esteem just don't recognize compliments in general. Other research finds they are just as enthusiastic about compliments in other couples, seeing them as just as sincere as people with higher self-esteem do. They just don't recognize them about themselves.

Think of a time when your partner told you how much he/she liked something about you. For example, a personal quality or ability you have that he/she thinks very highly of, or something you did that really impressed him/her.

CONTROL ⊖ PROMPT	CONCRETE ⊖ PROMPT	QUESTION ⊖ PROMPT	ABSTRACT ✓ REFRAMING PROMPT
Describe the event in the space below	Describe exactly what your partner said to you. Include any details you can recall about where you two were at the time, what you were doing, what you were both wearing, etc.	Explain whether you think what your partner said indicated that he/she admired you. Consider whether it was meaningful to you and significant for your relationship.	Explain why your partner admired you. Describe what it meant to you and its significance for your relationship.

Chris Hulleman, Judy Harackiewicz, and Elizabeth Canning saw that browbeating students with the importance of math and science wouldn't help. Students needed scaffolding. But then they needed to build out that connection for themselves. So, they created an opportunity for students to articulate the value math and science had for them personally. That's a guide for how a teacher or a parent can help a student.

Marigold saw that an outsider couldn't force a person to recognize a partner's love; nor would that be appropriate. What people needed was a structure that *assumed* a compliment meant something real about this love and gave people space to respond to that, to find evidence for their partner's love themselves. It's a less controlling approach, a lighter touch, more respectful, I think, and it's more effective. It's a guide for how friends can help each other in relationships.

One of my intellectual heroes is the developmental psychologist Urie Bronfenbrenner. Bronfenbrenner was a visionary co-founder of Head Start, the early childhood program that supports low-income kids with high-quality early learning opportunities. Bronfenbrenner famously wrote, "Every child needs at least one adult who is irrationally crazy about him or her." We'll see the depth of Bronfenbrenner's wisdom in school in chapter 7. But it's not just kids and it's not just in school. Every one of us needs someone who is irrationally crazy about us, who sees in you who you can become even before you do. It helps if you can accept that vision, if it's your vision too, and if you see your partner in turn in that light. These are visions that help us spiral upward, individually and together.

Working Through Conflicts

Congratulations! You've made it through the honeymoon stage. Maybe you've gotten married and enjoyed an actual honeymoon. Unfortunately, it seems, now you're on the downside of the slope.

When Eli Finkel, a social psychologist and relationship scientist at Northwestern University, reached out to me and my colleague James Gross about a study with married couples some years ago, I didn't know that it's common knowledge in the scientific literature that marriage just gets worse over time. Really. The very best studies, longitudinal studies that track couples over time, find that marital quality tracks negative, a never-ending slope downward. It's not as if that slope ends when the kids move out. It just keeps going. However your marriage is today, it seems, is as good as it ever will be. It's scheduled to be worse next year.

Say it ain't so!

But why? And need it be so?

At the time, Lisa and I were just a few years into our own marriage, so the question was personal. Obviously, I was eager to learn more. One of the reasons seems to involve a process Finkel calls "negative-affect reciprocity." Really, it's spirals gone wrong, cycles that start with the mundane complexities of living together, balancing jobs, money, kids, and everything else. Lisa tells me I'm spending too much time writing this book, so I feel bad and snap at her. She yells back, I storm off, and we're off to the races, a downward spiral, frittering away our love. If you're feeling insecure (*Do you love me?*), bad construals (*That means you don't!*) are especially likely to get calcified.

For many people, a good marriage is among the most cherished parts of life. The irony is that the stupidest things can imperil it. Just in time for Valentine's Day 2023, *The Washington Post* published a piece, "When the Dishes Mean War," with hilarious stories of readers' biggest and dumbest marital spats. One person wrote in, "We fight over how to put spoons in the dishwasher. I put them in so the handle is down and scoop is up. My husband does the opposite. It's gotten so bad that we will turn them around when the other person isn't looking." Is there anything more trivial? It reminds me of the Dr. Seuss classic *The Butter Battle Book,* where the Yooks and the Zooks approach mutual obliteration because one side butters its bread on the top and the other on the bottom. Perhaps love really is war.

The standard advice in conflicts is to understand the other person's perspective. But in marriage or any other long-standing relationship, you darn well know your partner's perspective—and they're crazy! Spoon side up? Insane! Spoon side down? Absurd! But of course, if that's all you know, conflict persists.

Sometimes, at least, conflicts can be revealing. If you're able to step back, you might understand yourself and your partner a little better, and learn to be better partners for each other. But if you don't, conflicts can spiral out of control. Here's another dirty dishes fight from a *Post* reader. (The kitchen, it seems, is ground zero for domestic squabbles.)

Luckily, my partner and I don't have huge fights. But oh my goodness do the dishes drive me crazy! I have asked many times over the six-plus years of our relationship that he please deal with his own dirty dishes. He is almost 41 years old and leaves dirty, crusty dishes in the sink without rinsing or soaking them constantly! I'm the type who makes sure the dishwasher is emptied every morning before we go to work so the sink can be free of dirty dishes. I always clean up after myself and our 5-year-old child. It drives me bananas that a fully functioning adult doesn't clean up after themselves.

Okay. Now I sympathize with the virtues of a clean kitchen. But let's play this one out. Suppose the man gets wind of the idea that his partner equates him with their five-year-old and sees her way of doing things as objectively right and his as objectively wrong. *Does she infantilize me? Does she look down on me?* The woman for her part seems to be asking, *Is my partner a slob? Is he disrespecting me? Is he taking advantage of me?* How's the next conversation going to go? I don't know about you, but I'm not feeling the love tonight; more a reverberation, a speeding car, lug nuts loosening, tires spinning out of control. *Kaboom!* I don't want to be in that room—or the next one either.

What's clear is that when we're fighting about trivialities, it's not really the trivialities we're fighting about. The dishes themselves aren't worth it. It's something else.

These are two-track fights. So, what are we really fighting over when we fight over spoon side up or spoon side down? Why do trivialities sometimes function as tifbits in relationships? What is it they signify?

More Than Words, Part 2.

Denise Marigold had a simple but profound idea: that sometimes, at root, there's just a basic insecurity about a partner's love and appreciation. *Does my partner truly love me? Do they respect me?* The fact is, the more you care, the more you have to lose. Absent that security, a conflict can start to cleave. Then a kitchen disagreement can come to represent something bigger.

A place to start is by surfacing those deeper worries, getting perspective with your partner. If the "dirty, crusty dishes" couple shared their respective concerns (for example, *Does she infantilize me? Is he taking advantage of me?*), if they said them out loud, so each person could understand what lay beneath, might their conversation go better?

To address those deeper concerns, Marigold suspected conflict conversations might be more productive if couples first felt their partner's love and regard. To test this idea, she conducted a lovely lab experiment, adapting the "more than words" intervention. She asked dating couples to identify the most significant conflict in their relationship. Soon they'd have a ten-minute conversation about this. But first, half the couples did the abstract-reframing exercise. Both people thought about a compliment their partner had given them and considered "what it meant to you and its significance for your relationship." So both people had the chance to reflect on the admiration their partner had for them. Then they talked through their conflict.

The result was better conversations, especially for couples with histories of worse conflict. Couples that reflected first were more likely to anticipate before the conversation that their partner would be responsive to them in the conversation (for example, "My desires will be important to my partner"). Afterward, they reported the conversation was less stressful. They also felt more love in the conversation and for each other. That improvement was even visible to outside coders who watched videotapes of the conversations. They saw less distress in couples who did the reflection first, less destructive behavior (for instance, anger, sarcasm, and defensiveness), and more constructive behavior (support, warmth, understanding, and humor). Overall, they rated the conversation as closer and more productive as a whole. (Of course, the coders didn't know which condition the couples were in, so their ratings couldn't be affected by any expectations they might have had.)

When we're entering a conflict conversation with a loved one, sometimes existential questions might lie beneath the surface. If we can get those worries off the table, it's easier to make progress on the conflict at hand. Another reader told the *Post* about yet another kitchen fight. But she began and ended the story by affirming her

love and the quality of their relationship. And she found a pragmatic solution:

> My husband and I have been married for 35 years. We have a great
> relationship and usually get along very well, except when it comes
> to loading the dishwasher. I rinse the dishes before putting them
> in the washer. He insists that the dishes do not have to be rinsed
> and puts them in straight from the table. Then the food adheres
> to the dishes and silverware and I go crazy when I am unloading
> the washer. . . . My solution is to not let him load the dishwasher.
> It is okay because he does most of the cooking (he used to be a
> chef), and I love him!

Marigold's study was just a lab study. She wasn't able to track couples over time. But every bone in my body tells me that if couples
can manage conflict better, their spirals will improve.

A Third-Person Perspective on Conflict.
We see evidence of that long-term improvement in two other studies. Both were premised on the idea that couples can get lost in
conflicts, and that a new lens to think about the conflict itself might
help. One was that study that Eli Finkel reached out to me and
James Gross about. Finkel was working with a group of 120 Chicago-
area couples, most in their thirties and forties, married an average
of eleven years. They weren't in any particular state of martial distress, just normal couples, but that meant spiraling slowly down.
Every four months, the couples reported on their marriage. It wasn't
even halfway through the two-year study, but already Finkel's team
was seeing that couples felt less satisfied, less love, less intimate,
less trust, less passion, and less commitment than when the study
began. Finkel suspected that a toxic cycle of conflict was at play: I
feel insecure and yell at you, you get mad and yell back, I sulk, you
sulk. . . . So he wanted to talk through whether there was something
you could do to head that off. There was a constraint: we'd have just
seven minutes to play with at the end of the surveys that would be
distributed at the twelve-, sixteen-, and twenty-month follow-ups.

What to do? We knew that telling people to "take your partner's perspective" would be about as helpful as telling the Yooks that the Zooks really do like their bread with the butter side down. *Duh.* It's not just that, if you're married, you already know your partner's perspective, which of course you think is crazy. That's why you're locked in a conflict. "Getting perspective" on the deeper issues might help but it could also revert to "take my perspective." *No, really, let me explain to you again why I'm right and you're wrong.* As much as I've tried, that's never quite worked for me.

So we took a different tack. Could couples develop a third way to see a conflict?

In Finkel's survey, all of the couples shared a "fact-based summary of the most significant disagreement" they'd had in the prior four months. Beginning at month twelve, we asked a lucky half of the couples (as it would turn out) three extra questions: how a "neutral third party who wants the best for all" would view their conflict; obstacles that could prevent them from taking that perspective in conflict conversations; and how they could overcome those obstacles to take that perspective. Here's the full text.

SEEING FIGHTS LIKE A BENEVOLENT THIRD PARTY

1. Think about the specific disagreement that you just wrote about having with your partner. Think about this disagreement with your partner from the perspective of a neutral third party who wants the best for all involved; a person who sees things from a neutral point of view. How might this person think about the disagreement? How might he or she find the good that could come from it?

2. Some people find it helpful to take this third-party perspective during their interactions with their romantic partner. However, almost everybody finds it challenging to take this third-party perspective at all times. In your relationship with your partner, what obstacles do you face in trying to take this

third-party perspective, especially when you're having a disagreement with your partner?

3. Despite the obstacles to taking a third-party perspective, people can be successful in doing so. Over the next four
months, please try your best to take this third-party perspective during interactions with your partner, especially
during disagreements. How might you be most successful in
taking this perspective in your interactions with your partner
over the next four months? How might taking this perspective help you make the best of disagreements in your relationship?

Both people answered these questions, but independently from
each other.

Couples who did the survey as usual continued their decline in
marital quality, spiraling slowly downward over the next year. But
those who answered these questions stabilized. The result was that
at the end of the two-year study they felt more satisfaction, more
love, more intimate, more trust, more passion, and more commitment than couples who did not. It was twenty-one minutes to stabilize a marriage.

That didn't happen because conflicts just went away. Conflict is
a fact of relationships. It was like the belonging intervention, where
college students still had bad days. Or it's like a growth-mindset intervention where you still fail a test sometimes. Couples who got
the extra three questions reported that their fights were just as severe as couples who didn't. But they were less distressed by those
fights. No longer did they invite questions like *Is my spouse a jerk?* or
Are we broken? That reduction in distress predicted better relationships over time.

A better marriage has all sorts of cascading benefits. So it's not
so surprising but still important that at the end of that second year
couples who got those extra questions were also less depressed, less
stressed, and more satisfied with their lives in general. I'm happier
too when my marriage is going well.

Seeing the Big Picture in Conflicts.

At Waterloo, I also became good friends with Karina Schumann, who is now a professor of psychology at the University of Pittsburgh. Later, Schumann and her husband, Omid Fotuhi, another good friend and collaborator, would join me at Stanford to do their own postdocs.

Schumann has many gifts, but one is a special ear for conflicts. If you're lost in a stupid fight, like how to load the dishwasher, Schumann asked, would it help to just step back and consider the big picture? To find out, she brought 152 couples, either living together, engaged, or married, into the lab and asked them to talk through a conflict. But first she asked half to keep in mind the big picture when they had a conflict. Each person had five minutes to reflect on their own on the following prompt, before they talked.

SEEING THE BIG PICTURE IN FIGHTS

Occasionally, you will experience conflict with your romantic partner. From now on, when you find yourself in a conflict situation with your partner, take a moment to reflect. Try to take a step back and *see the bigger picture*. Ask yourself: What matters most to you? What are *the important values* that guide your life? Then take a moment to *think about the conflict with your partner while considering these important values*. Try to do this every time you have a conflict with your partner.

To summarize, when you're in a conflict with your romantic partner, take a moment to:

1. Take a step back and see the bigger picture.
2. Ask yourself: What are the important values that guide your life?
3. Think about the conflict with your partner while considering these important values.

Then she tracked couples over a year. The results were, frankly, extraordinary. Let's take it step-by-step. First, in the lab right after the conversation, couples in the big picture group, as compared to those in the control group, said that they and their partner were more constructive in the conversation. They were more likely to agree with statements like "I felt open-minded toward my partner" and "My partner seemed open-minded toward me." They also felt more satisfied in the relationship and more love, less hostility, and less shame. A month later, people said that their partners were more responsive to their needs. A year later, they reported they were better at managing conflict in general as a couple and that they felt less anxious and avoidant in their relationship (for example, they disagreed more with statements like "I worry that my partner won't care about me as much as I care about them" and "I try to avoid getting too close to my partner"). They also felt more love, satisfaction, trust, and intimacy, a bump from 6.22 to 6.58, nearly reaching the top of the 7-point scale. That's *five minutes* now for more love *a year later.*

It's stunning.

Let's break it down. First, how in the heck could "take the big picture" even start a better process? Don't people already know this? But you might know it and not know it all at once—and not know it just when you need it. As we saw with the *Washington Post* readers, lots of people get caught up in massive fights over nothing at all. When you're at loggerheads with someone you're supposed to love, it's easy to lose sight of what's really important. Actually, I suspect part of the elegance of this approach is precisely that it's not new. What Schumann is doing is reminding people of a helpful idea, one they probably already endorse in the abstract. She's helping couples crystallize that idea at just the right time, right before a conflict conversation, and giving them a chance to practice putting it to work in that conversation.

The second thing that's stunning, of course, is that, hello, a year later! Once a better cycle began, it persisted. But maybe that's not so surprising. Once you're in a better cycle, a cycle with lots of affection and laughter, maybe some bad jokes, where you can talk through and resolve conflicts, then it's not so hard to keep it going. After all, this has been one of the big lessons of this book. Our lives are defined by spirals. We can shift them, and that shift can transform our lives.

Sometimes results like these can seem like magic. One side of that is to dismiss them, to think they're not real, that they're somehow illusory, that they lack substance, that they could never really help a couple. The other side is to herald them, to treat them as the magic bullet we've been waiting for. To immediately assign yourself and your partner, perhaps, to diligently do all three: Marigold's "more than words," Finkel's "third-party perspective," and Schumann's "seeing the big picture."

But what do we really learn from this work? And what should we take away? These studies aren't like an experiment in physics—how fast a ball of a given weight and dimension will roll down a ramp with a given incline, for example—which will deliver the same result, with a tiny error, every single time. The social world and our psychology are far more complex. There's no guarantee that if you and your spouse do, say, the third-party perspective, you'll be closer next year. Sorry!

These exercises are tools, sure. They give us things to try when they seem fitting for who you are and your circumstance. But as important, perhaps, is that they begin to teach us how relationships work. From the inside, it can be hard to see the dynamics in a relationship, like the virtues of idealization and how that can get short-circuited if you don't take a compliment, or how we can get lost in spirals of conflict. These studies help us to a broader view, a wisdom, as well as tools we might try to improve our relationships and some hope that we can use this wisdom and these tools to make things better.

And science doesn't stop. I call these demonstration studies for they show that an approach *can* help. But future studies will help us map their dimensions more clearly: When, how, for whom, and why might they work best, or not at all?

PART 2: PARENTS AND BABIES

I love the relationship interventions. But for me, the next intervention takes the cake. It's one of my very favorites, one of the most important lines of research I know, or can even imagine. For if there's any relationship that people value more than that with a romantic partner, or that's more important for everyone involved, it's the connection between a parent and a child.

When Lucy was born, she was healthy but small, five pounds, ten ounces of wonder. I was immediately smitten. A few hours after birth I brought Lucy to the maternity ward, where the nurses gave her her first bath. Soon she was screaming in outrage, a bright cooked-lobster red. I held her as close as could be. Lucy was born in the evening, at 6:21, and that first night in the hospital, whenever she woke, I took her for walks through the hallways so Lisa could rest. She was so small I could hold her on one arm, head nestled in my palm, tiny feet at the curve of my elbow. I marveled that inside her tiny body were countless capillaries and neurons, a tiny liver, two kidneys, three hundred some bones, a pumping heart, and a brain, all together and ready to grow.

As many babies do, Lucy lost weight over the first few days, as Lisa's milk came in and we stumbled to get the hang of feeding with the help of a skilled lactation consultant. Given this weight loss, we were tasked with feeding Lucy every two hours, around the clock, for two days. She was exhausted, and so were we. One bright afternoon it was time for Lucy to nurse, but she was fast asleep. We tried poking her, talking to her, rolling her over, all to no avail. She just would not wake up. It got so bad we actually called the advice nurse to inquire, "How do you wake a sleeping baby?" I'll always appreciate the kind woman on the other end who didn't laugh at us, though I think I could detect a smirk in her voice. But she gave us some good advice: take her clothes off and drip water on her face. It worked like a charm.

A few months later, my mother, observing our experience and other new parents', said to me, "What is it with your generation? In my generation, no one had 'lactation consultants.' We didn't have these problems. We just fed the babies."

This puzzled me, for almost every parent I knew had some sort of challenge feeding babies. How could just "my generation" have these problems? A few days later, I recalled an experience my mother had had when my brother Eric was a baby. So, the next time we talked, I said to her, "Didn't you tell me once that Eric had all these undiagnosed food allergies as a baby, that he threw up nearly every day and actually lost weight from six months to twelve months?"

"Yes."

"Wasn't that stressful?"

"It was incredibly stressful."

And she went on and on telling me how hard that had been, how it had made her feel like a bad parent, how many doctors she'd talked to until she figured out the problem. But before I'd asked, all she remembered decades later was the warm nostalgia of bringing a child into the world. There's truth in that. But it's not the only truth.

It's not just the pain of childbirth that gets forgotten. Parenting is hard, especially early parenting. Really hard. Suddenly you're in the deep end floundering, a baby to care for, a new identity to master. Lisa and I and other parents at our cooperative daycare regularly shared stories in an informal competition for the "worst parent of the week" award. My nominations included:

- the time I brought moldy pasta for my kids' lunch;
- the time I forgot Lucy's lunch entirely, got a call at 4:00 P.M. as I was leaving my class, and discovered her lunch buried in the bottom of my backpack;
- the time I misfired Tomato's Chuckit launcher and nailed Oliver square in the head;
- the time boarding a fourteen-hour flight I hoisted a wailing Lucy into the air—and bashed her head into an overhanging TV, causing the other passengers to gasp.

Among Lisa's nominations were these:

- the time she locked baby Lucy—and the keys—in the car;
- the time she felled an already-upset preschool-age Oliver with a hard-kicked soccer ball to the head, dropping him like a rock, and thereby receiving a permanent red card for all future family soccer games.

A wonderful part of our daycare was that many of the parents took a couple hours each week to volunteer in the classroom. That way, you could get to know all the kids. And there were regular potlucks, so you could get to know the other parents too. The community gave us space to tell these stories, to hear other people's stories, to laugh at ourselves.

When people are becoming parents, I've found they're thirsty to talk with other recent parents. *What's it like?* they want to know. These conversations help. For six months later, sleep deprived and in the middle of the night, you might not remember exactly how to swaddle a newborn or the "five S's" to calm a crying baby (shh, side, suck . . . ?). But you might remember that your friends had trouble too, that they got frustrated too, and that they too felt exhausted. Then you can take comfort in knowing that difficulties with a newborn are normal, that they won't last forever, and that there might be some things you could do to get better.

One evening, when Lucy was just a few months old and I was utterly sleep deprived, our pre-parent friends and colleagues Karina and Omid dropped by to pick up a few things. It was very late at night, as late as 8:30, and I'd fallen fast asleep on the couch. Hair askew, I answered the door. There they stood, fresh and energetic, in workout gear.

"Where have you been?" I asked.

"At the gym," they said.

"And where are you going?"

"To dinner."

"At this hour?" I asked, completely shocked.

Karina, Omid, Lisa, and I laugh now, but I think their image at the door helped me then. It let me see that this exhaustion would pass, that someday a 9:00 P.M. dinner might even be conceivable again. And I think my image helped them too. It gave them a vision of what might come: that with a newborn, they too might be exhausted, that this was normal, and that it was okay. And so it was, and so it would be.

I count myself and Lisa incredibly privileged when we became parents. There were many ways, but a big one was the community around us: friends like Karina and Omid, friends who'd become parents just before us and shared their experiences with us, our daycare community, that kind nurse. For at every turn, when we had troubles, we were supported in understanding that parenting is hard at first and that we were learning. Perfection was not the goal. Muddling through, recognizing mistakes, apologizing when necessary, and getting better—that would be enough.

For what if, instead, you were isolated when you became a parent? What if, then, you had a hard time getting your baby to take a nap, to take a bottle, or to stop crying, not just once, but time after time? What if you struggled just to get out the door? What if you're exhausted and haven't had a proper rest in weeks? What if every time you find a moment to take a shower, or to just have a second to yourself, your baby cries, as if on cue?

The Bay Area writer Anne Lamott (whose book on writing, *Bird by Bird,* I love) begins a classic essay for *Salon* by affirming her love for her son, "The truest thing in the world is that I love my son literally more than life itself. I would rather be with him, talk to him and watch him grow than anything else on earth." But that doesn't stop him from provoking in Lamott "something similar to road rage":

But the third time they call for you, you try to talk them out of needing you, only they seem to have this tiny problem with self-absorption, and they can't hear that you can't be there for them. And you become wordless with rage. You try to breathe, you try everything, and then you blow. You scream, "God fucking damnit! WHAT! WHAT? Can't you leave me alone for FOUR seconds?"

Deep breath. Lamott goes on:

> Of course, it helps if you can catch yourself before you blow up, if you give one of you a timeout. I'm sure it helps to have a spouse, and it also helps when people tell you their own terrible stories of blowing up, so you can laugh about it: At one of my lowest points, a friend—a teacher—told me that she looks at her child and thinks, "I gave you life. So if I kill you, it's a wash."

We have to surface these things. We have to be real. We have to be in community with each other. As Lamott writes, "Good therapy helps. Good friends help. Pretending that we are doing better than we are doesn't. Shame doesn't. Being heard does."

When I was becoming a new parent, a friend, the wife of a colleague, literally the kindest and gentlest person I know, told me of the rage she felt as a young mother years earlier when her baby would not stop crying hour after hour; how she called her husband at his office in tears, and how he told her to just put the baby in the crib, to leave him, to walk out of the room, and to shut the door while he came home. That he wouldn't hurt himself in the crib alone. This was a gift she gave me then, a marvelous one.

In March 2012, a few months before Lucy was born, I was invited to give a talk at the University of California, Santa Barbara. My kind host asked whom I might like to meet while there, and while many people came to mind, I knew immediately whom I wanted to talk with most: it was Daphne Bugental. Unfortunately, Bugental had recently retired and since, sadly, has passed away. It is to my everlasting regret that I never got to meet Bugental. For it is her research on parenting—and on the prevention of child abuse—that I admire so deeply.

Bugental conducted her research in Southern California, working mostly with Latinx families, many of them recent immigrants. She began by identifying families in difficult circumstances, where parenting is harder, situations that make abuse more likely. About half of the moms had been abused themselves as children. Other risk factors included experiences of unemployment or low income, unstable housing, a lack of education, a history of partner violence, or past involvement with child protective services. About half of the families didn't include a husband or partner, so mothers were the focus of Bugental's study.

When Bugental talked with moms, she found that they not infrequently explained challenges in parenting in ways that implicitly or explicitly blamed themselves or their child. "My baby cries no matter what I do," they might say, or "My baby likes my mother better than he likes me." One even said, "My baby is only three months of age and he's already talking back to me."

It was as if mothers daily faced two horrid questions: *Am I a bad mother?* and *Is my baby a bad baby?* Then they read the daily struggles of parenting through these lenses. Bugental suspected this could trigger a downward spiral, a spiral in which a mother becomes increasingly frustrated, powerless at the mercy of a tiny tyrant; the baby's needs increasingly unmet; the two locked in a conflict that erodes the most important relationship each person might have.

She wanted to learn if this pattern of thinking really did hurt families. And she wanted to help.

So, she developed the Family Thriving Program. In her original study, published in 2002, Bugental randomized families to one of three conditions. First was a no-treatment control condition, where families got no special services. Then there were two conditions where trained staff visited mothers an average of seventeen times over the baby's first year. In one case, the visits were based on an existing program. The visitors shared standard advice about parenting skills, resources, and family goals.

In the third condition, the Family Thriving Program, the visitors focused, instead, on the everyday challenges of parenting and how to make sense of them. They began by asking moms about the biggest challenge they had with their baby (for example, "My baby won't stop crying"). Then they asked why they thought they were having this problem. Whenever mothers gave reasons that implicitly or explicitly blamed themselves or their child, they never contradicted this reasoning. They just kept asking, "Could it be something else?" until the mother gave a reason that wasn't blaming (for example, "Maybe the baby needs a new bottle"). Then they asked how she could work on this ("What do you think you would like to try?"). They closed by affirming the mother's problem-solving ("Okay, great—that sounds good. Try it out. Next time you can tell me how it worked out"). On the next visit, they asked how this approach had gone.

As with the dating and marriage interventions, this approach doesn't tell people how to think. Nor does it tell mothers what to do. That's actually more what the standard visits did. But for a visitor to sweep in and tell moms what the "right" answer is ("To get your baby to take a bottle, you should . . .") takes away their agency in finding a solution. And it fundamentally misses the point: Whatever the immediate challenge is, solving that isn't the most important thing—just like deciding between spoon side up and spoon side down isn't actually the conflict.

It's not an outsider's place to tell a parent how to parent. But it could be an outsider's role to help a parent take the most pejorative ideas off the table, to help you see that everyday challenges are normal, that they don't make you a bad mom or your child a bad baby. That challenges are pragmatic, and you can make progress on them. That's what our friends, our daycare, and our community did for us. Then, when a problem comes up, a mother can ask, "How can I work on this?" This approach respects moms and empowers them to solve problems. As Bugental said, "We're not solving problems for them, we're helping them to become their own problem-solvers."

Bugental's approach was overwhelming in its impact. A primary goal of the research was to prevent child abuse, especially for families in the most difficult circumstances. In the no-visit condition and in the skill-and-resource condition, about one in four infants had experienced abuse (as reported by mothers themselves) by their first birthday: 26 percent in the former condition and 23 percent in the latter. That means the baby was hit with a fist or object, beaten up, kicked, bitten, shaken, or thrown or tossed down. But with the Family Thriving Program, the rate fell to 4 percent.

The numbers were even more dramatic for babies who presented greater challenges to caregivers: babies who were born premature (at least three weeks early) or who had lower Apgar scores five minutes after birth (<9). That's a first indicator of health, and it can be harder for caregivers to understand and respond to these babies. They might even withdraw from your touch, because they're not developed enough yet to accept social contact. Here Bugental reported a broader measure of "harsh parenting," which includes abuse but also legally nonabusive uses of force, like spanking, slapping, grabbing, or shoving. Fully 58 percent of these more challenging babies experienced harsh treatment by their first birthday absent Bugental's program. But with it, just 10 percent did.

Abuse is just one indicator of a family dynamic gone wrong. When Bugental looked, she found that her program also improved children's health at the age of one and reduced mothers' rate of depression. What could be more depressing, after all, than feeling you are in, and losing, a raging struggle with a nine-month-old and having to resort to hitting her? And that depression rebounds. It feeds back into the negative cycle. In fact, mothers' rate of depression was a strong predictor of harsh parenting.

Moms who got the Family Thriving Program felt more empowered too. When Bugental asked about factors that affected the success or failure of their interactions with their babies, moms in the program were more likely to endorse factors they could control, like the effort they put in or the approach they chose. She also included a lovely indirect measure to look at empowerment. She asked moms to draw separate pictures of themselves and their babies. In the two comparison conditions, mothers depicted their babies as nearly as large as them: tiny tyrants looming large. But moms in the Family Thriving Program drew their children considerably smaller, just 60 percent as large as themselves. That's healthy power, appropriate to the role of mother, and it predicted less harsh parenting.

A few years later, Bugental and her colleagues ran a replication study. In this new study, they tracked families longer, through the child's third birthday, and looked at broader outcomes of healthy development. In this sample, the rates of abuse in the first year were low in both conditions (4 percent in the treatment, 5 percent in the control). But the program reduced the rate of corporal punishment from 35 percent to 21 percent, reduced children's injuries, and improved safety in the home by the child's first birthday. By the time kids turned three, the program had increased mothers' investment in time and money in higher-risk children; improved children's health; reduced children's aggression; reduced children's level of stress, as assessed by a hormonal marker (basal cortisol); and improved children's cognitive functioning (short-term verbal memory). Moms were off to a better start in perhaps their most important relationship. Kids were off to a better start in life. Families were doing better. Everyone was spiraling up. That came at a cost of $4,000 per family per year. Is there anything more worth it?

I find this work overwhelming. It's so important, for all of us. When I share it in class, I always ask students what lessons they take from it, for with time of course many of my students will become parents themselves. What would you say to yourself if you can't get your baby to stop crying? What would you say to a friend? Here are some favorite bits of advice:

- *I'd think:* "It's hard to be a baby. How can I help?"
- *I'd remember:* "They change so fast—it's like you have a new baby every two weeks."
- *I'd think:* "It's like holding the hand of someone you love when they go through a painful procedure."

I particularly like this third bit of wisdom. In my experience, when I'm the only other person in a room and someone is yelling, they're usually yelling *at* me. But with a crying baby, that's not the case. It's just hard to be a baby. To have your ear ache and not know why. To have soiled yourself. To not be able to feed yourself. To not be able to reach that shiny toy. And it's hard to be a parent. To understand what your child needs, to read them, to make mistake after mistake until you find what works. And then to do it all over again as your baby changes.

When Lisa was pregnant with our second child, whom we named

Turkey Tom in utero, because he was due on Thanksgiving, we read some of the popular advice about how to introduce a new baby to an older sibling. One of the ideas out there was to give the older child a present purportedly from the new baby. But that seemed off to us. A new sibling isn't like the swim lessons I endured as a child only because I negotiated a visit to Dairy Queen after each and every class. It's not a sacrifice for which you deserve compensation. Anyway, two-year-old Lucy was smart enough to know that a blob who couldn't even roll over yet or burp without assistance couldn't give her a gift (now, of course, Oliver is well known for his ability to burp on command).

So, instead, we decided to ask Lucy to pick a gift to give to Oliver after he was born. So one day, at a toy store in a shopping center near our home, she found a crinkly little bear. We set it aside and waited. And sometimes in those last weeks before his birth we read Debra Frasier's classic picture book *On the Day You Were Born* with Lucy. It was a gift from a wise and kind colleague at Lucy's own baby shower:

> On the eve of your birth, word of your coming passed from animal to animal . . . and the marvelous news migrated worldwide. While you waited in darkness, tiny knees curled to chin, the Earth and her creatures with the Sun and the Moon all moved in their places, each ready to greet you the very first moment of the very first day you arrived.

Fast-forward. Oliver's born and we're home, and it's a typical busy night. I'm reading to Lucy, putting her to bed. Lisa is giving Oliver a diaper change, which he clearly does not like. *Wha! Wha! Wha!*

Lucy says, "*Blar blar!*" At first, I don't get it, but then I understand. "Bear bear!" So we find that crinkly bear, and go to the room where Oliver is lying on the floor, mid-change. And when Lucy gave him the bear, he stopped crying. For us, that was a way to help Lucy into the role of big sibling, to be agentic, to care for a little brother.

There was one other bit of advice we received then: wise words from my friend and colleague David Yeager, a dad several times over. Help the older sibling see every ambiguous act of the baby as an expression of their love, he said. So we told Lucy, "Whenever the baby looks at you, that's how the baby says, 'I love you.'"

Lucy and Oliver are still close today—so much so that Oliver, at least, is ready to be done with us. When he was about six, I was explaining to him what an orphan is. He announced that it'd be okay if both me and Lisa died, because he'd still have Lucy.

PART 3: FRIENDS

For love is not just for lovers. And it's not just for parents and children. It's also for siblings and for friends. Especially as we become older, these relationships become more and more important.

One of the absolute best parts of my job is when grad students defend their dissertations. It's a time to celebrate: what a student has accomplished, what they have learned and taught us, the steps to come for them and for the work, and what they have meant to our community. So, when it's the turn for a student I have advised, I survey other grad students, postdocs, and undergrads in our community a week or so in advance. I ask what has this person meant to you, what difference have they made in your life, both personally and professionally. And then I share some of these appreciations in introducing the candidate.

Doing science and growing scientists are both team efforts. Everyone recognizes the webs of connection, support, and learning that allow us to do our work well. So what people share to honor a milestone like the certification of a new doctor is always wonderful. March 9, 2022, was no different, for it was Kiara Sanchez's turn, and Sanchez is and was a special member of our community. One former grad student described Sanchez's "superpower of intentionally creating, building, and fostering meaningful relationships." A second wrote, "Her efforts in improving diversity and inclusion in the Department have been vast and widely impactful." A third, a student from Nigeria, shared, "Kiara is the first person at Stanford who understood and connected with me as a new grad student

6,000 miles from home. In fact, my first Thanksgiving dinner ever was at Kiara's home."

But superpowers don't come naturally. When Sanchez entered Rice University in 2012 as a kid from Laredo, Texas, a nearly all-Latinx town, she was eager to join a more diverse community. But she struggled to fit in. In one essay, she wrote, "When an acquaintance said that my border accent sounded 'so stupid,' why did my close White friend laugh? Why did White friends seem to clam up every time I tried to explain a fun part of Mexican culture? I quickly learned to downplay my Latina identity in front of White friends."

Experiences like these are painful. For Kiara, as for many social scientists, this personal pain gave rise to a scholarly interest—for her, an interest in friendships between people from different groups. This is important for all of us. For a diverse society to function well, we all need to make friends with people from other groups: so we can understand and integrate our different experiences, so many can become one. Yet it's not only that our schools and neighborhoods are structured so people have less opportunity to become friends with people from other backgrounds. Even when we form these friendships, they're less stable. Cross-race roommates in college, for example, are less close than same-race roommates. And these relationships are more likely to erode over time. Why might that be?

The essential fact of cross-race friendships, Sanchez saw, was that the two friends have different race-specific experiences. But people might struggle with sharing those experiences, both positive ones, like celebrations of in-group pride and culture, and negative ones, like experiences of bias. A question looms: *Can I be fully me with you?*

That might constrain friendships, for disclosure is like rocket fuel for relationships. Have you ever seen headlines, usually around Valentine's Day, like "The 36 Questions That Can Lead to Love?" It's not just a cheap pop quiz. It's based on actual research by the psychologist Arthur Aron. In a 1997 study, "The Experimental Generation of Interpersonal Closeness," Aron showed that having strangers take turns asking and answering questions that prompt increasing levels of self-disclosure makes people feel closer and closer to each other.

Here's a question from early in Aron's protocol: "Given the choice of anyone in the world, whom would you want as a dinner guest?" (For me? Kurt Lewin and Jacqueline Woodson for sure. Michelle Obama and Viet Thanh Nguyen. Jim Abbott and Dolly Parton.) Here's one from later, "If you were to die this evening with no opportunity to communicate with anyone, what would you most regret not having told someone? Why haven't you told them yet?" (Um . . .)

Sanchez knew that people of color had reason to hold back in sharing experiences specific to their racial identity with White people, even with White friends. She'd learned to clam up herself when she first got to Rice. But that holding back might be problematic. Being known is foundational in relationships. No one wants to feel like a stranger in their own relationship. Could the right procedure help cross-race friends begin to share?

A Threatening Opportunity.

Sanchez began by exploring how Black people feel about sharing experiences specific to their race with friends, especially White friends, and how White friends feel in return. Interviewing Black and White adults, she found that friends from both groups anticipated both risks and benefits in these conversations. Both said they'd feel closer and would understand each other better, if race-related experiences were shared. But everyone had worries. Black friends feared being disrespected or having their experiences dismissed. When Sanchez walked Black people through a situation in which they could share a race-related experience, they said they'd share their experiences with most of their White friends. They also *wanted* their White friends to understand their experiences just as much as their Black friends. But they also said they'd feel less comfortable sharing with White friends than with Black friends (or with other-race friends), and that they'd be less likely to do it. That was the case even when they felt just as close to their White friends.

For their part, White friends feared making a mistake in a conversation about race and being labeled racist. When asked how they'd respond if a Black friend shared an experience with race with them, they too said they'd feel less comfortable than if the conversation were about something else. But they also said this sharing would make them feel closer to their Black friend, almost as if they'd be honored to be entrusted with this experience. And they said they'd feel more comfortable if a Black friend shared their experience directly with them than if they learned about the same experience independently.

Sanchez called it "a threatening opportunity." Both Black and White friends wanted to talk about race, but both had concerns. *Will I be heard and respected? Will I make a mistake and be seen as racist?* These concerns are grounded in the reality of American race relations. Black people sometimes are disrespected, their experiences discounted. White people sometimes are called racist, a label that sticks. Other research had shown that these fears can muck up interactions between Black and White strangers. Sanchez was finding they were popping up even between friends. Actually, they might even be more troubling with friends. *Is there something wrong in our friendship?* It was easy to understand how friends might avoid race then, even friends who are close in other ways.

The concerns are real, but so are the costs. Sanchez quotes from the 2018 film *The Hate U Give*. The Black protagonist Starr Carter tells her White boyfriend, "If you do not see my Blackness, you do not see me."

At Stanford, Sanchez's dinner parties were legendary among grad students for their melding of Mexican and other cuisines (all spicy!). And she was a leader in our community in creating belonging for people from all groups, especially during the traumas following the murder of George Floyd, and in supporting younger students of color when they faced instances of discrimination. All of that involved talking, sharing experiences and feelings. So, Sanchez wanted to learn what might happen if you created a well-structured opportunity for Black people to share an experience with race with a good White friend. How would that conversation go?

What if Feeling Uncomfortable Meant You Care?
To learn, she developed a procedure for Black and White friends to have a personal conversation over Zoom. It was a lucky stroke be-

cause, as it turned out, most of the data had to be collected during the COVID-19 lockdown. She focused on college students, because it's in young adulthood when people often form lasting adult friendships. Because race plays a more direct role in the lives of Black people, Black friends would do the sharing. So, at every step, Sanchez gave them agency. First, Black college students identified friends with whom they'd be willing to share an experience from their life. If they listed a White friend, this person was then recruited. Then the Black friend was asked what they'd like to share with this friend. To learn how race-related conversations go, Sanchez asked one group to share an experience related to their "personal life" and a second to share an experience related to "their race or ethnicity."

Those two conditions explore just the effect of talking about race. But there was a third condition too. For Sanchez wanted to do everything she could to help friends make that conversation productive. She knew that talking about race provoked discomfort for both Black and White friends. That discomfort could serve as a tifbit. *Does discomfort mean the conversation is going to go badly? That we should avoid this topic? That our friendship is in trouble?* So, working with a team of racially diverse research assistants, Sanchez created a brief exercise to surface and address this question.

She called it a "friendship-affirming reflection." The materials were the same for both the Black and the White person in the friendship. They shared the findings from Sanchez's earlier research that most people recognize the benefits of talking about race with friends from other groups. They also surfaced the fact that people can feel uncomfortable in these conversations and described this as normal ("sometimes it can feel a bit awkward or uncomfortable at first. And that's reasonable because people have different experiences"). She included stories from other friends describing the anxiety they felt in talking about race but how they worked through this anxiety and how these conversations then strengthened their relationships.

Here's the design and one of the stories Sanchez shared in that third condition.

NON-RACE CONVERSATION 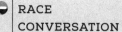	RACE CONVERSATION	RACE CONVERSATION + FRIENDSHIP-AFFIRMING REFLECTION
1. The Black friend chooses an experience "related to your personal life" to discuss. 2. The White friend knows this is the prompt the Black friend is responding to. 3. [No reflection exercise] 4. Friends talk.	1. The Black friend chooses an experience "related to your race or ethnicity" to discuss. 2. The White friend knows this is the prompt the Black friend is responding to. 3. [No reflection exercise] 4. Friends talk.	1. The Black friend chooses an experience "related to your race or ethnicity" to discuss. 2. The White friend knows this is the prompt the Black friend is responding to. 3. Both friends complete the friendship-affirming reflection. 4. Friends talk.

FRIENDSHIP-AFFIRMING REFLECTION

SAMPLE STORY

"I went and saw the movie *Black Panther* with a group of Black friends. I felt this huge collective sense of joy in the room watching a movie that so positively represented Black people. Later I hung out with my friend Emmy, who is White, and I wanted to share with her how good it felt as a Black person. I could see she was unsure what to say at first, but she had good intentions and was actually more open than I would have realized. So we talked more. Now it feels more normal to talk with her about things related to race, even negative experiences. Of course she doesn't know exactly what it's like to be me, but I do know she has my back. It's good to know I can be myself around her."

After reading these stories, both friends were asked three questions about the benefits that talking about race could have; challenges to these conversations; and what they could do to overcome these challenges. (These questions were inspired in part by the questions Eli Finkel used to "save marriages.") Here's how Sanchez put them:

1. What are some benefits you think can happen from talking about race with friends of different racial groups, including for yourself and/or your friendship?
2. What, if anything, might get in the way of you and a friend experiencing these benefits?
3. Considering your role in these conversations, what can you do to help overcome these obstacles and experience these benefits?

After the Black friend decided what to share and both friends did, or didn't do, the friendship-affirming reflection, the friends came together for an unscripted Zoom conversation.

What did friends talk about? Here's what one Black friend shared in the "race or ethnicity" condition:

> I think being biracial in a predominantly white area where there's no diversity . . . you see a bunch of white people. And then you see how the media portrays black people, and you're just like, black people are bad, white people are good, but then you see the way people treat you and . . . it's hard because they're always saying like these things that try to relate me to the people that they're saying are bad. . . . But they're also saying I'm a good one.

The first thing that was apparent when Sanchez watched the videos of these conversations was that they were, almost universally, amazing. Asked to talk for ten minutes, friends spoke on average for nearly twice as long. The conversations were deep and personal, both when they weren't about race and when they were. Afterward, both the Black person and the White person in the friendship rated the conversation as very positive—with scores nearly at the top of the scale—and reported having been highly engaged in it. And the two friends felt closer to each other after the conversation than they had before. It was just as positive when friends talked about race as when they didn't. One Black woman said afterward, "It was cathartic to open up and I feel like [friend name] may see me as a more complex person. My opinion of [friend name] was already good but it improved in terms of trust." A Black man said, "She listened to me and understood where I was coming from which was really all I wanted walking away. We aren't super close but I feel like that could change in the future and this conversation really showed me that." On those immediate outcomes, the friendship-affirming reflection didn't matter. It couldn't have made the conversations go better. Friends just needed a dedicated space to talk.

But fascinatingly, the reflection exercise began to matter over time. It stabilized the friendships, particularly for Black people. When Sanchez surveyed friends two to eight months later, she found that Black friends in the first two conditions showed declines in their feelings of authenticity over time and in their closeness. Compared with before the conversation, they felt they could be less authentic with their White friend "about aspects of yourself that are important to you." And they felt less "close," less "connected," and less "trust." That was the case when friends hadn't talked about race and, in Sanchez's data, even when they had. Friends were spiraling down.

But in the third condition, when both friends had had the opportunity to reflect on the value talking about race could have for them and their friendship and to consider how discomfort could be normal and reflect their commitment to each other, Black friends felt just as authentic and just as close with their White friend as they had months earlier. And they reported feeling somewhat more comfortable talking about race with this friend than Black friends did in the two comparison conditions.

So that exercise had improved the spiral between friends. But how? Was it because the reflection had affected Black friends directly, such as by helping them open up and share more in that first conversation or later? Or were White friends affected directly, such as to be more responsive and welcoming, then or later? Was it both? We don't yet know. And we don't know if these benefits will replicate in another test, or for other groups. But we'll learn.

In a classic series of studies, the psychologists Nicole Shelton and Jennifer Richeson found that both Black and White people wanted more contact with the other group. When asked why they didn't initiate that contact, each group said they were nervous about being rejected. But when asked why the other group didn't, both thought the other group just wasn't interested.

Getting beyond this assumption might take a little faith. It might take thinking through the discomfort you experience, and asking if you can experience that discomfort as a reflection of your care, not a reason to hold back, and something that can improve. It might also help to know that these conversations tend to go better than you'd expect. In the end, sharing our experiences and getting perspective with each other is one of the most effective ways to build better relationships. It's the day *we* begin.

You might feel as if you have no power if a relationship begins to get sucked downward, as if inexorably into a black hole. But Denise Marigold, Eli Finkel, Karina Schumann, Daphne Bugental, and Kiara Sanchez show we do have some control. There are things we can do, at different times and in different contexts, to stabilize our relationships and even to help them spiral up.

KNOW IT. OWN IT. USE IT.

Know your questions. Use your answers.

Here are some of the questions this chapter has covered.

Does my partner really love me?
Does my partner value and respect me?
Is our relationship in trouble?
Am I a bad parent?
Is my baby a bad baby?
Can I be fully me with a friend?
Can we talk about race (or identity or difference)?

Pick one of these questions. Then do either part 1 or part 2 or both with regard to this question.

Part 1: Think about yourself, your life and circumstance. *Then write down your answers to these questions.*

1. What's a tifbit you've experienced relevant to this question —something small that happened that you had a disproportionate response to? How does that tifbit reveal how this question comes up for you, what exactly the question is for you?
2. Why is that question normal and reasonable for you, given your circumstance—but not necessarily true (or not the only way to think about it)?
3. How can you answer that question in a way that will be healthy and productive and authentic for you? What's a better answer, and how can you *offer* yourself that answer and try it out?*

Part 2: Think about someone else, someone you care about: a friend, a family member, someone you work with or for. Consider their life and circumstance. *Then write down your answers to these questions.*

1. What's a tifbit they've shown relevant to this question? How does that tifbit suggest how this question comes up for them, what exactly the question is for them?

2. Why is that question normal and reasonable for them, given their circumstance—but not necessarily true (or not the only way to think about it)?

3. Given your role and relationship, how can you help this person answer that question in a way that will be healthy and productive and authentic for them? What's a better answer, and how can you gracefully *offer* that answer to them so they can build it out for themselves?* *For instance, describe your own experience with a question like this, and how you are or have worked through this.*

---

* Remember the principles for thinking through "bad" events:

Principle 1: Avoid negative labels (*I'm not bad*)

Principle 2: You're not the only one; you're never the only one (*It's normal*)

Principle 3: Recognize causes that don't malign you or others (*I/you face real obstacles*)

Principle 4: Forecast improvement (*It can get better*)

Principle 5: Recognize opportunities (*Silver lining*)

DIGGING DEEPER
REFLECTION EXERCISES FOR YOU AND
YOUR PARTNER

*Want to try one of the romantic relationship
interventions?*

Marigold's "More Than Words"

This exercise was designed for dating couples, but anyone in a long-term relationship could try it. This version is designed for both people to do before talking about a conflict. If you want to do it on your own, just do No. 2.

1. Independently, think of three to five issues or topics that have been a recent source of disagreement in your relationship. Write down a few words to identify the issue (for example, spending time together, other friendships, level of commitment). Then share with your partner and identify together what is the most significant area of unresolved disagreement in your relationship.
2. Working independently, think of a time when your partner told you how much he/she liked something about you. For example, a personal quality or ability you have that he/she thinks very highly of, or something you did that really impressed him/her. Explain why your partner admired you. Describe what it meant to you and its significance for your relationship. Write down your answer.
3. Think about the area of disagreement you identified. Think back to the last major disagreement you two had about this issue and then try to resolve it. Remember what you were arguing about and why you were upset with your partner. Remember what you were thinking about and how you felt during the disagreement. After remembering these things,

discuss this issue with each other. Tell the other person what it is about his or her attitudes, habits, or behaviors that bothers you.

Finkel's Benevolent Third-Party Perspective

This exercise was designed for married couples, but anyone in a long-term relationship could try it. It's designed for both people to do but independently of each other.

1. Briefly provide a fact-based summary of the most significant disagreement you have experienced with your spouse over the preceding four months, focusing on behavior, not on thoughts or feelings.
2. Think about the specific disagreement that you just wrote about having with your partner. Think about this disagreement with your partner from the perspective of a neutral third party who wants the best for all involved; a person who sees things from a neutral point of view. How might this person think about the disagreement? How might he or she find the good that could come from it?
3. Some people find it helpful to take this third-party perspective during their interactions with their romantic partner. However, almost everybody finds it challenging to take this third-party perspective at all times. In your relationship with your partner, what obstacles do you face in trying to take this third-party perspective, especially when you're having a disagreement with your partner?
4. Despite the obstacles to taking a third-party perspective, people can be successful in doing so. Over the next several months, please try your best to take this third-party perspective during interactions with your partner, especially during disagreements. How might you be most successful

in taking this perspective in your interactions with your partner over the next several months? How might taking this perspective help you make the best of disagreements in your relationship?

Repeat every few months.

Schumann's "Big Picture Perspective"

This exercise was designed for couples in committed relationships. It's designed for both people to do on their own before talking about a conflict in a relationship.

1. Occasionally, you will experience conflict with your romantic partner. From now on, when you find yourself in a conflict situation with your partner, take a moment to reflect. Try to take a step back and *see the bigger picture*. Ask yourself: What matters most to you? What are *the important values* that guide your life? Then take a moment to *think about the conflict with your partner while considering these important values*. Try to do this every time you have a conflict with your partner.

To summarize, when you're in a conflict with your romantic partner, take a moment to:

a. Take a step back and see the bigger picture.
b. Ask yourself: What are the important values that guide your life?
c. Think about the conflict with your partner while considering these important values.

Take five minutes to reflect. Feel free to jot down some notes or ideas.

2. Consider general areas in which couples may have conflicts (for example, money, communication, jealousy). Identify with your partner a problem area for you to discuss.

3. Discuss this problem area with your partner. Say whatever you would like to say to each other about the topic.

SANCHEZ'S FRIENDSHIP-AFFIRMING REFLECTION

Want to talk more about race-related experiences with friends from other racial or ethnic groups?

This exercise was originally designed to be done by Black and White friends, immediately before a conversation about a race-related experience. But outside a structured setting you can just try it yourself, or with a friend or group, before finding the right time and place for a conversation.

In general, this exercise assumes that most conversations about race begin with the experiences of people of color, because race can play a more direct role in their lives. If you're a person of color, you can think about an experience related to your race that you'd like to share.

But people of color don't always have to start these conversations. If you're White, how does Whiteness affect your life? What questions about your friend's experiences can you ask gently and appropriately? How can you open a space of learning and discovery for each of you?

The specific topic or experience you share could be positive or negative, in the past or ongoing, whatever you like.

Step 1: Read

When we've asked about conversations with friends about race, 86 percent of Black and Latinx people and 91 percent of White people said there were benefits to these conversations, for themselves or for the relationship. Sometimes there are important benefits that aren't even immediately visible.

Sometimes it feels normal to talk about race, and sometimes it can feel a bit awkward or uncomfortable at first. And that's reasonable, because people have different experiences. However you feel is okay.

Why can it be good to talk with friends about race?

Most of the time, friends have good intentions with each other. And as friends talk more, they can become more comfortable, learn more about each other, and become closer, or gain other benefits.

When we've asked people about their experiences, here is what a few of them said:

> I went and saw the movie *Black Panther* with a group of Black friends. I felt this huge collective sense of joy in the room watching a movie that so positively represented Black people. Later I hung out with my friend Emmy, who is White, and I wanted to share with her how good it felt as a Black person. I could see she was unsure what to say at first, but she had good intentions and was actually more open than I would have realized. So we talked more. Now it feels more normal to talk with her about things related to race, even negative experiences. Of course she doesn't know exactly what it's like to be me, but I do know she has my back. It's good to know I can be myself around her.

> I'm White and my friend Leon is Black. When we first started talking about race and he shared some of his experiences, I'll be honest, I felt a little awkward. I didn't want to say the wrong thing, or for him to think I was ignorant. But as we talked more, I realized that it didn't have to be awkward. The truth is, I didn't get it, but that was ok! Of course we've had different experiences. Nobody ever fully gets it but you can get closer to understanding when you listen and share. I think in the long run being open, and talking about our different experiences has made us better friends.

In general, friends are good people to talk with about personal experiences.

When people have experiences that matter to them, both positive and negative, they often turn to friends to share and listen. For most people, these conversations are about being able to share experiences and understand each other better.

When it comes to race, many friends say they want to be able to learn, to support each other, and to be able to be more of themselves. For example:

> In my experience, these conversations can go in a variety of ways. But what's most meaningful for me is when I feel like I'm really being heard, that my friend has been able to listen to me even if they don't always have answers.
>
> *(Latina woman, aged thirty-four, Estes Park, Colorado)*

> I see my goal in these conversations as listening and supporting my friend. I think it's important, because I know it can be difficult to talk about. I want my friend to feel comfortable sharing that part of their life with me, even though we have different experiences with race.
>
> *(White man, aged twenty-nine, Boston, Massachusetts)*

Step 2: Reflect

Write down your thoughts about these questions.

1. What are some benefits you think can happen from talking about race with friends of different racial groups, including for yourself and/or your friendship?
2. What, if anything, might get in the way of you and a friend experiencing these benefits?
3. Considering your role in these conversations, what can you do to help overcome these obstacles and experience these benefits?

Step 3: Have a Conversation

You can begin by sharing or asking a question. Sometimes it helps to clarify your intentions: "I've been thinking about . . . ," "This has been on my mind and I wanted to share . . . ," "I'm curious about . . ."

Chapter 7

Can I Trust You?

Leave it to the simple-minded to understand
only one side of a contradiction.
—VIET THANH NGUYEN, *THE COMMITTED*

"She Thought He Would Kill Her. Then She
Complimented His Orchids."
—*THE NEW YORK TIMES*, JULY 30, 2019

I t was a sunny afternoon years ago in the placid days before Lisa
and I had kids. I'd run an errand in the nearby town of Mountain
View and was gliding on my bike through a parking lot at the train
station to return to campus when a uniformed Caltrain employee
looked my way. "No biking on the platform!" she yelled.

"I'm *not*," I shouted back, furious. I was in the bus lane. At least
give me a chance to break the rules before you accuse me of breaking them. But already she was gone.

A big lesson of Sandra Murray's research on close relationships
is that it pays to assume the best in other people. If you treat people

as who you want them to be, more often than not they'll become that good person you envision. That doesn't mean sticking your head in the sand, ignoring problems, or being taken advantage of. It's just the place to start. And that's true not only for friends and lovers. It's also true for computer programs. Starting "nice" is the first move of the most famous four lines of code in the history of game theory. You might know it as tit for tat.

In 1980, while I was toddling about Ann Arbor in diapers, my fellow city resident Robert Axelrod, a political scientist at the University of Michigan, held a computer tournament. Axelrod was interested in the origins of cooperation. How do people (or other organisms, or institutions) come to cooperate in a dog-eat-dog world where each person can exploit another? He invited people to program responses for the game, which he called a Prisoner's Dilemma game. Imagine two prisoners accused of conspiring in the same crime, held in different cells. Each prisoner has a choice: To hold out, stay mum, and continue to cooperate with their partner. Or to confess, to sell out, to "defect" in Axelrod's terms.

The tricky part of the game is that what's best for you is worst for us. Suppose your partner continues to cooperate with you. If you confess, they'll get lots of prison time, and you very little. If your partner confesses, you're still better off confessing. So, no matter what your partner does, your personal outcome will be better if you defect. But together you'll get the least total time if you both keep cooperating, hold out, stay mum.

Axelrod wanted to learn what strategies work best in a game like this, and not just if you played once but if you played round after round with another player. So, he invited academics from diverse fields to write computer programs to guide the behavior of a player taking the role of one of the prisoners. Each round both players would get three points if both cooperated (little prison time, in Axelrod's analogy), and one point if both defected (lots of time). If they diverged, the defecting player got five points (very little time) and the cooperator none (tons of time). The goal was to get the most points.

In the first tournament, Axelrod received fourteen submissions. Each played against each other, against a program that responded randomly, and against itself. Each match extended over two hundred rounds. The programs varied widely. Many were complex, clever, seeking to exploit every advantage. But the tournament is famous because the absolute simplest submission won. Just four lines of code, the strategy is known as tit for tat: Cooperate on the first trial, and then do whatever your opponent did on the previous round. So, if your opponent cooperates, you keep cooperating. If your opponent defects, you defect next too.

Tit for tat was what Axelrod called "nice": it never defected first. In fact, the *eight* highest-scoring programs in Axelrod's tournament were all nice, and none of the lower-scoring programs were. In a second round of the tournament, among sixty-two entries, tit for tat won again. This time fourteen of the top fifteen performers were nice, and fourteen of the fifteen worst entries were not nice.

Suffice it to say that the Caltrain employee was not "nice." She did not begin by presuming the best in me. But I'm sure she had her reasons. I'll bet she'd seen countless bikers cruise right through the bus lane and onto the platform. Maybe there'd been some ugly accidents. Maybe, in her experience, this kind of rule breaking was most common in the middle of the day, when fewer commuters are about and people think there's no problem. Come to think of it, I'd seen cyclists break the rules myself.

So that context provokes questions for her: *Is this biker going to cause problems? Do I have to crack down on him to make sure no one gets hurt?* I'm sure she was just trying to do her job. Still, her presumption left me irate. I fumed all the way back to my office, where I kvetched to Jason Okonofua, one of my first grad students at Stanford and today a leading expert in how to mitigate bias and reduce conflict in school and policing. I'm sure my yelling back did no good for her view of bikers like me. But Okonofua calmed me down.

In Axelrod's tournament, niceness wasn't the only quality that mattered. If a program just cooperated every time, other programs could take advantage of it. So it was also important that tit for tat retaliated: if an opponent defected, tit for tat would defect on the next trial. But equally important was that tit for tat had a short memory. It forgave quickly. If an opponent stopped defecting, tit for tat immediately returned to cooperating. In essence, tit for tat won because it taught other programs to cooperate with it. It created the conditions for positive, cooperative cycles to begin and persist to the benefit of all.

As with computers, so with life. We would all do well to begin with trust, to stand up for helpful rules and good behavior when necessary, and to forgive transgressions quickly. That was one of the big lessons from Sandra Murray's work in chapter 6: Begin nice (idealize your partner), so an upward spiral can begin, but don't be blind. Sometimes you have to stand up for yourself too and demand change.

Axelrod's tournament and the game of love play by the same rules because in each case you're vulnerable to another person. In a romantic relationship, your partner can hurt you, maybe more than anyone else. That's why people sometimes build walls, even walls that might constrain your opportunities for growth or connection.

But it's not just romantic partners. It's authority figures too. The Caltrain employee didn't know me from Adam. But if I broke the rules, that could cause her problems. Nor did the fact that we were strangers make me any less resentful of her judgment. I didn't like how she enforced the rules.

This was just one of many interactions we have with authority figures in daily life. In this chapter, we'll focus on two of the most important: interactions between law enforcement officers and residents of a community, and those between teachers and students in a classroom. The incident with the Caltrain employee could not have been more trivial. Yet consider the frustration she felt with me, the anger I felt in return. How quickly an interaction can spiral out of control. What if people are treated discourteously not just once but time and again? What if this disrespect threatens a person's basic safety or their opportunities for growth? This is a recipe for rage.

We'll name the questions that come up in these interactions, on both sides. We'll look at how these questions work, and we'll follow their logic. Sometimes, they lead people to behave in truly terrible ways. Achingly, their logic can get in the way of the very purpose of these relationships: to keep communities safe and to teach and learn. Yet we'll find ways to get to better answers—answers that help us cooperate and work toward the goals we have and share.

Suppose you're in the Caltrain employee's circumstance. You have reason to wonder whether someone might think or do something bad, something that would violate a rule you're bound to enforce, something that could hurt you or others. Then you don't begin with what you hope another person will do. You begin with what you *fear* they might do.

These fears might come from personal experience, like seeing bikers break the rules. But they could also come from innuendo, whispers heard from established vets about asshole bikers like me. That cultivates fears about how a whole group might behave. It's not just the doubt that Iago sows about Desdemona. It's what "bikers do," like riding on train platforms, putting everyone at risk.

That's a tame one as they go. There are far more dangerous ideas in our society. One is "Black people are violent." That stereotype is powerfully built, well represented in our media, in the stories we tell, and in our minds. You might fully reject that idea. You might come up with a thousand counterexamples. You might find that notion morally offensive. It might make you nauseated. But still, it could provoke a question in a relevant situation. It's late at night and you're lost in a tough neighborhood. You've got $100 bucks in your pocket from a recent ATM stop. A Black man in dreadlocks is standing in a doorway looking your way. *Will he be dangerous?* And if that question is in your ear, you might start to see evidence for this danger. An interaction might escalate.

In this section, in exploring the interactions between law enforcement officers and residents of a community, we're going to center the perspective of the officers. That's because they're the ones walking around with guns; with the legal authority to confine people and, sometimes, to commit violence. Of course, everyone in an interaction contributes to its spiral. But it's officers who begin these interactions and are most responsible for their course.

PART 1: LAW ENFORCEMENT OFFICERS
AND RESIDENTS

How Interactions Can Go Wrong: *Are You a Threat?*
Will You Disrespect Me?

Long before the atrocities in which Michael Brown, Eric Garner, George Floyd, and others were killed, Amadou Diallo, a twenty-three-year-old Guinean student, was approached by police in New York City just after midnight on February 4, 1999. The officers were looking for a serial rapist. When they ordered him to show his hands, Diallo reached into his pocket and removed a wallet. They shot forty-one rounds, hitting him nineteen times. Diallo died at the scene. There was no weapon.

I think we can assume that Diallo, like any resident of New York, would want the cops to find the rapist. It wasn't that he had some contrary intention. The failure of the interaction was a failure of trust, a failure of cooperation.

At the time, Josh Correll, now a professor of social psychology at the University of Colorado at Boulder, was finishing his senior year at Stanford. The Diallo killing led Correll and his collaborators on a multiyear quest to understand how interactions between police and civilians can go wrong. Using a simplified first-person shooter game, Correll gave people a series of images of a single person in a public space holding either a neutral object (wallet, cellphone) or a gun. The task was simple: "shoot" if the person had a gun; don't shoot if they don't. In a seminal 2002 paper, Correll found that people were faster to shoot armed Black men than armed White men. And, when people had to respond quickly, they made the Diallo mistake: they were more likely to shoot unarmed Black men than unarmed White men.

Correll used the shooter game to begin to understand what leads to this bias. The first thing he found was that it's not prejudice, at least not in the way we usually understand it. More racist people didn't shoot Black people more or more quickly. Three separate measures of prejudice didn't predict the bias. In fact, Black people showed the bias too. What predicted the bias, instead, was people's perception of cultural stereotypes: the more people thought that White Americans saw Black people as "dangerous," "violent," and aggressive," the faster they were to shoot Black people.* We now know that other cues that make people think a situation is dangerous increase the bias. In other studies, when people were led to think about a more dangerous neighborhood (South Central Los Angeles versus Beverly Hills), and when the suspect was wearing clothing seen as more threatening (sweatshirt, headband, black baseball cap versus button-up shirt and tie), people were more likely to shoot at unarmed Black people.

If you're wondering whether a person might be dangerous, you might see a gun more quickly—or imagine one that isn't there. In fact, in one study using tools to track where people were looking, Correll found that people looked at objects held by Black people differently than the same objects held by White people, relying more on ambiguous cues. Then a gleam of light on a wallet might appear as a gun. Correll concluded, "The present data thus strongly suggest that participants can truly misperceive simple objects in a manner that is consistent with stereotypic or schematic expectations—that a cellphone or a wallet can actually look like a gun in the hands of a Black man." You're looking for a gun. There's a flash. You see a gun.

The shooter game examines a single dramatic decision: shoot or don't shoot. But that's at the end of an encounter. If an officer is pointing a gun and considering whether to shoot, the situation has already gone terribly wrong.

So, let's step back. How do these interactions begin, and how do they play out? How might they escalate, or how might they defuse?

You're on your normal commute home eager to see your kids when police lights flash in the mirror. *Why are they stopping me?* If you're a person of color, the history of police violence directed at

---

* Correll understood this measure as an indirect measure of participants' own stereotypes, which they might not be willing to fully admit when asked directly.

your community might flash before your mind, maybe some bad stories from family members too. Your fears become acute. *Will they harm me? Will they disrespect me? Will they handcuff me on the side of the road?*

Now say you're the officer. You've just left your kids to begin a 6:00 P.M. shift. Perhaps some of the old-timers have talked of the "thugs" on your beat. Maybe your social media feed has recently featured stories from other cops in scary situations. No doubt you've had your share of encounters with disrespectful motorists. Now you see an old clunker doing fifteen over the limit, a Black driver inside. You wonder, *Will this guy be dangerous? Do I need to take a tough line? Will they disrespect my authority?*

If that's where we begin, neither person starts "nice." But in a traffic stop it's the officer who's in control. They lead these interactions. How do they do it? To learn, my colleague Jennifer Eberhardt brought together a team of psychologists and computational linguists to look at data from body-worn cameras during routine traffic stops. In one study, Eberhardt's team found that officers in Oakland, California, treated Black motorists with less respect than White motorists, even for the same kinds of stops. With White motorists, they were more likely to use formal titles like "ma'am" and "sir," and more likely to assure drivers of their safety ("Drive safe"). With Black drivers, they used more informal titles ("All right, my man") and were more controlling ("Just keep your hands on the steering wheel"). It wasn't just a few bad apples, and it wasn't just White officers. Black officers showed the same disrespect to Black drivers. And that gap in respect emerged right away—in the first 5 percent of the interaction. For all drivers, officers became more respectful as the interaction went on. But that recovery was shallower if the driver was Black.

More disrespect in the first 5 *percent* of the conversation? "My man"? That doesn't keep people safe. In fact, Eberhardt's team found you could predict whether a stop of a Black driver escalated to an arrest, search, or handcuffing from just the officer's first forty-five words. The more officers issued commands and the less they told drivers why they'd been stopped, the more likely the stop ended with a driver in cuffs on the side of the road. Unsurprisingly, when Black men heard clips from the beginning of the interactions that escalated, they said they'd feel more fearful, confused, and unsafe. And they worried more that the officer would use force.

Millions of people have seen the video of a Minneapolis police officer killing George Floyd on May 25, 2020. But consider the first twenty-seven seconds of the interaction. Floyd apologized ("Hey, man. I'm sorry! I'm sorry"), asked why he'd been stopped ("What we do, Mr. Officer?"), expressed his innocence ("I do nothing! I do nothing!"), explained why he was scared ("I got shot before. I got shot"), exclaimed ("Oh, oh, oh!"), and pleaded ("Please, please, Mr. Officer!"). At every turn, the officers responded with orders: "Put your fucking hands up right now," "Jesus Christ, keep your fucking hands on the wheel." That's an interaction gone wrong before it began.

The George Floyd case was egregious. Thankfully, all four officers were convicted, the lead officer of murder, and are serving time in prison.

When an officer is as out of control as that, there might be little you can do in the moment. But Correll found the shooter bias was systematic. Eberhardt found the same in disrespect to Black motorists. Another study, which looked at use-of-force records in a large metropolitan police department on the West Coast, came to the same conclusion. It found that officers started interactions with Black and Latino suspects with greater force than they did with White suspects. With White suspects, officers increased their use of force over the course of the interaction, particularly if the suspect posed a threat to themselves or others. They were responsive. But with Black and Latino suspects, they just used more force from the start.

Why?

Were officers really lost in racial stereotypes? To learn, in one study, Correll asked people to read a newspaper article that described a series of armed robberies, including a police sketch of the suspects, before they played the shooter game. When the suspected robbers were Black men, people showed a large racial bias on the shooter game. But when they were White men, the bias vanished.

It's not just what you read in the media. It's also experiences you have. In another study, Correll gave people the opportunity to practice on the shooter game. When the game was rigged so Black people were more likely to be holding a gun than White people, people showed a larger shooter bias on a second, unrigged round. They also learned to associate Black people with words like "attack," "criminal," "danger," and "violence."

You learn what you're exposed to. You ask the questions that seem relevant. When a stereotype defines a group as dangerous, you ask if a member of that group might threaten you. But then you make the world too. If an officer is expecting an interaction to go wrong, that expectation can make it so. Eberhardt shows that expectation gets expressed in disrespect to Black community members, in ordering people around, in not telling a person why they've been detained, in not assuring them of their safety in a tense situation. No one likes that—especially if you're already worried an officer might harm you or disrespect you. A foundation of policing is that it is a kind of cooperation. "Policing by consent," as Sir Robert Peel, who founded the Metropolitan Police Service in London in 1829, put it. It depends on the legitimacy of officers to enforce rules, the opportunity for residents to express themselves, and the transparency and fairness of police procedures. When that's lacking, things can spiral out of control fast.

When Correll looked at how police officers behave in the shooter game, he found that they do better than regular people in general. They're faster and more accurate overall. They should be. They're trained to handle firearms and difficult situations. Officers do show a racial bias in some respects. They're faster to shoot armed Black people than armed White people. But they tend not to show the Diallo bias. While they sometimes make mistakes in the game and shoot unarmed people, they're not more likely to shoot unarmed Black people than unarmed White people. Good training seems to help.

Those officers, though, are regular "beat cops," people who patrol a particular area, often interacting with witnesses or victims of crime. As Correll and his colleagues write, "These officers have extensive contact with a variety of people, most of whom are (for lack of a better term) *good guys*." But Correll has also tested a small number of officers who served on special units that require them to interact with violent criminals. He writes, "Members of these special units (SUs), which deal primarily with gangs or street crime, may have much greater contact with *bad guys,* and to the extent that these units deal primarily with Blacks and other minorities, the officers' on-the-job experiences may tend to reinforce cultural stereotypes." Correll found that special unit officers show a far higher level of racial bias than beat officers in the shooter game. They were more biased even than untrained community members. Those officers who killed Amadou Diallo? They were members of New York City's special Street Crime Unit (motto: "We Own the Night"), which was disbanded soon after the Diallo killing.

Sometimes psychologists say that stereotypes thrive when we lack information. That implies that special unit officers are ignorant. But they're not. Like anyone, they're just responding to the world as it is presented to them. And sometimes what appears is a terrible idea: *Black people are dangerous.* But could we change that? One of the oldest traditions in social psychology, pioneered in the mid-twentieth century by the Harvard psychologist Gordon Allport, shows that positive contact between people from different groups can improve understanding. Drawing on this tradition, what may be Correll's most important finding is that White people who grew up with more Black friends, who went to school with more Black kids, who know more Black people, show a smaller bias on the shooter task. It's one reason why research like Kiara Sanchez's on how to strengthen friendships between people from different groups matters. From this perspective, the disrespect that officers show Black motorists is a symptom of a broader sickness in society, a reflection of extreme patterns of segregation in neighborhoods and schools and workplaces that make it harder for people from different groups to get to know each other and to build and maintain relationships—relationships that could help all of us set aside ugly questions, like *Will this person be a violent threat?*

How Interactions Can Start Right:
A Transparency Statement

Building and maintaining a truly diverse society is hard work, long-term work for all of us. In the meantime, what can a police department do? In elementary school, my music teacher taught us that the first and last songs of a musical are most important. The first one sets the course. The last is what the audience takes away. But, of course, interactions with police don't always begin or end well. Sometimes it's just a lack of basic courtesy. I've experienced this myself. Once I got pulled over by a Stanford sheriff for biking through a stop sign on campus. Here's how the deputy began our conversation:

> STANFORD SHERIFF: Do you see that octagon?
>
> ME: Yes.
>
> STANFORD SHERIFF: What does it say?
>
> ME: Stop.
>
> STANFORD SHERIFF: And what did you do?

Really? I could do without the sarcasm.

One way police departments have sought to improve trust is through community policing. These are programs in which officers try to build good relationships with a community, even when they aren't actively investigating a crime, and then work with community members to prevent and solve problems. In theory, it's a more respectful approach to policing than the dominant model, in which officers respond aggressively to suspected crimes with investigatory stops and hostile interrogations. Billions of dollars have been invested in community policing, but evaluations find no overall reduction in crime or increase in trust. Instead, it seems, some programs work and others don't.

Kyle Dobson is now a professor at the University of Virginia School of Leadership and Public Policy. As a postdoctoral fellow at

the University of Texas at Austin, Dobson suspected that *how* officers implement community policing might matter. In long hours of
field observations and ride-alongs, he found that even when officers
were trying to build good relations with community members, they
rarely told people this. Then conversations were stilted. In one case,
an officer drove through a city park and yelled out to a community
member sitting on a bench:

OFFICER: You okay?
RESIDENT: Yeah . . . why?
OFFICER: Just wanted to check—it's cold!

In another case, two White officers approached four Black residents having a picnic in a park. They asked, "How are you?" and
"What are you up to in the park today?" The residents responded
"with terse answers." After the officers left, Dobson's team approached the picnickers. They said they were "anxious and unsure
why the interaction was happening" and "felt threatened."

Beginning an interaction like that is a-psychological. It's insensitive to the worries a person might have when approached randomly
by a cop, especially a person of color.

But on occasion Dobson saw officers make their good intentions clear from the start. He wanted to know if that would make
a difference. Working in a community with recent accusations of
officer mistreatment, he approached adults and invited them to
participate in a study of "natural interpersonal interactions." If
they agreed, a few minutes later a fully uniformed officer carrying
a weapon approached the adult and engaged the person in a manner consistent with community policing. The interactions were
short, usually just a few minutes long. Just one thing varied:
whether the officer began the interaction with a transparency
statement—if they explicitly said *why* they were approaching the
person.

There wasn't a script, so officers described their goals in their
own words. Here are some examples.

TRANSPARENCY STATEMENTS IN COMMUNITY POLICING

EXPLAINING *WHY* YOU'RE BEGINNING AN INTERACTION

- "Hello, I'm just out and about walking around, talking to people in the community. Is it okay if I talk to you for a minute?"
- "Hey, my name is [name], and I'm just taking a walk, trying to get to know my community better. You mind if I sit and talk to you for a second?
- "I'm [name] with [department] and I'm just walking around getting to know like everybody that's hanging out in the area. [To] just introduce myself."

How'd it go? Without a transparency statement, the conversations were tense, often monosyllabic, just as Dobson had observed previously. Here's an example:

OFFICER: Hello.

RESIDENT: Hi.

OFFICER: Can I talk to you a second?

RESIDENT: Yeah, sure.

OFFICER: Sure. What's your name?

RESIDENT: [Name].

OFFICER: [Name]. My name is [name].

RESIDENT: Hi, nice to meet you.

OFFICER: I don't know if you can tell. I'm a, I'm, I'm a policeman.

RESIDENT: Mhm.

OFFICER: Um, are you a student here?

RESIDENT: Mhm.

. . .

OFFICER: Have a good rest of your day.

RESIDENT: You too.

OFFICER: Drink plenty of water.

RESIDENT: Yeah.

OFFICER: Refill that.

RESIDENT: Will do.

Afterward, this resident reported feeling threatened by the officer (for example, believed the officer "did not trust you") and little trust (unsure whether the officer would "care about you and your welfare" or "go out of their way to help you").

But when officers made their good intentions clear from the start, the conversations were completely different. Here's an example:

OFFICER: I'm [officer] with [police department]. I'm just walking around, talking to people in the community. Is it okay if I talk to you?

RESIDENT: Yeah, of course.

. . .

OFFICER: Yeah, I'm going to come in and just say hey to you now because I feel like—

RESIDENT: Yes, I'm at the front desk. Just come.

OFFICER: You'll just like need it to like—

RESIDENT: To get through the day. Honestly.

OFFICER: Yeah, to like just switch it up, flip it up.

RESIDENT: No, you should. You should definitely come in. I'm always at the front desk.

OFFICER: I will. I will. Next time, I'm, I'm working tomorrow. You work tomorrow?

RESIDENT: Yeah. No, I actually do.

OFFICER: I'm going to come say hey.

RESIDENT: Yeah, come say hi. Literally. Okay.

OFFICER: Well, it was nice to talk to you.

RESIDENT: It was nice meeting you. I'll see you later.

With transparency statements, the conversations were longer and with more rapport. They were more authentic. At the end of this conversation, the resident said, "At the beginning, I was nervous because I don't like police officers," but "at the end, I was feeling comfortable and like we were friends." Residents approached with the transparency statement felt less threatened and more trust. They reported more positive emotions like "comfortable" and "happy," and they were less than half as likely to express threatened emotions like "afraid," "nervous," or "upset." In later studies, Dobson found that transparency statements were effective for all demographic groups. If anything, they were most helpful for groups that trust police less such as people of color.

Dobson's work focuses on the experience of community members. But reflecting on research on the shooter bias, I wonder if it's just as important for officers. It gives them a chance to have better interactions with community members too, to see how good most people are and want to be.

How Bad Interactions Can End Right: An Apology

That's a way to start. But for police officers, not all interactions can begin well. Sometimes you're chasing down a suspect. But how might that interaction end?

In chapter 5, I introduced my grandmother Vendla and the beloved cabin that she and my grandfather built by hand in the White Mountains of Arizona in the 1930s. Over Memorial Day weekend in 2010, I took Lisa to the Cabin for the first time. We had a wonderful day hiking up and around the local hills, exploring canyons and washes, and admiring the views. The Cabin sits on nearly fifty acres of land, and there's no electricity (or running water), so it's quiet in the evening. We'd gone to bed about 9:00 P.M. But about an hour later we awoke to voices all around us. Flashlights probed every window. Who was it? Were they burglars? For a hot moment I wondered if we might hole up in the bedroom closet while they ransacked the place. But I knew they'd see us when they looked in the right place. Then the voices began shouting. "Come out! Come out with your hands up!"

"Okay!" I said. "We're coming out." I felt my way into the kitchen, blinded by the flashlights pointed in our eyes. It felt like a dozen guns were pointed our way.

"Put your hands up!" someone screamed. I put my hands up. Josh Correll's research, which I was scheduled to teach to several hundred Psych 1 students the following Wednesday, flashed before my mind. I was scared. But I knew it'd be more dangerous yet if Lisa or I were dark-skinned.

When I got to the door, I still didn't know who our visitors were, so I asked. "Who are you?" Only then did they say, "The sheriff." It was vaguely comforting. At least they weren't burglars. At least they had some training.

I said, "I'm going to unhook the door now." I slowly lowered my hand and opened the screen door. As soon as I stepped out onto the deck, they shouted, "Lie down! Lie down!" An officer shoved me down, Lisa right behind me, and clicked on handcuffs. There we were, face-planting the splintery old wooden deck, the one my parents had helped build back in the 1970s.

About eight officers circled us. All young men, all well built, all with bulletproof vests, all with guns drawn. They even had a dog.

"Is there anyone else here?"

"No."

"Is there anyone else here?" they shouted.

"No," I said again. "Not that we know of."

They combed every room and circled the grounds: "Clear!" "Clear!" "Clear!" At last they helped us up. It turns out it's very hard to stand up when you're handcuffed and lying flat on your tummy. We sat down on the recliner chairs on the deck, chilly now with the sun down. An officer found my hiking boots and demanded whose they were. "Mine," I said. "They match!" he cried gleefully.

What were we accused of? I wondered. It's true that we'd been in and out of barbed-wire fences all day. But that's routine in this high desert ranch land. Could some of the neighbors down on the flats have seen us and thought we were squatters?

"We have every right to be here," I said. "This is my family's cabin. This is my family's land. My grandparents built this place." Could we call someone? Could we show them Grandma's book, which described the building of the Cabin?

Then they separated us, Lisa in the kitchen, me on the deck. And then they Mirandized us. "You have the right to remain silent. Anything you say can and will be used against you in a court of law. You have the right to an attorney. If you cannot afford one, one will be appointed to you. Do you understand these rights as they have been read to you?"

It was surreal. *You have got to be kidding me,* I thought. This could be a huge problem. We were hours from the county seat. It was late at night on a long weekend. There was no way we could find a lawyer. And I was due to teach next week. So, I agreed to talk.

The deputy said, "Did you commit a burglary earlier today?"

"I committed no burglary."

It soon became clear that a burglary had been committed at a property on the flats, several miles away. The owner had walked in on the act and chased the burglar, but he'd gotten away. The deputy explained they'd been tracking the burglar for the past five hours, and the trail led directly to our driveway at the base of the hill. Moreover, he said, the prints matched my boots—with a distinctive oval right in the middle. And the dog had followed a scent right up the hill to the Cabin. It didn't look good. I imagined the *Stanford Daily* headline, "Psych Prof Jailed!"

The deputy began to interrogate me. Where were we from? California. Where in California? The Bay Area. Which bay? The San Francisco Bay Area. Where in the Bay Area? Stanford. Why were we in Arizona? What had we done that day? Lisa got even more specific questions. When did you arrive? What did you eat these last few days? Can you provide a receipt for the food you bought?

I gave a detailed account of our day, and little by little, it seems, the deputy began to trust me. At last, he decided to take off the handcuffs, and after a brief terrifying moment ("Do you have the keys?" "No, do you?") we were freed. Then the deputy asked me to walk down the hill with him to reconstruct exactly where we'd walked. I felt a lot better when he got a radio call from someone called the commander and heard him say that they had two suspects in custody but that he didn't think we'd done it. Phew!

As I showed the deputy where we'd walked, I realized he was trying to figure out where they'd lost the trail. As we later learned, my boot prints didn't quite match the suspect's. And the suspect had been described as five foot, nine inches with dirty-blond hair and a beard. Maybe my brother, scruffy after a few days at the Cabin. But he wasn't there. And I'm five foot eleven, brown hair, no beard.

Months later, my colleague Jennifer Eberhardt would ask me to record the story for a class she was teaching at San Quentin State Prison, just north of San Francisco. At the time it was called the Prison University Project, now Mount Tamalpais College, and she taught the same content as with Stanford undergraduates. I once had the opportunity to do a guest lecture with her at the prison. It was a Sunday afternoon, and it may be the most rewarding teaching experience of my life. I've never had students so engaged, so eager to learn, so eager to share.

When Eberhardt played my story for her students, they didn't bat an eye at the aggression of the officers, at the guns pointed in dark spaces, at the indignity of being handcuffed. Been there, done that. Nor were they surprised when the story continued, when the commander spun in and began interrogating me all over again: flashlight in my eyes, hostile questions.

But what happened next they had never experienced. For everything shifted. Soon the commander too seemed satisfied I wasn't the bad guy. After some milling about we all walked back up to the Cabin, where Lisa was hanging out with her guards. The deputy explained that there'd been a series of burglaries in the area and that they were trying to shut the operation down. He said that when they'd first come up, they thought the Cabin was abandoned, that it was the perfect hideaway. They'd tracked the trail to the base of the driveway, and the dog had led them all the way up. They thought they had their guy. I guess that's why they blustered in SWAT-team style, guns drawn, shouting.

I told him the Cabin was not at all abandoned, that it was much loved and used by the family, and that it needed their protection just as much as any fancy new house in the neighborhood.

He apologized for interrupting our evening and vacation. It was an explicit apology that he and the other officers repeated several times. The commander was particularly impressed with the Cabin. "When was the Cabin built?" he asked. It's a dynamic answer, I said, but it began in 1932. Looking at the bay window in the living room overlooking the valley, he said, "I could sit here with a glass of wine." He spotted the old cast-iron wood-burning stove and told me that he and his wife had one just like it. "This one was built in Tennessee in the 1910s," I said. "We still cook with it sometimes." Meanwhile, I saw the deputy leafing through a copy of my grandmother's book.

Eberhardt's students at San Quentin, mostly Black and brown men, told her they'd been accused countless times of crimes they hadn't committed.

But never had an officer apologized to them. *Not once.* Even when they realized they hadn't done whatever it was they'd been accused of doing, their attitude was more, "Well, even if you didn't do this, you probably did something else. We'll get you next time."

I had thought race mattered at the beginning of the interaction, in that dark moment in the kitchen, with guns drawn. "Hands up!" But maybe just as important was how we recovered from that bad start, how an interaction that started so badly could end well enough.

Later, when we told my parents the story, they were outraged. "Are you going to sue them?" they asked. (No.) A friend deemed the officers incompetent, noting they began questioning me before the *Miranda* warning and that they didn't identify themselves when they came in guns blazing. "That's how cops get killed," he proclaimed. Certainly, guns aren't wanting in rural Arizona. A few years later I would see a grandfather taking his granddaughter to the local library with a gun in his belt.

But by the time the officers left, we actually liked them. We respected them too, and felt respected by them. It was a new experience for me to be treated as a base physical threat, to be handcuffed and shoved to the floor. It was dehumanizing. But they repaired that: By explaining to us what they did and why. By inviting our help in solving the problem. By apologizing to us directly, explicitly, and repeatedly. By expressing interest in the things that were important to us. When they left, they warned us to lock the doors (which locks?), and to not leave keys in the car. They left their business cards and urged us to contact them for updates on the investigation. And they promised to protect the Cabin, especially when no one was there. If the officers hadn't done that, they would have become our enemy—for they would have left hanging the question that their actions had raised: *Are we members of the community in good standing?* But, as it was, we felt valued, citizens in good standing. They were doing their job, and part of that job was to protect us and the Cabin. In the end, the experience was deeply humanizing.

That's what the students at San Quentin never felt.

In Eberhardt's research, she finds that the single strongest sign of respect in traffic stops is whether officers apologize ("Sorry to stop you"). Apologies can do wonders to overcome conflict. They help victims feel validated, reduce retributive aggression, and promote forgiveness. It's not just in law enforcement. A case study at the University of Michigan Health Service found that moving from a deny-and-defend ethos in response to claims of medical malpractice to a disclose-and-apologize approach reduced the time to reach settlements from twenty months to eight and halved litigation costs. When states pass laws that protect doctors from liability if they apologize for mistakes, they see similar benefits.

The following Wednesday I was back at Stanford as scheduled, teaching Psych 1 students about Josh Correll's work, among other things. That night at home I was rapt to read the story of what had happened in the Detroit Tigers' game that day. The pitcher Armando Galarraga had thrown an imperfect perfect game. Having retired the first twenty-six Cleveland batters in a row, Galarraga got the last batter to hit a little dribbler to the first baseman Miguel Cabrera. Cabrera flipped the ball to Galarraga covering first. It was a bang-bang play, but the runner was out. Only the veteran umpire Jim Joyce signaled safe.

The Tigers' manager, Jim Leyland, came out to argue, but to no avail. After the next batter grounded out, Leyland yelled at the umpire, "Jimmy! You blew it! You blew it, go look at the video!" As soon as Joyce got to the locker room, he had the attendant dial up the replay. "I hope I got it right! I hope I got it right!" But it was clear. The runner was out. He'd blown the call.

Then Joyce did something extraordinary. He opened up the umpire room to the media and poured his heart out. "This is a history call." He's crying. "And I kicked the shit out of it. And there's nobody that feels worse than I do. And I took a perfect game away from that kid that worked his ass off all night." Joyce asks if he can talk with Galarraga. When Galarraga comes to the locker room, he hugs Joyce, saying, "We're all human." Joyce apologizes in English and in Spanish until he's overcome. As Galarraga would later say, "Nobody's perfect. Everybody's human. I understand. I give the guy a lot of credit for saying, 'I need to talk to you.' You don't see an umpire tell you that after a game." The next day, when Joyce served as home plate umpire, Galarraga brought him the lineup card before the game began and Joyce wiped away his tears. Later Joyce would say, "I can't even explain the feeling, because there are no words. It's almost worse than my dad's death. That's how bad I felt."

Anyone in a position of authority—whether a cop or a doctor, or an umpire or a teacher—will sometimes make mistakes. But you also have the power to repair that—to repair that trust.

In many communities, relationships between law enforcement officers and residents are fraught. Sometimes, they're broken. Yet I believe we have enormous opportunities to do better. One way to start is to look for inspiration at other kinds of relationships, where people are struggling to trust and overcome conflict, and approaches that have worked there. Consider Karina Schumann's "big picture" approach to romantic conflict. What if officers took five minutes, as a matter of regular practice, to reflect on the big picture values they hold dear and hope to advance through their work? Could that shift how they interact with residents on the beat? Might they be more likely to begin interactions with greater respect, or to end interactions that began badly with an appropriate apology? With time, could that help restore trust and keep everyone safer?

We don't know. But there is reason to hope.

Jason Okonofua developed an approach not dissimilar to this with probation and parole officers. These aren't police officers interacting with residents on a beat but professionals working with people returning to civil society following a period in prison. Okonofua gave probation and parole officers an opportunity to reflect on the value they placed on empathizing with and supporting their clients as they returned to civil life and how this could protect their community. It was a way to help officers set aside ugly questions like *Are all people who have done time bad?* or *Will ex-felons necessarily recidivate?*—questions that could get in the way of a positive relationship with a client. Randomized to 216 officers, this half-hour online "empathic supervision" exercise cut recidivism by 13 percent over ten months among the 20,478 adults the officers served.

That's stunning.

We don't know if something like that would work for regular police officers or for other kinds of law enforcement officials. But these are things we can try. And as we learn, we can begin to implement changes that help.

PART 2: TEACHERS AND STUDENTS

When trust breaks with police officers, things can go wrong in a blink. In school, the burn is slower but no less painful.

You know the dream. The one where you're in class stark naked. Or maybe in just your skimpy hot-night, no-AC tighty whities. If you're me in the fourth grade, you're squirming to get under your chair, desperate to hide. Exposed.

There's an intimacy to school, especially to the relationship of a student with a teacher. You're trying something new. You don't get it. Who sees you? You get mad and have a fit. Who judges you? Those watchful eyes are most often a teacher's. And in the classroom, at least, it might seem as if the teacher were all-powerful, godlike. You're vulnerable.

So, of course, children's literature is full of fearsome teachers. It's not just Harry Potter's Dolores Umbridge. Who can forget Miss Trunchbull, the tyrannical headmistress in Roald Dahl's *Matilda,* who swings Amanda Thripp over the schoolyard fence. "'But don't the parents complain?' Matilda asked. 'Would yours?' Hortensia asked. 'I know my parents wouldn't. She treats the mothers and fathers just the same as the children and they're all scared to death of her.'"

I adored my third-grade teacher. Ms. S. was a wonderful teacher for me. It was the year I came to love reading. She organized a play for us that year, *The Lion, the Witch, and the Wardrobe,* a book I read about half a dozen times. I played the part of Peter the High King and my best friend, Sam, was Aslan. But on a rainy day toward the end of the school year our class got rowdy, and I guess Ms. S. got frustrated. Our classroom had a high ceiling. She gestured up and announced to the whole class that she wished she could "just take some of us up there and just teach us." I knew she wasn't mad at me; I'd be up there with her. But it was crushing to hear. How might that feel to the other kids? The person who knows you best throws you away.

In the 2008 French movie *The Class,* Souleymane, a teenage immigrant from Mali, struggles with French and has various conflicts in class. Still, he thinks he has a strong relationship with his young French teacher François Marin. But two students imply that M. Marin has said something bad about Souleymane in a meeting with the principal. "Sir, sir, I have a question," Souleymane says. "I heard you really wiped me out at the meeting yesterday." M. Marin tries to stonewall Souleymane, but one of the students lays it out. "He said you were 'limited,'" she says, checking her notes. "I underlined it. I was so shocked." Souleymane slouches in his chair, seething: "I'm what? I'm limited?" A minute later, he erupts: "You don't talk to me, man! You don't talk to me like that, wacko!"

At the darkest hour, when the material you're trying to learn seems impossible (French verbs!), or when you're frustrated, angry, and fighting with the world at every turn, it helps if someone can see in you the skilled and good person you can become, and when they share this image with you. This is the gift that Jean Valjean receives at the beginning of *Les Misérables*. Rejected by all after his release from jail, Valjean has been cheated at work and excluded from an inn. Yet when he steals silver from the bishop who has given him refuge, the bishop allows him to keep it: "But remember this, my brother / See in this some higher plan / You must use this precious silver / To become an honest man." Valjean reflects, "I feel my shame inside me like a knife / He told me that I have a soul / How does he know? / What spirit comes to move my life? / Is there another way to go?"

When Urie Bronfenbrenner says, "Every child needs at least one adult who is irrationally crazy about him or her," this is the irrationality. It's a grace, a faith in possibility, treating people as they might become, even when nothing yet justifies that hope. That lets a young person set aside questions like *Am I dumb? Am I a bad person?* or *Will I always have conflicts?* It gives you an image to work up to.

People don't become teachers for the great pay or the comfy working conditions. They do it to be that person in a young person's life, the one who will make a difference. And we can see this difference in data. One longitudinal study of 18,924 students found that having a natural mentor in school during high school increased the rate at which students went to college by twelve to twenty-six percentage points. That's an enormous gain.

I've benefited from this kind of mentorship time and again. My sophomore year of college I took a small class with the eminent developmental psychologist Eleanor Maccoby. Maccoby was one of the first women to break into psychology and became a leading scholar of gender and gender roles. She was already retired at the time, but she'd written a new book, *The Two Sexes: Growing Up Apart, Coming Together*. In class, we read and discussed a draft of the book as she made final revisions. Later, she would give me a copy of it. On the inside front jacket, she wrote, "For Greg, Who *does* think like a psychologist, and may become one. Eleanor Maccoby."

I treasure that book. I've taken it everywhere. Today it sits in a place of honor in my office.

It means a lot when a person you admire so much believes in who you might become. I hope you've had this experience too.

But that's not the experience many students have in school. For many students, school edges closer to Souleymane's: lonely, isolating, judgy, one failure or conflict after another. In a 2021 survey, less than 60 percent of middle and high school students in California reported having a caring relationship with an adult in school. And that study of natural mentors? It found that just 15 percent of students had a school-based mentor—and fewer yet for kids from less well-off families, even as these relationships were especially valuable for them. This is tragic.

Teachers want to teach, and students want to learn. So, what goes wrong? The good news is we can identify critical turning points when relationships in school are at risk. Even better, in understanding the questions that flare up in these junctures, we can design "small" changes that make a world of difference. We're going to focus on three junctures: (1) when students get critical feedback on their work; (2) in transitions, like when students start a new school or grade; and (3) in conflicts, when kids misbehave and teachers have to discipline them. These are make-or-break moments. And they don't just happen in school. What's a time you got or received critical feedback at work; when you started a new job; when a conflict had to be managed at work or in your community?

Just as both people in a romantic relationship can have questions that feed a relationship spiral, so both students and teachers can have questions that feed their spiral. So some of the approaches I'll share will address the questions students face (how to understand critical feedback, how to understand a transition), some address the questions teachers face (how to work through a conflict with a student), and some address both (when students are most vulnerable to being mis-seen or unseen, in the Spotlight). In thinking about policing, we also saw the value of both starting and ending interactions well. Here too we'll see approaches that help students and teachers start right (feedback and transitions), recover from difficult interactions (conflict), or both (in the Spotlight).

It's become a truism that relationships are the foundation of education. But *how* can we build better teacher-student relationships? By focusing on key turning points, we can offer students and teachers better visions of who they can become, together.

Middle School

The joke is that middle school is a time of decline in all things: Kids' grades and motivation. Their self-esteem and body satisfaction. Teachers' patience. Peace and quiet on the home front. But there is one exception, sort of. It's also when conflict and disciplinary problems spike.

For me, a highlight of sixth grade was when a kid in my German-language class got bored one day and decided that the best way to exit our ground-floor classroom was via belly flop out the window. Our kind but hapless first-year teacher, Herr Schmidt, had no idea what to do. In seventh grade, a school-wide hero was the kid who got cut from the school soccer team because he wasn't showing up at practice (apparently it conflicted with his paper route). He took revenge by lighting the gym mats in the center of the school on fire, filling the building with noxious smoke. School was canceled for two weeks until the authorities deemed the air safe. Of course, I was no angel. Once in sixth grade friends and I determined the difference between walking and running was whether both feet are off the ground at the same time in your stride. We then speed walked down the hall, only to be caught by the nasty assistant principal. "No running in the hall!" she shouted. My friends all apologized, but I stood my ground. "I wasn't running," I said, "I was speed walking." "You have an attitude," she said. How could I not? Rumor had it our school had been designed by the same architect who had designed the state prison a few hours away. Sometimes, it felt that way.

The educational psychologist Jacquelynne Eccles calls middle school a "misfit" between development and schooling. It's when kids go from having one primary teacher who knows them well to having a new teacher for every subject—just as relationships with adults become more important and more fraught. It's when teachers increasingly try to control classrooms, just as young people are seeking to make their own choices. It's when social comparisons increase, such as with tracking, just as kids are becoming more sensitive to comparisons. It's when, some evidence suggests, classwork actually becomes less demanding and more rote, just as kids are ready to take on more and work toward becoming the kind of person who can make a difference in things they care about. And, of course, middle school is when everyone is flummoxed by the uneven arrival of puberty and the rearrangement of friendships.

Adolescence is also when young people become more aware of social stereotypes. In one study, my colleagues and I asked a group of middle schoolers if they worried that people in school would judge their "racial group based on the behavior or performance of other people in my race." In college, Black students almost always express worries like this more than White students. But through sixth grade, no one much worried about stereotypes. Only as seventh grade came to an end did worries about stereotypes begin to rise for Black students, especially Black boys. Maybe that's kids getting older and learning more about the world. Or maybe it's because stereotypes thrive more in the relative anonymity of middle school.

Either way it matters. It's a common pattern that students of color get in trouble more than White students. But it's not just kids acting out. In one school in suburban Connecticut, Black students were no more likely to get cited for objective violations like cheating or fighting. What they were cited for, at *three times* the rate for White students, was things like being "disobedient" or "disrespectful." Black students were getting in trouble when interactions went south, when teachers judged them poorly. They were getting disciplined for a bad relationship spiral. The more Black students were aware of this bias early in middle school, the more they lost trust in the school in seventh and eighth grades. In turn, that loss of trust predicted more disciplinary infractions in eighth grade and, even, lower odds of enrolling in college on time at the end of high school. That's the shit hitting the fan. It's Souleymane in a longitudinal data set.

Like any relationship, there are two sides to the relationship between a student and a teacher, and two ways into a system that can go so wrong. You're the student, worried how you'll be treated. *Will I be disrespected, controlled, treated unfairly, put in a box?* You're a teacher, worried about teaching. *Will I be able to get through the next lesson? Is this kid a troublemaker? Do I need to crack down if he misbehaves?* Put those questions together and the dynamic becomes toxic. No wonder middle school can become a mini war zone.

Turning Point 1: Critical Feedback

Why are you criticizing me? Do you think I can't do it? Are you biased against me?

You're a new teacher, fresh out of ed school. You've learned that one of the best resources for learning is good critical feedback: feedback from someone who really knows what they're doing, who takes the time to go through your work and show you what you've done well and how you can improve. You know that's gold for learning.

It's early in the school year, and you've given your students their first writing assignment. You get their essays back and they're all right, but you know they can do better. So, you get to work, going through each student's paper, filling each page with comment after comment, "Yes!" "More of this." "Too long." "I don't follow here." "Confusing." "Doesn't fit here." "Wrong word." "What about . . . ?" "Did you think of . . . ?"

You're up late, and the next day you proudly hand back the marked-up essays. You announce that anyone who wants to use your feedback to revise their work can raise their grade.

The first clue that this isn't going to go well is in your students' body language. They're not leaning in. They're slouching back. When the due date comes, just a trickle of revisions appear in your inbox. One . . . Two . . . To make matters worse, almost no students of color take up the opportunity. You're discouraged, demoralized.

What happened?

Feedback might be gold for learning. But receiving critical feedback can feel like a ton of bricks. Say you're the student. You're already worried, just a little, *Am I dumb at school?* and nervous about your writing especially. You work hard on the first writing assignment, but then your new teacher hits you with a bloodbath of red ink. It feels as if she hates you. She probably thinks you're an idiot. Maybe you are.

If you're a student of color and your teacher is White, that feedback might map onto social stereotypes. Then more questions might flood your mind. *Does she think people "like me" are limited? Is she biased against me?*

Just giving feedback like this is a-psychological; it is insensitive to a student's predictable concerns. But the solution isn't just to not give feedback. How can a teacher (or a mentor, or a manager) give tough feedback without demotivating the recipient? While still in grad school, Geoff Cohen called this "the mentor's dilemma."

Sometimes White people seem to intuit that Black students won't respond well to unvarnished criticism. In one study, Kent Harber, a psychologist at Rutgers University, found that White evaluators sugarcoated feedback on bad work from Black students. It's as if you don't want to seem racist, so you hold back. But that does no one any good. If a student hasn't performed well, they need to know that.

So, a teacher could have the best intentions. You might work hard for your students, give them great feedback, want them to improve, believe they can do it, but still face mistrust. Why? The fact is you never told your students *why* you were giving them feedback. Geoff Cohen realized you needed what Kyle Dobson would later call a transparency statement.

Cohen was inspired by educators like Jaime Escalante, the real-life Los Angeles teacher portrayed in the 1988 film *Stand and Deliver,* whose high standards inspired his Latinx students to take and pass the Advanced Placement Calculus exam at such high rates they were accused of cheating. Escalante told his students he believed in them—that's why he worked his butt off for them.

Cohen thought making those good intentions clear from the start might help. To find out, as a grad student at Stanford in the late 1990s he ran a series of lab studies. He asked Black and White undergrads to write an essay describing a favorite teacher and then had a character, "Dr. Gardiner Lindsay," give the students tough, critical feedback. What varied was just the preface of that feedback.

When there was no preface and Dr. Lindsay just launched into his critique, Black students were suspicious of his motives. They saw him as somewhat biased, and felt equivocal about revising the essay for him, much less enthusiastic than were White students. It wasn't much better when Dr. Lindsay began with generic praise ("Overall, nice job. Your enthusiasm for your teacher really shows through"). Sometimes that's called a shit sandwich. It might feel a bit better, but it's still ambiguous in a critical respect.

What helped was when Dr. Lindsay said exactly why he was giving the critical feedback—because he had high standards and he believed in the student's ability to meet those standards: "The comments I provide in the following pages are quite critical but I hope helpful. Remember, I wouldn't go to the trouble of giving you this feedback if I didn't think, based on what I've read in your letter, that you are capable of meeting the higher standard I mentioned." It was a way to disambiguate his intentions.

Cohen called it "high standards and assurance." Same criticism. But that preface inverts the meaning. It's *because* Dr. Lindsay has high standards and believes you can meet them! No longer did Black students see Dr. Lindsay as biased. And now they were just as motivated to revise their essay as White students, if not more so.

As a young assistant professor at Yale, Cohen took these ideas back to school. Working with a local middle school, he partnered with social studies teachers to create an assignment in which students would write a five-paragraph essay about their hero. Midway through seventh grade, before declines in trust had taken root, teachers gave out the assignment, got students' essays back, and marked them up as usual. But before returning the essays, they gave them to Cohen's team, which appended one of two paper-clipped notes at random. Both notes were handwritten by teachers in advance, so they'd be authentic to students. But teachers didn't know which students got which note, so the study could isolate the effect of the note itself, apart from any shift in teachers' beliefs or behavior. One of the notes was placebic. But the other told students exactly why the teacher was giving them feedback. It was wise to a student's predictable concerns.

PLACEBIC NOTE

I'm giving you these comments so you have feedback on your essay.

MY HERO

My hero is Dr. Martin Luther king JR. My hero has ①*had the*
②*had* ③*had* ④
courage to do what he has to and when he has to do it. He
define
hero
is a testimony to others, and when he was tested he over
⑤ *met the test*
came it. He went through trials after trials and he did not
hold a grudge. ⑥*had or was*
courageous
First, Dr. Martian Luther kin JR has courage. He did
Give
Good- use not have to speak for "his people" but he did it because he *more*
this earlier
w/courage cares. King lead some civil rights movements in his time. *details*
maybe
Dr. King also gave a speech in front of 200, 000 of his

supporters. — *where?*

WISE FEEDBACK NOTE

I'm giving you these comments because I have high standards and I know you can meet them.

MY HERO

My hero is Dr. Martin Luther king JR. My hero has ①*had the*
②*had* ③*had* ④
courage to do what he has to and when he has to do it. He
define
hero
is a testimony to others, and when he was tested he over
⑤ *met the test*
came it. He went through trials after trials and he did not
hold a grudge. ⑥*had or was*
courageous
First, Dr. Martian Luther kin JR has courage. He did
Give
Good- use not have to speak for "his people" but he did it because he *more*
this earlier
w/courage cares. King lead some civil rights movements in his time. *details*
maybe
Dr. King also gave a speech in front of 200, 000 of his

supporters. — *where?*

This study focused on students earning intermediate grades (B's and C's), for whom an emphasis on the opportunity for improvement would be most fitting. The first outcome was just whether students took up their teacher's invitation to revise their essay for a higher grade. With the placebic note, just 27 percent of Black students did so. Imagine you've burned the midnight oil to give your students high-quality feedback. *They didn't even use it. Do they even care?* But it wasn't that students didn't care. For with the wise feedback note, that rose to 64 percent. White students too were more likely to revise their essay: 82 percent did, up from 64 percent.

Of course, school and relationships don't stop at one assignment. Combining data from this study and a second, similar one, the research team found that single note midway through seventh grade headed off a decline in trust among Black students in school over the rest of the year. In turn, it reduced disciplinary citations the next year in eighth grade for Black students by half. It even increased the rate at which Black students enrolled in a four-year college on time after high school from 45 percent to 64 percent. That's seventeen words, at the right time and place, to increase college-going six years later.

I once presented this research to a group of business leaders in Silicon Valley. A man came up to me afterward and introduced himself as a manager in a tech company. "That wise feedback research," he said, "it's so amazing. I have a lot of people who report to me. Do I have to say it every time?"

Of course not! That would be ridiculous. I give critical feedback to grad students almost every day. If I said "I have high standards and I know you can meet them" every time, it'd be absurd. Quickly it'd become patronizing.

They're not magic words. There's a time and place to be explicit. But the larger point is to develop a culture in which it's obvious that that's why you give feedback. That's why Carol Dweck and I called our lab half-baked. It's a way to make the purpose of feedback clear: that feedback is for growth and because we believe you can reach a high standard. You want that understanding to become common sense, the common ground between you and the people you work with, the default assumption. Then, trust secured, you can each set to work on the task at hand.

It's not just teachers or managers. Sometimes it's just two professionals. After the screenwriter Scott Frank tried his hand as a director, his close friend the director Steven Soderbergh had a "very blunt" conversation with him: "Look, you are a writer who has directed now, but you are not yet a director. You documented what you wrote. But that's not the same as being a director." Soderbergh emphasized that "he loved Frank too much to offer disingenuous enthusiasm, and that he wouldn't have said what he did if he hadn't thought that Frank could ultimately 'get there.'" That's wise feedback: it's explaining why. It was a gift Frank later returned when Soderbergh was stuck editing his 2011 film *Contagion*. "He watched the movie and said, 'You've got huge problems. I don't even know where to start,'" said Soderbergh. Frank's assessment helped Soderbergh cut forty-five minutes from the film. "The fact that he was right, coupled with the fact that he got to be tough on me, was probably a necessary and helpful step in our reconnecting."

There are many ways to build a culture in which everyone knows that tough feedback is because you care, because you believe in each other. One way is just to talk about the meaning of feedback in general. In other studies, researchers have shared stories from older students who describe learning that feedback "is like a treasure," that "teachers who give me feedback that corrects my mistakes are the ones who really care," and that "critical feedback is a sign that the teacher believes in your ability to be really good someday." Sometimes, students get a marked-up essay and practice this way of thinking by imagining its their essay and describing why the teacher provided that feedback. These exercises can raise grades for students in high school and college, especially students of color, reducing inequality.

There's a curious detail in the paper-clipped note studies. The note came from a single teacher, yet it protected students' trust in school *in general*. Students who got that one note were more likely to agree at the end of seventh grade that they were "treated fairly by teachers and other adults at my school" and that "students in my racial group are treated fairly by the teachers and other adults [in my school]." And they were caught in fewer conflicts with *all* teachers the next year. How could a note from a single teacher shift students' views of, and experiences with, teachers in general?

There are at least two ways to think about this question. One is to consider the tremendous importance of going from zero to one. It's much easier to go to a party when you have just one friend there. What's it like to go to school when you know for sure that one teacher believes in you, as opposed to none? Bronfenbrenner emphasized that kids need "at least one adult." In *Matilda,* Miss Honey is the saving grace; she's enough for Matilda to survive Miss Trunchbull. Perhaps the image a single teacher gives of who you might be and who you could become is enough.

Another way to think about this is that as we grow, we develop models of teachers—just as we develop models of police officers or any other group. *What are teachers like? How do I relate to them? Are they good and want the best for me? Or not?* Maybe a well-timed note, just when kids are trying to make sense of all the teachers around them, spurs kids to entertain the idea that if one teacher believes in you, maybe others do too. A young person might carry that model with them.

In the spring of 2023, a photograph brought this idea home to me in the most vivid way. For several years, I'd been working with a team, including a postdoc, Dave Kalkstein, and the group Leading Educators, to create a professional learning series on wise feedback: Teachers learned about the science of wise feedback and then began to implement wise feedback with their students. They surveyed their students about how they thought about feedback, led a class discussion about why they gave feedback, and began to write wise feedback notes to students. The goal was to come full circle from Jaime Escalante, to help teachers use wise feedback flexibly to help their students succeed.

One of the participants in our pilot was a high school Spanish teacher in Grand Rapids, Michigan. Walking through the classroom one day, she saw that one of her students had slipped the wise feedback note she'd written him under his transparent phone case. She snapped a photo and sent it to us. It's not a great photo. Just the back of a cellphone. There's some glare. But you can see her note inside the case, words facing out: "I'm giving you extra help because I have very high standards and know that you can meet . . ."). This child will carry that note with him everywhere he goes. It will be his guide for understanding the feedback he receives, not just from her but from every teacher. It makes me tear up. I could feel the upward shift.

These are moments of exquisite beauty: times you can see things change. And it's not just wise feedback. We'll see the power of one teacher to change the life of a student again and again.

Turning Point 2: School Transitions for Tweens

Can I trust teachers?

In grad school, I spent part of the summer of 2004 in a school library listening to seventh graders tell stories about their transition to middle school. I asked what they liked, what was hard, how their experience changed over time. Kids told me they'd worried they'd get lost, that they'd forget their locker combination, that no one would show them the way. One said, charmingly, "There was a whole lot more people and they were very tall in size." There was the classic peer drama: "I got along with everyone except for one kid. I did not like him and he did not like me. After a few weeks we became good friends." But many of the children's worries focused on teachers. One child was scared teachers "would yell at me." Another said, "I was afraid of them before I knew them for myself." But they also described progress. A third said, "In sixth grade I didn't want to talk to my teachers very much, because I didn't want them to make any impressions. Toward the end of the year when I learned more about them I was more comfortable talking to them." A fourth said that despite not fitting in at first, "I learned everyone felt that way. You just have to be brave and talk to the people around you."

Listening to the kids helped me remember how huge my middle school had seemed at first, how nervous I'd been. So, when Lucy was on the eve of middle school, I showed her my old transcripts from these conversations. She summarized "the main thing" as "things get better." She particularly liked one child, who said that he'd become more confident talking to teachers, "for I've gotten use[d] to them and sometimes I think of them as like extra parents."

Then, at back-to-school night that year, I was delighted when an experienced gym teacher told all of us sixth-grade parents that he'd been walking down the hall in the first week and saw a girl trying to open her locker. When he came back a few minutes later, she was still there. He asked if she needed help and she exploded, crying. "Yes," she said, unable to get her lock to work. He got it. He understood how lost she felt. He knew how overwhelmed kids can feel when they start at a big new school. *Will people here help me and show me the way?*

So that summer back in grad school, Geoff Cohen and I put the stories we heard together in a little package for new sixth graders. We'd have two twenty-five-minute class sessions in the fall to work with. We told students that "almost all 7th graders said they had worried at first that they did not 'fit in' or 'belong' in 6th grade" but "almost all say that now they know that they 'fit in' and belong.'" Then we gave students a few stories from seventh graders. In each story, a student worried at first about middle school and their relationships with teachers, but this got better with time. The stories were surrounded by images of diverse seventh graders to show that these experiences were common for everyone. It was a way to offer students more hopeful ideas about middle school, a bit like the interventions I described in chapter 3 to help college students work through questions of belonging as they came to college. On the following page are two of the stories we told.

We then asked students to put these ideas into their own words. When we asked why sixth graders might worry at first in middle school, one child wrote, "They might thinck [sic] they're dumb and everyone will laugh at them. They might get lost and forget their locker combination." When we asked why this might get better with time, he wrote, "Because their teachers respect you. Because they now have really close friends." I think of this as a trust and belonging exercise, for these issues are closely linked in school. In fact,

TRUST AND BELONGING IN THE TRANSITION TO MIDDLE SCHOOL

SAMPLE STORIES FROM "TYPICAL 7TH GRADERS"

1. "I felt like I had a knot in my stomach in my first few months at [school name]. I was afraid to talk to my teachers. I didn't know them, and the classes are harder. I worried that they thought I was dumb. But they believe in you even when you get bad grades. They want to help you get better, and they helped me do better."

2. "Middle school is scary at first but it gets better. [School name] is big. You have to be more independent and change classes. I worried I wouldn't find my classes, and that I'd forget my locker combination. But [school name] teachers and staff care about you. Once I got lost but the people I asked showed me the way. Even when I got in trouble or didn't do well in class the teachers showed me respect."

one of the best predictors of students' experience of belonging in middle and high school is support from teachers.

This was a randomized experiment, because we wanted to see if this would actually make a difference for kids. In the control group, the materials were similar but focused on mundane topics, like getting used to the school cafeteria. In the end, we tracked students all the way through the end of high school. As each year passed and students' experience in school unfolded, we were more and more astonished. At one point, we applied for a small grant to better grasp what we were seeing and got rejected out of hand. No way this could be, the reviewers said. They didn't believe it.

What we'd seen was that the two twenty-five-minute sessions in the first two months of sixth grade had reduced the number of disciplinary citations Black boys received over the next *seven* years, all the way through the end of high school. It was a reduction from an average of nearly three citations per year to one. In the control condition, Black boys had the highest rate of disciplinary citations of any group by far. But with the structured opportunity to think through issues of trust and belonging, the discipline gap with White boys had closed by 75 *percent.*

If that was all we had, it might not have seemed real, like a fluke. But fortunately, we had a series of measures that let us look more closely at kids' experience. And critically, we were able to bring on to the team a postdoctoral scholar, Parker Goyer, with both terrific statistical chops and analytic skills. What Goyer's analyses would reveal was a toxic dynamic brewing between Black boys and teachers in the control condition—one that the trust and belonging exercise had interrupted.

The first thing Goyer did was to pull out those subjective, relational offenses, like getting cited for being "disobedient" or "disrespectful." Goyer found that in the control condition Black boys started both sixth and seventh grades with low levels of these offenses, but then these offenses spiked as the year went on. It wasn't that Black boys were just behaving badly. Objective offenses like cheating or fighting didn't show this pattern. It looked like relationships spiraling down one year and then again the next year.

Next, Goyer looked at regular reports from students about their experience in school. By the end of seventh grade, after two years of this cycle, Black boys had come to believe that people in their school saw them as a token of a stereotype. They'd also begun to feel that they didn't belong. Then they started eighth grade with high levels of citations for "disobedience" and "disrespect." And then their discipline citations as a whole stayed high all the way through the end of high school. They'd spiraled down.

But with the trust and belonging exercise, Black boys never suffered that spike in citations for offenses like "disrespect" in sixth and seventh grades. With greater faith that relationships with teachers could improve, those relationships didn't erode. Nor did Black boys develop elevated worries about stereotypes or come to feel they didn't belong: their belonging stayed high through eighth grade. And then they got in trouble less all the way through the end of high school.

It had taken fifty minutes to address the questions *Can I trust teachers? Will they have my back?* at the beginning of sixth grade. That had reversed a downward spiral for Black boys over seven years.

Goyer's analyses helped us understand. But it was a small sample. And it was just one spiral in one school. Another study, with a much larger sample, reinforced our confidence in the potential of the trust and belonging exercise. A team led by Geoffrey Borman and Chris Rozek at the University of Wisconsin implemented the same exercise with sixth graders in eleven middle schools in a district in the Midwest. Tracking 1,304 students over one year, they found the exercise reduced disciplinary citations over sixth grade (by 34 percent), increased attendance (by 12 percent), and reduced course failures (by 18 percent) for all students, with some of these improvements larger for students of color and for boys. It's not just middle school. Another team led by Lee Williams and Tim Wilson at the University of Virginia developed a similar exercise for students in the transition to high school. It boosted attendance and helped students develop more friends over ninth grade. It also reduced course failures, raised grades, and reduced disciplinary citations for students of color, cutting racial disparities by 86 to 100 percent. Starting school on the right path can take you to a very different place.

Turning Point 3: Conflict

Is this student a troublemaker? Do I need to crack down?
These results are fantastic. They're life-changing for students. But they work with just one side of the coin. Can we help teachers too with the questions they face, and help them make school better for kids? For even as both parties influence relationship cycles, it's ultimately teachers' responsibility to get this right.

Sometimes I think about my sixth-grade German teacher, Herr Schmidt. I really liked him. I could tell he was sincere about teaching us German. But he had no clue how to handle rowdy tweens. When the class clown flopped his way out the window, I'd forgive Herr Schmidt for wondering, *Do I need to punish him to get back control of the class?*

In many ways, we live in a world dominated by a perversion of behaviorism, the idea developed by psychologists like John Watson and B. F. Skinner in the early and mid-twentieth century that behavior is just the product of rewards and punishments. That tradition leads to the simplistic notion that if someone is doing something wrong, they just need to know there will be consequences for that misbehavior. It's the basis for school policies like "zero tolerance" for minor misbehaviors. It's what I suffered when I got put in "time-out" in preschool day after day. We express this punitiveness even with those we love. Good luck finding a parent who hasn't gotten fed up at one point and snapped at their own child, "That's it. Go to your room!" You might know even as you shout that out that it's not the right approach, that it's not who you want to be, that it won't accomplish what you want. But you might do it anyway.

It was appropriate when I got yelled at by the Caltrain employee that I was returning to campus to meet with Jason Okonofua. Now a professor of psychology at Brown University, Okonofua was raised in Memphis, Tennessee, where he and his two brothers were in and out of trouble. Okonofua himself was suspended in middle school, before leaving for a boarding school in Rhode Island. So, when he entered our graduate program at Stanford in 2009, one of the things he wanted to learn was how punitiveness and racial bias might work in school.

Okonofua and I suspected that punitiveness is a cultural default, that it wouldn't take much to prompt it. To test this, in one study, we just reminded teachers of the idea. Experienced teachers read how "consequences lead students to appropriately conduct themselves in the classroom" and "how punishment allows teachers to take control of the class." We asked teachers how this approach could help them "maintain control." Then we shared a real disciplinary record from a student who had disrupted class by repeatedly throwing trash away. We asked teachers how they would respond. Would evoking that punitiveness make teachers more punitive? It sure did. In this case, teachers said they'd give the kid detention, that they'd threaten him, and that they might involve administrators. One said,

He would be given one warning. Once he left his seat the second time, he would be sent to the hall. If he continues to disrupt from the hall, he would be sent to the office.

Maybe that feels right: a warning followed by escalating consequences. But if I'm a kid and that's how my teacher responds, just because I threw some trash away, I'd sure be pissed. In fact, when we gave college students a description of this situation and asked how they would feel about a teacher who treated them like that, they held little respect for the teacher and, ironically, felt little motivation to behave well in class in the future. The punitiveness is self-defeating.

Of course, no one goes into teaching to send kids to the principal's office. People want to make a difference for kids. And, certainly, there's an older tradition in education that prioritizes developing strong relationships with students, especially when they struggle, to help them improve.

So, in a second condition, we prompted teachers with this relational approach. Teachers read how "good teacher-student relationships help students learn how to appropriately conduct themselves in the classroom." When we asked teachers how they'd respond to the very same misbehavior, they were far kinder. One said,

> I would give the class some work to do and then I would talk to [the student] privately. He has a need that is not being met. I would try to understand the need and try to meet it.

Now that's lovely!

It's like teachers are on a knife's edge as they respond to kids who misbehave. A culture guided by behaviorism prompts the question *Do I need to crack down to maintain control?* That's pushing kids away. But a culture focused on relationships implies the opposite, pulling kids closer, talking to them, listening to them, understanding them. And just a little prompt can lead even experienced teachers one way or the other.

From 1973 to 2010, the rate at which students in the United

States got suspended nearly tripled. In the 2017–18 school year, 2.5 million kids lost a total of 11.2 million school days to suspensions. The burden of this conflict and loss of opportunities is grossly inequitable. Black students, in particular, are three to four times more likely to be suspended than White students. For when a punitive mindset gets mixed with racial stereotypes, it's an especially unlovely cocktail.

A police officer sees a Black person in a tense circumstance. He wonders, *Will this person pose a threat?* Then a flash of light might appear to be a gun. A teacher sees a Black student act out. Does she wonder, even in the back of her mind, *Will this student be a troublemaker?* Will she be quicker to see a pattern in his behavior, and quicker to crack down?

To learn how racial stereotypes work in school, Okonofua and Jennifer Eberhardt developed a procedure in which teachers responded to a series of minor classroom misbehaviors. They also manipulated the first name of the student so teachers would think the student was White ("Greg"—how'd they come up with that name?) or Black ("Darnell").

After a first incident, teachers were evenhanded in their response. They were equally troubled by Greg and Darnell's misbehaviors and meted out similar punishment. They weren't willy-nilly biased. But if the student misbehaved a second time, teachers escalated their response to Darnell more. They felt more troubled by Darnell's second misbehavior than by Greg's. They wanted to punish Darnell more, and they were more apt to deem Darnell a "troublemaker." Greg's misbehaviors seemed more like separate incidents. Darnell's seemed like a pattern.[*]

Of course, in the real world, that's how teachers and students interact—over and over again, in close quarters, through good and bad. Then, if you're faster to see a pattern in incidents of misbehav-

---

[*] A methodological note: It wasn't that teachers thought that one particular misbehavior was more severe than the other. Which misbehavior was presented first or second varied for different teachers; in technical terms, it was counterbalanced, isolating the effect of a second misbehavior, whichever it was.

ior, that's consequential. In fact, Okonofua and Eberhardt see a similar pattern in national suspension data. Among students suspended once, Black students are more likely to get suspended a second time than are White students. They called it two strikes and you're out.

When a stereotype provokes a question (*Will this student be a troublemaker?*), we're more likely to see a pattern. But if a teacher cracks down at the slightest misbehavior, that only exacerbates the disrespect and lack of trust students feel—especially if it seems racially biased. *Will I get a fair shot here? Are you racist?* Then students respond in kind, and the two are off to the races, spiraling down.

It's easy to be outraged at teachers' role in this cycle. Those punitive, racist bastards! But going in guns blazing does no one any good. Teachers want nothing more than to make a difference for kids. Just calling them names is simplistic, for even when there is racism, that's not all teachers are, nor all they can be or want to be. That's true for all of us: we're all vulnerable to the influence of bias. And impugning the teacher's character doesn't help. It would end the conversation before it begins. Countless "implicit bias" programs teach people about bias and offer cognitive strategies to reduce it. In school, you might teach teachers about racial bias and then ask them to think about students of color who aren't troublemakers. But I guarantee you that wouldn't help me set aside the worry that another student of color might be. Nor does it help me think through how best to approach a student who is misbehaving. Evaluations find that these programs are often ineffective. Sometimes they're counterproductive. The blame game doesn't help. It only puts more questions on the table, and we're already overloaded.

Okonofua is a calm and wise man. So, together we decided to do the opposite: to focus on the good, not the bad. We took a page from the bishop in *Les Misérables:* we described the wonderful people teachers could be for their students and asked them how they were or were working toward becoming this person. In the "empathic discipline" intervention, using articles and stories from other teachers and from students, we described an ideal approach to working with students when they misbehave: a focus on maintaining strong relationships, even when students misbehave; on listening to and understanding students, even when they're irrational; and on helping students improve within the context of strong relationships. Here are some of the stories we shared.

EMPATHIC-DISCIPLINE EXERCISE FOR MIDDLE SCHOOL TEACHERS

SAMPLE STORIES

From a middle school student

"In middle school, I didn't feel like I belonged. It seemed like the teachers always called on the other students. So I didn't pay attention in class and sometimes I got in trouble. One day I got detention and, instead of just sitting there, my teacher talked with me about what happened. He really listened to me. And then he told me that he had trouble sometimes in middle school but that it gets better. It felt good to know I had someone I could trust in school."

From a middle school teacher

"When I was a child, I remember worrying about how I would be treated by teachers at my school. But I will always remember Ms. McBride, who treated me with respect and trust. She showed me that teachers could make all the difference in how students feel about school."

There's nothing radical here, nothing new even. This isn't rocket science. It's just reminding teachers of who they really want to be with their students, the kinds of relationships that probably brought them into teaching in the first place. It's inviting teachers to bring this model to interactions with their own students when they misbehave.

So, after reading these materials, we asked teachers how they build and maintain strong relationships with students, especially students who are struggling, who aren't participating, or who are getting in trouble ("saying is believing"). Then they shared advice for future teachers about how to work with students when they struggle. That way teachers could begin to translate the basic ideas into their own practice.

There are some details in the empathic-discipline exercise that, I think, are especially important. One is that the materials don't say not to discipline kids. All of us need good rules sometimes to stay in line. They just say to discipline in ways that pull kids closer, not push them away.

The second is that, even as the materials never accuse teachers of being racist, they're not blind to race. Okonofua and I knew that teachers could well look around their class and see that kids of color really were acting out more than other kids. We'd seen that in our own data. In a teacher's experience, that might be true year after year. But what teachers might not see is the worries about belonging and respect that contribute to this. And if they don't see that, their observation could just feed a suspicion, *Maybe kids of color really are troublemakers?*

We wanted to help teachers think about misbehaving kids of color without blaming the kids (troublemakers) or teachers themselves (racist bastards). So, we told teachers the truth: that kids of color can have legitimate concerns about how they're seen and treated, and that means it's especially important to take an empathic approach with them when they misbehave.

Sometimes, when I present the empathic-discipline work, I cry. There are several reasons. One is because of how beautifully teachers responded to our materials. Here are some examples.

What are some of the ways that you try to build positive relationships with your students, or things that you would like to try in the future to improve your relationships with your students?

[I] greet every student at the door with a smile every day no matter what has occurred the day before.

[I] answer their questions thoughtfully and respectfully no matter what their academic history with me has been.

I NEVER hold grudges. I try to remember that they are all the son or daughter of someone who loves them more than anything in the world. They are the light of someone's life!

Yes! Now, that's how I'd want to be treated, how I'd want my kids to be treated. I think about the radical contrast between this gorgeous statement, which so deeply reflects the highest professional values of teachers, and the punitiveness that teachers showed when just prompted with the idea that "punishment" could help keep control of class.

And I think about teachers. No teacher wants to be that jerk, to send kids to the principal's office. That's a failure. It's demoralizing. But here's a way for teachers to get back to who they really want to be for their kids.

I think about Jason Okonofua and all of the other millions of children, parents, and families for whom these issues are so personal, for whom school has become a place of conflict and exclusion. I think about boys, especially; about kids of color; and about kids with disabilities, each more likely to suffer suspensions in school than others.

And last, I cry because I think about our results. Okonofua, Dave Paunesku, and I first tested the empathic-discipline exercise in three school districts in San Jose, California, reporting the results in 2016. We gave thirty-one middle school math teachers the treatment materials or a control, which took the same form but focused on using technology in class. The whole thing happened online, in two sessions, a total of seventy minutes. Our thirty-one math teachers taught 1,580 students that year, mostly Latinx kids. When we tracked students over the rest of the school year, we found that 9.6 percent of students whose math teacher had gotten the control materials had been suspended over the year. That dropped to 4.8 percent if the student's math teacher had gotten the empathic-discipline exercise.

Later, we conducted a large replication in a district in Florida under court orders to reduce racial disparities in its disciplinary practices. There were sixty-six math teachers and 5,822 students in this sample. Its size and diversity let us look at which students benefited most. As predicted, Black and Hispanic students had the largest drop in suspension rates, from 27 percent to 21 percent. It was a 45 percent reduction in the racial inequality in suspension rates. Students who'd been suspended before, and students with disabilities, also had fewer suspensions.

Remember that I said we'd see the power of one teacher to change the life of a student again? You might think that students benefited from the empathic-discipline exercise only when they were interacting with their math teacher—the one person who'd been prompted to take an empathic stance. But when we looked, we found it went much deeper than that. Suspensions issue from every context in school. It's not just math class but every class and the bus, the hallway, the cafeteria, the playing fields. Students' risk of being suspended *anywhere* was dropping. In one analysis in the San Jose study, even when we entirely eliminated suspensions referred by math teachers from the data, we found the exact same reduction in students' risk of suspension for incidents referred by all other adults in school.

Was having one teacher take an empathic stance shifting students' entire models of who teachers could be? Can I trust teachers? Was it helping them in their interactions with everyone in school?

It was an exciting idea. And a powerful one. For if that was happening, students' risk of suspensions might be lower even the next school year, when they had entirely new teachers.

The Florida study let us test this question. In the main analysis, we looked at all seventh and eighth graders during the current school year, when their math teachers were randomly assigned to condition. But we also tracked seventh graders into eighth grade. We saw the exact same reduction in suspension rates as we'd seen in seventh grade, and especially for Black and Hispanic students. That's a year later, with all new teachers, and no new implementation of the empathic-discipline exercise.

If you're a teacher, it's exhilarating to think of the impact you can have on kids: how a positive, empathic stance can help kids not just today and not just with you but with all their teachers and into the future.

But there's a more sobering way to think about this too: How lonely and universally punitive must school be for students that a more empathic stance from a single teacher makes such a difference? Why is this needed? Why is even one empathic teacher not the norm?

The Florida study also let us look at next-year effects for teachers. Just as interesting, we didn't see the same pattern for them. If you're teaching seventh grade and you got the empathic-discipline exercise last year, your kids showed, in our data, a lower risk of suspension that year (and the next). But now you have a new batch of seventh graders coming in. Will they show the same drop in suspension rates? The answer was no. There was no carryover effect for teachers. Teachers aren't developing new mental models of kids. These are experienced professionals. They've taught cohort after cohort. It's easy for a teacher to just assume that last year was a good crop, this year not so much. It's easy to fall back on that punitive approach and maybe not even know it. As adults, we might have to be reminded to get back in touch with who we really want to be. That's why structured, intentional exercises help.

The empathic-discipline intervention assumes that even if teachers have some bias in them or some punitiveness, this is not all they are. It treats people as who they could become. But sometimes this faith could seem naïve.

There's a moment in Harper Lee's classic novel *To Kill a Mockingbird* I've always loved. It's late in the evening. Eight-year-old Scout, led by her big brother, Jem, and friend Dill, has come upon her father, Atticus, sitting outside the local jail. Atticus is guarding his client Tom Robinson, an African American man accused of rape in the small fictional town of Maycomb, Alabama. A lynch mob has formed. Men are crowding in. Violence hangs in the air. But Scout finds a familiar face and calls out, "Hey, Mr. Cunningham." When Mr. Cunningham doesn't respond, Scout tries again:

"Don't you remember me, Mr. Cunningham? I'm Jean Louise Finch. You brought us some hickory nuts one time, remember?" I began to sense the futility one feels when unacknowledged by a chance acquaintance.

"I go to school with Walter," I began again. "He's your boy, ain't he? Ain't he, sir?"

Mr. Cunningham was moved to a faint nod. He did know me, after all.

"He's in my grade," I said, "and he does right well. He's a good boy," I added, "a real nice boy. We brought him home for dinner one time. Maybe he told you about me, I beat him up one time but he was real nice about it. Tell him hey for me, won't you?"

Scout goes on and on, chitchatting and offering legal advice. Only slowly does she sense that something is amiss.

"What's the matter?" I asked.

Atticus said nothing. I looked around and up at Mr. Cunningham, whose face was equally impassive. Then he did a peculiar thing. He squatted down and took me by both shoulders.

"I'll tell him you said hey, little lady," he said.

Then he straightened up and waved a big paw. "Let's clear out," he called. "Let's get going, boys."

Scout doesn't get it. The next day she asks Atticus:

"I thought Mr. Cunningham was a friend of ours. You told me a long time ago he was."

"He still is."

"But last night he wanted to hurt you."

Atticus placed his fork beside his knife and pushed his plate aside. "Mr. Cunningham's basically a good man," he said, "he just has his blind spots along with the rest of us."

In *Song of Myself,* Walt Whitman writes, "Do I contradict myself? / Very well then I contradict myself, / (I am large, I contain multitudes.)." People, all of us, are complicated mixtures of good and bad. So it's like tit for tat. In the most difficult situations, our goal has to be to elicit from other people their best selves. It's not primarily an act of charity or kindness. It's equally an act of self-interest. It's so other people can become the best people they can be for you. Especially when it's hardest.

In July 2019, Nathalie Birli, a professional cyclist and new mom, was abducted near her home in southern Austria on a training run. A man rammed her with his car, pulled her into his vehicle, and bound and blindfolded her. "Part of me had already thought my life was over," Birli would later say.

When she came to, her captor tried to force her into a cold bath, holding her head underwater. But later, in a quiet moment "when he was not beating or threatening me," she looked around and noticed his orchids. "I just threw it out there, that his orchids were so beautiful," and that she knew how much went into growing orchids, how hard it was to keep them alive. "Suddenly, he started talking about how he cared for them, using water from his aquarium. Suddenly, he was a completely different person."

That created the space for the man to share the relationships he'd had that had betrayed him, for Birli to share that she was a new mom and that her baby needed her mother. And with that, the man retrieved her bike, tried to repair it, loaded it in his car, and brought her home.

KNOW IT. OWN IT. USE IT.

Know your questions. Use your answers.

This chapter has focused on pairs of specific roles, so we're going to change this reflection a bit.

Pair 1: Residents (Role 1) and Officers (Role 2)

Here are some of the questions these roles face:

RESIDENTS: *Will a law enforcement officer disrespect me? Am I treated as a lesser member of the community?*
OFFICERS: *Will this civilian threaten me or my control of the situation? Will they disrespect my authority?*

Pair 2: Students (Role 1) and Teachers (Role 2)

Here are some of the questions these roles face:

STUDENTS: *Do teachers think I or people "like me" are "limited"? Do teachers think I or people "like me" are bad?*
TEACHERS: *Will this student be a troublemaker? Do I need to punish this student to get back control?*

Pick one of the pairs. *Write down your answers.*

1. What's a tifbit a person in Role 1 might experience relevant to the question(s) they face—something "small" that a person could have a disproportionate response to? How does that tifbit reveal how this question comes up for them, what exactly the question is for them?

2. What's a tifbit a person in Role 2 might experience relevant to the question(s) they face? How does that tifbit reveal how this question comes up for them, what exactly the question is for them?

3. Are there ways this question is normal and reasonable for each person, given their circumstance, but not necessarily true (or not the only way to think about it)?

4. What agency does each person have to answer both the question they face and the question the other person faces in a way that will be healthy and productive and authentic for both people? How can they do this? And given who you are, including your identity and any personal or professional role, how can you develop this answer for yourself and/or gracefully *offer* another person this answer so they can build it out for themselves?*

---

* Remember the principles for thinking through "bad" events:

Principle 1: Avoid negative labels (*I'm not bad*)

Principle 2: You're not the only one; you're never the only one (*It's normal*)

Principle 3: Recognize causes that don't malign you or others (*I/you face real obstacles*)

Principle 4: Forecast improvement (*It can get better*)

Principle 5: Recognize opportunities (*Silver lining*)

DIGGING DEEPER
BEING A GREAT PROFESSIONAL

If you'd like to build your professionalism.

This exercise is designed to be done on your own. But you could also do a version with others who share your profession. Once each person has answered the questions, share your responses, either anonymously, by not identifying yourself and crumpling up your papers and tossing them in the middle of the table to be read aloud, or non-anonymously, with each person reading their own. Then discuss the themes you are hearing. What is similar? What is the range? What are you learning? How can you build on what you are already doing?

For this exercise, begin by naming your profession. Then write down your answer to these questions.

Question 1: Values

What are the highest ideals of your profession? What is the way you want to serve others, such as clients, the people you work with and for, or the general public? Think of what drew you to the profession in the first place.

Question 2: Challenges and Progress

What challenges come up in working toward these ideals as a member of this profession? When is it hard? How have you learned to make progress when faced with challenges? What has worked for you and what are you working on? Be sure to consider how you want to show up for others, who you want to be for others, the difference you want to make for others.

A Letter: Share Your Expertise

What does a new person just entering the profession now need to know? Describe the challenges they are likely to face in working toward their professional ideals, and how they can make progress to succeed.

Improving School for the Most Vulnerable Children

In the most difficult circumstances, when people look at you and all they see is something horrible, there must be space to tell your own story; a chance to tell that story in a way that other people can hear; a way to make that story real together.

For a decade, our team has worked in Oakland with groups of young people most vulnerable to being mis-seen or unseen in school. Working hand in hand with educators and youth groups, we created a platform for children to introduce or reintroduce themselves to an adult in school who could support them in their learning and growth. This approach draws on the trust and belonging work that helped tweens forecast and then build better relationships with teachers. It incorporates the empathic-discipline work too, in that it seeks to help teachers get back to who they really want to be with their kids. But it integrates these into a single coherent experience for both students and teachers. It's a way for children to speak and adults to hear, setting the stage for a better relationship. It is the single most powerful approach I know to remedy mistrust in school.

MORE THAN THAT: "I'M HAPPY TO SUPPORT. I'M READY TO GET STARTED."

In years of work, Rhana Hashemi has come face-to-face with the challenges educators have working with kids with substance use issues. One principal in Oakland, a friend of Hashemi's, told her that he'd just about had it with kids smoking weed in school. An African American man and a dedicated educator, he himself had smoked weed on occasion as a teenager. All he wanted, really, was for kids to do what they would do—just not at school. *Just go up the damn street!* he thought. But nothing he did or said seemed to work. When a child who'd been caught with drugs sat in his office, he told Hashemi that, honestly, he didn't know what to say. Yelling and cracking down wouldn't help. He knew that. But what else was there? His frustration was boiling.

Hashemi knew from her own experience, and from her interviews with young people in Oakland, the devastation a punitive approach could bring. The feeling of being "a bad kid," of "always and forever" being "a drug-dealing, drug-addicted high school dropout." Of being thrown away. She'd seen administrators give up. Once another principal bragged to Hashemi that he'd "cleared the boys out," expelling a group of teens with substance use issues, even as they were also taking steps to lead drug education efforts in school. She shared that news with me in a text with a single teardrop emoji.

So when Hashemi came to graduate school at Stanford, one of her goals was to restore trust between students caught with drugs and educators. It was thrilling, then, early one morning in January 2024 when she sent me a text with a bull's-eye emoji. For Hashemi was seeing the spiral begin to reverse.

Earlier that week she'd given an assistant principal in Oakland a one-page letter introducing a student who'd been caught with drugs. The principal said he was "moved" by the letter and that he felt a "sense of pride and responsibility to a young person who identified me as a support." He anticipated that his relationship with the student would "grow," and he shared that already he and the student had "agreed to regular check-ins." This principal was not "clearing out" another "bad kid." He was opening his arms and pulling a child closer, ready to partner with a teen facing a challenge. This was a day to begin. I immediately texted Hashemi back a big red heart emoji.

It was only the latest extraordinary response. That fall, Hashemi had come bounding into my office to report that a second educator had "literally jiggled with joy" when she'd delivered another letter regarding a drug-using student. A third responded, "[I] loved receiving the letter," said that it "helped me realize that the work I am doing is actually effective," and that it "makes me feel more confident that they would like me to be a mentor in their lives, and there to support them. I felt happy and wanted to make sure to support them more."

What was this letter? How did this happen? What magic words could transform frustration and dread into inspiration and opportunity?

To answer these questions, I need to take you back to where it all began. For Rhana Hashemi is only one of a long line of innovative social psychologists, educators, and young people determined to get this right. To fully understand how a single sheet of paper can work ordinary magic into the lives of children too close to the edge, I need to take you back to the woman who inspired it all.

LIFTING THE BAR: "I'M A GOOD KID"

It was late in the fall of 2014, just a few weeks after Oliver was born, that I first met Ms. Hattie Tate. Today I think of Ms. Tate as an extraordinary educator, partner, and mentor. She's a woman I deeply admire, a person of great warmth, courage, and wisdom. She ends every meeting, no matter how difficult a situation or an interlocutor, by saying, "I look forward to our success." And she means it. For sometimes it takes faith that things can improve. Faith even when there's no justification yet. That faith, I've learned, is not optional.

Tate grew up in Oakland and is a proud graduate of the Oakland schools. She'd left a career in business to teach and then to serve as a principal in the district. By 2014, she'd become a leader in the district's efforts to support youth caught up in the juvenile justice system. That November she gave Jason Okonofua, Jennifer Eberhardt, and me a tour of the Juvenile Justice Center in Alameda County. That's where kids in Oakland are sent if they get in trouble with the law. It was her job to help children return to school in Oakland successfully.

The justice center is a beautiful facility. It sits up on a hill, just a few exits down 580 from the Oakland Zoo. It has million-dollar views over the San Francisco Bay. Inside, it feels safe and secure. There's even a dentist's office for when kids need cleanings. Yet on that tour I saw children in cages, their hands hanging through bars or reaching out. I learned that if you acted out while in detention, a punishment could be a "no-contact visit" with your parents. With baby Oliver at home, that was very hard for me. A child might not get a hug from his or her mom or dad.

As I saw that space, I remembered that awful language from the 1990s, "superpredator." I knew viscerally the stereotypes these kids would face in school. But walking through the building with Ms. Tate, I saw the love—the love—that she showed every child. It was in her greeting, in her hug. And I saw, in her eyes, the faith in every child's essential goodness, in their potential.

With Tate's support, our team spent fifteen months interviewing young people in schools and through youth groups in Oakland. We asked children about experiences in the justice system, in the community, and in schools. We learned a great deal about their community, their goals and values. More than one child told me of seeing a friend get shot by the age of eleven. I knew those who'd been locked up had all gotten caught up in something. But I also heard stories of who they wanted to be, the places they wanted to go, the good they wanted to do.

Sometimes, when we asked children about their experiences in school, with teachers, they became quiet. They'd mumble. I'd lean in, just to catch a word or two. I could feel the pain. For this is a group for whom trust has been broken. These children have been told, more or less definitively, that they do not belong in school, that they are not wanted: "troublemaker," "violent," "out of control," "doesn't care," "thug." *Will anyone support me? Am I a "bad kid"? Will I be seen as one?* And I knew the questions teachers faced. A few years later, when we asked a teacher in a survey for her thoughts if a child entered her class from juvenile detention, she wrote, "First thoughts, in complete honesty, would be 'oh great' or 'why me.' I would think about what problems he may add to my class." *Will they even try? Or will they just disrupt my class?*

But we knew the kids were more than that. Could we give them a platform to help a teacher see that too?

Ultimately, with feedback from young people, we developed a forty-five-minute one-on-one experience for kids several days after they left the justice facility and returned to school. We call it "Lifting the Bar," because the goal is to lift the social and psychological bars that children face even after they return to school.

The session begins with children reflecting on and sharing their personal values and goals in school. These are genuine values of inherent importance, like making your parents proud or being a good role model for a younger brother or sister. As one student wrote, "I wanna help and support my family because I know some of them need help (!!) It's important because I want the best for my little sister." Another child wanted to be a good role model "because you don't want your little brother or sister grow up to be going to jail in and out messing up their future."

Then we share stories from older students about their experiences returning to school after a time in juvenile detention. The stories are blunt about the difficulties of this transition, but they also describe how developing relationships with adults can help. Students then have the chance to share their advice for future students, how relationships with adults could help them make progress toward their goals in school, and what students can do to build these relationships (saying is believing). This portion borrows from the trust and belonging exercise.

At the end, we give students a platform. We ask them to name an adult in school who isn't yet but could be an important source of support for them. We ask them what they would like this adult to know about who they are as a person: what is important to them, their values, the goals they have in school, and what is hard for them that the adult could help with.

Children's responses to these questions are the most moving expressions of vulnerability and hope I've seen in my career. They bring me to tears, every time. They're also practical. Students use this platform to describe their commitment to school, interests they have, and specific ways they would like support.

One child wanted his sixth-grade math teacher "to know [that] I'm a good kid and likes to learn new things and like to have fun and I like talkin a lot," that his goals were "one to graduate from middle school [and] two is to not have any problems with no one," and that he wanted help with "turning in my homework" and "wearing [his] uniform or [not] sleeping in class."

A second child wanted his teacher "to know that I care about make people happy. and that I respect them," that "[I] want them to know everything about my goals in life. I want them to know I'm for real," and he wanted their help because of "how bad I stink at read. How bad I am at computation."

A third wanted his teacher to know "I'm a smart person when it comes to math but I haven't really been to school so it's kinda hard to focus," that his goals were "to graduate and go to college at LSU," and that he wanted help because "like some of the work in class I don't understand sometimes."

Children are telling adults they care. They are asking adults to be a partner for them in their learning and growth. And they are showing adults where to begin.

We told students we might be able to share these responses with one of the adults they had named. For a random group of students, we did share these introductions—in that one-page letter I mentioned earlier. The letter emphasizes that the child had chosen the adult specifically. It asks for their support, and it includes the child's self-introduction. For educators, it is honorific. It doesn't tell them to do anything in particular. There is no accountability; no specific requirements have to be met. It respects their professional expertise and their inherent motivation to support young people. It just asks them to reach out to the student soon. And it says thank you: "Teachers like you are on the front lines and are the most important people for the success of your students. Thank you for your work."

It's a way to invite educators to bring their best self to bear for a student in need. In this first pass, when our research staff implemented the protocol, we put the letter on Stanford letterhead (what better use of the brand?). Today, as we work with district staff to incorporate the protocol in their work, we use joint Stanford and school district letterhead. Here's the full letter.

THE LIFTING THE BAR LETTER

Dear Mr./Ms. [teacher name],

We hope that your school year is going well.

Your student, [student name], decided to participate in a program to improve [his/her] transition back to school from the Juvenile Justice Center. As part of this program, students have the opportunity to identify an adult in school whom they would like to be a partner for them in this transition. As you know, one of the most important factors in any student's development is having a trusting and positive relationship with an adult in school.

[Student name] would like for you to be this adult for them.

The transition back to school from the JJC is difficult for many students. Some days will be easier and some days will be harder.

We hope that you will be able to be there for this student and to help [him/her] grow and overcome the challenges that [he/

she] faces. We also hope that a strong relationship with you will help [student] develop better relationships with other teachers and have a better school experience as a whole.

As part of our process, we asked [student name] what [he/she] would like you to know about [himself/herself]. Here is what [he/she] said:

- I'm a serious person about my school and graduating and play football, but I just have a problem catching up fast.
- I want to have all A's or B's and I want to graduate and play college football.
- I would like to help myself and get help from other people by understanding it one by one and growing slowly through the process.

Piped in from student

We encourage you to reach out and talk to [him/her] within the next week. For example, you could . . .

At the end of the day, teachers like you are on the front lines and are the most important people for the success of [student name] and all your students.

Thank you for your work,
    The Stanford University Lifting the Bar Project

A *Forty* Percentage-Point Reduction in Recidivism

In a first field trial in Oakland, there were three randomized groups. In the first, students completed control materials focused on study skills. In the second, students did the Lifting the Bar exercise, but we didn't share the letter. In the third, we delivered the letter. (Remember, we'd told everyone we *might* be able to share their responses with one of the adults they named.)

Months later, we looked at our data. The question was simple:

Would children be able to stick the landing and succeed in school? We tracked students in the semester in which they were released and through the next full academic term. In these months, fully 69 percent of children in the first group were sent back to juvenile detention. When students completed our exercise but the letter wasn't delivered, the outcome wasn't much better: 64 percent. Let's stop and take that in. This is where we are at baseline, and this is terrible.

But when we delivered the letter to the teacher, students' risk of recidivism dropped to 29 percent. Nearly three in ten children still returned to juvenile detention. But that's a reduction of more than half. Another four in ten children who would have gone back to jail without the letter did not. With the letter, they were in school, where they could learn and make progress.

Today, we see the impact of the letter in nearly every case. One teacher in Chicago Public Schools wrote that he was "proud and excited" to receive the letter, that he hoped "to support the student's academic and social-emotional well-being," and to help the student "build leadership, accountability, academic grit, and confidence." Asked to partner, this teacher stood up.

In experimental studies, we have formally tested the impact of the letter for teachers. In one case, we asked nearly 350 experienced teachers to imagine a student coming back to class from juvenile detention, and randomized them to get the letter or not. Then we asked teachers what they would think, feel, and do. Remember that teacher who worried "why me" about a student joining her class from juvenile detention? She was actually a teacher in this study. But earlier, I gave you only the first part of her response. Here's the whole thing:

> First thoughts, in complete honesty, would be "oh great" or "why me." I would think about what problems he may add to my class. But, as I read more of the letter and see that [student name] CHOSE ME to be his mentor/confidant, I am immediately reminded that he is a child that has made some mistakes and wants to change. He deserves that chance and, if I can, I want to help.

Reading about his passions made me see him more as a person than just another student with problems.

You can feel her thinking begin to shift, a bias slip away, and a new, healthier, empowered, and positive stance begin to emerge.

With that new perspective, that new way of seeing, small victories begin to stand out as progress to build upon, and small setbacks are less conspicuous, less ill omens. Teachers who got the letter saw the student as more committed to school, and felt more committed to them in turn. They were more confident the student could succeed. They were more eager to serve as a mentor, advocate, and guide for the student, to nominate the student for opportunities in school, to integrate them in class, and to build a positive relationship with them. They even felt more love and respect for a justice-involved youth. They were less likely to wonder what crime the child had committed, and less likely to leap to negative conclusions, to judge a student "a troublemaker" if, say, they fell asleep in class one day and refused to do their work. No longer were these kids "criminals." They were kids—kids with a future. And teachers were ready to do their part to make that future real.

That stance transforms school. Hattie Tate describes Lifting the Bar this way: "A lot of that has to do with building positive adult relationships where students feel protected, listened to, cared for, and heard. All that feeds into a sense of belongingness, and feeling like this is where I can be successful. Someone here cares for me, someone here is guiding me, someone here is concerned about my success. . . . It's focused on building a relationship between the person responsible for the academic learning and the learner."

This initial field trial was just a pilot. There were only forty-seven children. We'll learn more from future studies, both with justice-involved youth and in adaptations for kids in other populations, including Rhana Hashemi's work with students with substance use issues. But there is a fundamental truth here: a truth about voice, about listening, and about "the day you begin."

It's hard to overstate how important relationships are in school. It's not just Urie Bronfenbrenner. One ethnography concluded that the experience of "being known" by adults in school is "ordinary magic" for adolescents, given all the functions these relationships serve. Some of the barriers to improving relationships are structural. School and class sizes might be large, teaching loads high. There are only twenty-four hours in a day. But the most fundamental barriers, I think, are stereotypes—"dumb," "troublemaker," "doesn't care," "biased." These drive wedges between students and teachers. They predefine another person. They make us start not nice, and then we infer the worst. But when we see the questions stereotypes prompt, we can create tools that set them aside, with simplicity and grace.

Lifting the Bar creates space for a young person to make themselves known to an adult who could matter for them. It assumes that students—all students—have good, prosocial goals, and they'll pursue these goals if only a teacher partners with them. And it assumes that teachers really want to help their students succeed, even students who are struggling, and that they'll do their best for every kid. With that space both people can start nice. That doesn't guarantee success. But it's the place to begin.

PART 4

Us

Chapter 8

Toward a Better World

We do not look to distant ages, or amuse ourselves with brilliant,
though delusive dreams concerning the infinite improveability of
man, the annihilation of labour, disease, and even death. But we
reason by analogy with simple facts. We consider only a state of
human progression arising out of its present condition. We look
for a time that we may reasonably expect, for a bright day of
which we already behold the dawn.

—SIR HUMPHRY DAVY, JANUARY 21, 1802

I have a dream.

—DR. MARTIN LUTHER KING JR., AUGUST 28, 1963

Through the first half of the nineteenth century, the United
States was mostly a nation of farms and farmers. Almost everyone lived near the source of food production. The cream for your
morning coffee came straight from the cow. But as the country industrialized, people began to move to cities. By 1900, 40 percent of

Americans lived in cities, up from 15 percent in 1850. In the Northeast, two in three people did.

The country had seen a long decline in child mortality rates, but this began to falter. In the 1870s, the death rate for kids under five actually rose nationwide by 10 percent. In New York City that same decade, the death rate spiked in the month of July, especially for the youngest children under one. Every year it was twice the rate for the rest of the year. The same thing was happening in Chicago.

It was no mystery. As early as 1866, a physician reported to the New York City Board of Health, "It was seldom that an artificially fed infant under the age of six months or even ten months residing within the city limits escaped the summer diarrhea." One cause was contaminated water supplies. But it was also that the rapidly expanding factory jobs took people out of their homes. It was harder now for new mothers to breast-feed their infants. And when they couldn't, the cow milk used to substitute had to be brought in by horse cart, barge, and steam train from far-off dairies. So, milk was going bad, especially when it had to sit out for long periods in the summer sun.

The solution was at hand. By 1865, Louis Pasteur, a French chemist and microbiologist, had already conducted the basic research to understand that growing microbes were the culprit. And, working with wine, Pasteur had found the solution: heating wine to 130 degrees and then cooling it quickly would kill the microbes and prevent spoilage while preserving flavor. Yet it took until 1908 for any major American city, the first was Chicago, to begin to require the pasteurization of milk. That's forty-three years later.

Babies died while adults dithered.

Let's repeat that.

Babies died while adults dithered.

What a waste. And what a waste when a child fails algebra because he asks, *Am I smart enough?;* when a student drops out of college because she fears "people like me" don't belong, and so never raises her hand, never goes to office hours, never joins a student group; when a good marriage deteriorates because a couple struggles to contend with a troubling question about a conflict. And how tragic when the relationship between a mother and her baby is corrupted by the question, *Am I a bad mom?*

It's hard enough to create good structures that give people opportunities to succeed, like a strong algebra curriculum or a good partner in marriage. When psychological questions then get in the way, it's all the more frustrating—especially when we know how to offer better answers. But the truth is, know-how is only the first step.

In this book, I've shared some of the most amazing science I know. I could not have imagined the changes I've seen when I first started this journey in grad school twenty-five years ago. But these studies, mostly, are demonstrations. They show us what might be possible. They invite us to imagine a new world, a wiser world. In this world, wise interventions weave their way through our daily lives and institutional policies and practices. Important settings are organized in ways that anticipate troubling questions as they come up, and offer each person good answers they can use to spiral up. School is organized around belonging and growth, and teachers always take an empathic stance with kids when they misbehave. Every student knows that teachers give critical feedback because they believe in the student's potential to reach a high standard. In this world, we're "nice" to one another; we always begin with cooperation. We stand up for good rules, but we forgive transgressions quickly. We have faith in one another. We believe in who each of us can become. It's tantalizing.

Science gives us the contours of this world. It shows us what it might look like. It gives us tools to help us get there. It offers glimmers of a flourishing we can yet achieve. But demonstrations alone don't make it real. It's not understanding pasteurization that saves babies. It's actually pasteurizing the milk. Know-how has to meet can-do. We have to roll up our sleeves and get to work. Otherwise, wise interventions will be orphaned, unsponsored, promises unfulfilled.

How can we get there?

To move toward this better world, we have to understand how psychological tools fit and how we can get them to fit: to fit in contexts, and to fit with the individuals and institutions that will need to act to realize their potential. And in the end, we'll need precise ways to change specific aspects of our culture.

You'd be forgiven for being dubious. It's not usually psychology we turn to for solutions to massive social problems. Years ago, I presented research on growth mindset and social belonging to a group of Stanford administrators. As a new assistant professor and as an alumnus, I was trying to build a partnership with Stanford to implement exercises to create a healthier, more equitable environment for students. The staff who worked most closely with students were all enthusiastic. Every day, they saw students struggle with those interlocking worries, *Do I belong?* and *Can I do it?* But the most senior administrator there, the trusted right hand for a generation of Stanford leadership, just looked at me and said, "I don't believe it." She thought it was magic, and she didn't believe in magic. Our project was delayed a year.

I get it. Psychology can seem too squishy to pin down, psychological exercises too "small" to actually affect things that matter.

As a society we invest billions of dollars annually developing, evaluating, and disseminating biomedical tools of change. It's commonplace to take a wonder drug and expect to receive a benefit for your health, well-being, and functioning long into the future. We'll literally take a "poop pill" if the doctor says it will improve GI function. Equally, today most of us have come to be confident that basic public health measures like pasteurizing milk or adding fluoride to water will protect us from harm. Yet it can seem so improbable that a few well-designed minutes considering and reflecting on the things that matter most could improve our collective lives. Then our investment in social and psychological tools of change pales; our urgency to implement these innovations flags.

Ironically, one of the barriers, I think, is our own experience. When you're caught up in your own head, it's easy to think there's nothing you could do to help everyone with all their myriad worries. But as we've seen, people aren't snowflakes. We're not paranoid. Our concerns aren't random or amorphous. We can predict the questions people ask. They're concrete and discrete, like the first-generation student who wants to know, *Can people like me belong in college?* We can name these questions. Can we create structures to answer them en masse?

FITTING

To answer psychological questions, we have to get these answers to fit: with who we are and with the institutions that structure our lives. In describing this fitting, I'm going to focus on examples from school for two reasons: it's inherently important, and this is where the research is most developed.

Fitting with Individuals. The first level of fitting is with each individual person. For even if there are common questions, they take different forms for each of us. That's why we *offer* people answers; we don't hand them out fully formed, fixed, and rigid. This is not "take it or leave it" but "how does this play out for you?" It's why wise interventions often express the same basic idea in multiple forms. A social-belonging exercise shares the general truth that everyone worries at first if they belong when they come to a new school, and this gets better with time. But it gains power by sharing multiple stories of this experience. That way more people can find resonance with their own experience. Then students have a chance to tell their own story in return, to share how that general truth applies to them and their circumstance (that is, saying is believing). It's a way for people to customize an idea for themselves, to build it out for themselves, an answer they can use to chart a path of growth from where they are. It creates grease so the same materials can work for many people.

Fitting with Populations. At the second level, the fitting is with populations. When we wanted to work with women to support their belonging in engineering, we didn't just use the same materials Geoff Cohen and I had developed previously for Black and White college students. We adapted them. And when we wanted to work with sixth graders and the issues of trust and belonging they faced in the transition to middle school, we adapted them again.

On December 1, 2011, I was with David Yeager and Shannon Brady and a large group at the Stanford d.school trying to better understand the experiences of students who had graduated from "high-performing" urban charter schools going to college. Together Claude Steele and I had a memorable conversation with a young Latina woman I'll call Jasmine, a student in the first year at San Francisco State University. Soft-spoken and petite, Jasmine told us she commuted to campus from her home in San Jose with her brother. So, I asked her what she did on campus while her brother was in class.

"I sit in my car."

"You sit in your car?"

"I sit in my car and look out at all the people going by. I wonder how they met each other."

I was incredulous. Here she was, at a critical crossroads in life, a young person in college, a time when people are as open and available to make friends as ever. Yet she was sequestering herself off, alone and isolated.

I didn't get it. But as I learned more about the charter school world she'd come from, it began to make sense. These schools are so highly structured essentially nothing is left to chance. Everything—including, in some respects, your friend group—is given to you. That might work in high school but it left students adrift in college. College, after all, is a big, wide world, with little structure. You have to be proactive to find your path. That led us to introduce one of several simple but potentially critical revisions in the belonging exercise: to emphasize the active steps a student needs to take to build relationships with professors and fellow students in college, even small steps, and that these take time to pay off. Later, we delivered that exercise to 584 students in a half-hour online module in May of students' senior year of high school in partnership with the charter school networks. That raised the rate at which students completed the first year of college full-time enrolled, by eleven percentage points over a randomized control condition.

Fitting with Organizations: How to Reach People En Masse. As important, that online module was a low-cost exercise the charter schools could use year after year, reaching thousands of kids going forward.

I'm a big believer in the power of psychological knowledge, in understanding yourself and others more deeply, in why you react the way you do, in figuring out what your tifbits are and why. It's a big reason I've written this book. This knowledge has helped me in my life, and I hope it helps you in yours. But to create change on a mass scale, we also have to figure out who's going to do what and when. Only then can everyone who needs a space to reflect get the right thing at the right time. Typically, that means working within the capacities and constraints of organizations. Sometimes, it entails compromises between the optimal time or way to offer a psychological exercise and what is practical to reach large numbers of people. It could mean a trade-off between impact (how much you can help a given person) and scale (how many people you can reach).

Before the charter school study, my collaborators and I had always implemented belonging exercises ourselves, always in person, and always during the school year. That way we knew students would pay attention. They'd be fully immersed. And people could apply the basic ideas to whatever challenges they were experiencing right then. But hand delivery is no way to scale. There just aren't enough of us to go around.

As I mentioned earlier, one of my first grad students at Stanford, Dave Paunesku, saw these problems early. He knew we needed to get beyond bespoke solutions that require a researcher in every room to something more like a public health approach. As a first step, Paunesku developed online methods to scale wise interventions. These are modules that share social-belonging stories, ideas like growth mindset, and other exercises along with interactive experiences to help students take on these ideas and connect them to their own lives (saying-is-believing exercises). Critically, these modules can be accessed by anyone with a computer anywhere. And it's easy to randomize students to condition, to test the causal effects. Together with another grad student, Carissa Romero, Paunesku first developed this method for growth mindset in high school. Cold-calling dozens of schools, Paunesku and Romero asked, Are you interested in growth mindset? Could you get your students to the school computer lab? Could you share their academic records? Reporting the results in a landmark 2015 paper, we found that among 1,594 students in thirteen geographically diverse high schools the online growth-mindset module, as compared with a control condition, had raised students' GPA the next semester, especially for academically struggling students. It also cut the likelihood that students received poor grades (D or lower) in core academic classes by six percentage points.

These are the methods that would set tens of thousands of high school and college students into rigorous randomized controlled trials of growth-mindset and belonging exercises.

So, in the charter school study, and in two concurrent studies with university partners, we implemented belonging exercises online, months before students started college. We didn't know if this would work. Would students coast through the exercise, distracted by social media? Even if they paid attention, would the materials seem abstract to the point of irrelevance months before starting college? But maybe, we hoped, it might work like a road map for psychology. Perhaps it could help students anticipate challenges and preplan how to make sense of them, as normal and as capable of improving, and how to respond when they occurred.

With the charter schools, we had no choice. The charter schools controlled the high school environment, but they had no influence on the dozens of colleges their graduates entered every year, or how they welcomed students. Their window to act was in May of students' senior year of high school, after required standardized testing and college admissions and before graduation. That's when they could bring students to the computer lab for a half-hour session. (It was also when students' attention began to turn toward college.) So, part of the question was whether the belonging exercise—as implemented in a way the charter schools could actually use—would improve college outcomes. Now that we've seen the benefits, it's a tool they have used going forward.

But at the end of the day it's not high schools but colleges and universities that are most responsible for students' college experience. We learned it's also often easier for universities to reach an entire incoming class before students get to campus. In the summer before starting college, students get innumerable tasks. You might have to upload a photo for your ID card, provide health insurance information, write an introduction to an adviser, or indicate your interest in various optional first-year programs. And new students are eager beavers to start college, so it's easier then to get their attention. But once students get to campus, they splinter into a million communities.

So, working with two universities, one public and one private, we also integrated belonging and related exercises (for example, a growth-mindset intervention) into their online pre-matriculation systems. Students might log on to complete "Form 15: Social and Academic Life at [college name]. What is it like to come to [college name]?" Using these methods, we reached 90 percent of the incoming class at each university, nearly nine thousand students in total. A year later, looking at students' academic records, we found the half-hour online session had reduced institutional inequality, in persistence or in grades over the first year, by 30 to 40 percent at each university relative to a control condition. And these tools were easy and cheap for universities to use with all students going forward. In fact, when we conducted a formal analysis at the public university after it implemented the exercises for everyone (with no control group), we saw continued improvement in persistence rates.

Obviously, there is far more schools can and should do to support their students than offering an online module. We'll dig into this in a moment. But these are tools to help students begin their college journey on the right path. They unlock students' agency. And they're freely available and easy to implement for all four-year colleges and universities in North America. Already, they've been accessed hundreds of thousands of times.

What can be hardest for people like that Stanford administrator to understand is the power of wise interventions to cause change over time. How can something so brief change people's lives? If you don't get spirals, it seems like magic and, then, not real. These studies helped us see that spiral. In the charter school study, students who got the belonging exercise instead of the control materials were more likely to live on campus in the fall of their first year (76 percent versus 53 percent); more likely to use academic support services, such as attending office hours, talking with older students, or meeting with an adviser (91 percent versus 60 percent); and more likely to join a student group (77 percent versus 63 percent). In the private university, students of color and first-generation students who'd gotten a pre-matriculation belonging exercise said they'd made more close friends in college by the end of the first year, that they'd used academic support services more, and that they were more involved in student groups. They were also more likely to have developed a mentor relationship. These are concrete steps an administrator can appreciate. They're vehicles for sustained growth.

Fitting with Opportunities: Understanding Affordances. But there's a catch. These spirals depend on the opportunities for growth that people actually have. This is the fourth level of fitting. For wise interventions don't work on their own. They clear barriers that hold people back. They unleash potential. But people have to be able to put positive answers to work.

My colleagues and I call these opportunities affordances. What does a situation afford? What does it make possible?

One kind of affordance is objective. What does a situation let you *do*? Take an English-speaking student who gets a great growth-mindset intervention about learning Chinese. She's totally bought in. Only she's not taught Chinese. That won't do any good. The situation doesn't afford learning Chinese. Some research, for example, finds that wise interventions don't move the needle in school if the quality of instruction is poor.

The second kind of affordance is more subtle. It's psychological. What does a situation let you *think*? For if, in the end, the answer a wise intervention offers to a troubling question you face seems illegitimate, inapplicable, or not useful in a context, you'll drop it. We see this boundary condition in massive trials of both growth-mindset and social-belonging interventions.

Early in 2013, I was deep in the weeds with David Yeager, planning a meeting for May at the White House on "learning mindsets," when we realized we needed a headline idea. In a breakthrough happy-hour phone call, we thought about that high school study that Dave Paunesku and Carissa Romero had just run. Could we use those methods to conduct a nationally representative trial of a growth-mindset intervention? That way we could learn: If this scalable method were used everywhere, what kinds of gains would we see? And where would that be more effective, and where would it be less effective?

Six years later, having brought together an interdisciplinary team of psychologists, sociologists, economists, education scholars, and statisticians, Yeager would report the primary results of the National Study of Learning Mindsets. Following a careful redesign process and several test runs, we had implemented the study during the critical transition to high school with a nationally representative sample of 12,512 ninth-grade students in sixty-five public high schools in the United States. As compared with the randomized controlled exercise, the online module offering students a growth mindset had raised grades over the school year among students who entered high school with lower achievement. It reduced the risk that students earned a D or F average in ninth grade by five percentage points. At a cost of less than $1 per student, that module, if implemented nationally, could get 105,000 students in the United States above that threshold every year. Paunesku's results had replicated, and they generalized to the entire country.

But just as we anticipated, the intervention was not a magic bullet; there are no magic purple crayons. It didn't work everywhere. If you're a ninth grader, I'll bet you care about being cool, maybe more than anything else. But what if acting on a growth mindset would make you "a nerd"? Not every school celebrates "nerd nation." We found that in high schools where peer norms opposed taking on academic challenges, students considered the idea of a growth mindset, but then dropped it like a hot potato. They didn't use it to improve academically. Or what if your math teacher rejects the basic idea that intelligence can grow? In another analysis, we found that, in general, students got higher grades in math when they'd been offered a growth mindset—but not when their math teacher endorsed a fixed mindset. If Mr. E. treats some students as "math kids" and others as not, it's hard to hold fast to your growth mindset and apply it in math class.

A massive scale-up of the social-belonging intervention came to the same conclusion: you need a supportive context. Following publicity around the success of the pre-matriculation belonging interventions, Christine Logel, Mary Murphy, David Yeager, and I built an organization called the College Transition Collaborative (now Equity Accelerator). Together, we partnered with 22 colleges and universities to test the online belonging exercise. A total of 26,911 incoming students in two cohorts were randomized to the belonging exercise or a control experience before college and tracked through the first year. To understand where the belonging exercise would be effective and where not, we looked at the opportunity students had to belong at their college: whether their identity group attained at least a moderate level of belonging on the local campus as reported in a survey toward the end of the first year without the intervention. For students in these groups, the belonging exercise raised the rate at which students completed the first year full-time enrolled. The largest gains were for students in groups that had historically performed poorly and had more room for improvement. The 22 colleges and universities in our sample were representative of 749 postsecondary institutions in the United States, which welcome 1.02 million new students to college every year. If all these institutions offered their students the ten-to-thirty-minute online belonging exercise, we estimate that more than 12,000 students would complete the first year of college full-time enrolled each year.

But it wasn't good for everyone, everywhere. Some students don't have adequate opportunities to belong in college. Opportunities to find community on campus might be lacking. They might face discrimination. Some research, for instance, finds that faculty can be less responsive to requests for mentorship from students of color. Regardless of the cause, students in identity groups that did not have this opportunity to belong did not benefit from the belonging exercise.

As studies go, the National Study of Learning Mindsets and the CTC Belonging Trial were massive. These are among the largest randomized controlled longitudinal experiments with representative samples ever conducted. But still, they reached just a sliver of the population. The NSLM reached just 0.31 percent of the more than four million students entering ninth grade in the United States that year; the CTC trial reached 1.32 percent of the more than two million students starting at those 749 representative colleges those two years. And fundamentally, these trials showed that we can't just work with students alone. Online modules are not enough. For students and schools to achieve their full potential also requires change in the culture and practice of education as a whole.

Wise interventions seed a way of thinking that could be useful in a context. But good seeds require fertile soil. If the hopeful message an intervention offers is discredited or illegitimate so people can't act on it, then that's the problem to be solved. That's where the fitting ends and we need broader reforms—reforms that empower the people who lead contexts, like teachers or administrators, to make these contexts better. In school, that means treating everyone in ways that truly include them and support them in their growth.

LEADERSHIP: HOW WE CAN IMPROVE EXPERIENCES FOR OTHERS

So, we move from the individual to the interpersonal and the institutional levels of analysis. An advantage is that shifting the behavior of a few leaders can shape the experiences of many.

We've already seen this potential. Catherine Thomas worked with leaders in 322 villages in rural Niger to accelerate economic development among 4,712 households, reaching 22,507 people. It was part of a government-led program that ultimately reached more than 1 million people out of a rural population in poverty of 7 million. Jason Okonofua's empathic-mindset intervention reached dozens of teachers to reduce suspensions among thousands of students, especially students of color and those with disabilities. And his empathic-supervision intervention, randomized to 216 officers, cut recidivism among 20,478 adults reentering civil society from prison. These are incredible opportunities for reform.

In school, a rapidly expanding focus of research in the last few years has been on the costs an exclusionary and judgy culture imposes on students. One study led by Elizabeth Canning at Washington State University surveyed 150 science, technology, engineering, and mathematics professors at a large public university about their beliefs about intelligence. Collectively, these professors taught more than fifteen thousand students. Canning found that the more professors endorsed a fixed mindset about intelligence, the worse their students' experience and grades. It's not just the douchebag who gazes out over two hundred students and says, "Look to your right, look to your left. At the end of the term, only one of you will be left." It's also the routine reflections of a culture focused on performance, like the premium placed on timed tests and the default presumption that students should not be able to revise their work for a higher grade. That culture hurts everyone, but especially students of color. In fact, Canning found that racial achievement gaps were twice as large when professors endorsed that fixed mindset. This culture even pervades elementary school. Another study found that the more teachers endorsed the crazy view that elementary school math requires innate ability, the lower the motivation of fourth graders, especially kids who were lower achieving.

Seriously? We can do better.

Remember that White House meeting David Yeager and I co-organized in 2013 on "learning mindsets"?

Educators told story after story of students they served, the worries they had (*Do I belong? Can I do it?*), and how these worries got in the way of learning. They were thirsty for practices that could help their kids succeed. It was an incredibly productive meeting, and it led to all sorts of collaborations.

But just a week later Yeager and I went to a second meeting, this one in Chicago. A group of academics had convened at a fancy downtown hotel to discuss inequality. With no sense of irony, a man carved meat for lunch. One person flew in from Switzerland for the event. Yet our hosts rejected the social-belonging and growth-mindset interventions we described out of hand because, they implied, intelligence really is fixed at age twelve and students of color actually kind of don't belong in college. To tell people otherwise, they said, would be dishonest. One attendee proposed a "five-year moratorium" on these interventions while we "figure out the normative issues." Needless to say, this did not end well. I thought of those educators and their kids. I thought of Chicago, an incredibly unequal city, of kids within a mile of our meeting dropping out of school right now because they felt they didn't belong and were judged as dumb. If these were your children, could you dither? The reason we do this work, I said, is that it is moral.

The changes we try won't always work. But we have a world of opportunity to do better. My view is we have to. That trying should be guided by listening to people and thinking through what questions reasonably come up in a situation. Leaders in contexts can take concrete steps to offer people good answers to these questions. The details here matter. Intuitions can lead us astray (consider the self-esteem movement). Even good ideas poorly implemented might backfire. But if we try things systematically, if we collect rigorous data and randomize where possible, we can learn what works best where, when, and for whom. In the Floodlight, I've gathered some of the most exciting and practical steps researchers, teachers, and administrators can and are taking to address the questions that students predictably face. It's a way to make school wise.

And these things are "easy," so then we can just do them.

Right?

JUST DO IT?

Pasteurization was easy too.

So, change is within reach. But will we do it? For there are challenges to acting both for individuals and for institutions. Take teachers. It's an incredibly difficult profession. Five classes, 125 kids, 200 parents, and a vice-principal breathing down your neck. Your paycheck is too small and rent is due next month. Teachers are often stretched so thin they have little capacity left. How can we help them create classrooms that truly support students' belonging and growth?

Jason Okonofua didn't reduce suspension rates by incentivizing teachers, by monitoring them closely, or by giving them some form of "diversity training." He didn't make teachers feel bad, judged, or inadequate. Quite the opposite. He held up for teachers their own ideal of who a teacher is and how that person could relate to their students. Then he gave teachers a chance to describe how they were working toward becoming this person for their students. He invited them to share their advice for future teachers who might learn from them. That's a playbook that could help any service professional. (It's the basis for the exercise at the end of chapter 7, "Being a Great Professional.") That way professionals *want* the ideas you're offering; these ideas feel good and fitting and help them do what they want to do and become who they want to be. As Hattie Tate says, "Nobody signs up every day to go to work and fail. Sometimes you actually inspire, motivate adults to bring their best self to the success of one student."

It's not hard to imagine how an approach like this could work in other settings too. A police department could integrate Dobson's "transparency statements" in its training and practice for community policing. A probation department could integrate Okonofua's empathic-supervision intervention.

In health contexts, a doctor's office could incorporate Lauren Howe's work on the representation of side effects of exposure therapy for children with peanut allergies (it's my body getting stronger!). As another example, my colleague Alia Crum led a team of psychologists and oncologists to offer people newly diagnosed with cancer the idea that their body is strong; that it's working with them, not against them; that cancer is manageable; and that it might even present opportunities. That improved the quality of life patients reported over ten weeks, improved coping, and reduced distress.

That's an approach oncologists could take up—and health insurance should fund.

Police officers, probation officers, and medical professionals all want to do better by those they serve. But what would motivate a school, a police department, or a health system to make sure change happens?

The question of organizational change goes well beyond this book. For it must be incentivized, planned for, regulated, budgeted, hired for, and committed to. It takes money, organizational structures, and good management. In some cases, market forces may prod organizations to change to meet our needs, but often these forces are sorely inadequate, in supporting both the development (supply) and the uptake (demand) of wise interventions. On the supply side, the value wise interventions create is typically not monetized. These exercises aren't sold like a new drug. They're not cash cows. When a team creates a new innovation, for instance, it generally makes no money off it. Rather, researchers and funders usually do everything they can to make their innovations freely accessible. That's great, but it means profit motives don't fuel the development, marketing, and distribution of wise interventions. Perhaps performance-based funding models, where funding is provided contingent on outcomes achieved, could help here.

On the demand side, the market forces to drive the improvements that wise interventions aid are often indirect at best. Certainly, it's not direct financial incentives that are pushing schools to reorganize around growth and belonging; it's a broader cultural change.

The consequence is that too often we're stuck with stasis, how things have always been done, a perception of risk in any change that holds organizations back from doing anything at all, even if this stasis perpetuates mediocre outcomes. Sometimes, then, change must be impelled, by social movements, by political processes, and by legal pressures. I've seen the role of external pressures in my own work. When we recruited partners for the CTC Belonging Trial, we received particular enthusiasm from universities in states where legislatures were making noise about holding back financial aid if universities didn't improve graduation rates. And it wasn't just be-cause the first trial of the empathic-discipline intervention worked so well that Okonofua was able to scale up that program. The dis-trict he partnered with in the second trial was under a consent de-cree to reduce racial disparities in the rate at which students were suspended. That motivated them to find a positive and science-based approach to improve practice. Could organizational incen-tives be more systematic and widespread? Can they drive proactive improvement for everyone?

At least in these cases there are relevant institutions. For some-times, there aren't. For some of the most important aspects of human flourishing, no specific organization supports us. Certainly, no one wants Big Brother breathing down their marriage. The qual-ity of our most intimate relationships is a matter usually left to fam-ily, to friends, and to faith. But how, then, can we help more people access innovations like Kiara Sanchez's to strengthen cross-race friendships; Denise Marigold's to help dating couples truly take compliments; Eli Finkel's or Karina Schumann's approaches to help couples in long-term relationships work through conflicts; or Daphne Bugental's to support new moms with their babies? These relationships can define a person's life. Are there ways schools, faith communities, nonprofit organizations, or government programs can integrate these approaches in their efforts to support couples and families? Are there market solutions? Can you tell a friend?

Sometimes, it seems, the magic is all around us. Here is one time, not so long ago, for my brother.

For much of his twenties, my brother worked as a piano player, piecing together auditions, music director and arranging gigs, sum-mer camps and cruise ship contracts, and the occasional big-tent production. For a while he lived in a tiny basement apartment in Astoria, New York, near LaGuardia Airport. A closed-off stairway served as his closet (shorter items to the left, longer to the right). But he got his laughs in. Once on a cruise ship he was asked to play background music during a ceremony to change captains. He played "My Heart Will Go On" from *Titanic* at low volume as the old captain gave a pompous speech. None of the passengers seemed to notice, but the new captain heard: "If you ever do that again, you're outta here!" A highlight for me in grad school was seeing Eric perform for the first time in an Off-Broadway production, *I Love You, You're Perfect, Now Change.* The show placed the music pit in a perch high above the stage. *That's my brother up there!* I kept thinking, *That's Eric!* remembering all the shows I'd seen him perform in back in Michigan. Afterward, two friends and I took him to dinner and gave him an obscenely large bouquet of flowers. Another time Lisa and I saw him play *Mary Poppins* on the North American tour twice in eighteen hours.

Eric loved the music, but the life wasn't sustainable. The money is thin, and stable jobs like a tour, even if you get it, put you in a new city every week or so, with the same small group of often high-strung people. It's hard to build a life. So eventually Eric decided to make a change. He'd always enjoyed computer programming, once writing from scratch a program to play Bill Clinton's favorite card game, oh hell. He took most of a year off, living back home with our parents and taking online courses to build his skills. When he was ready, I introduced him to a friend from college, Neil, who introduced him to his friend, also named Neil, who had a job opening. As Eric got ready for the interview, he was nervous. He hadn't majored in computer science, or anything relevant. He had no experience in the industry. But Neil No. 2 hired him. And when he did, he told him something important. "We look for two things in people," he said. "First, we want people who work well in small groups. You've spent a decade doing that in music. Wow. And second, we look for people who can learn. And you've learned all these skills on your own. You're exactly the kind of person we want." That let Eric set aside those questions. He was free to start a new upward spiral.

You are enough. You can do it. You do belong. Now go for it!

Making School Wise

Many of us have complicated relationships with school. Some wonderful experiences, but some very painful.

I think of school as sacred. It's what we create to help people become. We use tax dollars to fund school. We require young people to attend. We want the learning opportunities school offers to help people become happy and productive citizens, to lead secure lives, and to contribute back to our communities and to the next generation. So, it's most important to me to get school right: to make sure schooling is wise to the questions that come up, that could get in the way of a young person's growth, to integrate cultures and practices that will reflexively help students to better answers.

DISCRETE PRACTICES EDUCATORS CAN USE TO FREE STUDENTS FROM TROUBLING QUESTIONS

Sometimes educators ask, "Which should I do? A growth-mindset intervention or a social-belonging intervention? Utility value or something else?"

I think it's more useful to ask what to do when, for it is at specific intervals that questions come up. Here I'll track the trajectory of a student through school. What might a wise school look like as a student navigates its twists and turns? For at every juncture, wise educators can make changes to free students to succeed. These examples are not just ideas. All of them have been developed in basic research and evaluated in rigorous trials. As I've said, data matter.

Welcoming Students to Class. You enter class. You wonder, *Do I belong here?*

A basic way to welcome anyone, whether to a party, a school, or a workplace, is to be very intentional in saying you're glad they're there. Hattie Tate, who defines her career in part as "a lifetime focused on warm welcomes," greets new partners with this: "I welcome your experience and your expertise." How simple. How lovely.

Sohad Murrar is now a professor at the University of Illinois Chicago. But in grad school, Murrar and Markus Brauer, a psychologist at the University of Wisconsin, led a project to simply post posters and share videos depicting the norm that everyone is welcome in classrooms. "We are all Wisconsin Badgers. We embrace diversity and welcome people from all backgrounds into our UW-Madison community," they said. This created a more inclusive climate for all students, improved a sense of belonging in class for ethnic- and religious-minority students, and, among 763 students in STEM courses, fully eliminated an achievement gap in course grades.

A second way is to create space so people can share who they are as a person, their values. That way, students can know their whole selves are welcome in class. In a series of studies, a team led by Geoff Cohen worked with middle school teachers to give an assignment early in seventh grade inviting students to share their values with them. The thought was that this might be most helpful for students who face negative stereotypes in school, who might otherwise feel seen just as a token of a stereotype. Indeed, Black students felt more secure in their belonging in school and earned higher grades. In some cases, the benefits lasted years into the future as that early success helped students get on to more rigorous academic tracks. This can help in higher education too. When physics professors invited college students to share what was important to them, women earned higher grades; when biology professors did the same, first-generation students did better; and when massive open online courses included such opportunities, learners from less developed countries were more likely to persist and complete the course successfully.

In another case, Eric Smith at the University of Texas revised a syllabus in a large university lecture course to say that the purpose of office hours wasn't just to ask questions about class material but because the instructors cared about students and wanted to learn about their broader values and goals. That raised grades for first-generation students and students of color. It wasn't that students actually went to office hours more. It was just the signal that all parts of them were welcome in class. So I smiled when Oliver's third-grade teacher started the year by asking every child to fill a "Me Bag" and bring it in for show-and-tell ("We can't wait to learn more about you! Put five things in this bag that describe something about yourself"). That kind of welcome isn't just good for third graders. It's good for all of us. Every team should do something like this.

Social-belonging interventions, which convey to students that worries about belonging are normal in a school transition and improve with time, can be delivered in online modules that reach tens of thousands of students. But they can also be implemented by educators in courses. At the University of Pittsburgh, the psychologist Kevin Binning has led a collaboration with science faculty to create a culture in gateway courses in which everyone recognizes belonging worries as normal and as improving with time. Faculty describe their own experiences, students write reflections, and everyone shares in small groups and class-wide. With an initial 1,822 students randomized to condition, this eliminated a large gender gap in grades in an introductory physics course, and a large race gap in grades in biology. It's an effort that's rapidly expanding.

Communicating the Value of Learning and Making Learning for Students. That's welcoming. But now you open the textbook, look at the list of course readings, begin the first problem set. You wonder, *If I make mistakes, will I be judged?*

Among the most important values to set clearly is that the purpose of school is to support growth—nothing else. That might mean being intentional in describing what you value on the first day, or being explicit in a syllabus. It might mean publicly valuing mistakes as learning opportunities ("That's a great mistake! What can we learn from that?"), something expert tutors do to great effect. It might mean creating assignments that let students revise their work and show progress, rather than just relying on one-off timed tests. It might mean having a class discussion about why you give tough critical feedback—because you believe in students' potential to reach a high standard with feedback and more work, not because you doubt or judge them. In the next section, we'll see how motivating educators to create this kind of intentional growth-mindset culture can help students thrive.

Or you might look at the course and wonder, *Does this content fit with me and who I want to be and what I want to do?* As an instructor, it's critical to make sure that the learning *is* relevant to your students, that it speaks to their lives, where they've been and where they're going. But even when the course material has that value, students might need space to draw that connection out for themselves. So, Judy Harackiewicz and her collaborators have learned to integrate brief written reflections for college students to consider the usefulness of course content for themselves and for their friends and families in gateway science courses. In one case, a team led by Elizabeth Canning found that this space boosted grades in an introductory biology course among 577 students, and raised the rate at which students persisted in a math, science, or engineering major at the end of the semester (from 89 percent to 96 percent). A similar approach in chemistry raised the rate at which 2,505 students majored in STEM two and a half years later from 70 percent to 74 percent, with the largest gain for students of color, from 55 percent to 69 percent.

Helping Students Prepare and Perform. Now, say, a big test is coming. A student wonders, *How will I study?*

As a grad student at the University of Michigan, Patricia Chen created an opportunity for college students to think through what resources were available for them to study and when and how they could best use these resources. Randomized to several hundred statistics students, that opportunity raised test performance and course grades. Next Chen leveraged technology to make this tool easily available to 12,065 college students enrolled in a variety of STEM and economics courses. When students made use of this resource, they did better in class, with the largest gains in classes where instructors and course norms supported its use.

Or you wonder, *Is anxiety a sign I'm about to fail?* In a collaboration with the faculty in a large university lecture class, Shannon Brady added a single paragraph to the email sent to students the day before a midterm reminding them of the test logistics. The paragraph conveyed that test anxiety is your body getting ready to take on a challenge and succeed. For first-year students, who felt most anxious, that reduced anxiety and raised test scores and course grades. Chris Rozek, a psychologist at Washington University in St. Louis, took a similar approach with 1,175 ninth-grade science students. He randomized students to get a short reminder of this same idea ten minutes before taking a final exam. That reminder raised scores, especially for students from lower-income backgrounds, and the rate at which low-income students passed the course from 61 percent to 82 percent.

A third study addressed the stress and anxiety of preparing for the bar exam—a canonical high-stress test. Our group built a team of legal scholars and psychologists led by Victor Quintanilla and Heidi Williams that partnered with the State Bar of California to create a forty-five-minute exercise to represent this stress as normal and useful and as a tool that can be harnessed for learning and performance. Three months later, this "situated stress-mindset" intervention raised bar exam passage rates by seven percentage points among 1,693 test takers, with the greatest gains for students of color and first-generation college students. That closed the gap with White continuing-generation students by more than a third. More students were able to pursue their dreams of becoming an attorney and support their families and serve their communities through law. And this exercise was built to be scalable. Following the randomized trial, the state bar has continued to make it available to test takers in cohort upon cohort, ultimately reaching more than 1,500 additional students with continued benefits.

Helping Students Recover from Setbacks. Now the test is over. You bombed it. *Am I dumb at this class? Do I not belong here?*

At the University of California, Davis, the economist Scott Carrell and the higher education scholar Michal Kurlaender crafted a sequence of emails for professors to send to students expressing their concern and support following struggles on early assignments. Here's one:

> Dear [student name], We are approaching the midpoint in the semester. I am concerned that based on your performance on the [prior assignment] you may be struggling in this course. However, don't be discouraged, there is still plenty of time to recover. To do well in the upcoming [next assignment] I encourage you to [come to class regularly, review lecture notes, go to office hours].
>
> Sincerely, Professor [name]

There's nothing special about these emails. But it's the right thing at the right time. One student wrote back, "I'd . . . like to thank you for offering your help in such a kind manner, I've rarely seen teachers at this school respond to missed assignments the way you have. I'll be sure to complete future assignments in a timely manner, the first practice homework was indeed pretty helpful."

In two trials in introductory microeconomics, this raised students' grades on subsequent course assignments. In a scale-up with forty-three classes and 3,922 students at a large broad-access university, it improved students' experience in class (for example, the belief that the professor cared about their success) and course grades for first-year students from underrepresented racial groups. Why is this rare?

Or remember that research I mentioned in chapter 2 to help universities write wiser probation letters? Shannon Brady created a free tool kit to help university administrators rewrite their own probation letters. That tool kit has now been accessed by administrators at 241 universities around the globe, which collectively enroll nearly three million students.

HELPING EDUCATORS CREATE WISE CLASSROOMS

Know-how is not can-do. How can we motivate and position educators to take the next step?

Motivating Educators to Create Belonging-Supportive, Growth-Mindset Cultures. To help middle school teachers in their interactions with kids when they misbehave, Jason Okonofua did not lecture teachers. He gave them space to articulate the teacher they truly wanted to be for their students.

In a similar spirit, another study found that inviting teachers to reflect on their mission as educators led them to endorse a growth mindset more. And in a massive field trial, Cameron Hecht, Chris Bryan, and David Yeager at the University of Texas used this values-aligned approach to help teachers endorse growth-mindset practices, like conveying a belief in the potential of all their students to improve and emphasizing improvement over time, not students' current level of performance. In one trial, Hecht randomized 319 high school teachers who taught 11,560 students to a forty-five-minute online session focused on growth-mindset practices or a control condition. He anticipated that a shift in classroom culture could be most helpful for students from lower social-class backgrounds, kids who don't have a parent with a college degree, because these children might feel most judged if a teacher implies that only some students can learn. The treatment increased the odds teachers intended to implement growth-mindset practices in their class, as they reported in a survey several weeks later. And, as anticipated, this raised achievement especially in classes with more students from lower social-class backgrounds. On one bottom-line measure, that forty-five-minute session raised the rate at which students in these classes passed the course over the next six to seven months by six to eleven percentage points. This is a road map toward better schooling.

One reason teaching is hard is that students don't pay attention, disengage, or even launch themselves out the window like my sixth-grade German classmate. So, when teachers implement practices that support belonging and growth for students, their work should become more manageable. In fact, one study found that the more teachers invited students of color to share their personal values at the beginning of class, the better the class environment as a whole and the more everyone learned.

Teachers have little spare capacity. But approaches that honor them and draw on their deepest values and strengths may ease their work.

Platforms That Let Teachers Hear Their Students. It's not just stand-alone trainings that can help. It's also making it easier for teachers to hear their students.

As I reflect on this work, I come back to the importance of listening. Listening more informally, like in conversations with students, or in structured ways, like in well-designed laboratory experiments. It's the only way we can understand another person's experience, their reality, the questions they face. It's what we need to move from a-psychological to psychologically wise. In chapter 7, I described the most powerful intervention I know to repair mistrust, the Lifting the Bar exercise. All that did was give kids a platform to introduce themselves on their terms to a teacher of their choosing. It was a chance for a teacher to hear a child's request to partner with them in their learning and growth.

We can create these platforms systematically and proactively, as Dave Paunesku is showing. I've always considered Paunesku visionary. He's always a step ahead of me at least. While I was wallowing in the success of the first small-scale tests of social-belonging interventions, Paunesku feared that interventions like that could be hothouse flowers: beautiful to look at but impractical in the real world, where it really counts. That's when he led the way to deliver belonging and growth-mindset interventions online, letting us reach students at an order of magnitude larger than anything done before. But when I was bowled over by the success of those trials, Paunesku was still dissatisfied. For what about the other 99.99 percent of the school year? he asked. It's the teacher's job to create a strong climate in class. Yet online modules sidestep their role and expertise. All a teacher does is bring kids to the school computer lab.

We could do so much more.

Today, one of the leading programs Paunesku created through PERTS, the organization he co-founded and leads, is Elevate. It's a structured way for teachers to hear from students about the learning conditions in their classroom. In Elevate, teachers give out very brief regular surveys. These are straightforward and obviously important statements about class that students can endorse, or not. Students' responses are anonymous so they can be completely honest. Here are some examples.

PERTS ELEVATE

SAMPLE LEARNING CONDITIONS

	CLASSROOM COMMUNITY	MEANINGFUL WORK	AFFIRMING IDENTITIES	FEEDBACK FOR GROWTH
SAMPLE ITEM	This class is a welcoming place for everyone.	In this class, we do meaningful work, not busy work.	I see positive examples of people like me in the things we learn in this class.	I get specific suggestions about how to improve my work.

This feedback isn't for research or for the vice-principal to peer at or for anyone else. It's not for holding teachers accountable or for evaluating them. There is only one purpose: to help teachers listen to their students.

So teachers get short, regular reports. You see what percentage of kids in your class endorse each learning condition. The numbers are broken down by demographic groups (gender and race-ethnicity), as long as the groups are large enough to keep kids anonymous. That way you can see where you're reaching kids and where you're not. Then you get space to reflect and access to practice guides to decide what you'd like to try to improve the learning conditions in your class. It's a way to surface problems and drive improvement.

One teacher, Hirvelt Megie, who taught technology to high school juniors in Brooklyn, found his results were lower than he'd anticipated, especially on two dimensions, Teacher Caring and Meaningful Work. "That first report was an eye-opener," he said. But he redesigned a unit on genetic engineering and saw a 15 to 20 percent improvement in these learning conditions. The PERTS team has found that the more the learning conditions are met, the greater students' learning. And the more learning conditions *improve,* the more students' grades rise.

Elevate has now reached more than 160 schools in twenty-five states. It's a way to harness children and teachers together, to support their communication and mutual understanding, to align and organize their efforts to create classrooms that help children become.

Burned in my memory is an image of Lucy on the first day of kindergarten, sitting on the class rug with her new classmates, back straight, eyes on the teacher. *Ready to learn.* I snapped a photo. Babies enter the world eager to learn: to learn to nurse; to sit up; to crawl; to walk; to talk; to read; to do math; to ride a bike; to speak up at a school board meeting; to contribute to a community group; to work toward a fairer, more secure, more equitable, and freer world; and then to teach a new generation.

How can we maintain this joy at every stage?

Acknowledgments

For generations, everyday people, alongside members of professional and scientific communities, have sought to understand the psychological barriers that hold people back, and worked diligently and in good faith to learn how we can dodge, overcome, blast out, or slip by these barriers to thrive. Often this work is quiet. It's typically dogged, marked by repeated failures, but there are occasional breakthroughs—and these breakthroughs we share. It's the individual who struggles with a challenge she faces, but finds a productive way to think about that challenge and writes down her experience in an essay; the teacher who reflects on his own doubts in school to understand his students better, comes up with a turn of phrase that inspires a student to take on work that seems impossibly hard, and then shares this success with a colleague; the physician who learns from a mentor how to help her patients understand an illness in a better way. And it is the young social scientist who learns how to think about a social problem from leaders in the field, what might underlie it, and then step-by-step figures out a way to remedy that problem, formalizes that solution, tests it, and learns to scale it.

This book would not have been possible without the ingenuity, dedication, and sheer hard work of these countless people. It is their work we lean on and learn from, whose dividend we cash today.

Education, in particular, is the field dedicated most directly to helping people become. It is no surprise, then, that wisdom from educators is veined throughout this book. My home field of social psychology, too, was born in the crucible of social problems, in the conflicts and horrors of the mid-twentieth century, and the need for a deeper and more useful understanding of our nature. It is the wisdom honed by generations of social psychologists, from founding scholars like Kurt Lewin into the present, that gives members of my generation novel conceptual tools and powerful methods to understand and solve problems of modern life.

Nor would this book have been possible without the love, care, and expertise of many individual people. I am forever grateful to my agents Celeste Fine and Alison MacKeen, who saw the potential for a book like this well before I did and supported it in its long becoming. I did most of the writing on a fellowship at the Center for Advanced Study in the Behavioral Sciences at Stanford University. I am indebted to CASBS for its support, to the 2022–23 CASBS community for its fellowship, as well as to other invaluable professional communities, especially the College Transition Collaborative, the Dweck-Walton Lab, the Mindset Scholars Network, SPARQ, Stanford Impact Labs, and the Stanford Psychology Department. I also owe deep debts of gratitude to my editors, first Shannon Welch, who helped set the course, and then Ann Marie Healy, for the craft, care, and partnership she brought to this project, which improved the book immensely, and to Marnie Cochran and the whole team at Harmony Books and at Penguin Random House for their support. The book also benefited enormously from feedback and suggestions big and small from my first readers, Carol Dweck and Kiara Sanchez, and specific points of feedback from Christina Bauer, Shannon Brady, Nick Camp, Maithreyi Gopalan, Rob MacCoun, Gregg Muragishi, Steve Spencer, and Catherine Thomas. All errors that remain are my own.

When Lucy was about three, I was trying to teach her to hit a ball off a tee. "Keep your eyes on the ball," I said. She looked at me quizzically, and I saw then just how absurd that metaphor is. Your eyes on the ball? "Open your eyes and see the ball," she translated. What better language! I love the directness and clarity of children. In just the same way, the best children's literature can help us see some of the hardest, most obscure issues more clearly, what they are, what they aren't, and what we can do with them. I am indebted to all of the children's authors referenced in this book, and to many who aren't (including my sister-in-law, Nicole Chen).

For me personally, this book would not have been possible without the opportunity to learn from and with so many incredible mentors (Geoff Cohen, Carol Dweck, Eleanor Maccoby, Steve Spencer, Claude Steele, Tim Wilson) and students, colleagues, and collaborators (Lauren Aguilar, Mahzarin Banaji, Christina Bauer, Danielle Boles, Shannon Brady, Tiffany Brannon, Eddie Brummelman, Chris Bryan, Luke Butler, Nick Camp, Priyanka Carr, Patricia Chen, Alia Crum, Ayo Dada, Angela Duckworth, Jennifer Eberhardt, Sam Erman, Eli Finkel, Omid Fotuhi, Mike Frank, Maithreyi Gopalan, Parker Goyer, Valerie Purdie Greenaway, James Gross, Kyla Haimovitz, Rhana Hashemi, Cayce Hook, Zainab Hosseini, Lauren Howe, Veronika Job, Dave Kalkstein, Toni Kenthirarajah, Katie Kroeper, Mark Lepper, Cedric Lim, Christine Logel, Hazel Rose Markus, Allison Master, Benoît Monin, Gregg Muragishi, Mary Murphy, Paul O'Keefe, Jason Okonofua, Gábor Orosz, Dave Paunesku, Victor Quintanilla, Leslie Remache, Steven Roberts, Lee Ross, Chris Rozek, Kimia Saadatian, Kiara Sanchez, Karina Schumann, Eric Smith, Gregg Sparkman, Hattie Tate, Valerie Jones Taylor, Catherine Thomas, Eric Uhlmann, Heidi Williams, David Yeager, and many others). It's a privilege to be a social psychologist. Thank you for having me.

Nor would this book have been possible without the love, support, and wisdom of my family. Thank you to my parents, Ken and Susan, to my brother, Eric, and to Lisa, Lucy, and Oliver. And Tomato too.

Notes

PROLOGUE

xiv **"21 Minutes to Save a Marriage"** Jennifer Welsh, "It Takes Just 21 Minutes a Year to Save Your Marriage," *Business Insider,* Feb. 5, 2013, www.business insider.com/21-minutes-could-save-your-marriage-2013-2; Eli J. Finkel et al., "A Brief Intervention to Promote Conflict Reappraisal Preserves Marital Quality over Time," *Psychological Science* 24, no. 8 (Aug. 2013): 1595–601, doi .org/10.1177/0956797612474938.

xiv **So, yes, the "tricks"** Gregory M. Walton et al., "Lifting the Bar: A Relationship-Orienting Intervention Reduces Recidivism Among Children Reentering School from Juvenile Detention," *Psychological Science* 32, no. 11 (Nov. 2021): 1747–67, doi.org/10.1177/0956797621101380I; Jerome A. Motto and Alan G. Bostrom, "A Randomized Controlled Trial of Postcrisis Suicide Prevention," *Psychiatric Services* 52, no. 6 (June 2001): 828–33, doi.org/10.1176/appi.ps.52 .6.828.

xv **It's ordinary magic** The term draws inspiration from several sources, including Confucius, who is often credited with the saying "A common man marvels at uncommon things. A wise man marvels at the commonplace." The author Edward Abbey, too, wrote, "I now find the most marvelous things in the everyday, the ordinary, the common, the simple and tangible." Most directly, Vichet Chhuon and Tanner LeBaron Wallace describe the feeling of "being known" by adults in school as "ordinary magic" for adolescents, given all the functions these relationships serve young people. Vichet Chhuon and Tanner LeBaron Wallace, "Creating Connectedness Through Being Known: Fulfilling the Need to Belong in U.S. High Schools," *Youth and Society* 46, no. 3 (2014): 379–401, doi.org/10.1177/0044118X11436188.

I first began to think about how wise interventions can seem like magic together with David Yeager. David S. Yeager and Gregory M. Walton, "Social-

Psychological Interventions in Education: They're Not Magic," *Review of Educational Research* 81, no. 2 (June 2011): 267–301, doi.org/10.3102/0034654311405999.

xvii   **We call them wise interventions** Gregory M. Walton, "The New Science of Wise Psychological Interventions," *Current Directions in Psychological Science* 23, no. 1 (2014): 73–82, doi.org/10.1177/0963721413512856; Gregory M. Walton and Alia J. Crum, eds., *Handbook of Wise Interventions: How Social Psychology Can Help People Change* (New York: Guilford Press, 2020), www.guilford.com/books/Handbook-of-Wise-Interventions/Walton-Crum/9781462551002; Gregory M. Walton and Timothy D. Wilson, "Wise Interventions: Psychological Remedies for Social and Personal Problems," *Psychological Review* 125, no. 5 (2018): 617–55, doi.org/10.1037/rev0000115.

xvii   **In one case, my colleagues** Gregory M. Walton and Geoffrey L. Cohen, "A Brief Social-Belonging Intervention Improves Academic and Health Outcomes of Minority Students," *Science* 331, no. 6023 (2011): 1447–51, doi.org/10.1126/science.1198364; Shannon T. Brady et al., "A Brief Social-Belonging Intervention in College Improves Adult Outcomes for Black Americans," *Science Advances* 6, no. 18 (2020): eaay3689, doi.org/10.1126/sciadv.aay3689.

xviii   **Dweck calls it "a journey"** Carol Dweck, "Carol Dweck Revisits the 'Growth Mindset,'" *Education Week*, Sept. 23, 2015, www.edweek.org/leadership/opinion-carol-dweck-revisits-the-growth-mindset/2015/09; Greg Walton, "Stop Telling Students, 'You Belong!,'" *Education Week*, Nov. 17, 2021, www.edweek.org/leadership/opinion-stop-telling-students-you-belong/2021/11.

CHAPTER 1: SPIRALING DOWN

5   **Do you know the white bear study?** Daniel M. Wegner et al., "Paradoxical Effects of Thought Suppression," *Journal of Personality and Social Psychology* 53, no. 1 (1987): 5–13, doi.org/10.1037/0022-3514.53.1.5.

6   **Even by preschool** One 2014 report found that Black children, who represent 18 percent of preschoolers, composed 42 percent of preschoolers who got suspended once and 48 percent of those suspended more than once. "Civil Rights Data Collection: Data Snapshot (School Discipline)," U.S. Department of Education Office for Civil Rights, March 21, 2014, www2.ed.gov/about/offices/list/ocr/docs/crdc-discipline-snapshot.pdf; Walter S. Gilliam et al., "Do Early Educators' Implicit Biases Regarding Sex and Race Relate to Behavior Expectations and Recommendations of Preschool Expulsions and Suspensions?," Yale University Child Study Center, Sept. 28, 2016, www.jsums.edu/scholars/files/2017/03/Preschool-Implicit-Bias-Policy-Brief_final_9_26_276766_5379.pdf.

6   **One of my all-time favorite studies** Sandra L. Murray et al., "When Rejection Stings: How Self-Esteem Constrains Relationship-Enhancement Processes," *Journal of Personality and Social Psychology* 83, no. 3 (2002): 556–73, doi.org/10.1037/0022-3514.83.3.556.

11   **And now they can't "hear"** Patricia K. Kuhl, "Early Language Acquisition: Cracking the Speech Code," *Nature Reviews Neuroscience* 5, no. 11 (Nov. 2004): 831–43, doi.org/10.1038/nrn1533.

12   **Construal is like a kind of focus** You can think about this focus literally. Say you're doing a jigsaw puzzle. You first seek out pieces with a particular wavy

line. You look and look for that line. Once you've put those wavy-line pieces together, you go back through the pile for, say, pieces with a certain hue of blue. Those blue pieces were there all along, but you didn't "see" them when you were looking for the wavy line. For a classic treatment of construal, see Lee Ross and Richard E. Nisbett, *The Person and the Situation: Perspectives of Social Psychology* (New York: McGraw-Hill Book Company, 1991).

16 **When you start to look** In the natural world too. As the biologist Deborah Gordon writes, "All organisms respond to changing situations, which they in turn modify." Deborah M. Gordon, *The Ecology of Collective Behavior* (Princeton, N.J.: Princeton University Press, 2023).

CHAPTER 2: SPIRALING UP

20 **This use of the word "wise"** Erving Goffman, *Stigma: Notes on the Management of Spoiled Identity* (Englewood Cliffs, N.J.: Prentice-Hall, 1963); Claude M. Steele, "A Threat in the Air: How Stereotypes Shape Intellectual Identity and Performance," *American Psychologist* 52, no. 6 (1997): 613–29, doi.org /10.1037/0003-066X.52.6.613.

21 **In one study I ran** Walton and Cohen, "Brief Social-Belonging Intervention Improves Academic and Health Outcomes of Minority Students."

24 **There was, in fact** W. R. Thompson and Dalbir Bindra, "Motivational and Emotional Characteristics of 'Bright' and 'Dull' Rats," *Canadian Journal of Psychology / Revue Canadienne de Psychologie* 6, no. 3 (1952): 116–22, doi.org /10.1037/h0083561.

24 **When Rosenthal looked at the data** Robert Rosenthal and Kermit L. Fode, "The Effect of Experimenter Bias on the Performance of the Albino Rat," *Behavioral Science* 8, no. 3 (1963): 183–89, doi.org/10.1002/bs.3830080302.

25 **Teachers had elicited the growth** Robert Rosenthal and Lenore Jacobson, "Teachers' Expectancies: Determinants of Pupils' IQ Gains," *Psychological Reports* 19, no. 1 (1966): 115–18, doi.org/10.2466/pro.1966.19.1.115; Robert Rosenthal and Lenore Jacobson, "Pygmalion in the Classroom," *Urban Review*, Sept. 1968, 16–20.

25 **That might backfire** Claudia M. Mueller and Carol S. Dweck, "Praise for Intelligence Can Undermine Children's Motivation and Performance," *Journal of Personality and Social Psychology* 75 (1998): 33–52, doi.org/10.1037/0022 -3514.75.1.33.

25 **In fact, in later studies** Stephen W. Raudenbush, "Magnitude of Teacher Expectancy Effects on Pupil IQ as a Function of the Credibility of Expectancy Induction: A Synthesis of Findings from 18 Experiments," *Journal of Educational Psychology* 76, no. 1 (1984): 85, doi.org/10.1037/0022-0663.76.1.85.

25 **The bloomer label** In Rosenthal's original report, he paid particular attention to the results for Mexican American youth, finding that the more "Mexican" boys appeared, the greater their gains with the "bloomer" label. Rosenthal writes, "We can speculate that teachers' pre-experimental expectancies of the more Mexican-looking boys' intellectual performance was probably lowest of all. These children may have had the most to gain by the introduction of a more favorable expectation into the minds of their teacher." Rosenthal and Jacobson, "Pygmalion in the Classroom."

In calling this work "Pygmalion in the Classroom," Rosenthal drew upon a rich current in the mid-twentieth century exploring how labels can help people become or, conversely, hold us back. In 1956, *My Fair Lady* premiered on Broadway, a retelling of the 1912 George Bernard Shaw play *Pygmalion*. It's the story of how Professor Henry Higgins teaches the Cockney-speaking flower seller Eliza Doolittle an upper-class accent, gaining her entrance into high society and his own affection. His expectations empower her upward mobility. John Steinbeck's classic 1952 family saga, *East of Eden*, too, contends with labels. As the novel comes to a close, the protagonist, Adam, worries that his evil wife Cathy's genes will poison the blood of his children. "I would like to know what kind of blood is in my boys. When they grow up—won't I be looking for something in them?" he asks. His wise neighbor, Samuel, advises, "Yes you will. And I will warn you now that not their blood but your suspicion might build evil in them. They will be what you expect of them." When Adam protests, Samuel goes on to say, "I don't very much believe in blood. I think when a man finds good or bad in his children he is seeing only what he planted in them after they cleared the womb."

In science too, the Stanford psychiatrist David Rosenhan explored the stickiness of mental illness labels (that is, diagnoses), showing in a famous study that completely healthy volunteers who checked into mental hospitals with vague symptoms (for example, hearing a voice saying "empty") were never detected as sane by hospital staff, had their personal histories and everyday behaviors reinterpreted as evidence of their illness (for example, staff described pseudo-patients waiting in line for lunch as evidence of the "oral acquisitive nature of their syndromes"), and, upon release, were not deemed cured or as never having been ill in the first place but, often, as "paranoid schizophrenic in remission." D. L. Rosenhan, "On Being Sane in Insane Places," *Science* 179, no. 4070 (1973): 250–58, doi.org/10.1126/science.179 .4070.250.

26   **Sitting on the old white couch** Claude M. Steele, "Race and the Schooling of Black Americans," *Atlantic Monthly,* April 1992; Claude M. Steele and Joshua Aronson, "Stereotype Threat and the Intellectual Test Performance of African Americans," *Journal of Personality and Social Psychology* 69, no. 5 (1995): 797, doi.org/10.1037/0022-3514.69.5.797.

26   **It's a disparity found so often** Steele, "Threat in the Air."

26   **In fact, equating for students' preparation** Gregory M. Walton and Steven J. Spencer, "Latent Ability: Grades and Test Scores Systematically Underestimate the Intellectual Ability of Negatively Stereotyped Students," *Psychological Science* 20, no. 9 (Sept. 2009): 1132–39, doi.org/10.1111/j.1467-9280 .2009.02417.x.

27   **Now, hundreds of experiments later** Toni Schmader, Michael Johns, and Chad Forbes, "An Integrated Process Model of Stereotype Threat Effects on Performance," *Psychological Review,* 115, no. 2 (2008): 336–56, doi.org/10.1037 /0033-295X.115.2.336; Toni Schmader and Sian Beilock, "An Integration of Processes that Underlie Stereotype Threat," in *Stereotype Threat: Theory, Process, and Application* (Oxford University Press, 2012), 34–50.

27   **In just the same way** Steven J. Spencer, Claude M. Steele, and Diane M. Quinn, "Stereotype Threat and Women's Math Performance," *Journal of Experimental Social Psychology* 35, no. 1 (1999): 4–28, doi.org/10.1006/jesp .1998.1373; Thomas M. Hess et al., "The Impact of Stereotype Threat on Age Differences in Memory Performance," *Journals of Gerontology: Series B, Psy-*

chological Sciences and Social Sciences 58, no. 1 (Jan. 2003): P3–11, doi.org /10.1093/geronb/58.1.p3; Jeff Stone et al., "Stereotype Threat Effects on Black and White Athletic Performance," *Journal of Personality and Social Psychology* 77, no. 6 (1999): 1213–27, doi.org/10.1037/0022-3514.77.6.1213.

27   **Research finds these mutual questions** Hilary B. Bergsieker, J. Nicole Shelton, and Jennifer A. Richeson, "To Be Liked Versus Respected: Divergent Goals in Interracial Interactions," *Journal of Personality and Social Psychology* 99, no. 2 (2010): 248–64, doi.org/10.1037/a0018474; Priyanka B. Carr, Carol S. Dweck, and Kristin Pauker, " 'Prejudiced' Behavior Without Prejudice? Beliefs About the Malleability of Prejudice Affect Interracial Interactions," *Journal of Personality and Social Psychology* 103, no. 3 (2012): 452–71, doi.org /10.1037/a0028849; Phillip Atiba Goff, Claude M. Steele, and Paul G. Davies, "The Space Between Us: Stereotype Threat and Distance in Interracial Contexts," *Journal of Personality and Social Psychology* 94, no. 1 (2008): 91–107, doi.org/10.1037/0022-3514.94.1.91; J. Nicole Shelton and Jennifer A. Richeson, "Interracial Interactions: A Relational Approach," in *Advances in Experimental Social Psychology* (San Diego: Elsevier Academic Press, 2006), 38:121–81, doi.org/10.1016/S0065-2601(06)38003-3.

28   **Could that help kids succeed** Drawing inspiration from real-life schools and educators, Steele created a program at the University of Michigan called the 21st Century Program sensitive to the burden posed by stereotypes in the transition to college (what he called "wise schooling"). This improved grades for African American students. Steele, "Threat in the Air."

29   **"Kidneys or certain viscera"** Kurt Lewin, "Forces Behind Food Habits and Methods of Change," in *The Problem of Changing Food Habits: Report of the Committee on Food Habits, 1941–1943* (Washington, D.C.: National Academies Press, 1943), 35–65, www.ncbi.nlm.nih.gov/books/NBK224347/.

29   **"Perhaps one might expect"** Kurt Lewin, "Group Decision and Social Change," in *Readings in Social Psychology,* ed. Theodore M. Newcomb and Eugene L. Hartley (Washington, D.C.: Henry Holt, 1948), 330–41.

31   **A few years ago, a team** Tal Eyal, Mary Steffel, and Nicholas Epley, "Perspective Mistaking: Accurately Understanding the Mind of Another Requires Getting Perspective, Not Taking Perspective," *Journal of Personality and Social Psychology* 114, no. 4 (2018): 547–71, doi.org/10.1037/pspa0000115.

33   **"And it all starts with a conversation"** As Oluo anticipates, perspective getting is one of the most powerful ways to bridge group divides and overcome prejudice. Emile G. Bruneau and Rebecca Saxe, "The Power of Being Heard: The Benefits of 'Perspective-Giving' in the Context of Intergroup Conflict," *Journal of Experimental Social Psychology* 48, no. 4 (2012): 855–66, doi.org /10.1016/j.jesp.2012.02.017; Joshua L. Kalla and David E. Broockman, "Which Narrative Strategies Durably Reduce Prejudice? Evidence from Field and Survey Experiments Supporting the Efficacy of Perspective-Getting," *American Journal of Political Science* 67, no. 1 (2023): 185–204, doi.org/10.1111 /ajps.12657.

33   **That May, Lewin wrote** Ludy T. Benjamin Jr., *A History of Psychology in Letters,* 2nd ed. (Malden, Mass.: Blackwell, 2006).

33   **Sometimes when people are trying** Ariana Orvell, Ethan Kross, and Susan A. Gelman, "How 'You' Makes Meaning," *Science* 355, no. 6331 (2017): 1299–302, doi.org/10.1126/science.aaj2014; Ariana Orvell, Ethan Kross, and Susan A. Gelman, " 'You' Speaks to Me: Effects of Generic-You in Creating Resonance

Between People and Ideas," *Proceedings of the National Academy of Sciences* 117, no. 49 (2020): 31038–45, doi.org/10.1073/pnas.2010939117.

34   **He speaks almost entirely** "Essay B," *This American Life*, National Public Radio, Sept. 8, 2017, www.thisamericanlife.org/625/essay-b.

37   **In the first study I ran** Gregory M. Walton and Geoffrey L. Cohen, "A Question of Belonging: Race, Social Fit, and Achievement," *Journal of Personality and Social Psychology* 92, no. 1 (2007): 82–96, doi.org/10.1037/0022-3514.92 .1.82.

40   **In another study, my good friend** Christine Logel et al., "The Perils of Double Consciousness: The Role of Thought Suppression in Stereotype Threat," *Journal of Experimental Social Psychology* 45, no. 2 (2009): 299–312, doi.org /10.1016/j.jesp.2008.07.016.

41   **Later studies used a more direct approach** Michael Johns, Toni Schmader, and Andy Martens, "Knowing Is Half the Battle: Teaching Stereotype Threat as a Means of Improving Women's Math Performance," *Psychological Science* 16, no. 3 (March 2005): 175–79, doi.org/10.1111/j.0956-7976.2005.00799.x; Avi Ben-Zeev et al., "'Speaking Truth' Protects Underrepresented Minorities' Intellectual Performance and Safety in STEM," *Education Sciences* 7, no. 2 (June 2017): 65, doi.org/10.3390/educsci7020065.

42   **When bad things happen** Gregory M. Walton and Shannon T. Brady, "'Bad' Things Reconsidered," in *Applications of Social Psychology*, ed. Joseph P. Forgas, William D. Crano, and Klaus Fiedler (New York: Routledge, 2020), 58–81, doi.org/10.4324/9780367816407-4.

43   **In the victim-impact statement** Chanel Miller, "Victim Impact Statement," June 2, 2016, www.americanyawp.com/reader/30-the-recent-past/emily-doe -victim-impact-statement-2015/.

46   **In fact, I think that if you're a professional** Walton and Brady, "'Bad' Things Reconsidered."

46   **The Sean. N. Parker Center** Lauren C. Howe et al., "Changing Patient Mindsets about Non-Life Threatening Symptoms During Oral Immunotherapy: A Randomized Clinical Trial," *The Journal of Allergy and Clinical Immunology in Practice* 7, no. 5 (May 2019): 1550–59, doi.org/10.1016/j.jaip.2019.01.022.

47   **How could medical professionals help** Sean R. Zion, Lidia Schapira, and Alia J. Crum, "Targeting Mindsets, Not Just Tumors," *Trends in Cancer* 5, no. 10 (Oct. 2019): 573–76, doi.org/10.1016/j.trecan.2019.08.001; Sean R. Zion et al., "Changing Cancer Mindsets: A Randomized Controlled Feasibility and Efficacy Trial," *Psychooncology* 32, no. 9 (Sept. 2023): 1433–42, doi.org/10 .1002/pon.6194.

48   **our team, led by Shannon Brady** Shannon T. Brady et al., "A Scarlet Letter No More: Psychologically Attuned Notifications About Academic Probation Improve Students' Response and Recovery," 2024.

49   **five saddest country songs** "Whiskey Lullaby" includes these cheer-me-up lyrics: "She put him out like the burnin' end of a midnight cigarette / She broke his heart, he spent his whole life tryin' to forget / We watched him drink his pain away a little at a time / But he never could get drunk enough to get her off his mind." The other saddest songs were "The Little Girl" recorded by John Michael Montgomery, "He Stopped Loving Her Today" by George Jones, "I'm So Lonesome I Could Cry" by Hank Williams, and "Concrete Angel" by Martina McBride. Cady Drell et al., "40 Saddest Country Songs of

All Time," *Rolling Stone* (blog), Sept. 17, 2019, www.rollingstone.com/music /music-lists/40-saddest-country-songs-of-all-time-158907/.

53   **Sometimes it might be a sign** Sapna Cheryan et al., "Designing Classrooms to Maximize Student Achievement," *Policy Insights from the Behavioral and Brain Sciences* 1, no. 1 (2014): 4–12, doi.org/10.1177/2372732214548677.

54   **One of the best ways** Lauren Eskreis-Winkler, Ayelet Fishbach, and Angela L. Duckworth, "Dear Abby: Should I Give Advice or Receive It?," *Psychological Science* 29, no. 11 (2018): 1797–806, doi.org/10.1177/0956797618795472.

54   **The next day he was sullen** This story draws on a story told by Maisha Winn, a professor of education at Stanford University. Maisha T. Winn, *Justice on Both Sides: Transforming Education Through Restorative Justice* (Cambridge, Mass.: Harvard Education Press, 2020).

55   **We call this technique "saying is believing"** Elliot Aronson, "The Power of Self-Persuasion," *American Psychologist* 54 (1999): 875–84, doi.org/10.1037 /h0088188.

55   **In fact, this approach** Jason A. Okonofua, David Paunesku, and Gregory M. Walton, "Brief Intervention to Encourage Empathic Discipline Cuts Suspension Rates in Half Among Adolescents," *Proceedings of the National Academy of Sciences* 113, no. 19 (2016): 5221–26, doi.org/10.1073/pnas.1523698113; Jason A. Okonofua et al., "A Scalable Empathic-Mindset Intervention Reduces Group Disparities in School Suspensions," *Science Advances* 8, no. 12 (2022): eabj0691, doi.org/10.1126/sciadv.abj0691.

55   **The right space might involve** Denise C. Marigold, John G. Holmes, and Michael Ross, "More Than Words: Reframing Compliments from Romantic Partners Fosters Security in Low Self-Esteem Individuals," *Journal of Personality and Social Psychology* 92, no. 2 (2007): 232–48, doi.org/10.1037/0022 -3514.92.2.232.

56   **When people have had traumatic experiences** When left to your own devices, it's easy to ruminate: *Why did I do that? . . . That was so embarrassing . . . I'm such an idiot . . . Why did I do that? . . . That was so embarrassing . . . I'm such an idiot . . . Why did I do that? . . .* That's not productive. Each bad thought prompts the next bad thought, pushing you further down. But writing gives you a structure that helps build a narrative: you can look back on what you've written and decide what something really means, and what it doesn't; where a story starts, and where it ends. And then you can begin to find closure.

Showing the power of writing, Pennebaker, a psychologist at the University of Texas at Austin, asked college students in a classic 1988 study to write for twenty minutes a day for four days about their "deepest thoughts and feelings" about "the most traumatic and upsetting experiences of your entire life." That improved students' immune system and reduced doctor visits over the next six weeks. In a later study, when first-year students wrote about their "deepest thoughts and feelings" about coming to college, they earned higher grades. In a third, when laid-off middle-aged professionals wrote about their "deepest thoughts and feelings" about their job loss, they drank less and were more likely to find a new full-time job over the next eight months (up to 53 percent, from 19 percent in two comparison conditions). James W. Pennebaker, Janice K. Kiecolt-Glaser, and Ronald Glaser, "Disclosure of Traumas and Immune Function: Health Implications for Psychotherapy," *Journal of Consulting and Clinical Psychology* 56, no. 2 (1988): 239–45, doi.org/10.1037

/0022-006X.56.2.239; James W. Pennebaker and Martha E. Francis, "Cognitive, Emotional, and Language Processes in Disclosure," *Cognition and Emotion* 10, no. 6 (1996): 601–26, doi.org/10.1080/026999396380079; Stefanie P. Spera, Eric D. Buhrfeind, and James W. Pennebaker, "Expressive Writing and Coping with Job Loss," *Academy of Management Journal* 37, no. 3 (1994): 722–33, doi.org/10.2307/256708; James W. Pennebaker and Joshua M. Smyth, *Opening Up by Writing It Down: How Expressive Writing Improves Health and Eases Emotional Pain*, 3rd ed. (New York: Guilford Press, 2016), www.guilford.com/books/Opening-Up-by-Writing-It-Down/Pennebaker-Smyth/9781462524921.

CHAPTER 3: DO I BELONG?

63   *Science News* Sujata Gupta, "A Simple Exercise on Belonging Helps Black College Students Years Later," *Science News*, May 5, 2020, www.sciencenews.org/article/black-college-students-social-belonging-intervention.

64   **At the time and still today** Martha A. Sandweiss, "Princeton & Slavery Project," accessed Feb. 9, 2024, slavery.princeton.edu; Liam O'Connor, "A Brief History of Princeton Admissions," *Daily Princetonian*, June 25, 2020, www.dailyprincetonian.com/article/2020/06/brief-history-of-admissions-princeton-diversity-representation-gender-race.

64   **Yet her introduction** Michelle LaVaughn Robinson, "Princeton-Educated Blacks and the Black Community" (bachelor's thesis, Princeton University, 1985).

64   **Forty-one years later** Sonia Sotomayor, *My Beloved World* (New York: Vintage Books, 2014).

64   **And just in the spring of 2022** Dialynn Dwyer, "Watch: Ketanji Brown Jackson Shares the Message She Received from a Stranger in Harvard Yard," Boston.com, March 24, 2022.

66   **Who belongs in the United States** Sapna Cheryan and Benoît Monin, "Where Are You Really From? Asian Americans and Identity Denial," *Journal of Personality and Social Psychology* 89, no. 5 (2005): 717–30, doi.org/10.1037/0022-3514.89.5.717; Thierry Devos and Mahzarin R. Banaji, "American = White?," *Journal of Personality and Social Psychology* 88, no. 3 (2005): 447–66, doi.org/10.1037/0022-3514.88.3.447; Sam Erman, *Almost Citizens: Puerto Rico, the U.S. Constitution, and Empire* (Cambridge, U.K.: Cambridge University Press, 2018), doi.org/10.1017/9781108233866.

66   **At its founding** "Bicentennial Edition: Historical Statistics of the United States, Colonial Times to 1970," U.S. Census Bureau, accessed Feb. 11, 2024, www2.census.gov/library/publications/1975/compendia/hist_stats_colonial-1970/hist_stats_colonial-1970p1-chA.pdf?#.

66   **Thomas Jefferson, the lead author** Thomas Jefferson, *Notes on the State of Virginia* (Richmond: J. W. Randolph, 1853), www.loc.gov/item/01006564/.

66   **Policies of exclusion** James Baldwin, "Letter from a Region in My Mind," *New Yorker*, Nov. 9, 1962, www.newyorker.com/magazine/1962/11/17/letter-from-a-region-in-my-mind; Luke Mogelson, "Among the Insurrectionists at the Capitol," *New Yorker*, Jan. 15, 2021, www.newyorker.com/magazine/2021/01/25/among-the-insurrectionists.

66   **Dr. Martin Luther King Jr.** Martin Luther King Jr., "I Have a Dream" (March

on Washington for Jobs and Freedom, Washington, D.C., Aug. 28, 1963), www.americanrhetoric.com/speeches/mlkihaveadream.htm.

67   **From 1922 to 1945** Lewis M. Terman, *The Measurement of Intelligence* (Boston: Houghton, Mifflin, 1916), 91, doi.org/10.1037/10014-000.

67   **Among the questions** Robert V. Guthrie, *Even the Rat Was White: A Historical View of Psychology*, 2nd ed. (Upper Saddle River, N.J.: Pearson Education, 2004).

70   **This when we know** Walton and Spencer, "Latent Ability." For discussion of policy and legal implications, see Gregory M. Walton, Steven J. Spencer, and Sam Erman, "Affirmative Meritocracy," *Social Issues and Policy Review* 7, no. 1 (Jan. 2013): 1–35, doi.org/10.1111/j.1751-2409.2012.01041.x; Sam Erman and Gregory M. Walton, "Stereotype Threat and Antidiscrimination Law: Affirmative Steps to Promote Meritocracy and Racial Equality in Education," *Southern California Law Review* 88 (2015): 307–78; Rachel D. Godsil, Stuart Banner, and Jerry Kang, "Brief of Experimental Psychologists as Amici Curiae in Support of Respondents, Fisher v. University of Texas," Aug. 13, 2012, blackfreedom.proquest.com/fisher-v-university-of-texas-at-austin-brief-of -experimental-psychologists-as-amici-curiae-in-support-of-respondents/; Rachel D. Godsil, Jerry Kang, and John V. Wintermute, "Brief of Experimental Psychologists as Amici Curiae in Support of Respondents, Fisher v. University of Texas," Nov. 2015, perception.org/publications/brief _amici/.

70   **It echoed at my alma mater** Scott Jaschik, "Yale Worker Breaks Stained Glass Depicting Slaves," *Inside Higher Ed*, July 11, 2016, www.insidehighered.com /quicktakes/2016/07/12/yale-worker-breaks-stained-glass-depicting-slaves; Sara Tabin and Jingyi Cui, "200 Gather in Coalition Protest Against Calhoun," *Yale Daily News*, Oct. 13, 2016, yaledailynews.com/blog/2016/10/31 /200-gather-in-coalition-protest-against-calhoun/; Brandon Griggs, "A Black Yale Graduate Student Was Reported to Police for Napping in Her Dorm," CNN.com, May 12, 2018, www.cnn.com/2018/05/09/us/yale-student-napping -black-trnd/index.html.

70   **It echoed one week earlier** Sam Levin, " 'They Don't Belong': Police Called on Native American Teens on College Tour," *Guardian,* May 4, 2018, www .theguardian.com/us-news/2018/may/04/native-american-students-colorado -state-college-tour-police.

70   **That same year** Institutional Research, Planning, and Effectiveness, Colorado State University, "FY21 Fact Book," n.d., irpe-reports.colostate.edu/pdf /fbk/2021/Fact_Book_Partial_FY21.pdf.

71   **Sotomayor was mentored** Sheryl Gay Stolberg, "Sotomayor, a Trailblazer and a Dreamer," *New York Times,* May 27, 2009, www.nytimes.com/2009/05/27 /us/politics/27websotomayor.html.

71   **Michelle Obama shared a story** Michelle Obama, "Remarks by the President and First Lady at College Opportunity Summit" (College Opportunity Summit, Washington, D.C., Jan. 16, 2014), obamawhitehouse.archives.gov/the-press -office/2014/01/16/remarks-president-and-first-lady-college-opportunity -summit.

72   **It's a feeling of unsettledness** Neil A. Lewis, "On a Supreme Court Prospect's Résumé: 'Baseball Savior,' " *New York Times,* May 15, 2009, www.nytimes .com/2009/05/15/us/15sotomayor.html.

72   **As the sociologist Erving Goffman wrote** Goffman, *Stigma.*

72   **Justice Sotomayor wrote** *Schuette v. Coalition to Defend Affirmative Action,* 572 U.S. 291, No. 12-682 (U.S. Supreme Court, April 22, 2014).

73   **Later, we'd do research** Gregory M. Walton et al., "Mere Belonging: The Power of Social Connections," *Journal of Personality and Social Psychology* 102, no. 3 (2012): 513–32, doi.org/10.1037/a0025731.

73   **When Cohen and I looked at the results** Walton and Cohen, "Question of Belonging."

75   **We asked students to describe** Walton and Cohen, "Question of Belonging"; Walton and Cohen, "Brief Social-Belonging Intervention Improves Academic and Health Outcomes of Minority Students." For a replication, see Mary C. Murphy et al., "A Customized Belonging Intervention Improves Retention of Socially Disadvantaged Students at a Broad-Access University," *Science Advances* 6, no. 29 (2020): eaba4677, doi.org/10.1126/sciadv.aba4677.

77   **Then we gave out two more** Originally, we also included a third question ("When something good happens, I feel that I really belong at [college name]"), but nowadays we often drop it, because it doesn't always go with the first two.

78   **I decided to start** Mary C. Murphy, Claude M. Steele, and James J. Gross, "Signaling Threat: How Situational Cues Affect Women in Math, Science, and Engineering Settings," *Psychological Science* 18, no. 10 (2007): 879–85, doi.org/10.1111/j.1467-9280.2007.01995.x.

79   **Together with two of his grad students** Gregory M. Walton et al., "Two Brief Interventions to Mitigate a 'Chilly Climate' Transform Women's Experience, Relationships, and Achievement in Engineering," *Journal of Educational Psychology* 107, no. 2 (2015): 468–85, doi.org/10.1037/a0037461.

83   **We made them into parables** Walton and Cohen, "Question of Belonging"; Gregory M. Walton and Shannon T. Brady, "The Social-Belonging Intervention," in Walton and Crum, *Handbook of Wise Interventions,* 36–62.

84   **We'd treat our participating students** The procedure was inspired by earlier lines of research led by Tim Wilson and Josh Aronson. Timothy D. Wilson and Patricia W. Linville, "Improving the Academic Performance of College Freshmen: Attribution Therapy Revisited," *Journal of Personality and Social Psychology* 42, no. 2 (1982): 367, doi.org/10.1037/0022-3514.42.2.367; Timothy D. Wilson and Patricia W. Linville, "Improving the Performance of College Freshmen with Attributional Techniques," *Journal of Personality and Social Psychology* 49, no. 1 (1985): 287, doi.org/10.1037/0022-3514.49.1.287; Joshua Aronson, Carrie B. Fried, and Catherine Good, "Reducing the Effects of Stereotype Threat on African American College Students by Shaping Theories of Intelligence," *Journal of Experimental Social Psychology* 38, no. 2 (2002): 113–25, doi.org/10.1006/jesp.2001.1491.

90   **If anything, the processes** Walton and Cohen, "Brief Social-Belonging Intervention Improves Academic and Health Outcomes of Minority Students."

90   **But with the belonging exercise** We also found statistical evidence that change in the construal of daily events contributed to the gain in Black students' grades. The more resilient Black students' fit was in the first week after the intervention—the more it stayed high even on worse days—the more their grades improved over the next three years. That change in social construal predicted ("mediated") the gain in grades. These results point to the importance of that psychological process for academic gains, but there's no doubt other factors also contribute, including the kinds of relationships

(friendships, mentor relationships) students were able to develop once worries about belonging had been addressed.

90   **Because our sample was small** When we compared Black students in our control condition with those campus-wide, their grades were almost identical. There were also dramatic improvements in students' placement in the class distribution. With the belonging exercise, Black students were far more likely to be in the top 25 percent of the class both in GPA from sophomore through senior year and in growth in GPA from the fall semester of the first year (prior to the intervention) to the rest of their college careers. They were also far *less* likely to end up in the bottom 25 percent of the class on both metrics.

91   **Later, when we got** Another trial found the belonging intervention reduced clinical diagnoses of depression through the second year of college, from 26 percent to 13 percent. Hae Yeon Lee et al., "A Brief Social-Belonging Intervention Reduces Health Center Visits in College over 3–4 Years Among Socially Disadvantaged Students," 2023 (under review); Erin S. Sheets and Denise Young, "A Brief Group Social-Belonging Intervention to Improve Mental-Health and Academic Outcomes in BIPOC and First-Generation-to-College Students," *Clinical Psychological Science*, Feb. 19, 2024, doi.org/10 .1177/21677026231220060.

92   **So, the belonging exercise went under the radar** Still, when I looked more deeply at students' responses at the end of college, I found a psychological mark. One question asked students to "guess" what the key message in that first-year session was. Then fully half of Black students in the belonging condition guessed it described how students' social experience in college improved with time, as compared with just 20 percent of students in the control condition. One student wrote, "I think it described the process of growing into the community here." And when I asked students how their own experience in college had changed over time, I saw something similar. Again, half of Black students in the belonging condition spontaneously reported that their belonging had improved with time, as compared with 20 percent in the control condition. One said, "When I first got here I didn't feel as if I fit in very well. As time passed, I found my niche." Another shared, "At first I thought I had gotten [in] by accident and didn't deserve to be here. My first semester Freshman year was tough. As I went along and succeeded academically, I realized that I did belong here and that I could excel." It was as if the idea had become part of the zeitgeist, the received wisdom, the background assumption about what coming to college is like.

93   **How were they doing** Brady et al., "Brief Social-Belonging Intervention in College Improves Adult Outcomes for Black Americans."

95   **By comparison, winning $100,000** Robert Östling and David Cesarini, "Long-Run Effects of Lottery Wealth on Psychological Well-Being," *Review of Economic Studies* 87, no. 6 (2020): 2703–26, doi.org/10.1093/restud/rdaa006.

100   **If you wanted to belong** Emily Pronin, Claude M. Steele, and Lee Ross, "Identity Bifurcation in Response to Stereotype Threat: Women and Mathematics," *Journal of Experimental Social Psychology* 40, no. 2 (2004): 152–68, doi.org/10.1016/S0022-1031(03)00088-X; Sapna Cheryan et al., "Ambient Belonging: How Stereotypical Cues Impact Gender Participation in Computer Science," *Journal of Personality and Social Psychology* 97, no. 6 (2009): 1045–60, doi.org/10.1037/a0016239.

100   **Logel knew from** Christine Logel et al., "Interacting with Sexist Men Triggers Social Identity Threat Among Female Engineers," *Journal of Personality and Social Psychology* 96, no. 6 (2009): 1089–103, doi.org/10.1037/a0015703.

101   **As we reflected** Walton et al., "Two Brief Interventions to Mitigate a 'Chilly Climate' Transform Women's Experience, Relationships, and Achievement in Engineering."

104   **Today, belonging interventions have been tested** Walton and Brady, "Social-Belonging Intervention"; David S. Yeager et al., "Teaching a Lay Theory Before College Narrows Achievement Gaps at Scale," *Proceedings of the National Academy of Sciences* 113, no. 24 (2016): E3341–48, doi.org/10.1073/pnas .1524360113; Murphy et al., "Customized Belonging Intervention Improves Retention of Socially Disadvantaged Students at a Broad-Access University"; Gregory M. Walton et al., "Where and with Whom Does a Brief Social-Belonging Intervention Promote Progress in College?," *Science* 380, no. 6644 (2023): 499–505, doi.org/10.1126/science.ade4420; Kevin R. Binning et al., "Changing Social Contexts to Foster Equity in College Science Courses: An Ecological-Belonging Intervention," *Psychological Science* 31, no. 9 (2020): 1059–70, doi.org/10.1177/0956797620929984; J. Parker Goyer et al., "Targeted Identity-Safety Interventions Cause Lasting Reductions in Discipline Citations Among Negatively Stereotyped Boys," *Journal of Personality and Social Psychology* 117, no. 2 (Aug. 2019): 229–59, doi.org/10.1037/pspa0000152; Geoffrey D. Borman et al., "Reappraising Academic and Social Adversity Improves Middle School Students' Academic Achievement, Behavior, and Well-Being," *Proceedings of the National Academy of Sciences* 116, no. 33 (2019): 16286–91, doi.org/10.1073/pnas.1820317116; Kevin R. Binning et al., "Unlocking the Benefits of Gender Diversity: How an Ecological-Belonging Intervention Enhances Performance in Science Classrooms," *Psychological Science*, Feb. 12, 2024, doi.org/10.1177/09567976231221534; C. Lee Williams et al., "A Brief Social Belonging Intervention Improves Academic Outcomes for Minoritized High School Students," *Motivation Science* 6, no. 4 (2020): 423–37, doi.org/10.1037/mot0000175.

106   **Sacks once wrote** Oliver Sacks, *The River of Consciousness* (New York: Vintage Books, 2018).

106   **As the Native American activist** Tristan Ahtone, "Native Americans Are Recasting Views of Indigenous Life," *National Geographic*, Dec. 2018, www .nationalgeographic.com/magazine/article/native-americans-recasting -views-indigenous-life.

106   **Not all belonging trials** Michael Broda et al., "Reducing Inequality in Academic Success for Incoming College Students: A Randomized Trial of Growth Mindset and Belonging Interventions," *Journal of Research on Educational Effectiveness* 11, no. 3 (2018): 317–38, doi.org/10.1080/19345747.2018.1429037.

113   **Then a team** Binning et al., "Changing Social Contexts to Foster Equity in College Science Courses"; Binning et al., "Unlocking the Benefits of Gender Diversity."

CHAPTER 4: CAN I DO IT?

118   **Verlander described** Ken Rosenthal, "How Justin Verlander, After 516 Starts, Earned His First World Series Win—'I Can Say I Got One,'" *Athletic*, Nov. 4,

2022, theathletic.com/3762453/2022/11/04/verlander-astros-phillies-world -series/.

119   **Then creating a structure to plan** Howard Leventhal, Robert Singer, and Susan Jones, "Effects of Fear and Specificity of Recommendation upon Attitudes and Behavior," *Journal of Personality and Social Psychology* 2, no. 1 (1965): 20–29, doi.org/10.1037/h0022089; Katherine L. Milkman et al., "Using Implementation Intentions Prompts to Enhance Influenza Vaccination Rates," *Proceedings of the National Academy of Sciences* 108, no. 26 (2011): 10415–20, doi.org/10.1073/pnas.1103170108; Patricia Chen et al., "Strategic Resource Use for Learning: A Self-Administered Intervention That Guides Self-Reflection on Effective Resource Use Enhances Academic Performance," *Psychological Science* 28, no. 6 (2017): 774–85, doi.org/10.1177/0956797617 696456; Angela Lee Duckworth et al., "From Fantasy to Action: Mental Contrasting with Implementation Intentions (MCII) Improves Academic Performance in Children," *Social Psychological and Personality Science* 4, no. 6 (2013): 745–53, doi.org/10.1177/1948550613476307.

120   **One study found that using kid-friendly** Another study conducted during the 2003 SARS epidemic in Hong Kong taught fourth graders about the germ theory of disease—that germs are too small to see but are alive and cause disease and have to be killed with soap and, thus, getting a cold isn't caused by being cold and can't be prevented by putting on a sweater. With that kids were more likely to wash their hands with soap at snack time. Social systems too can be opaque. A third study taught low-income students about the importance of education for career success. That increased the likelihood students completed a school extra credit assignment, from 3 percent to 23 percent. Sarah J. Gripshover and Ellen M. Markman, "Teaching Young Children a Theory of Nutrition: Conceptual Change and the Potential for Increased Vegetable Consumption," *Psychological Science* 24, no. 8 (2013): 1541–53, doi.org/10.1177/0956797612474827; Terry Kit-fong Au et al., "Folkbiology Meets Microbiology: A Study of Conceptual and Behavioral Change," *Cognitive Psychology* 57, no. 1 (Aug. 2008): 1–19, doi.org/10.1016/j.cogpsych .2008.03.002; Mesmin Destin and Daphna Oyserman, "Incentivizing Education: Seeing Schoolwork as an Investment, Not a Chore," *Journal of Experimental Social Psychology* 46, no. 5 (2010): 846–49, doi.org/10.1016/j.jesp .2010.04.004.

Sometimes the problem is not that people don't know what actions matter but that they forget at the key time. Then well-placed reminders can help. In one memorable study, a safe sex video had no effect on whether Canadian undergrads used a condom over the next two months. Probably, they'd already heard about safe sex. But when they also got a bracelet to wear to remind them of this idea, the number who used a condom when having sex jumped from 27 percent to 55 percent. The bracelet was especially effective when students had sex after drinking. That might seem surprising; lay psychology says that being drunk just makes people seek out risks. But actually, drinking makes people more sensitive to local cues. Usually those cues say "take risks"; then you might do something dumb, like waterslide out of a second-story window (not you?). But when the bracelet became a salient cue, it said, *Danger! Unsafe sex! Use condom!* So, students did. Sonya Dal Cin et al., "Remembering the Message: The Use of a Reminder Cue to Increase Condom Use Following a Safer Sex Intervention," *Health Psychology* 25, no. 3

(2006): 438–43, doi.org/10.1037/0278-6133.25.3.438; Claude M. Steele and Robert A. Josephs, "Alcohol Myopia: Its Prized and Dangerous Effects," *American Psychologist* 45, no. 8 (1990): 921–33, doi.org/10.1037/0003-066X.45.8 .921.

Well-placed reminders can also remind people of healthy-eating goals, reducing snack consumption. Warning labels can remind people of the risks of smoking and, it seems, cut smoking. And mask wearing in China during the COVID-19 pandemic seemed to serve as a moral symbol, promoting other prosocial behaviors. Esther K. Papies and Petra Hamstra, "Goal Priming and Eating Behavior: Enhancing Self-Regulation by Environmental Cues," *Health Psychology* 29, no. 4 (2010): 384–88, doi.org/10.1037/a0019877; Sabrina Stöckli et al., "An (Un)Healthy Poster: When Environmental Cues Affect Consumers' Food Choices at Vending Machines," *Appetite* 96 (2016): 368–74, doi.org/10.1016/j.appet.2015.09.034; David Hammond et al., "Graphic Canadian Cigarette Warning Labels and Adverse Outcomes: Evidence from Canadian Smokers," *American Journal of Public Health* 94, no. 8 (Aug. 2004): 1442–45; Jackson G. Lu et al., "Masks as a Moral Symbol: Masks Reduce Wearers' Deviant Behavior in China During COVID-19," *Proceedings of the National Academy of Sciences* 119, no. 41 (2022): e2211144119, doi.org /10.1073/pnas.2211144119.

122   **That's a catchy notion** It reflects our inclination to explain behaviors in terms of the qualities of individuals. Lee Ross, "The Intuitive Psychologist and His Shortcomings: Distortions in the Attribution Process," in *Advances in Experimental Social Psychology*, ed. Leonard Berkowitz (New York: Academic Press, 1977), 10:173–220, doi.org/10.1016/S0065-2601(08)60357-3; Hazel R. Markus and Shinobu Kitayama, "Culture and the Self: Implications for Cognition, Emotion, and Motivation," *Psychological Review* 98, no. 2 (1991): 224–53, doi .org/10.1037/0033-295X.98.2.224.

122   **It's present in the habitual ways** Elizabeth A. Gunderson et al., "Parent Praise to 1–3 Year-Olds Predicts Children's Motivational Frameworks 5 Years Later," *Child Development* 84, no. 5 (Sept. 2013): 1526–41, doi.org/10.1111/cdev.12064; Elizabeth A. Gunderson et al., "Parent Praise to Toddlers Predicts Fourth Grade Academic Achievement via Children's Incremental Mindsets," *Developmental Psychology* 54, no. 3 (2018): 397–409, doi.org/10.1037/dev0000444; Mia Radovanovic, Antonia Soldovieri, and Jessica A. Sommerville, "It Takes Two: Process Praise Linking Trying and Success Is Associated with Greater Infant Persistence," *Developmental Psychology* 59, no. 9 (2023): 1668–75, doi .org/10.1037/dev0001584; Aneeta Rattan, Catherine Good, and Carol S. Dweck, " 'It's Ok—Not Everyone Can Be Good at Math': Instructors with an Entity Theory Comfort (and Demotivate) Students," *Journal of Experimental Social Psychology* 48, no. 3 (2012): 731–37, doi.org/10.1016/j.jesp.2011.12.012; Mary C. Murphy and Carol S. Dweck, "A Culture of Genius: How an Organization's Lay Theory Shapes People's Cognition, Affect, and Behavior," *Personality and Social Psychology Bulletin* 36, no. 3 (2010): 283–96, doi.org/10.1177 /0146167209347380.

122   **Featuring such questions as** John Greenwood, "Psychologists Go to War," *Behavioral Scientist* (blog), May 22, 2017, behavioralscientist.org/psychologists -go-war/; *Army Mental Tests* (New York: H. Holt, 1920).

123   **After the war, the Princeton psychologist** The relationship of the SAT to inequality in educational opportunities is complex. In some cases, the SAT has

been used by colleges to identify talented students they would not otherwise recognize, including students from lower social-class backgrounds, students of color, and students from high schools and communities less well known to selective colleges. Yet standardized tests like the SAT are also subject to systematic biases that underestimate the potential of students from groups that face negative stereotypes in schooling. Nicholas Lemann, *The Big Test: The Secret History of the American Meritocracy* (New York: Farrar, Straus and Giroux, 1999); Walton and Spencer, "Latent Ability."

123   **It's absurd, but Terman** Lewis M. Terman, "Were We Born That Way?," *World's Work* 44 (1922): 649–60.

123   **James Baldwin wrote** James Baldwin, *The Price of the Ticket: Collected Nonfiction, 1948–1985* (Boston: Beacon Press, 2021).

123   **A few years ago, the Stanford Graduate** *Rethinking Giftedness* (Citizen Film), accessed Feb. 12, 2024, www.youcubed.org/rethinking-giftedness -film/.

124   **In 1998, Dweck published a classic** Mueller and Dweck, "Praise for Intelligence Can Undermine Children's Motivation and Performance."

125   **That's spiraling down in thirty minutes** You don't need Mueller and Dweck to know that a culture that venerates smartness promotes cheating. Just watch episode 2 of *The Simpsons*. Bart's teacher introduces an IQ test by saying, "Now, I don't want you to worry, class. These tests will have no effect on your grades. They merely determine your future social status and financial success. If any." Bart responds by cheating. Of course he does. "Bart the Genius," *The Simpsons*, Fox, Jan. 14, 1990.

127   **The year Lucy started kindergarten** For many years, the building housing our psychology department was named after David Starr Jordan, Stanford's first president, but also another noted eugenicist. Among Jordan's contributions to public life was to inspire an early physician at San Quentin prison, Dr. Leo Stanley, to perform at least six hundred sterilizations of prisoners in the early twentieth century, "to illustrate the value of preventing propagation of the unfit." In 2019, our department and a student group petitioned Stanford to change the name. What would it be like to attend classes, meet with advisers, or work with community groups in a building that venerates a man who thought people from your community were not worthy to reproduce? As one student said in a community meeting, "[The building's name] communicates that Stanford does not care that much about marginalized groups." It was especially ironic given how many students' research focused on supporting belonging for people from diverse communities. The request was granted in October 2020. Marc Chappelle et al., "Reports of the Advisory Committee on Renaming Jordan Hall and Removing the Statue of Louis Agassiz," Stanford University, Sept. 14, 2020, campusnames.stanford.edu /wp-content/uploads/sites/14/2020/10/Jordan-report.pdf.

128   **"In the early two-thousands, Nvidia"** "How Jensen Huang's Nvidia Is Powering the A.I. Revolution," *New Yorker*, Dec. 4, 2023, www.newyorker.com /magazine/2023/12/04/how-jensen-huangs-nvidia-is-powering-the-ai -revolution.

130   **"Dear Jenny"** John McPhee, "Draft No. 4," *New Yorker*, April 22, 2013, www .newyorker.com/magazine/2013/04/29/draft-no-4.

130   **One of my first grad students** The notion of a vomit draft plays on an old insight in psychology: that breaking a big task into little parts and then accom-

plishing each one in turn can build confidence. Research finds that such "proximal goals" can help kids struggling with arithmetic and increase industrial productivity, among other things. Albert Bandura and Dale H. Schunk, "Cultivating Competence, Self-Efficacy, and Intrinsic Interest Through Proximal Self-Motivation," *Journal of Personality and Social Psychology* 41, no. 3 (1981): 586–98, doi.org/10.1037/0022-3514.41.3.586; Gary P. Latham and J. James Baldes, "The 'Practical Significance' of Locke's Theory of Goal Setting," *Journal of Applied Psychology* 60, no. 1 (1975): 122–24, doi.org/10.1037/h0076354.

131 **In 1970, two psychologists at Yale** Michael D. Storms and Richard E. Nisbett, "Insomnia and the Attribution Process," *Journal of Personality and Social Psychology* 16 (1970): 319–28, doi.org/10.1037/h0029835.

133 **These exercises consistently raise grades** Wilson and Linville, "Improving the Academic Performance of College Freshmen"; Wilson and Linville, "Improving the Performance of College Freshmen with Attributional Techniques"; Timothy D. Wilson, Michelle Damiani, and Nicole Shelton, "Improving the Academic Performance of College Students with Brief Attributional Interventions," in *Improving Academic Achievement*, ed. Joshua Aronson (San Diego: Academic Press, 2002), 89–108, doi.org/10.1016/B978-012064455-1/50008-7.

133 **Modern-day growth-mindset interventions** Carol S. Dweck and David S. Yeager, "A Growth Mindset About Intelligence," in Walton and Crum, *Handbook of Wise Interventions*, 9–35.

133 **Josh Aronson, Carrie Fried** Aronson, Fried, and Good, "Reducing the Effects of Stereotype Threat on African American College Students by Shaping Theories of Intelligence."

134 **In another early trial** Lisa S. Blackwell, Kali H. Trzesniewski, and Carol S. Dweck, "Implicit Theories of Intelligence Predict Achievement Across an Adolescent Transition: A Longitudinal Study and an Intervention," *Child Development* 78, no. 1 (2007): 246–63, doi.org/10.1111/j.1467-8624.2007.00995.x.

135 **Today, rigorous growth-mindset interventions** Ingo Outes-Leon, Alan Sánchez, and Renos Vakis, "The Power of Believing You Can Get Smarter: The Impact of a Growth-Mindset Intervention on Academic Achievement in Peru," World Bank Policy Research Working Paper No. 9141, Feb. 4, 2020, papers.ssrn.com/abstract=3531336; Eric Bettinger et al., "Increasing Perseverance in Math: Evidence from a Field Experiment in Norway," *Journal of Economic Behavior and Organization* 146 (2018): 1–15, doi.org/10.1016/j.jebo.2017.11.032; Mari Rege et al., "How Can We Inspire Nations of Learners? An Investigation of Growth Mindset and Challenge-Seeking in Two Countries," *American Psychologist* 76, no. 5 (2021): 755–67, doi.org/10.1037/amp0000647; David S. Yeager et al., "A National Experiment Reveals Where a Growth Mindset Improves Achievement," *Nature* 573, no. 7774 (Sept. 2019): 364–69, doi.org/10.1038/s41586-019-1466-y.

135 **First, in grad school, he pioneered** David Paunesku et al., "Mind-Set Interventions Are a Scalable Treatment for Academic Underachievement," *Psychological Science* 26, no. 6 (June 2015): 784–93, doi.org/10.1177/0956797615571017; Yeager et al., "Teaching a Lay Theory Before College Narrows Achievement Gaps at Scale."

135 **These methods would ultimately power** Walton et al., "Where and with Whom Does a Brief Social-Belonging Intervention Promote Progress in Col-

lege?"; Yeager et al., "National Experiment Reveals Where a Growth Mindset Improves Achievement."

137   **As Oliver and I whooped and cheered** A few years later I got a beautiful coda to this story from Oliver, actually two of them. One evening when Oliver was seven, we were biking home together after a late soccer practice. It was after 7:00 P.M., well after the sun had gone down, and Oliver was pedaling very slowly. I thought back on those conversations.

"Do you remember what I used to tell you when we biked home?"

"No."

"I used to say that when you're tired and you keep going, that's when your muscles get stronger," I said. "What do you think about that?"

Oliver paused. "It means you have to exercise," he said, and then added, "I can go faster now."

He zoomed ahead.

Two years later, just as I was finishing this book, Oliver and I were playing soccer on a field near our house. "You're so strong," I said to Oliver, "How'd you get so strong?"

"Magic!" he declared.

137   **The very notion** Ever Meister, "Coffee History: The Coffee Break," *Serious Eats* (blog), Aug. 9, 2018, www.seriouseats.com/coffee-history-the-coffee-break.

137   **The campaign has been credited** James Miller, "Case Study: How Fame Made Snickers' 'You're Not You When You're Hungry' Campaign a Success," Oct. 26, 2016, www.campaignlive.com/article/case-study-fame-made-snickers-youre-not-when-youre-hungry-campaign-success/1413554?utm_source=website&utm_medium=social.

137   **In a famous 1998 study** Roy F. Baumeister et al., "Ego Depletion: Is the Active Self a Limited Resource?," *Journal of Personality and Social Psychology* 74, no. 5 (1998): 1252–65, doi.org/10.1037/0022-3514.74.5.1252.

139   **Job ran a series of studies** Veronika Job, Carol S. Dweck, and Gregory M. Walton, "Ego Depletion—Is It All in Your Head? Implicit Theories About Willpower Affect Self-Regulation," *Psychological Science* 21, no. 11 (2010): 1686–93, doi.org/10.1177/0956797610384745.

140   **In one study, Job tracked** Veronika Job et al., "Implicit Theories About Willpower Predict Self-Regulation and Grades in Everyday Life," *Journal of Personality and Social Psychology* 108 (2015): 637–47, doi.org/10.1037/pspp0000014.

141   **Now we know that** Eric M. Miller et al., "Theories of Willpower Affect Sustained Learning," ed. Joy J. Geng, *PLoS ONE* 7, no. 6 (2012): e38680, doi.org/10.1371/journal.pone.0038680; Katharina Bernecker et al., "Implicit Theories About Willpower Predict Subjective Well-Being," *Journal of Personality* 85, no. 2 (April 2017): 136–50, doi.org/10.1111/jopy.12225; Veronika Job et al., "Implicit Theories About Willpower Predict the Activation of a Rest Goal Following Self-Control Exertion," *Journal of Personality and Social Psychology* 109, no. 4 (2015): 694–706, doi.org/10.1037/pspp0000042; Katharina Bernecker and Veronika Job, "Too Exhausted to Go to Bed: Implicit Theories About Willpower and Stress Predict Bedtime Procrastination," *British Journal of Psychology* 111, no. 1 (2020): 126–47, doi.org/10.1111/bjop.12382; Katharina Bernecker and Veronika Job, "Beliefs About Willpower Are Related to Therapy Adherence and Psychological Adjustment in Patients with Type 2

Diabetes," *Basic and Applied Social Psychology* 37, no. 3 (2015): 188–95, doi.org /10.1080/01973533.2015.1049348.

141 **In one study, when Job prompted** Veronika Job et al., "Beliefs About Will-power Determine the Impact of Glucose on Self-Control," *Proceedings of the National Academy of Sciences* 110, no. 37 (2013): 14837–42, doi.org/10.1073 /pnas.1313475110.

142 **"For [nineteenth-century school superintendents]"** Kenneth Mark Gold, *School's In: The History of Summer Education in American Public Schools* (New York: Peter Lang, 2002).

142 **But that view is not dominant everywhere** Krishna Savani and Veronika Job, "Reverse Ego-Depletion: Acts of Self-Control Can Improve Subsequent Per-formance in Indian Cultural Contexts," *Journal of Personality and Social Psy-chology* 113 (2017): 589–607, doi.org/10.1037/pspi0000099.

143 **In one study, the psychologist** Kyla Haimovitz, Carol S. Dweck, and Gregory M. Walton, "Preschoolers Find Ways to Resist Temptation After Learning That Willpower Can Be Energizing," *Developmental Science* 23, no. 3 (May 2020), doi.org/10.1111/desc.12905.

143 **"I don't think we thought"** Christopher Clarey, "Serena and Venus Williams Are Siblings Forever, but Rivals for Not Much Longer," *New York Times,* July 6, 2015, www.nytimes.com/2015/07/07/sports/tennis/wimbledon-2015 -serena-williams-defeats-venus-williams-in-straight-sets.html.

144 **Or as James Bond puts it** Prefer other heroes? Sherlock Holmes puts it this way in *The Sign of the Four:* "I never remember feeling tired by work, though idleness exhausts me completely." Or, as Rhyme and Reason advise Milo in *The Phantom Tollbooth,* "So many things are possible just as long as you don't know they're impossible." William James, "The Energies of Men," *Philosoph-ical Review* 16, no. 1 (1907): 1–20, doi.org/10.2307/2177575.

146 **A clue as to how fundamental** Rodolfo Cortes Barragan and Carol S. Dweck, "Rethinking Natural Altruism: Simple Reciprocal Interactions Trigger Chil-dren's Benevolence," *Proceedings of the National Academy of Sciences* 111, no. 48 (2014): 17071–74, doi.org/10.1073/pnas.1419408111; Felix Warneken and Michael Tomasello, "Altruistic Helping in Human Infants and Young Chimpanzees," *Science* 311, no. 5765 (2006): 1301–3; Felix Warneken and Michael Tomasello, "Helping and Cooperation at 14 Months of Age," *Infancy: The Official Journal of the International Society on Infant Studies* 11, no. 3 (May 2007): 271–94, doi.org/10.1111/j.1532-7078.2007.tb00227.x; Lara B. Aknin, J. Kiley Hamlin, and Elizabeth W. Dunn, "Giving Leads to Happiness in Young Children," *PLoS ONE* 7, no. 6 (2012): e39211, doi.org/10.1371 /journal.pone.0039211.

146 **Following smaller-scale experiments** In one study, a team led by Elizabeth Dunn at the University of British Columbia gave adults $5 or $20 and in-structed them to spend it on themselves or others. When she asked people to predict what would make people happier, they said more money and spend-ing it on yourself. But that was doubly wrong. Spending on others increased happiness the most, and the amount didn't matter. Lara B. Aknin et al., "Pro-social Spending and Well-Being: Cross-Cultural Evidence for a Psychological Universal," *Journal of Personality and Social Psychology* 104, no. 4 (2013): 635–52, doi.org/10.1037/a0031578; Elizabeth W. Dunn, Lara B. Aknin, and Michael I. Norton, "Spending Money on Others Promotes Happiness," *Sci-ence* 319, no. 5870 (2008): 1687–88, doi.org/10.1126/science.1150952.

146   **If helping is fundamental** Adam M. Grant and David A. Hofmann, "It's Not All About Me: Motivating Hand Hygiene Among Health Care Professionals by Focusing on Patients," *Psychological Science* 22, no. 12 (Dec. 2011): 1494–99, doi.org/10.1177/0956797611419172; Adam M. Grant, "The Significance of Task Significance: Job Performance Effects, Relational Mechanisms, and Boundary Conditions," *Journal of Applied Psychology* 93, no. 1 (2008): 108–24, doi.org/10.1037/0021-9010.93.1.108; Adam M. Grant et al., "Impact and the Art of Motivation Maintenance: The Effects of Contact with Beneficiaries on Persistence Behavior," *Organizational Behavior and Human Decision Processes* 103, no. 1 (2007): 53–67, doi.org/10.1016/j.obhdp.2006.05.004.

148   **They called this the "utility-value" intervention** Chris S. Hulleman and Judith M. Harackiewicz, "Promoting Interest and Performance in High School Science Classes," *Science* 326, no. 5958 (2009): 1410–12, doi.org /10.1126/science.1177067; Chris S. Hulleman and Judith M. Harackiewicz, "The Utility-Value Intervention," in Walton and Crum, *Handbook of Wise Interventions*, 100–125.

149   **Next, Harackiewicz and her collaborators** Elizabeth A. Canning et al., "Improving Performance and Retention in Introductory Biology with a Utility-Value Intervention," *Journal of Educational Psychology* 110, no. 6 (2018): 834–49, doi.org/10.1037/edu0000244; Michael W. Asher et al., "Utility-Value Intervention Promotes Persistence and Diversity in STEM," *Proceedings of the National Academy of Sciences* 120, no. 19 (2023): e2300463120, doi .org/10.1073/pnas.2300463120; Judith M. Harackiewicz et al., "A Prosocial Value Intervention in Gateway STEM Courses," *Journal of Personality and Social Psychology* 125, no. 6 (2023): 1265–307, doi.org/10.1037/pspa0000356; Judith M. Harackiewicz et al., "Closing Achievement Gaps with a Utility-Value Intervention: Disentangling Race and Social Class," *Journal of Personality and Social Psychology* 111, no. 5 (Nov. 2016): 745–65, doi.org/10.1037 /pspp0000075.
      A related approach, the pro-social-purpose intervention, goes beyond the usefulness of specific course content to help students connect learning in school to the kind of person they want to become and the impact they want to have for others. First, students reflect on a social problem that matters to them. Next, they review stories from other students who describe how a growing awareness of social problems motivated them to work hard in school. Last, they write their own story for future students about their purposes for learning. This can help students sustain focus on boring but foundational learning tasks, and raise grades in math and science, especially for students who start off performing at lower rates. David S. Yeager et al., "Boring but Important: A Self-Transcendent Purpose for Learning Fosters Academic Self-Regulation," *Journal of Personality and Social Psychology* 107, no. 4 (Oct. 2014): 559–80, doi.org/10.1037/a0037637.

149   **She's also found that** Judith M. Harackiewicz et al., "Helping Parents to Motivate Adolescents in Mathematics and Science: An Experimental Test of a Utility-Value Intervention," *Psychological Science* 23, no. 8 (2012): 899–906, doi.org/10.1177/0956797611435530; Christopher S. Rozek et al., "Utility-Value Intervention with Parents Increases Students' STEM Preparation and Career Pursuit," *Proceedings of the National Academy of Sciences* 114, no. 5 (2017): 909–14, doi.org/10.1073/pnas.1607386114.

149   **In one study, Elizabeth Canning** Elizabeth A. Canning and Judith M. Harack-

iewicz, "Teach It, Don't Preach It: The Differential Effects of Directly-Communicated and Self-Generated Utility-Value Information," *Motivation Science* 1, no. 1 (2015): 47–71, doi.org/10.1037/mot0000005.

150   **It's also doing together** Felix Warneken, Frances Chen, and Michael Tomasello, "Cooperative Activities in Young Children and Chimpanzees," *Child Development* 77, no. 3 (2006): 640–63, doi.org/10.1111/j.1467-8624.2006.00895.x; Warneken and Tomasello, "Helping and Cooperation at 14 Months of Age"; Lucas P. Butler and Gregory M. Walton, "The Opportunity to Collaborate Increases Preschoolers' Motivation for Challenging Tasks," *Journal of Experimental Child Psychology* 116, no. 4 (Dec. 2013): 953–61, doi.org/10.1016/j.jecp.2013 .06.007; Priyanka B. Carr and Gregory M. Walton, "Cues of Working Together Fuel Intrinsic Motivation," *Journal of Experimental Social Psychology* 53 (2014): 169–84, doi.org/10.1016/j.jesp.2014.03.015.

151   **In one study, Lauren Howe** Lauren C. Howe, Priyanka B. Carr, and Gregory M. Walton, "Normative Appeals Motivate People to Contribute to Collective Action Problems More When They Invite People to Work Together Toward a Common Goal," *Journal of Personality and Social Psychology* 121 (2021): 215–38.

152   **The paper towel study was inspired** Noah J. Goldstein, Robert B. Cialdini, and Vladas Griskevicius, "A Room with a Viewpoint: Using Social Norms to Motivate Environmental Conservation in Hotels," *Journal of Consumer Research* 35, no. 3 (2008): 472–82, doi.org/10.1086/586910.

153   **This is an industry that spends** "The Facts on Junk Food Marketing and Kids," Prevention Institute, accessed Feb. 15, 2024, www.preventioninstitute .org/facts-junk-food-marketing-and-kids.

153   **Working in a large public middle school** Christopher J. Bryan et al., "Harnessing Adolescent Values to Motivate Healthier Eating," *Proceedings of the National Academy of Sciences* 113, no. 39 (2016): 10830–35, doi.org/10.1073/pnas .1604586113; Christopher J. Bryan, David S. Yeager, and Cintia P. Hinojosa, "A Values-Alignment Intervention Protects Adolescents from the Effects of Food Marketing," *Nature Human Behaviour* 3, no. 6 (June 2019): 596–603, doi.org /10.1038/s41562-019-0586-6; Christopher J. Bryan, "Values-Alignment Interventions: An Alternative to Pragmatic Appeals for Behavior Change," in Walton and Crum, *Handbook of Wise Interventions*, 259–85.

156   **Harwood had a problem** Bernard Burnes, "The Role of Alfred J. Marrow and the Harwood Manufacturing Corporation in the Advancement of OD," *Journal of Applied Behavioral Science* 55, no. 4 (2019): 397–427, doi.org/10.1177 /0021886319865270.

156   **So two of Lewin's students** Lester Coch and John R. P. French Jr., "Overcoming Resistance to Change," *Human Relations* 1, no. 4 (1948): 512–32.

157   **It led to headlines such as** " 'Human Relations' Raises Sales 300%; 'Experiments' with Personnel in Marion, Va., Textile Mill Found to Pay Dividends," *New York Times*, Feb. 16, 1948, www.nytimes.com/1948/02/16/archives /human-relations-raises-sales-300-experiments-with-personnel-in.html.

157   **In a 2022 study** Sherry Jueyu Wu and Elizabeth Levy Paluck, "Having a Voice in Your Group: Increasing Productivity Through Group Participation," *Behavioural Public Policy*, April 8, 2022, 1–20, doi.org/10.1017/bpp.2022.9.

157   **In modern-day tech companies too** Gregg A. Muragishi et al., "Microinclusions: Treating Women as Respected Work Partners Increases a Sense of Fit

in Technology Companies," *Journal of Personality and Social Psychology*, Aug. 21, 2023, doi.org/10.1037/pspi0000430.

159   **In one study, when struggling** Sade Bonilla, Thomas S. Dee, and Emily K. Penner, "Ethnic Studies Increases Longer-Run Academic Engagement and Attainment," *Proceedings of the National Academy of Sciences* 118, no. 37 (2021): e2026386118, doi.org/10.1073/pnas.2026386118.

159   **One exhibit showcased a project** Richard Rothstein, *The Color of Law: A Forgotten History of How Our Government Segregated America* (New York: Liveright, 2017), www.epi.org/publication/the-color-of-law-a-forgotten-history-of-how-our-government-segregated-america/.

159   **This is called culturally relevant pedagogy** Gloria Ladson-Billings, "Toward a Theory of Culturally Relevant Pedagogy," *American Educational Research Journal* 32, no. 3 (1995): 465–91, doi.org/10.3102/00028312032003465.

160   **In some cases, Indian families resisted** As Ned Blackhawk writes, "In 1919, only 2,089 out of an estimated 9,613 children from the Navajo Nation attended schools. In countless acts of everyday resistance, families hid their children from government officials to limit the damaging effects of assimilation." Ned Blackhawk, *The Rediscovery of America: Native Peoples and the Unmaking of U.S. History* (New Haven, Conn.: Yale University Press, 2023), 402.

160   **In other cases** In January 2024, on a family road trip, we were listening to a podcast recommended by our daughter's friend Lena, *Cautionary Tales*, in which Jim Gray, the former principal chief of the Osage Nation in Oklahoma, describes the experience of his great-grandfather Henry Roan in an Indian boarding school. Gray said,

> Assimilation. This is where they actually took children out of their homes, often times against the will of their parents, and sent them off to these reeducation camps called Indian boarding schools. They were there for years often without communication back to their families. Their clothes were burned. They were replaced with military uniforms. Their hair was shaved. They were paraded around in these photographs of kind of before and after pictures that these schools used to perpetuate the success of the programs. What was behind those photographs was a series of beatings for Indian children who spoke their language. They were forced into servitude to local families that lived in the area to do menial labor. They were abused. Some were molested. Some were raped. Some committed suicide. Some tried to run away and were beaten severely. My great-grandfather was one such story. He spent his early years of his life in a boarding school in Pennsylvania, which is about a thousand miles away. He spent I think seven years there. Basically robbed of a traditional Osage upbringing, and not really having much of a human connection. I don't know whether or not he was beaten or molested or any of that. I do know that through some historical documents it was pretty clear he just wanted to be left alone when he got back.

The host, Tim Harford, then says, "I'm looking at a photograph of him now as a schoolboy, with short hair. He's wearing a suit and he's wearing a tie. I'm sure you've seen the same photograph, and what it says to you when you see that image?" Gray responds,

Well, ah, they tried to remove the Osage that was a part of him, and turn him into something else, often against his will. So, I think that the image it tells me is that he probably didn't have the agency to be able to make his own choices about whether or not he wanted to be there. He married and had a family. But I, I feel like he struggled with his identity. I think that's one of the outcomes of the boarding school experience. Not just Henry Roan. But Indian children throughout the United States who went through this experience came back, I guess you could say damaged, and not really fitting into the traditional Indian world that they came from but certainly not fitting into the white world because to them they were just another Indian. Henry's is just one of many stories from that period of time. And others were treated worse and some never survived that experience. So, the fact that he came back, albeit maybe confused or at worst damaged because of it psychologically, he struggled to reclaim his Osage identity, as you can tell. As a young man, there's a picture of him where he's grown his hair out. He's refusing to allow that boarding school experience to define you. I take some measure of comfort in knowing that that policy failed to achieve its goals.

Thus, Henry Roan fought back. Tim Harford, "Killers of the Flower Moon: Osage Chief Jim Gray in Conversation," *Cautionary Tales,* accessed Feb. 15, 2024, www.pushkin.fm/podcasts/cautionary-tales/killers-of-the-flower-moon -osage-chief-jim-gray-in-conversation.

CHAPTER 5: WHO AM I?

170   **It's better to ask** William J. McGuire et al., "Salience of Ethnicity in the Spontaneous Self-Concept as a Function of One's Ethnic Distinctiveness in the Social Environment," *Journal of Personality and Social Psychology* 36, no. 5 (1978): 511–20, doi.org/10.1037/0022-3514.36.5.511; Richard L. Miller, Philip Brickman, and Diana Bolen, "Attribution Versus Persuasion as a Means for Modifying Behavior," *Journal of Personality and Social Psychology* 31, no. 3 (1975): 430–41, doi.org/10.1037/h0076539; Gregory M. Walton, David Paunesku, and Carol S. Dweck, "Expandable Selves," in *Handbook of Self and Identity*, ed. Mark R. Leary and June Price Tangney, 2nd ed. (New York: Guilford Press, 2012), 141–54; Steele, "Threat in the Air."

170   **In our family is a book** Vendla Sides Walton, *View from Dutch Hill* (2012); Vendla Sides Walton, *Chalk, Pottery, Pennies, and Dust: Vignettes of the Thirties* (2000).

171   **That's irksome to say the least** It's also what got my eighth-great-grandmother, Martha Carrier, killed. Over the course of a few months in the summer of 1692, Carrier was accused of witchcraft, tried, convicted, and then hanged, one victim among many in the Salem witch trials. Perhaps Carrier was accused because she'd been suspected of having brought smallpox to the community two years earlier. Perhaps it was because she had inherited land as a result of this tragedy, threatening the patriarchy in colonial New England. Yet Martha was a tough cookie. She never confessed. I have the transcript of her trial, dated August 2, 1692. It's just three and a half pages long. The conclusion pulls no punches:

> This rampant Hag, *Martha Carrier,* was the person, of whom the Confessions of the Witches, and of her own children among the rest, agreed, That the Devil had promised her, she should be *Queen of Hell.*

That's our relation, I tell our kids—the Queen of Hell! We're part witch.

171   **A generation earlier Charles Darwin** Charles Horton Cooley, *Human Nature and the Social Order* (New York: C. Scribner's Sons, 1908); Charles Darwin, *The Expression of the Emotions in Man and Animals,* 3rd ed. (Oxford: Oxford University Press, 1998).

173   **As the nineteenth century turned to the twentieth** W.E.B. Du Bois, "Strivings of the Negro People," *Atlantic,* Aug. 1, 1897, www.theatlantic.com/magazine/archive/1897/08/strivings-of-the-negro-people/305446/.

174   **The rate at which Black girls** Kelly Danaher and Christian S. Crandall, "Stereotype Threat in Applied Settings Re-examined," *Journal of Applied Social Psychology* 38, no. 6 (2008): 1639–55, doi.org/10.1111/j.1559-1816.2008.00362.x.

174   **It's the insidiousness** In one study, when African Americans read about a situation of blatant racial discrimination, they showed no drop at all in their performance on a subsequent challenging cognitive task (a Stroop task), as compared with when the situation involved no discrimination. *What was that? That was discrimination. Nothing new.* But when the discrimination was ambiguous, African Americans scored worse. *What was that? Was it discrimination? Was it not? I'm not sure . . .* It's the *questions* that get in the way. Jessica Salvatore and J. Nicole Shelton, "Cognitive Costs of Exposure to Racial Prejudice," *Psychological Science* 18, no. 9 (2007): 810–15, doi.org/10.1111/j.1467-9280.2007.01984.x.

176   **A prominent theory** Barbara L. Fredrickson et al., "That Swimsuit Becomes You: Sex Differences in Self-Objectification, Restrained Eating, and Math Performance," *Journal of Personality and Social Psychology* 75, no. 1 (1998): 269–84, doi.org/10.1037/0022-3514.75.1.269; Barbara L. Fredrickson and Tomi-Ann Roberts, "Objectification Theory: Toward Understanding Women's Lived Experiences and Mental Health Risks," *Psychology of Women Quarterly* 21, no. 2 (1997): 173–206, doi.org/10.1111/j.1471-6402.1997.tb00108.x.

177   **In one example, Erin Strahan** Erin J. Strahan et al., "Victoria's Dirty Secret: How Sociocultural Norms Influence Adolescent Girls and Women," *Personality and Social Psychology Bulletin* 34, no. 2 (2008): 288–301, doi.org/10.1177/0146167207310457; Emma Halliwell and Phillippa C. Diedrichs, "Testing a Dissonance Body Image Intervention Among Young Girls," *Health Psychology* 33, no. 2 (2014): 201–4, doi.org/10.1037/a0032585.

177   **After the fatwa was issued** David Remnick, "The Defiance of Salman Rushdie," *New Yorker,* Feb. 6, 2023, www.newyorker.com/magazine/2023/02/13/salman-rushdie-recovery-victory-city.

178   **As the Black Lives Matter founder** Michel Martin, "The #BlackLivesMatter Movement: Marches and Tweets for Healing," NPR, June 9, 2015, www.npr.org/2015/06/09/412862459/the-blacklivesmatter-movement-marches-and-tweets-for-healing.

178   **One 1997 study found** Steve W. Cole, Margaret E. Kemeny, and Shelley E. Taylor, "Social Identity and Physical Health: Accelerated HIV Progression in Rejection-Sensitive Gay Men," *Journal of Personality and Social Psychology* 72, no. 2 (1997): 320–35, doi.org/10.1037/0022-3514.72.2.320.

178   **In one study, the social psychologist** Pronin, Steele, and Ross, "Identity Bifurcation in Response to Stereotype Threat."

179   **In another study, the psychologist Sapna** Cheryan and Monin, "Where Are
You Really From?"

179   **To find out, my colleagues** The *Vogue* cover shows James screaming with an
arm around the model Gisele Bündchen. It echoes a World War I recruit-
ment poster, where a brutish gorilla runs off with a blond woman. Our ad
was less extreme, but it raised the same themes. An African American security guard appeared next to a gorilla in an ad for "Jungle Source Security"
with the tagline "It's a jungle out there." Lauren C. Howe, Karina Schumann,
and Gregory M. Walton, "'Am I Not Human?': Reasserting Humanness in
Response to Group-Based Dehumanization," *Group Processes and Intergroup
Relations* 25, no. 8 (2022): 2042–65, doi.org/10.1177/13684302221095730.

179   **This fight is healthy** Research finds that support for the Black Lives Matter
movement predicts better mental health and better intergenerational health
for African Americans: lower rates of depression and anxiety and greater
happiness among African American adults and lower rates of low birth
weight and mortality among African American infants. Tiffany N. Brannon,
"Racism Hurts, Can Antiracism Heal? Positive Mental Health Correlates of
Antiracist Engagement," *PNAS Nexus* 2, no. 10 (2023): pgad309, doi.org
/10.1093/pnasnexus/pgad309; Tiffany N. Brannon, "Antiracism and Positive
Intergenerational (Infant) Outcomes: A County-Level Examination of Low
Birth Weight and Infant Mortality," *Proceedings of the National Academy of Sci-
ences* 121, no. 15 (2024): e2320299121, doi.org/10.1073/pnas.2320299121.

180   **Instead, I show a video** "Jacqueline Woodson Reads *The Day You Begin*,"
Bookmarks, Netflix Jr., 2020, www.youtube.com/watch?v=KDs5d_qFbEs.

183   **When Taylor-Lind took the photo** "2022: The Pictures of the Year," *National
Geographic*, Dec. 2022, www.nationalgeographic.com/magazine/issue
/december-2022.

183   **A charity solicits** Tess McClure, "Australia–New Zealand Refugee Deal: UN
Blames Mental Health Toll After Just 36 People Take Up Offer," *Guardian*,
Sept. 30, 2022, www.theguardian.com/world/2022/sep/30/australia-new
-zealand-refugee-deal-un-criticises-canberra-after-just-36-people-take-up
-offer; "Change Lives—Donate Monthly," Oxfam, accessed Feb. 16, 2024,
give.oxfamamerica.org/page/26643/donate/1?locale=en-US.

184   **Perhaps one reason *Casablancaca* works** Aljean Harmetz, *Round Up the
Usual Suspects: The Making of "Casablanca"* (New York: Hyperion, 1992).

185   **she began to interview students** Christina A. Bauer, Raphael Boemelburg,
and Gregory M. Walton, "Resourceful Actors, Not Weak Victims: Reframing
Refugees' Stigmatized Identity Enhances Long-Term Academic Engagement," *Psychological Science* 32, no. 12 (Dec. 2021): 1896–906, doi.org/10.1177
/09567976211028978.

187   **But if that's all we see** All the time we miss the strengths people develop
contending with challenges. In the early years of the twenty-first century,
when rates of peanut allergies among children began to rise, how did we respond? We got all protective. Public health officials got on their soapbox and
urged parents to withhold peanuts from babies. What happened? Peanut allergy rates went through the roof, more than tripling in the United States
from 1997 to 2008. It turns out a bit of exposure helps the immune system
learn that peanuts are safe. Now the advice is to expose babies to peanuts

early even if, especially if, they're at high risk of an allergy. We underestimated how tough babies are—specifically because we didn't appreciate how they learn and grow. American Academy of Pediatrics, Committee on Nutrition, "Hypoallergenic Infant Formulas," *Pediatrics* 106, no. 2, pt. 1 (Aug. 2000): 346–49; George Du Toit et al., "Randomized Trial of Peanut Consumption in Infants at Risk for Peanut Allergy," *New England Journal of Medicine* 372, no. 9 (2015): 803–13, doi.org/10.1056/NEJMoa1414850.

187   **In a 2015 study** Arielle M. Silverman, Jason D. Gwinn, and Leaf Van Boven, "Stumbling in Their Shoes: Disability Simulations Reduce Judged Capabilities of Disabled People," *Social Psychological and Personality Science* 6, no. 4 (2015): 464–71, doi.org/10.1177/1948550614559650.

188   **In his memoir,** *Imperfect* Jim Abbott and Tim Brown, *Imperfect: An Improbable Life* (New York: Ballantine Books, 2013).

188   **After the first batter reached base** Rick Swaine, "Jim Abbott," *Society for American Baseball Research* (blog), accessed Feb. 16, 2024, sabr.org/bioproj /person/jim-abbott/.

188   **If you ask people** Lulu Miller and Latif Nasser, "The Right Stuff," *Radiolab*, n.d.; "Forum from the Archives: 'Life on Delay' Examines Life with a Stutter," KQED, Feb. 20, 2023, www.kqed.org/forum/2010101892268/forum-from -the-archives-life-on-delay-examines-life-with-a-stutter.

189   **And what could hearing these stories** Kalla and Broockman, "Which Narrative Strategies Durably Reduce Prejudice?"

189   **Depression affects** Ronald C. Kessler et al., "Twelve-Month and Lifetime Prevalence and Lifetime Morbid Risk of Anxiety and Mood Disorders in the United States," *International Journal of Methods in Psychiatric Research* 21, no. 3 (2012): 169–84, doi.org/10.1002/mpr.1359.

189   **We then reworked** Christina A. Bauer et al., "The Strength in Mental Illness: A Targeted Identity-Reframing Exercise Improves Goal Pursuit Among People Who Have Experienced Depression," 2023 (under review).

191   **If you talk with people** Bill Clinton credits his experience standing up to the abuse of a stepfather in helping him develop the empathy and values that guided his public service. In her autobiography, *Love, Pamela,* Pamela Anderson writes that she "became a warrior, a destroyer of old beliefs, slaying dragons," that she "embraced the illuminating thought: I am 'good enough.' I am powerful—Oh am I," in part through the challenges she faced as a child in rural Vancouver Island, including the horrific drowning of her beloved kittens. "I didn't say much to anyone about my home life. It was sensitive, and I innately understood that it was just what we had been dealt. I was grateful for what we had. I could not have survived my adult life without the strength I learned to muster early on."

In reviewing *Love, Pamela,* the journalist Jessica Bennett echoes Jacqueline Woodson in emphasizing the power of telling your own story:

> We forget sometimes, when we talk about the idea of agency, that it's as much about the stories we tell ourselves as it is about the actions we take. It's not just about what happened to us; it's about the role we feel we played in what happened. It's the difference between posing for Playboy and a stolen sex tape. It's why hearing someone recount your life to you can make you feel sick, while telling your own story, in your own words, can feel like a matter of survival.

Pamela Anderson, *Love, Pamela* (New York: Dey Street Books, 2023); Jessica Bennett, "Pamela Anderson Doesn't Need Your Redemption. She's Just Fine," *New York Times*, Jan. 13, 2023, www.nytimes.com/2023/01/13/opinion /sunday/pamela-anderson-pamela-and-tommy.html.

191   **Building on earlier laboratory studies** Ivan A. Hernandez, David M. Silverman, and Mesmin Destin, "From Deficit to Benefit: Highlighting Lower-SES Students' Background-Specific Strengths Reinforces Their Academic Persistence," *Journal of Experimental Social Psychology* 92 (2021): 104080, doi.org /10.1016/j.jesp.2020.104080; Christina A. Bauer et al. (in press), "The Strengths of People in Low-SES Positions: An Identity-Reframing Intervention Improves Low-SES Students' Achievement over One Semester," *Social Psychological and Personality Science.*

191   **It's a result that echoes** Nicole M. Stephens, MarYam G. Hamedani, and Mesmin Destin, "Closing the Social-Class Achievement Gap: A Difference-Education Intervention Improves First-Generation Students' Academic Performance and All Students' College Transition," *Psychological Science* 25 (2014): 943–53, doi.org/10.1177/0956797613518349; Nicole M. Stephens, MarYam G. Hamedani, and Sarah S. M. Townsend, "Difference-Education: Improving Disadvantaged Students' Academic Outcomes by Changing Their Theory of Difference," in Walton and Crum, *Handbook of Wise Interventions*, 126–47.

192   **From birth, we're utterly dependent** Elliot Aronson, *The Social Animal* (New York: Worth, 2004); Harriet Over, "The Origins of Belonging: Social Motivation in Infants and Young Children," *Philosophical Transactions of the Royal Society B: Biological Sciences* 371, no. 1686 (2016): 20150072, doi.org/10.1098 /rstb.2015.0072; M. H. Johnson et al., "Newborns' Preferential Tracking of Face-Like Stimuli and Its Subsequent Decline," *Cognition* 40, no. 1–2 (Aug. 1991): 1–19, doi.org/10.1016/0010-0277(91)90045-6; H. F. Harlow, R. O. Dodsworth, and M. K. Harlow, "Total Social Isolation in Monkeys," *Proceedings of the National Academy of Sciences* 54, no. 1 (July 1965): 90–97; Charles A. Nelson, Nathan A. Fox, and Charles H. Zeanah, *Romania's Abandoned Children: Deprivation, Brain Development, and the Struggle for Recovery* (Cambridge, Mass.: Harvard University Press, 2014); John Bowlby, *Attachment* (New York: Basic Books, 2008).

192   **In one clever study** Erica J. Boothby, Margaret S. Clark, and John A. Bargh, "Shared Experiences Are Amplified," *Psychological Science* 25, no. 12 (Dec. 2014): 2209–16, doi.org/10.1177/0956797614551162.

193   **Another study found** Carr and Walton, "Cues of Working Together Fuel Intrinsic Motivation"; Allison Master and Gregory M. Walton, "Minimal Groups Increase Young Children's Motivation and Learning on Group-Relevant Tasks," *Child Development* 84, no. 2 (March 2013): 737–51, doi.org /10.1111/j.1467-8624.2012.01867.x; Butler and Walton, "Opportunity to Collaborate Increases Preschoolers' Motivation for Challenging Tasks."

193   **It's what allows us** Michael Tomasello et al., "Understanding and Sharing Intentions: The Origins of Cultural Cognition," *Behavioral and Brain Sciences* 28, no. 5 (Oct. 2005): 675–91, discussion 691–735, doi.org/10.1017 /S0140525X05000129; Michael Tomasello, *Becoming Human: A Theory of Ontogeny* (Cambridge, Mass.: Harvard University Press, 2019); Joseph Henrich, *The Secret of Our Success: How Culture Is Driving Human Evolution, Do-*

mesticating Our Species, and Making Us Smarter (Princeton, N.J.: Princeton University Press, 2015).

193   **That makes the feeling** Kipling D. Williams, "Ostracism," *Annual Review of Psychology* 58 (2007): 425–52, doi.org/10.1146/annurev.psych.58.110405 .085641; Roy F. Baumeister et al., "Social Exclusion Impairs Self-Regulation," *Journal of Personality and Social Psychology* 88, no. 4 (2005): 589–604, doi .org/10.1037/0022-3514.88.4.589; John T. Cacioppo and William Patrick, *Loneliness: Human Nature and the Need for Social Connection* (New York: W. W. Norton, 2008).

In *Love, Pamela,* Pamela Anderson describes her own experience of invisibility: "I started passing out. . . . They called me 'Pass-Out-Pam' at school. Once, at the mall with friends, I had to lie down and put my feet up in the middle of the walkway, people stepping over me, oblivious to a kid lying there. *I felt invisible at times. Just particles of energy that people walked through—I felt like I had no edges, no borders to contain me—melting, spilling everywhere—.*"

193   **Terrell Jones** Jeneen Interlandi, "One Year Inside a Radical New Approach to America's Overdose Crisis," *New York Times,* Feb. 22, 2023, www.nytimes .com/2023/02/22/opinion/drug-crisis-addiction-harm-reduction.html.

194   **Years later, an evaluation team** Motto and Bostrom, "Randomized Controlled Trial of Postcrisis Suicide Prevention."

194   **But then I read another** Hossein Hassanian-Moghaddam et al., "Postcards in Persia: Randomised Controlled Trial to Reduce Suicidal Behaviours 12 Months After Hospital-Treated Self-Poisoning," *British Journal of Psychiatry* 198, no. 4 (April 2011): 309–16, doi.org/10.1192/bjp.bp.109.067199; Gregory L. Carter et al., "Postcards from the EDge: 5-Year Outcomes of a Randomised Controlled Trial for Hospital-Treated Self-Poisoning," *British Journal of Psychiatry* 202, no. 5 (May 2013): 372–80, doi.org/10.1192/bjp.bp.112.112664.

195   **That's a leftover** A leader in the self-esteem movement, Nathaniel Braden, said, "[I] cannot think of a single psychological problem—from anxiety and depression, to fear of intimacy or of success, to spouse battery or child molestation—that is not traced back to the problem of low self-esteem." Nathaniel Branden, "In Defense of Self," *Association for Humanistic Psychology,* Sept. 1984, 12–13; Roy F. Baumeister et al., "Does High Self-Esteem Cause Better Performance, Interpersonal Success, Happiness, or Healthier Lifestyles?," *Psychological Science in the Public Interest* 4, no. 1 (2003): 1–44, doi .org/10.1111/1529-1006.01431.

196   **Brummelman is good** Eddie Brummelman et al., "My Child Is God's Gift to Humanity: Development and Validation of the Parental Overvaluation Scale (POS)," *Journal of Personality and Social Psychology* 108, no. 4 (April 2015): 665–79, doi.org/10.1037/pspp0000012; Eddie Brummelman et al., " 'That's Not Just Beautiful—That's Incredibly Beautiful!': The Adverse Impact of Inflated Praise on Children with Low Self-Esteem," *Psychological Science* 25, no. 3 (2014): 728–35, doi.org/10.1177/0956797613514251; Eddie Brummelman et al., "When Parents' Praise Inflates, Children's Self-Esteem Deflates," *Child Development* 88, no. 6 (Nov. 2017): 1799–809, doi.org/10.1111/cdev.12936.

196   **Instead, Brummelman argues** Eddie Brummelman and Constantine Sedikides, "Raising Children with High Self-Esteem (but Not Narcissism)," *Child Development Perspectives* 14, no. 2 (2020): 83–89, doi.org/10.1111/cdep .12362.

196   **One of my first projects** Eddie Brummelman et al., "Unconditional Regard Buffers Children's Negative Self-Feelings," *Pediatrics* 134, no. 6 (2014): 1119–26, doi.org/10.1542/peds.2013-3698.

198   **An adviser, Mahzarin Banaji** Susan A. Gelman and Gail D. Heyman, "Carrot-Eaters and Creature-Believers: The Effects of Lexicalization on Children's Inferences About Social Categories," *Psychological Science* 10, no. 6 (1999): 489–93, doi.org/10.1111/1467-9280.00194.

198   **To find out, Banaji and I** Gregory M. Walton and Mahzarin R. Banaji, "Being What You Say: The Effect of Essentialist Linguistic Labels on Preferences," *Social Cognition* 22, no. 2 (2004): 193–213, doi.org/10.1521/soco.22.2.193.35463.

201   **Turnout rose again** Christopher J. Bryan et al., "Motivating Voter Turnout by Invoking the Self," *Proceedings of the National Academy of Sciences* 108, no. 31 (2011): 12653–56, doi.org/10.1073/pnas.1103343108.

201   **These effects have held up** Christopher J. Bryan, David S. Yeager, and Joseph M. O'Brien, "Replicator Degrees of Freedom Allow Publication of Misleading Failures to Replicate," *Proceedings of the National Academy of Sciences* 116, no. 51 (2019): 25535–45, doi.org/10.1073/pnas.1910951116.

201   **In a series of lab studies** Here's how the task worked: People were told that controversial recent research suggested that people could influence events with their minds alone. They were then asked to flip a coin ten times, trying to make it land heads each time. They were told they'd get paid $1 for each heads. However, they were urged "PLEASE DON'T CHEAT" or "PLEASE DON'T BE A CHEATER" (or neither). Last, people reported how many times out of ten their coin tosses had in fact turned up heads. In the control condition, people reported an average of 6.31 heads out of ten. In the "Please don't cheat" condition, they reported 6.22. Those numbers don't differ from each other significantly, and both are well above the predicted average of 5—so at least some people are cheating. But with the "Please don't be a cheater" message, the number dropped to 5.23, which was not significantly different from 5. Christopher J. Bryan, Gabrielle S. Adams, and Benoît Monin, "When Cheating Would Make You a Cheater: Implicating the Self Prevents Unethical Behavior," *Journal of Experimental Psychology: General* 142, no. 4 (2013): 1001–5, doi.org/10.1037/a0030655.

202   **It's important to note here** William James, *The Principles of Psychology*, vol. 1 (New York: Henry Holt, 1890), doi.org/10.1037/10538-000; Dacher Keltner and James J. Gross, "Functional Accounts of Emotions," *Cognition and Emotion* 13, no. 5 (1999): 467–80, doi.org/10.1080/026999399379140; Dacher Keltner and Jonathan Haidt, "Social Functions of Emotions at Four Levels of Analysis," *Cognition and Emotion* 13, no. 5 (1999): 505–21, doi.org/10.1080/026999399379168.

202   **I saw this for myself** Kimia Saadatian and Gregory M. Walton, "Secure Discipline: A Scalable Intervention to Mitigate Negative Outcomes of University Honor Code Investigations," 2023 (Manuscript in Preparation, Stanford University).

203   **Far better is to hold up** Here are examples of how to hold up this mirror in two of the most challenging circumstances. The first was designed by a team of psychologists working to mitigate extremism in the conflict between Israel and Palestinians. The second is from an ingenious filmmaker working in the wake of a genocide.

A technique in motivational interviewing is to reflect back to a person their own problematic views—but in a more extreme and, in fact, absurd form. For example, if a smoker says, "Anyone can get cancer," a doctor might reply, "Yes, cancer just happens. Smoking has nothing to do with it." The goal is to showcase a view so extreme the person argues back and moderates.

Inspired in part by this technique, a team of psychologists led by Boaz Hameiri at Tel Aviv University spent years developing a satirical media campaign depicting an absurd pro-Israel view of the Israel/Palestinian conflict. One twenty-second video Hameiri's team created, "For Justice," depicts bombs exploding, buses destroyed, and victims screaming. The tagline reads, "Without it we would never be just. . . . For justice, we probably need the conflict." The goal is to create content so extreme that an Israeli hawk might wonder, *Am I joke? Are my views absurd?* and then begin to pull back.

Beginning on September 10, 2015, just as a new wave of violence between Israel and Palestinians began (the "Knife Intifada" or "Lone Wolves Intifada"), Hameiri and his colleagues blanketed a small city in central Israel with this campaign. Over a six-week period, there were 4.4 million exposures to online banner ads, nearly a million views of the twenty-second videos, billboard posters in twenty central locations, and hundreds of themed T-shirts, balloons, and brochures handed out in the city center. As compared with a matched control city and residents' own pre-campaign reports, this campaign did, in fact, temper attitudes among rightists that perpetuate conflict (for example, "Peaceful resolution is unattainable because there is no partner on the other side"), reduce support for aggressive government policies (for instance, "Security forces should shoot to kill any suspect of a terror attack, even if s/he has not yet attacked"), and increase support for conciliatory policies (for example, "Israel must do its utmost to resume the negotiations with the Palestinians as soon as possible").

These results are encouraging. Yet this approach also raises concerns, at least for me. For example, would highlighting such extremist views pull centrists further out, making a more aggressive response seem less brutal? In fact, Hameiri found that the very same campaign *reduced* support among centrists for conciliatory policies. And how might content like this land on the other side? I'm not confident Palestinians would be in on "the joke." Certainly, one can imagine the memes bad actors could create to weaponize content like this to confirm the worst stereotypes about either side in a conflict.

When I teach undergraduates about Hameiri's work, I sometimes show the trailer for the most remarkable documentary I have ever seen: Joshua Oppenheimer's 2012 *The Act of Killing.* Oppenheimer travels to Indonesia to interview the right-wing gangster Anwar Congo, who served as an executioner in the killings of nearly a million people during political upheaval in Indonesia in 1965–66. Many of these perpetrators later became well-respected members of Indonesian society, leaders in media and government, heralded as national heroes. Oppenheimer invites Congo to show him exactly what he did, to join him in making a commemorative film, to showcase the hero that he is. Congo shows Oppenheimer just how he lured victims to a rooftop patio, how he strangled them. Children in thick makeup play victims screaming, fleeing fires and bombs. As Congo sees the footage he helped create, will he see himself in a new light? "I never expected it to look this brutal. I did this to so many people. Have I sinned?" Could this be the mirror that is needed for a person to begin to take responsibility for the most awful acts?

Boaz Hameiri et al., "Paradoxical Thinking as a New Avenue of Intervention to Promote Peace," *Proceedings of the National Academy of Sciences* 111, no. 30 (2014): 10996–11001, doi.org/10.1073/pnas.1407055111; Boaz Hameiri et al., "Moderating Attitudes in Times of Violence Through Paradoxical Thinking Intervention," *Proceedings of the National Academy of Sciences* 113, no. 43 (2016): 12105–10, doi.org/10.1073/pnas.1606182113.

204   **How can we have grace** Karina Schumann and Gregory M. Walton, "Rehumanizing the Self After Victimization: The Roles of Forgiveness Versus Revenge," *Journal of Personality and Social Psychology* 122, no. 3 (March 2022): 469–92, doi.org/10.1037/pspi0000367.

Spotlight: Reducing Global Poverty

210   **She read a famous thought experiment** Peter Singer, "Famine, Affluence, and Morality," *Philosophy and Public Affairs* 1, no. 3 (1972): 229–43; Peter Singer, "The Drowning Child and the Expanding Circle," *New Internationalist,* April 5, 1997, newint.org/features/1997/04/05/peter-singer-drowning-child-new-internationalist.

210   **Inspired by a feminism** Esther Duflo, "Women Empowerment and Economic Development," *Journal of Economic Literature* 50, no. 4 (Dec. 2012): 1051–79, doi.org/10.1257/jel.50.4.1051.

212   **One refugee, resettled in Britain** Lada Timotijevic and Glynis M. Breakwell, "Migration and Threat to Identity," *Journal of Community and Applied Social Psychology* 10, no. 5 (2000): 355–72, doi.org/10.1002/1099-1298(200009/10)10:5%3C355::AID-CASP594%3E3.0.CO;2-Y.

212   **In one study, Thomas looked at** Catherine C. Thomas et al., "Toward a Science of Delivering Aid with Dignity: Experimental Evidence and Local Forecasts from Kenya," *Proceedings of the National Academy of Sciences* 117, no. 27 (2020): 15546–53, doi.org/10.1073/pnas.1917046117.

213   **In the best help** Research among couples in which one person is studying for the bar exam and the other is supporting them finds that the less the test taker recognizes the support their partner gives them, the better their adjustment. Niall Bolger, Adam Zuckerman, and Ronald C. Kessler, "Invisible Support and Adjustment to Stress," *Journal of Personality and Social Psychology* 79, no. 6 (2000): 953–61, doi.org/10.1037/0022-3514.79.6.953.

214   **In a 2020 study** Thomas et al., "Toward a Science of Delivering Aid with Dignity."

214   **In the next step** Thomas Bossuroy et al., "Tackling Psychosocial and Capital Constraints to Alleviate Poverty," *Nature* 605, no. 7909 (May 2022): 291–97, doi.org/10.1038/s41586-022-04647-8. See also Abhijit Banerjee et al., "A Multifaceted Program Causes Lasting Progress for the Very Poor: Evidence from Six Countries," *Science* 348, no. 6236 (2015): 1260799, doi.org/10.1126/science.1260799.

CHAPTER 6: DO YOU LOVE ME?

226   **But Sandra Murray** Sandra L. Murray, John G. Holmes, and Dale W. Griffin, "The Self-Fulfilling Nature of Positive Illusions in Romantic Relationships: Love Is Not Blind, but Prescient," *Journal of Personality and Social Psychology* 71, no. 6 (1996): 1155–80, doi.org/10.1037/0022-3514.71.6.1155; Sandra L. Murray, John G. Holmes, and Dale W. Griffin, "The Benefits of Positive Illusions: Idealization and the Construction of Satisfaction in Close Relationships," *Journal of Personality and Social Psychology* 70 (1996): 79–98, doi.org/10.1037/0022-3514.70.1.79; Samantha Joel et al., "Expect and You Shall Perceive: People Who Expect Better in Turn Perceive Better Behaviors from Their Romantic Partners," *Journal of Personality and Social Psychology* 124, no. 6 (2023), doi.org/10.1037/pspi0000411.

227   **"As time passed, intimates"** Murray, Holmes, and Griffin, "Self-Fulfilling Nature of Positive Illusions in Romantic Relationships."

230   **In one study, he tracked** James K. McNulty, "Forgiveness in Marriage: Putting the Benefits into Context," *Journal of Family Psychology* 22, no. 1 (2008): 171–75, doi.org/10.1037/0893-3200.22.1.171. See also James K. McNulty, "Forgiveness Increases the Likelihood of Subsequent Partner Transgressions in Marriage," *Journal of Family Psychology* 24, no. 6 (2010): 787–90, doi.org/10.1037/a0021678; James K. McNulty, Erin M. O'Mara, and Benjamin R. Karney, "Benevolent Cognitions as a Strategy of Relationship Maintenance: 'Don't Sweat the Small Stuff' . . . but It Is Not All Small Stuff," *Journal of Personality and Social Psychology* 94, no. 4 (2008): 631–46, doi.org/10.1037/0022-3514.94.4.631; James K. McNulty, "The Dark Side of Forgiveness: The Tendency to Forgive Predicts Continued Psychological and Physical Aggression in Marriage," *Personality and Social Psychology Bulletin* 37, no. 6 (2011): 770–83, doi.org/10.1177/0146167211407077.

231   **A team led by Michelle Russell** V. Michelle Russell et al., " 'You're Forgiven, but Don't Do It Again!' Direct Partner Regulation Buffers the Costs of Forgiveness," *Journal of Family Psychology* 32, no. 4 (2018): 435–44, doi.org/10.1037/fam0000409.

231   **McNulty warns that** James K. McNulty, "When Positive Processes Hurt Relationships," *Current Directions in Psychological Science* 19, no. 3 (2010): 167–71, doi.org/10.1177/0963721410370298.

234   **What Marigold did** Marigold, Holmes, and Ross, "More Than Words"; Denise C. Marigold, "The Abstract Reframing Intervention: Helping Insecure Individuals Benefit from Romantic Partners' Positive Feedback," in Walton and Crum, *Handbook of Wise Interventions*, 385–402.

234   **In fact, earlier research** Joanne V. Wood, W. Q. Elaine Perunovic, and John W. Lee, "Positive Self-Statements: Power for Some, Peril for Others," *Psychological Science* 20, no. 7 (July 2009): 860–66, doi.org/10.1111/j.1467-9280.2009.02370.x; Sandra L. Murray et al., "Through the Looking Glass Darkly? When Self-Doubts Turn into Relationship Insecurities," *Journal of Personality and Social Psychology* 75, no. 6 (1998): 1459–80, doi.org/10.1037/0022-3514.75.6.1459.

236   **A single well-put question** Marigold, Holmes, and Ross, "More Than Words"; Denise C. Marigold, John G. Holmes, and Michael Ross, "Fostering Relation-

ship Resilience: An Intervention for Low Self-Esteem Individuals," *Journal of Experimental Social Psychology* 46, no. 4 (2010): 624–30, doi.org/10.1016/j .jesp.2010.02.011; Marigold, "Abstract Reframing Intervention."

237   **Other research finds** Lisa B. Hoplock et al., "Self-Esteem, Epistemic Needs, and Responses to Social Feedback," *Self and Identity* 18, no. 5 (2019): 467–93, doi.org/10.1080/15298868.2018.1471414.

238   **The very best studies** Norval D. Glenn, "The Course of Marital Success and Failure in Five American 10-Year Marriage Cohorts," *Journal of Marriage and the Family* 60, no. 3 (1998): 569–76, doi.org/10.2307/353529; Jody VanLaningham, David R. Johnson, and Paul Amato, "Marital Happiness, Marital Duration, and the U-Shaped Curve: Evidence from a Five-Wave Panel Study," *Social Forces* 79, no. 4 (2001): 1313–41; Janina Larissa Bühler, Samantha Krauss, and Ulrich Orth, "Development of Relationship Satisfaction Across the Life Span: A Systematic Review and Meta-analysis," *Psychological Bulletin* 147, no. 10 (Oct. 2021): 1012–53, doi.org/10.1037/bul0000342.

239   **Just in time for Valentine's Day 2023** Marisa Kashino, "When the Dishes Mean War: Couples Share Their Fights About the Home," *Washington Post,* Feb. 13, 2023, www.washingtonpost.com/home/2023/02/13/couples-fights -over-living-together/.

241   **To address those deeper concerns** Denise C. Marigold and Joanna E. Anderson, "Shifting Expectations of Partners' Responsiveness Changes Outcomes of Conflict Discussions," *Personal Relationships* 23, no. 3 (2016): 517–35, doi .org/10.1111/pere.12141.

242   **Finkel was working with a group** Finkel et al., "Brief Intervention to Promote Conflict Reappraisal Preserves Marital Quality over Time"; Erica B. Slotter and Laura B. Luchies, "The Couples Activity for Reappraising Emotions Intervention: A 7-Minute Marital Conflict Intervention Benefits Relational and Individual Well-Being," in Walton and Crum, *Handbook of Wise Interventions,* 366–84. For a replication, see Lindsey M. Rodriguez, Sherry H. Stewart, and Clayton Neighbors, "Effects of a Brief Web-Based Interpersonal Conflict Cognitive Reappraisal Expressive-Writing Intervention on Changes in Romantic Conflict During COVID-19 Quarantine," *Couple and Family Psychology: Research and Practice* 10, no. 3 (2021): 212–22, doi.org/10.1037 /cfp0000173.

245   **To find out, she brought 152 couples** Karina Schumann, Emily G. Ritchie, and Anna Dragotta, "Adapted Self-Affirmation and Conflict Management in Romantic Relationships," PsyArXiv, May 30, 2021, doi.org/10.31234/osf.io /j3hyk.

247   **Sometimes results like these can seem like magic** Yeager and Walton, "Social-Psychological Interventions in Education: They're Not Magic."

251   **The Bay Area writer** Anne Lamott, "Mother Rage: Theory and Practice," *Salon,* Oct. 29, 1998, www.salon.com/1998/10/29/29lamo_2/; Minna Dubin, "The Rage Mothers Don't Talk About," *New York Times,* April 16, 2020, www .nytimes.com/2020/04/15/parenting/mother-rage.html.

253   **In her original study** Daphne Blunt Bugental et al., "A Cognitive Approach to Child Abuse Prevention," *Journal of Family Psychology* 16 (2002): 243–58, doi .org/10.1037/0893-3200.16.3.243.

254   **As Bugental said** Bill Schlotter, "UCSB Child Abuse Studies Lead to Successful Prevention," *Current,* Sept. 27, 2001, news.ucsb.edu/print/pdf/node /11502.

255   **A few years later** Daphne Blunt Bugental and Alex Schwartz, "A Cognitive Approach to Child Mistreatment Prevention Among Medically At-Risk Infants," *Developmental Psychology* 45, no. 1 (2009): 284–88, doi.org/10.1037 /a0014031; Daphne Blunt Bugental, David A. Beaulieu, and Amelia Silbert-Geiger, "Increases in Parental Investment and Child Health as a Result of an Early Intervention," *Journal of Experimental Child Psychology* 106, no. 1 (2010): 30–40, doi.org/10.1016/j.jecp.2009.10.004; Daphne Blunt Bugental, Randy Corpuz, and Alex Schwartz, "Preventing Children's Aggression: Outcomes of an Early Intervention," *Developmental Psychology* 48, no. 5 (2012): 1443–49, doi.org/10.1037/a0027303; Daphne Blunt Bugental, Alex Schwartz, and Colleen Lynch, "Effects of an Early Family Intervention on Children's Memory: The Mediating Effects of Cortisol Levels," *Mind, Brain, and Education* 4, no. 4 (2010): 159–70, doi.org/10.1111/j.1751-228X.2010.01095.x.

259   **Cross-race roommates in college** Natalie J. Shook and Russell H. Fazio, "Roommate Relationships: A Comparison of Interracial and Same-Race Living Situations," *Group Processes and Intergroup Relations* 11, no. 4 (2008): 425–37, doi.org/10.1177/1368430208095398; Natalie J. Shook and Russell H. Fazio, "Interracial Roommate Relationships: An Experimental Field Test of the Contact Hypothesis," *Psychological Science* 19, no. 7 (2008): 717–23, doi.org/10.1111/j.1467-9280.2008.02147.x; Rebecca M. Carey et al., "Is Diversity Enough? Cross-Race and Cross-Class Interactions in College Occur Less Often Than Expected, but Benefit Members of Lower Status Groups When They Occur," *Journal of Personality and Social Psychology* 123 (2022): 889–908, doi.org/10.1037/pspa0000302.

259   **It's based on actual research** Arthur Aron et al., "The Experimental Generation of Interpersonal Closeness: A Procedure and Some Preliminary Findings," *Personality and Social Psychology Bulletin* 23, no. 4 (1997): 363–77, doi .org/10.1177/0146167297234003.

260   **Being known is foundational** Juliana Schroeder and Ayelet Fishbach, "Feeling Known Predicts Relationship Satisfaction," *Journal of Experimental Social Psychology* 111 (March 2024): 104559, doi.org/10.1016/j.jesp.2023.104559.

260   **Sanchez began by** Kiara L. Sanchez, David A. Kalkstein, and Gregory M. Walton, "A Threatening Opportunity: The Prospect of Conversations About Race-Related Experiences Between Black and White Friends," *Journal of Personality and Social Psychology* 122, no. 5 (2022): 853–72, doi.org/10.1037 /pspi0000369.

261   **Other research had shown that these fears** For instance, the belief that racism is fixed—that either you're racist or you're not—can lead White people to avoid interactions with Black people, it seems because they fear a mistake might make them racist. That's the case even for White people who, by all measures, are not particularly racist. Carr, Dweck, and Pauker, " 'Prejudiced' Behavior Without Prejudice?"; Goff, Steele, and Davies, "Space Between Us"; Bergsieker, Shelton, and Richeson, "To Be Liked Versus Respected"; Shelton and Richeson, "Interracial Interactions."

261   **To learn, she developed** Kiara L. Sanchez et al., "Friendship-Affirming Appraisals of Race Talk: A Longitudinal Intervention Field Experiment to Strengthen Black-White Friendships," 2024 (under review).

266   **In a classic series of studies** J. Nicole Shelton and Jennifer A. Richeson, "Intergroup Contact and Pluralistic Ignorance," *Journal of Personality and Social Psychology* 88, no. 1 (2005): 91–107, doi.org/10.1037/0022-3514.88.1.91.

266   **It might also help to know** Studying commuters on public transit in Chicago, Nick Epley and Juliana Schroeder found that people believe that sitting alone will be more pleasant than talking with strangers. But when people engage strangers, they find that the interactions are actually much more positive. People hold back, it seems, precisely because they underestimate the interest that other people have in connecting. But once we take that step, conversations that open us up and connect us can make us happier and we can learn from them, more even than we would expect. Nicholas Epley and Juliana Schroeder, "Mistakenly Seeking Solitude," *Journal of Experimental Psychology: General* 143, no. 5 (2014): 1980–99, doi.org/10.1037/a0037323; Gillian M. Sandstrom and Erica J. Boothby, "Why Do People Avoid Talking to Strangers? A Mini Meta-analysis of Predicted Fears and Actual Experiences Talking to a Stranger," *Self and Identity* 20, no. 1 (2021): 47–71, doi.org/10.1080/15298868.2020.1816568; Gillian M. Sandstrom and Elizabeth W. Dunn, "Social Interactions and Well-Being: The Surprising Power of Weak Ties," *Personality and Social Psychology Bulletin* 40, no. 7 (July 2014): 910–22, doi.org/10.1177/0146167214529799; Gillian M. Sandstrom and Elizabeth W. Dunn, "Is Efficiency Overrated? Minimal Social Interactions Lead to Belonging and Positive Affect," *Social Psychological and Personality Science* 5, no. 4 (2014): 437–42, doi.org/10.1177/1948550613502990; Stav Atir, Kristina A. Wald, and Nicholas Epley, "Talking with Strangers Is Surprisingly Informative," *Proceedings of the National Academy of Sciences* 119, no. 34 (2022): e2206992119, doi.org/10.1073/pnas.2206992119.

266   **In the end** Aron et al., "The Experimental Generation of Interpersonal Closeness: A Procedure and Some Preliminary Findings"; Eyal et al., "Perspective Mistaking: Accurately Understanding the Mind of Another Requires Getting Perspective, Not Taking Perspective"; Kalla and Broockman, "Which Narrative Strategies Durably Reduce Prejudice?"

CHAPTER 7: CAN I TRUST YOU?

276   **"She Thought He Would Kill Her"** Melissa Eddy, "She Thought He Would Kill Her. Then She Complimented His Orchids," *New York Times*, July 30, 2019, www.nytimes.com/2019/07/30/world/europe/austria-cyclist-abducted.html.

277   **In 1980, while I was toddling** Robert Axelrod, *The Evolution of Cooperation*, rev. ed. (New York: Basic Books, 2009).

280   **That stereotype is powerfully built** Jennifer L. Eberhardt et al., "Seeing Black: Race, Crime, and Visual Processing," *Journal of Personality and Social Psychology* 87, no. 6 (2004): 876–93, doi.org/10.1037/0022-3514.87.6.876; Patricia G. Devine and Andrew J. Elliot, "Are Racial Stereotypes Really Fading? The Princeton Trilogy Revisited," *Personality and Social Psychology Bulletin* 21, no. 11 (1995): 1139–50, doi.org/10.1177/01461672952111002; Brian A. Nosek et al., "Pervasiveness and Correlates of Implicit Attitudes and Stereotypes," *European Review of Social Psychology* 18 (2007): 36–88, doi.org/10.1080/10463280701489053; Mary Beth Oliver, "African American Men as 'Criminal and Dangerous': Implications of Media Portrayals of Crime on the 'Criminalization' of African American Men," *Journal of African American Studies* 7, no. 2 (2003): 3–18; Dennis Rome, *Black Demons: The Media's Depic-*

tion of the African American Male Criminal Stereotype (Westport, Conn.: Praeger, 2004); David J. Johnson and William J. Chopik, "Geographic Variation in the Black-Violence Stereotype," *Social Psychological and Personality Science* 10, no. 3 (2019): 287–94, doi.org/10.1177/1948550617753522.

281   **The Diallo killing led Correll** Joshua Correll, Bernadette Park, et al., "The Police Officer's Dilemma: Using Ethnicity to Disambiguate Potentially Threatening Individuals," *Journal of Personality and Social Psychology* 83, no. 6 (2002): 1314–29, doi.org/10.1037/0022-3514.83.6.1314; Joshua Correll, Sean M. Hudson, et al., "The Police Officer's Dilemma: A Decade of Research on Racial Bias in the Decision to Shoot," *Social and Personality Psychology Compass* 8, no. 5 (2014): 201–13, doi.org/10.1111/spc3.12099.

282   **In fact, Black people** See also Kimberly Barsamian Kahn and Paul G. Davies, "Differentially Dangerous? Phenotypic Racial Stereotypicality Increases Implicit Bias Among Ingroup and Outgroup Members," *Group Processes and Intergroup Relations* 14, no. 4 (2011): 569–80, doi.org/10.1177/1368430210374609.

282   **In other studies, when people** Kimberly Barsamian Kahn and Paul G. Davies, "What Influences Shooter Bias? The Effects of Suspect Race, Neighborhood, and Clothing on Decisions to Shoot," *Journal of Social Issues* 73, no. 4 (2017): 723–43, doi.org/10.1111/josi.12245.

282   **In fact, in one study using tools** Another study led by my colleague Jennifer Eberhardt came to a similar conclusion. Simply exposing people to images of Black faces made them quicker to detect crime-relevant objects like a gun. Joshua Correll et al., "Stereotypic Vision: How Stereotypes Disambiguate Visual Stimuli," *Journal of Personality and Social Psychology* 108, no. 2 (2015): 219–33, doi.org/10.1037/pspa0000015; Eberhardt et al., "Seeing Black."

282   **If you're a person of color** Cynthia J. Najdowski, Bette L. Bottoms, and Phillip Atiba Goff, "Stereotype Threat and Racial Differences in Citizens' Experiences of Police Encounters," *Law and Human Behavior* 39, no. 5 (2015): 463–77, doi.org/10.1037/lhb0000140.

283   **You wonder** Rick Trinkner, Erin M. Kerrison, and Phillip Atiba Goff, "The Force of Fear: Police Stereotype Threat, Self-Legitimacy, and Support for Excessive Force," *Law and Human Behavior* 43, no. 5 (Oct. 2019): 421–35, doi.org/10.1037/lhb0000339.

283   **In one study, Eberhardt's team** Rob Voigt et al., "Language from Police Body Camera Footage Shows Racial Disparities in Officer Respect," *Proceedings of the National Academy of Sciences* 114, no. 25 (2017): 6521–26, doi.org/10.1073/pnas.1702413114.

283   **In fact, Eberhardt's team** Another study found that officers used a more negative tone with Black drivers than White drivers. That tone alone led people to anticipate more negative and less respectful interactions, and it undermined trust in the police department as a whole. Eugenia H. Rho et al., "Escalated Police Stops of Black Men Are Linguistically and Psychologically Distinct in Their Earliest Moments," *Proceedings of the National Academy of Sciences* 120, no. 23 (2023): e2216162120, doi.org/10.1073/pnas.2216162120; Nicholas P. Camp et al., "The Thin Blue Waveform: Racial Disparities in Officer Prosody Undermine Institutional Trust in the Police," *Journal of Personality and Social Psychology* 121, no. 6 (2021): 1157–71, doi.org/10.1037/pspa0000270.

284   **Another study, which looked at use-of-force** Kimberly Barsamian Kahn et al.,

"How Suspect Race Affects Police Use of Force in an Interaction over Time," *Law and Human Behavior* 41, no. 2 (2017): 117–26, doi.org/10.1037/lhb0000218.

284 **To learn, in one study** Joshua Correll et al., "The Influence of Stereotypes on Decisions to Shoot," *European Journal of Social Psychology* 37, no. 6 (2007): 1102–17, doi.org/10.1002/ejsp.450. See also Jessica J. Sim, Joshua Correll, and Melody S. Sadler, "Understanding Police and Expert Performance: When Training Attenuates (vs. Exacerbates) Stereotypic Bias in the Decision to Shoot," *Personality and Social Psychology Bulletin* 39, no. 3 (March 2013): 291–304, doi.org/10.1177/0146167212473157.

285 **"Policing by consent"** Tom R. Tyler, Phillip Atiba Goff, and Robert J. MacCoun, "The Impact of Psychological Science on Policing in the United States: Procedural Justice, Legitimacy, and Effective Law Enforcement," *Psychological Science in the Public Interest* 16, no. 3 (2015): 75–109, doi.org/10.1177/1529100615617791.

285 **When Correll looked at how** Joshua Correll et al., "Across the Thin Blue Line: Police Officers and Racial Bias in the Decision to Shoot," *Journal of Personality and Social Psychology* 92, no. 6 (2007): 1006–23, doi.org/10.1037/0022-3514.92.6.1006; E. Ashby Plant and B. Michelle Peruche, "The Consequences of Race for Police Officers' Responses to Criminal Suspects," *Psychological Science* 16, no. 3 (March 2005): 180–83, doi.org/10.1111/j.0956-7976.2005.00800.x.

285 **As Correll and his colleagues** Sim, Correll, and Sadler, "Understanding Police and Expert Performance."

286 **Drawing on this tradition** Correll, Park, et al., "Police Officer's Dilemma."

287 **Billions of dollars have been invested** Charlotte Gill et al., "Community-Oriented Policing to Reduce Crime, Disorder, and Fear and Increase Satisfaction and Legitimacy Among Citizens: A Systematic Review," *Journal of Experimental Criminology* 10, no. 4 (2014): 399–428, doi.org/10.1007/s11292-014-9210-y.

287 **As a postdoctoral fellow** Kyle Dobson, Andrea Dittmann, and David Yeager, "A Transparency Statement Transforms Community-Police Interactions," June 4, 2022, doi.org/10.13140/RG.2.2.12294.24642.

296 **In Eberhardt's research** Voigt et al., "Language from Police Body Camera Footage Shows Racial Disparities in Officer Respect."

296 **Apologies can do wonders** Craig W. Blatz, Karina Schumann, and Michael Ross, "Government Apologies for Historical Injustices," *Political Psychology* 30, no. 2 (2009): 219–41, doi.org/10.1111/j.1467-9221.2008.00689.x; Karina Schumann, "The Psychology of Offering an Apology: Understanding the Barriers to Apologizing and How to Overcome Them," *Current Directions in Psychological Science* 27, no. 2 (2018): 74–78, doi.org/10.1177/0963721417741709; Ryan Fehr, Michele J. Gelfand, and Monisha Nag, "The Road to Forgiveness: A Meta-Analytic Synthesis of Its Situational and Dispositional Correlates," *Psychological Bulletin* 136, no. 5 (2010): 894–914, doi.org/10.1037/a0019993; Richard C. Boothman et al., "A Better Approach to Medical Malpractice Claims? The University of Michigan Experience," *Journal of Health and Life Sciences Law* 2, no. 2 (Jan. 2009): 125–59; Benjamin Ho and Elaine Liu, "What's an Apology Worth? Decomposing the Effect of Apologies on Medical Malpractice Payments Using State Apology Laws," *Journal of Empirical Legal Studies* 8, no. S1 (2011): 179–99, doi.org/10.1111/j.1740-1461.2011.01226.x.

298   **Jason Okonofua developed an approach** Jason A. Okonofua et al., "A Scalable Empathic Supervision Intervention to Mitigate Recidivism from Probation and Parole," *Proceedings of the National Academy of Sciences* 118, no. 14 (2021): e2018036118, doi.org/10.1073/pnas.2018036118.

300   **One longitudinal study** It's from a base of 54 percent. Participants were asked, "Other than your parents or step-parents, has an adult made an important positive difference in your life at any time since you were 14 years old?" Matthew A. Kraft, Alexander J. Bolves, and Noelle M. Hurd, "How Informal Mentoring by Teachers, Counselors, and Coaches Supports Students' Long-Run Academic Success," *Economics of Education Review* 95 (2023): 102411, doi.org/10.1016/j.econedurev.2023.102411.

301   **In a 2021 survey** Gregory Austin et al., *Student Engagement and Well-Being in California, 2019–21: Results of the Eighteenth Biennial State California Healthy Kids Survey, Grades 7, 9, and 11* (WestEd, 2023).

302   **The educational psychologist** Jacquelynne S. Eccles et al., "Development During Adolescence: The Impact of Stage-Environment Fit on Young Adolescents' Experiences in Schools and in Families," *American Psychologist* 48, no. 2 (1993): 90–101, doi.org/10.1037/0003-066X.48.2.90.

303   **Adolescence is also when** Goyer et al., "Targeted Identity-Safety Interventions Cause Lasting Reductions in Discipline Citations Among Negatively Stereotyped Boys."

303   **But it's not just kids acting out** Russell J. Skiba et al., "The Color of Discipline: Sources of Racial and Gender Disproportionality in School Punishment," *Urban Review* 34, no. 4 (2002): 317–42, doi.org/10.1023/A:1021320817372; Goyer et al., "Targeted Identity-Safety Interventions Cause Lasting Reductions in Discipline Citations Among Negatively Stereotyped Boys"; David S. Yeager et al., "Loss of Institutional Trust Among Racial and Ethnic Minority Adolescents: A Consequence of Procedural Injustice and a Cause of Life-Span Outcomes," *Child Development* 88, no. 2 (March 2017): 658–76, doi.org/10.1111/cdev.12697.

305   **While still in grad school** Geoffrey L. Cohen, Claude M. Steele, and Lee D. Ross, "The Mentor's Dilemma: Providing Critical Feedback Across the Racial Divide," *Personality and Social Psychology Bulletin* 25, no. 10 (1999): 1302–18, doi.org/10.1177/0146167299258011.

305   **In one study, Kent Harber** Kent D. Harber, "Feedback to Minorities: Evidence of a Positive Bias," *Journal of Personality and Social Psychology* 74, no. 3 (1998): 622–28, doi.org/10.1037/0022-3514.74.3.622.

305   **Cohen thought making those good** Cohen, Steele, and Ross, "Mentor's Dilemma."

306   **It was a way to disambiguate** Here's the full text: "It's obvious to me that you've taken your task seriously and I'm going to do likewise by giving you some straightforward, honest feedback. The letter itself is okay as far as it goes—you've followed the instructions, listed your teacher's merits, given evidence in support of them, and importantly, produced an articulate letter. On the other hand, judged by a higher standard, the one that really counts, that is, whether your letter will be publishable in our journal, I have serious reservations. The comments I provide in the following pages are quite critical but I hope helpful. Remember, I wouldn't go to the trouble of giving you this feedback if I didn't think, based on what I've read in your letter, that you are capable of meeting the higher standard I mentioned."

306   **And now they were just as** One of the great social psychologists of the second half of the twentieth century, Elliot Aronson, tells a powerful story about perhaps the most famous grad seminar in the history of the field (famous as they go, that is). It's an old-school story, and a story of wise feedback.

It was the late 1950s at Stanford, taught by Leon Festinger. There were just six students in the class including Aronson, among them a brilliant undergrad, Merrill Carlsmith. The seminar was held just before Festinger and Carlsmith would revolutionize the field with a 1959 paper on cognitive dissonance, based in part on Carlsmith's senior thesis. Aronson felt the tide coming. "The six of us in the seminar felt like we were part of something important," he writes. "We were contributing to the development of an idea that would permanently change social psychology." Festinger had come to Stanford as a new professor in 1955, a student of Kurt Lewin's. He could be tough; cruel, in fact, even by the standards of the day. Aronson describes him as "brilliant and scary. His questions were razor sharp, and he made it clear we had better answer knowledgeably and not leave any loose ends. It was like having a tiger in the classroom. He could pounce on you at any time without warning, often for reasons that were baffling or trivial to us."

Halfway through the term, Festinger assigned a term paper on the Salem witch trials. Aronson describes his first attempt, "I read the material, wrote the paper, and handed it in." A few days later, Festinger returned the paper to him with nary a comment.

Aronson writes he was "devastated." He gathers the courage to ask Festinger, "How am I supposed to know what I got wrong?"

"This is graduate school, not kindergarten," said Festinger, "You're supposed to tell *me* what's wrong with it."

Aronson, a young father at the time with a baby at home and another on the way, writes he was "confused and furious." Yet he got it together to read the paper "through Festinger's eyes" and found it lacking: "poorly reasoned, incompletely analyzed, imperfectly argued. The son of a bitch was right!" So Aronson devotes the next few days ("it seemed like seventy-two consecutive hours") to rewriting the paper. Twenty minutes after he drops the revision in Festinger's office, Festinger comes to Aronson, sits on his desk, puts his hand on his shoulder, and says, "Now, this is worth criticizing."

For Aronson, that incident was "a gift of incalculable value." He was worth Festinger's criticism. It meant he was a person who could become. And so he did. Elliot Aronson, *Not by Chance Alone: My Life as a Social Psychologist* (New York: Basic Books, 2010).

306   **As a young assistant professor** David S. Yeager et al., "Breaking the Cycle of Mistrust: Wise Interventions to Provide Critical Feedback Across the Racial Divide," *Journal of Experimental Psychology: General* 143, no. 2 (2014): 804–24, doi.org/10.1037/a0033906.

308   **Of course, school and relationships don't stop** Yeager et al., "Loss of Institutional Trust Among Racial and Ethnic Minority Adolescents."

309   **Sometimes it's just two professionals** Patrick Radden Keefe, "How a Script Doctor Found His Own Voice," *New Yorker*, Dec. 25, 2023, www.newyorker.com/magazine/2024/01/01/how-a-script-doctor-found-his-own-voice.

309   **In other studies, researchers** Yeager et al., "Breaking the Cycle of Mistrust"; Yeager et al., "Teaching a Lay Theory Before College Narrows Achievement Gaps at Scale."

312   **So that summer** Goyer et al., "Targeted Identity-Safety Interventions Cause Lasting Reductions in Discipline Citations Among Negatively Stereotyped Boys."

313   **In fact, one of the best predictors** Kelly Allen et al., "What Schools Need to Know About Fostering School Belonging: A Meta-analysis," *Educational Psychology Review* 30, no. 1 (2018): 1–34, doi.org/10.1007/s10648-016-9389-8.

314   **Then they started eighth grade** For more on the dynamic nature of discipline citations, see Sean Darling-Hammond et al., "The Dynamic Nature of Student Discipline and Discipline Disparities," *Proceedings of the National Academy of Sciences* 120, no. 17 (2023): e2120417120, doi.org/10.1073/pnas.2120417120.

315   **Another study, with a much larger sample** Borman et al., "Reappraising Academic and Social Adversity Improves Middle School Students' Academic Achievement, Behavior, and Well-Being"; Jaymes Pyne and Geoffrey D. Borman, "Replicating a Scalable Intervention That Helps Students Reappraise Academic and Social Adversity During the Transition to Middle School," *Journal of Research on Educational Effectiveness* 13, no. 4 (2020): 652–78, doi.org/10.1080/19345747.2020.1784330; Williams et al., "Brief Social Belonging Intervention Improves Academic Outcomes for Minoritized High School Students."

316   **To test this, in one study** Okonofua, Paunesku, and Walton, "Brief Intervention to Encourage Empathic Discipline Cuts Suspension Rates in Half Among Adolescents."

317   **From 1973 to 2010** Melanie Leung-Gagné et al., "Pushed Out: Trends and Disparities in Out-of-School Suspension," Learning Policy Institute, Sept. 30, 2022, learningpolicyinstitute.org/product/crdc-school-suspension-report; "Civil Rights Data Collection: Data Snapshot (School Discipline)"; Jason A. Okonofua, Gregory M. Walton, and Jennifer L. Eberhardt, "A Vicious Cycle: A Social-Psychological Account of Extreme Racial Disparities in School Discipline," *Perspectives on Psychological Science* 11, no. 3 (May 2016): 381–98, doi.org/10.1177/1745691616635592.

318   **To learn how racial stereotypes work** Jason A. Okonofua and Jennifer L. Eberhardt, "Two Strikes: Race and the Disciplining of Young Students," *Psychological Science* 26, no. 5 (2015): 617–24, doi.org/10.1177/0956797615570365; Shoshana N. Jarvis and Jason A. Okonofua, "School Deferred: When Bias Affects School Leaders," *Social Psychological and Personality Science* 11, no. 4 (2020): 492–98, doi.org/10.1177/1948550619875150; Christina L. Rucinski, Tara M. Mandalaywala, and Linda R. Tropp, "Escalation Effects in Teacher Perceptions of Classroom Behavior in a U.S. Context: The Intersecting Roles of Student Race, Gender, and Behavior Severity," *Social Psychology of Education*, July 11, 2023, doi.org/10.1007/s11218-023-09822-x.

319   **Evaluations find that these programs** Jason A. Okonofua, Lasana T. Harris, and Gregory M. Walton, "Sidelining Bias: A Situationist Approach to Reduce the Consequences of Bias in Real-World Contexts," *Current Directions in Psychological Science* 31, no. 5 (2022): 395–404, doi.org/10.1177/09637214221102422; Patrick S. Forscher et al., "A Meta-analysis of Procedures to Change Implicit Measures," *Journal of Personality and Social Psychology* 117, no. 3 (2019): 522–59, doi.org/10.1037/pspa0000160; Calvin K. Lai et al., "Reducing Implicit Racial Preferences: II. Intervention Effectiveness Across Time," *Journal of Experimental Psychology: General* 145, no. 8 (2016): 1001–16, doi.org

/10.1037/xge0000179; Elizabeth Levy Paluck et al., "Prejudice Reduction: Progress and Challenges," *Annual Review of Psychology* 72, no. 1 (2021): 533–60, doi.org/10.1146/annurev-psych-071620-030619.

319   **So, together we decided** Okonofua, Harris, and Walton, "Sidelining Bias"; Okonofua, Paunesku, and Walton, "Brief Intervention to Encourage Empathic Discipline Cuts Suspension Rates in Half Among Adolescents"; Jason A. Okonofua and Michael Ruiz, "The Empathic-Discipline Intervention," in Walton and Crum, *Handbook of Wise Interventions,* 324–45.

323   **Later, we conducted** Okonofua et al., "Scalable Empathic-Mindset Intervention Reduces Group Disparities in School Suspensions."

323   **In one analysis** Only 7 percent of referrals for suspensions were even from math teachers.

326   **In July 2019** Eddy, "She Thought He Would Kill Her."

Spotlight: Improving School for the Most Vulnerable Children

331   **It is the single most powerful** Walton et al., "Lifting the Bar."

340   **Hattie Tate describes** Melissa De Witte, "Stanford Researchers Develop an Intervention That Cuts Recidivism Among Children Reentering School from the Justice System," *Stanford News* (blog), Oct. 5, 2021, news.stanford .edu/2021/10/05/supporting-students-involved-justice-system/.

340   **One ethnography concluded** Chhuon and Wallace, "Creating Connectedness Through Being Known."

CHAPTER 8: TOWARD A BETTER WORLD

345   **Sir Humphry Davy** Sir Humphry Davy, *A Discourse, Introductory to a Course of Lectures on Chemistry: Delivered in the Theatre of the Royal Institution on the 21st of January, 1802* (London: Press of the Royal Institution, 1802); King, "I Have a Dream."

345   **By 1900, 40 percent** U.S. Census Bureau, 2010 Census of Population and Housing, *Population and Housing Unit Counts* (Washington, D.C.: U.S. Government Printing Office, 2012), www2.census.gov/library/publications /decennial/2010/cph-2/cph-2-1.pdf.

346   **The country had seen** "United States: Child Mortality Rate, 1800–2020," Statista, accessed Feb. 18, 2024, www.statista.com/statistics/1041693/united -states-all-time-child-mortality-rate/; Gretchen A. Condran and Harold R. Lentzner, "Early Death: Mortality Among Young Children in New York, Chicago, and New Orleans," *Journal of Interdisciplinary History* 34, no. 3 (2004): 315–54.

346   **The solution was at hand** Alan Czaplicki, " 'Pure Milk Is Better Than Purified Milk': Pasteurization and Milk Purity in Chicago, 1908–1916," *Social Science History* 31, no. 3 (2007): 411–33; Steven Johnson, "How Humanity Gave Itself an Extra Life," *New York Times Magazine,* April 27, 2021, www.nytimes.com /2021/04/27/magazine/global-life-span.html.

347   **Otherwise, wise interventions** Susan H. Evans and Peter Clarke, "Disseminating Orphan Innovations," *Stanford Social Innovation Review* (Winter 2011).

348   **We'll literally take a "poop pill"** Dina Kao et al., "Effect of Oral Capsule– vs Colonoscopy-Delivered Fecal Microbiota Transplantation on Recurrent *Clos-*

tridium difficile Infection: A Randomized Clinical Trial," *JAMA* 318, no. 20 (2017): 1985–93, doi.org/10.1001/jama.2017.17077.

350   **You have to be proactive** J. Parker Goyer, Gregory M. Walton, and David S. Yeager, "The Role of Psychological Factors and Institutional Channels in Predicting the Attainment of Postsecondary Goals," *Developmental Psychology* 57, no. 1 (Jan. 2021): 73–86, doi.org/10.1037/dev0001142.

350   **That raised the rate** It was an increase from 32 percent to 43 percent. The study also included a separate growth-mindset intervention. This had no effect on college persistence, perhaps because the charter schools had already doubled down on teaching a growth mindset. Yeager et al., "Teaching a Lay Theory Before College Narrows Achievement Gaps at Scale."

352   **So, part of the question was** We were cautiously optimistic when we saw how students used the saying-is-believing prompt. They were forecasting challenges they were likely to experience, and preplanning how to understand and respond to them. One student wrote, "The initial worries about belonging to a college are likely to go away over time because once the student becomes more involve[d] with social groups on campus that interest them they later found friends with the same interest[s] as them. Also when student[s] understand that they can go to office hours to meet with their professor to discuss a situation, they later feel that the professors are there for them and want them to succeed."

353   **A year later** Yeager et al., "Teaching a Lay Theory Before College Narrows Achievement Gaps at Scale."

353   **Obviously, there is far more** Kathryn M. Kroeper et al., "Who Gets to Belong in College? An Empirical Review of How Institutions Can Expand Opportunities for Belonging on Campus," 2023 (under review).

353   **And they're freely available** "Social Belonging for College Students," PERTS, accessed Feb. 18, 2024, www.perts.net/programs/cb.

354   **My colleagues and I call these** Gregory M. Walton and David S. Yeager, "Seed and Soil: Psychological Affordances in Contexts Help to Explain Where Wise Interventions Succeed or Fail," *Current Directions in Psychological Science* 29, no. 3 (2020): 219–26, doi.org/10.1177/0963721420904453. See also James J. Gibson, "The Theory of Affordances," in *Perceiving, Acting, and Knowing*, ed. Robert Shaw and John Bransford (Hillsdale, N.J.: Erlbaum, 1977), 67–82.

354   **Some research, for example** Thomas S. Dee, "Social Identity and Achievement Gaps: Evidence from an Affirmation Intervention," *Journal of Research on Educational Effectiveness* 8, no. 2 (2015): 149–68, doi.org/10.1080/19345747 .2014.906009.

355   **Early in 2013, I was deep** David S. Yeager et al., "How Can We Instill Productive Mindsets at Scale? A Review of the Evidence and an Initial R&D Agenda," May 10, 2013, gregorywalton-stanford.weebly.com/uploads/4/9/4 /4/49448111/yeagerpauneskuwaltondweck_-_white_house_r&d_agenda _-_5-9-13.pdf.

355   **Six years later** Yeager et al., "National Experiment Reveals Where a Growth Mindset Improves Achievement"; David S. Yeager et al., "Teacher Mindsets Help Explain Where a Growth-Mindset Intervention Does and Doesn't Work," *Psychological Science* 33, no. 1 (2022): 18–32, doi.org/10.1177/095679 76211028984.

356   **A massive scale-up** Walton et al., "Where and with Whom Does a Brief Social-Belonging Intervention Promote Progress in College?"

356   **Following publicity** Paul Tough, "Who Gets to Graduate?," *New York Times Magazine*, May 15, 2014, www.nytimes.com/2014/05/18/magazine/who-gets-to-graduate.html.

356   **Some research, for instance** Katherine L. Milkman, Modupe Akinola, and Dolly Chugh, "What Happens Before? A Field Experiment Exploring How Pay and Representation Differentially Shape Bias on the Pathway into Organizations," *Journal of Applied Psychology* 100, no. 6 (2015): 1678–712, doi.org/10.1037/apl0000022.

357   **But still, they reached just** The NSLM reached 12,512 of approximately 4,036,000 students entering ninth grade that school year. The CTC trial reached 26,911 of 2,039,580 students entering representative colleges those two years.

357   **But good seeds require fertile soil** Walton and Yeager, "Seed and Soil"; Jamie M. Carroll et al., "Mindset × Context: Schools, Classrooms, and the Unequal Translation of Expectations into Math Achievement," *Monographs of the Society for Research in Child Development* 88, no. 2 (2023): 7–109, doi.org/10.1111/mono.12471; Cameron A. Hecht et al., "When Do the Effects of Single-Session Interventions Persist? Testing the Mindset + Supportive Context Hypothesis in a Longitudinal Randomized Trial," *JCPP Advances* 3, no. 4 (Dec. 2023): e12191, doi.org/10.1002/jcv2.12191.

357   **We've already seen** Bossuroy et al., "Tackling Psychosocial and Capital Constraints to Alleviate Poverty"; Okonofua, Paunesku, and Walton, "Brief Intervention to Encourage Empathic Discipline Cuts Suspension Rates in Half Among Adolescents"; Okonofua et al., "Scalable Empathic-Mindset Intervention Reduces Group Disparities in School Suspensions"; Okonofua et al., "Scalable Empathic Supervision Intervention to Mitigate Recidivism from Probation and Parole."

358   **One study led by Elizabeth Canning** Elizabeth A. Canning et al., "STEM Faculty Who Believe Ability Is Fixed Have Larger Racial Achievement Gaps and Inspire Less Student Motivation in Their Classes," *Science Advances* 5, no. 2 (Feb. 2019): eaau4734, doi.org/10.1126/sciadv.aau4734; Anke Heyder et al., "Teachers' Belief That Math Requires Innate Ability Predicts Lower Intrinsic Motivation Among Low-Achieving Students," *Learning and Instruction* 65 (2020): 101220, doi.org/10.1016/j.learninstruc.2019.101220.

359   **Even good ideas poorly implemented** For other examples of intuitions gone wrong, see Richard Schulz, "Effects of Control and Predictability on the Physical and Psychological Well-Being of the Institutionalized Aged," *Journal of Personality and Social Psychology* 33, no. 5 (1976): 563–73, doi.org/10.1037/0022-3514.33.5.563; Richard Schulz and Barbara H. Hanusa, "Long-Term Effects of Control and Predictability-Enhancing Interventions: Findings and Ethical Issues," *Journal of Personality and Social Psychology* 36, no. 11 (1978): 1194–201, doi.org/10.1037/0022-3514.36.11.1194; Joan McCord, "A Thirty-Year Follow-Up of Treatment Effects," *American Psychologist* 33, no. 3 (1978): 284–89, doi.org/10.1037/0003-066x.33.3.284. For discussion see Timothy D. Wilson, *Redirect: Changing the Stories We Live By* (New York: Little, Brown, 2011).

360   **As another example, my colleague Alia Crum** Zion, Schapira, and Crum, "Targeting Mindsets, Not Just Tumors"; Zion et al., "Changing Cancer Mindsets."

Floodlight: Making School Wise

365   **But in grad school, Murrar** Sohad Murrar, Mitchell R. Campbell, and Markus Brauer, "Exposure to Peers' Pro-diversity Attitudes Increases Inclusion and Reduces the Achievement Gap," *Nature Human Behaviour* 4, no. 9 (Sept. 2020): 889–97, doi.org/10.1038/s41562-020-0899-5.

365   **A second way is to create space** David K. Sherman et al., "Self-Affirmation Interventions," in Walton and Crum, *Handbook of Wise Interventions*, 63–99.

365   **In a series of studies** Geoffrey L. Cohen et al., "Reducing the Racial Achievement Gap: A Social-Psychological Intervention," *Science* 313, no. 5791 (Sept. 2006): 1307–10, doi.org/10.1126/science.1128317; Geoffrey L. Cohen et al., "Recursive Processes in Self-Affirmation: Intervening to Close the Minority Achievement Gap," *Science* 324, no. 5925 (2009): 400–403, doi.org/10.1126/science.1170769; Jonathan E. Cook et al., "Chronic Threat and Contingent Belonging: Protective Benefits of Values Affirmation on Identity Development," *Journal of Personality and Social Psychology* 102, no. 3 (2012): 479–96, doi.org/10.1037/a0026312; David K. Sherman et al., "Deflecting the Trajectory and Changing the Narrative: How Self-Affirmation Affects Academic Performance and Motivation Under Identity Threat," *Journal of Personality and Social Psychology* 104, no. 4 (2013): 591–618, doi.org/10.1037/a0031495; J. Parker Goyer et al., "Self-Affirmation Facilitates Minority Middle Schoolers' Progress Along College Trajectories," *Proceedings of the National Academy of Sciences* 114, no. 29 (2017): 7594–99, doi.org/10.1073/pnas.1617923114; Akira Miyake et al., "Reducing the Gender Achievement Gap in College Science: A Classroom Study of Values Affirmation," *Science* 330, no. 6008 (2010): 1234–37, doi.org/10.1126/science.1195996; Judith M. Harackiewicz et al., "Closing the Social Class Achievement Gap for First-Generation Students in Undergraduate Biology," *Journal of Educational Psychology* 106, no. 2 (2014): 375–89, doi.org/10.1037/a0034679; Walton et al., "Two Brief Interventions to Mitigate a 'Chilly Climate' Transform Women's Experience, Relationships, and Achievement in Engineering"; René F. Kizilcec et al., "Closing Global Achievement Gaps in MOOCs," *Science* 355, no. 6322 (2017): 251–52, doi.org/10.1126/science.aag2063; René F. Kizilcec et al., "Scaling Up Behavioral Science Interventions in Online Education," *Proceedings of the National Academy of Sciences* 117, no. 26 (2020): 14900–905, doi.org/10.1073/pnas.1921417117.

366   **In another case, Eric Smith** Eric N. Smith et al., "An Organizing Framework for Teaching Practices That Can 'Expand' the Self and Address Social Identity Concerns," *Educational Psychology Review*, Nov. 17, 2022, doi.org/10.1007/s10648-022-09715-z.

366   **Social-belonging interventions, which convey** Walton et al., "Where and with Whom Does a Brief Social-Belonging Intervention Promote Progress in College?"; Yeager et al., "Teaching a Lay Theory Before College Narrows Achievement Gaps at Scale"; Binning et al., "Changing Social Contexts to Foster Equity in College Science Courses"; Binning et al., "Unlocking the Benefits of Gender Diversity."

367   **It might mean publicly valuing** Mark R. Lepper et al., "Motivational Techniques of Expert Human Tutors: Lessons for the Design of Computer-Based Tutors," in *Computers as Cognitive Tools,* ed. Susanne P. Lajoie and Sharon J.

Derry (Hillsdale, N.J.: Lawrence Erlbaum Associates, 1993), 75–105; Yeager et al., "Breaking the Cycle of Mistrust."

367 **So, Judy Harackiewicz and her collaborators** Canning et al., "Improving Performance and Retention in Introductory Biology with a Utility-Value Intervention"; Asher et al., "Utility-Value Intervention Promotes Persistence and Diversity in STEM."

368 **As a grad student** Chen et al., "Strategic Resource Use for Learning"; Patricia Chen et al., "Real-World Effectiveness of a Social-Psychological Intervention Translated from Controlled Trials to Classrooms," *Npj Science of Learning* 7, no. 1 (2022): 1–9, doi.org/10.1038/s41539-022-00135-w; Patricia Chen, "The Strategic Resource Use Intervention," in Walton and Crum, *Handbook of Wise Interventions*, 166–90.

368 **Or you wonder** Shannon T. Brady, Bridgette Martin Hard, and James J. Gross, "Reappraising Test Anxiety Increases Academic Performance of First-Year College Students," *Journal of Educational Psychology* 110, no. 3 (2018): 395–406, doi.org/10.1037/edu0000219; Jeremy P. Jamieson et al., "Turning the Knots in Your Stomach into Bows: Reappraising Arousal Improves Performance on the GRE," *Journal of Experimental Social Psychology* 46, no. 1 (2010): 208–12, doi.org/10.1016/j.jesp.2009.08.015; Jeremy P. Jamieson and Emily J. Hangen, "Stress Reappraisal Interventions: Improving Acute Stress Responses in Motivated Performance Contexts," in Walton and Crum, *Handbook of Wise Interventions*, 239–58; Christopher S. Rozek et al., "Reducing Socioeconomic Disparities in the STEM Pipeline Through Student Emotion Regulation," *Proceedings of the National Academy of Sciences* 116, no. 5 (2019): 1553–58, doi.org/10.1073/pnas.1808589116.

368 **A third study addressed** Victor D. Quintanilla et al., "A Situated-Stress Mindset Intervention Improves Bar Passage Rates Among Socially Disadvantaged Bar Exam Applicants," 2022 (in preparation).

369 **At the University of California, Davis** Scott E. Carrell and Michal Kurlaender, "My Professor Cares: Experimental Evidence on the Role of Faculty Engagement," *American Economic Journal: Economic Policy* 15, no. 4 (Nov. 2023): 113–41, doi.org/10.1257/pol.20210699; Scott E. Carrell and Michal Kurlaender, "My Professor Cares: Experimental Evidence on the Role of Faculty Engagement," Working Paper, Working Paper Series, National Bureau of Economic Research, June 2020, doi.org/10.3386/w27312.

369 **Shannon Brady created a free tool kit** Shannon Brady, Amy Henderson, and Katie Mathias, "StanfordOnline: How You Say It Matters: A Toolkit for Improving Communications About Academic Standing," accessed Feb. 9, 2024, www.edx.org/learn/education/stanford-university-how-you-say-it-matters-a-toolkit-for-improving-communications-about-academic-standing.

370 **In a similar spirit** Anke Heyder, Ricarda Steinmayr, and Andrei Cimpian, "Reflecting on Their Mission Increases Preservice Teachers' Growth Mindsets," *Learning and Instruction* 86 (Aug. 2023): 101770, doi.org/10.1016/j.learninstruc.2023.101770; Cameron A. Hecht, Christopher J. Bryan, and David S. Yeager, "A Values-Aligned Intervention Fosters Growth Mindset–Supportive Teaching and Reduces Inequality in Educational Outcomes," *Proceedings of the National Academy of Sciences* 120, no. 25 (2023): e2210704120, doi.org/10.1073/pnas.2210704120.

371 **In fact, one study** Joseph T. Powers et al., "Changing Environments by Changing Individuals: The Emergent Effects of Psychological Intervention,"

Psychological Science 27, no. 2 (2016): 150–60, doi.org/10.1177/0956797615614591; Elizabeth Levy Paluck, Hana Shepherd, and Peter M. Aronow, "Changing Climates of Conflict: A Social Network Experiment in 56 Schools," *Proceedings of the National Academy of Sciences* 113, no. 3 (2016): 566–71, doi.org/10.1073/pnas.1514483113; David A. Kalkstein et al., "Social Norms Govern What Behaviors Come to Mind—and What Do Not," *Journal of Personality and Social Psychology* 124, no. 6 (2023): 1203–29, doi.org/10.1037/pspi0000412.

372   **Today, one of the leading programs** "Elevate," PERTS, accessed Feb. 18, 2024, www.perts.net/elevate.

373   **The PERTS team has found** Sarah Gripshover et al., "Learning Conditions Are an Actionable, Early Indicator of Math Learning," Dec. 2022, consortium.uchicago.edu/publication/learning-conditions-are-an-actionable-early-indicator-of-math-learning.

Index

ABOUT THE AUTHOR

GREGORY M. WALTON, PHD, is the co-director of the Dweck-Walton Lab, the Michael Forman University Fellow in Undergraduate Education, and a professor of psychology at Stanford University. Dr. Walton's research is supported by many foundations, including Character Lab, the Bill and Melinda Gates Foundation, the Jeff and Tricia Raikes Foundation, and the William and Flora Hewlett Foundation as well as the National Science Foundation. He has been covered by major media outlets including *The New York Times, Harvard Business Review, The Wall Street Journal*, NPR, *The Chronicle of Higher Education, The Washington Post, San Francisco Chronicle*, and *Los Angeles Times*.